Flann O'Brien

PROBLEMS WITH AUTHORITY

Flann O'Brien

PROBLEMS WITH AUTHORITY

EDITED BY

Ruben Borg, Paul Fagan

AND

John McCourt

CORK UNIVERSITY PRESS

First published in 2017 by
Cork University Press
Youngline Industrial Estate
Pouladuff Road, Togher
Cork
T12 HT6V
Ireland

British Library Cataloguing in Publication Data
A CIP record for this book is available from the British Library.

ISBN: 978-1-78205-230-2

Printed in Poland by Hussar Books
Print origination & design by Carrigboy Typesetting Services, www.carrigboy.com

www.corkuniversitypress.com

for Werner

Contents

Acknowledgements

A portion of the essays collected in this volume have their origins in papers delivered at *Problems with Authority: The II International Flann O'Brien Conference*, which was held at the Dipartimento di Lingue, Letterature, e Culture Straniere, Università Roma Tre, from 19–21 June 2013. Neither the conference itself nor this edited collection would have been possible without the generous support of various individuals and institutions. The editors would like to express their sincere gratitude to His Excellency Mr Patrick Hennessy, Irish Ambassador to Italy, to Amal Kaoua, cultural attaché, and to the staff of the Dipartimento di Lingue, Letterature, e Culture Straniere. We are particularly grateful to David O'Kane for graciously providing the collection's artwork and to Maria O'Donovan and Mike Collins at Cork University Press for their work in bringing this volume to fruition.

November 2016
RUBEN BORG
PAUL FAGAN
JOHN MCCOURT

Textual note

The following abbreviations are used throughout:

ABB   Myles na gCopaleen, *An Béal Bocht* (Cork: Mercier, 1999)

AW   Flann O'Brien, *Flann O'Brien at War: Myles na gCopaleen 1940–1945*, John Wyse Jackson (ed.) (London: Duckworth, 1999)

BM   Flann O'Brien, *The Best of Myles*, Kevin O'Nolan (ed.) (London: Harper Perennial, 2007)

CL   Myles na gCopaleen/Gopaleen, 'Cruiskeen Lawn', *The Irish Times*

CN   Flann O'Brien, *The Complete Novels: At Swim-Two-Birds, The Third Policeman, The Poor Mouth, The Hard Life, The Dalkey Archive*, Keith Donohue (introd.) (New York, NY: Everyman's Library, 2007)

FC   Flann O'Brien, *Further Cuttings from Cruiskeen Lawn* (Normal, IL: Dalkey Archive, 2000)

MAD   Flann O'Brien, *Myles Away from Dublin: Being a Selection from the Column Written for The Nationalist and Leinster Times, Carlow, under the name of George Knowall*, Martin Green (ed.) (London: Granada, 1985)

MBM   Flann O'Brien, *Myles Before Myles*, John Wyse Jackson (ed.) (Dublin: Lilliput Press, 2012)

PT   Flann O'Brien, *Plays and Teleplays*, Daniel Keith Jernigan (ed.) (Champaign, IL: Dalkey Archive Press, 2013)

SF   Flann O'Brien, *The Short Fiction of Flann O'Brien*, Neil Murphy and Keith Hopper (eds), Jack Fennell (trans.) (Champaign, IL: Dalkey Archive Press, 2013)

SP   Flann O'Brien, *Stories and Plays*, Claud Cockburn (introd. and ed.) (London: Hart-Davis, MacGibbon, 1973)

Notes on contributors

Ruben Borg is an Alon Fellow (2008–11) and Head of the Department of English at the Hebrew University of Jerusalem. He has published articles in *Journal of Modern Literature*, *Modern Fiction Studies*, *Poetics Today*, *Joyce Studies Annual* and *Narrative* and has contributed chapters to collaborative volumes on Deleuze and Literature, on Deleuze and Beckett and on Posthumanism. He is the author of *The Measureless Time of Joyce, Deleuze and Derrida* and co-editor, with Paul Fagan and Werner Huber, of *Flann O'Brien: Contesting Legacies* (listed in the *Irish Times* top ten non-fiction books of 2014). He is currently working on a book titled *Fantasies of Self-Mourning: Modernism, the Posthuman and the Problem of Genre*.

Ronan Crowley is fwo [pegasus][2] Marie Skłodowska-Curie Fellow at the University of Antwerp. He received his PhD in English from the University at Buffalo in 2014 for a dissertation on transatlantic copyright regimes, genetic criticism and Irish modernism. He is currently writing a book on the composition of *Ulysses*.

Louis de Paor is Director of the Centre for Irish Studies at the National University of Ireland, Galway. His published works include *Faoin mBlaoisc Bheag Sin* (1991), a study of the short fiction of Máirtín Ó Cadhain, critical editions of the poems of Máire Mhac an tSaoi, Liam S. Gógan and Michael Davitt, and a bilingual anthology of twentieth-century poetry in Irish, *Leabhar na hAthghabhála: Poems of Repossession* (2016). He has been a Visiting Professor at Boston College, New York University and the University of California, Berkeley and is currently working on a monograph on the Irish language element in the work of Flann O'Brien.

Katherine Ebury is lecturer in modern literature at the University of Sheffield. Her first monograph, *Modernism and Cosmology*, appeared with Palgrave in 2014 and she is the editor, with James Fraser, of *Outside His*

Jurisfiction: James Joyce's Nonfiction Writings (forthcoming with Palgrave). Her articles have appeared in journals such as *Irish Studies Review*, *Joyce Studies Annual* and *Society and Animals*, and she is the guest editor of a special issue of *Humanities* on Joyce, animals and the nonhuman. She is currently working on a second book project on literary responses to capital punishment in the twentieth century, particularly in late modernism.

PAUL FAGAN is a lecturer in cultural studies and modernism at the University of Vienna and a Senior Scientist at Salzburg University. He is the co-founder and president of the International Flann O'Brien Society, as well as co-founder and series editor of the peer-reviewed society journal *The Parish Review*. He is the co-editor, with Ruben Borg and Werner Huber, of *Flann O'Brien: Contesting Legacies*, which was listed in the *Irish Times* top ten non-fiction books of 2014. He is currently working on the edited volumes *Flann O'Brien: Gallows Humour* (with Ruben Borg) and *Irish Modernisms: Gaps, Conjectures, Possibilities* (with John Greaney and Tamara Radak), and is completing a monograph titled *Positions of Distrust: The Literary Hoax and the Irish Tradition*.

CATHERINE FLYNN is Assistant Professor of English at UC Berkeley. She received her PhD from Yale University and was a Postdoctoral Fellow at Stanford University's Introduction to the Humanities Program. Her book project, *James Joyce, Walter Benjamin and the Matter of Paris*, considers Joyce and Benjamin's radical rejections of the conventions of fiction and theory within a context of urban writing that ranges from nineteenth-century realist fiction to twentieth-century *avant-garde* works. Flynn is co-editor, with Richard Brown, of a special issue of *James Joyce Quarterly* on 'Joycean Avant-Gardes'. She has also published articles on Joyce, Benjamin, Brecht, Kafka, De Stijl, surrealism and Marxist literary criticism, and is currently at work with David Wheatley on a scholarly edition of *Cruiskeen Lawn*.

DIETER FUCHS is full-time lecturer at the Department of English and American Studies of the University of Vienna. He received his doctorate from LMU Munich, where his PhD thesis on James Joyce and Menippean satire was supervised by Hans Walter Gabler. He has recently finalised the manuscript of his second book on *Elizabethan Revenge Drama and the Rise of Reformation Discourse*.

ALANA GILLESPIE is a lecturer at the English Department and affiliated researcher with the Institute for Cultural Inquiry at Utrecht University, where she earned a PhD for her thesis on Brian O'Nolan's comic critique of tropes of tradition and modernity in independent Ireland. She contributed an article on controversy about science in *Cruiskeen Lawn* to *Flann O'Brien: Contesting Legacies*. In addition to a number of forthcoming articles on O'Nolan, Gillespie is completing a monograph on the subject of comedy and cultural remembrance in O'Nolan's work and is working on bringing an animated adaptation of *Rhapsody in Stephen's Green* to the screen.

MARIA KAGER is a lecturer in modern English literature at Utrecht University, The Netherlands. She holds a double doctorate in comparative literature from Rutgers University in the US and from the University of Antwerp in Belgium. Her work has appeared in the *James Joyce Quarterly*, the *Journal of Modern Literature, Studies in the Novel* and *L2Journal*. She is currently at work on a book about bilingualism and cognition in modernist fiction.

MAEBH LONG is a senior lecturer in English literature at the University of Waikato. Her principal areas of research are modernist and contemporary literature in Ireland, Britain and Oceania, as well as literary theory and continental philosophy. She is the author of *Assembling Flann O'Brien* (London: Bloomsbury, 2014) and is currently editing O'Nolan's letters. She is also co-investigator of *Oceanic Modernism*, a project which explores creative expressions of modernity in the South Pacific.

R.W. MASLEN is a senior lecturer at the University of Glasgow, where he convenes the new Masters Programme in Fantasy. He has published extensively on early modern literature and modern fantasy, and his books include *Elizabethan Fictions, Shakespeare and Comedy* and editions of the poetry and nonsense of Mervyn Peake.

JOHN MCCOURT is professor of English literature at the Università di Macerata (Italy). He previously taught for many years at Università Roma Tre and the Università di Trieste. He is the author of *James Joyce: A Passionate Exile* (1999) and of *The Years of Bloom: Joyce in Trieste 1904–1920* (2000). An extended Italian version of the latter, *James Joyce: gli anni di Bloom*, was published by Mondadori in 2004 and won the Comisso Prize. A founder of the Trieste Joyce School, he has guest edited the *James Joyce Quarterly* and is currently a Trustee of the International James Joyce Foundation and a member of the academic board of the International Yeats Summer School. In 2009 he published *James Joyce in Context* (Cambridge University Press) and *Questioni biografiche: le tante vite di*

Yeats e Joyce appeared the following year along with a second edited collection, *Roll Away the Reel World: James Joyce and Cinema* (Cork University Press). His most recent book, *Writing the Frontier: Anthony Trollope between Britain and Ireland* was published by Oxford University Press in 2015. He is currently editing a collection of essays on Brendan Behan.

IAN Ó CAOIMH is doing a PhD on the work of Ciarán Ó Nualláin in the School of Irish, Celtic Studies and Folklore in University College Dublin, where he also works as a research editor on the dúchas.ie folklore digitisation project. He has previously worked as a translator with the Houses of the Oireachtas, on the editorial staff of the publisher An Gúm, as a journalist with RTÉ and as the editor of *Comhar* magazine, including a commemorative Flann O'Brien number in December 2011.

DAVID O'KANE is an Irish artist whose work is included in collections such as the Kunsthalle der Sparkasse in Leipzig, the Zabludowicz Collection in London, the CAP Foundation collection in Dublin, the Trapaga-Fonalledas collection in Puerto Rico, the Starke Foundation collection in Berlin. His short film *Babble*, which stages a multilingual conversation between Flann O'Brien, Franz Kafka and Jorge Luis Borges, won an e v + a open award (2008) from Hou Hanru and a still from his animated artwork *Dieselbe Noman* adorned the inaugural issue of *The Parish Review* (Summer 2012). In addition to receiving the R.C. Lewis-Crosby Award at the Royal Dublin Society (2006), O'Kane has been awarded residencies at the British School at Rome (2009), the Stiftung Starke in Berlin (2010–13) and is currently undertaking a long-term residency at the Fire Station Artists Studios in Dublin (2014–17). He is represented by Gallery Baton in Seoul (South Korea), Cavanacor Gallery in Lifford (Ireland), Galerie Maïa Muller in Paris (France) and the Josef Filipp Galerie in Leipzig (Germany).

TAMARA RADAK is a lecturer and PhD candidate at the University of Vienna. Her thesis, titled *No(n)Sense of an Ending?: Aporias of Closure in Modernist Fiction*, is concerned with endings in the works of James Joyce, Flann O'Brien, Virginia Woolf and Ernest Hemingway which transgress traditional notions of closure and question teleological plot development. She was the host organiser of *Irish Modernisms: Gaps, Conjectures, Possibilities* (University of Vienna, 2016) and has published in *James Joyce Quarterly*, *European Joyce Studies*, *James Joyce Literary Supplement* and *The Parish Review*.

CAROL TAAFFE is the author *of Ireland Through the Looking-Glass: Flann O'Brien, Myles na gCopaleen and Irish Cultural Debate* (Cork University Press, 2008) and articles on Flann O'Brien for *Irish University Review*, *Canadian Journal of Irish Studies* and the Four Courts Press collection *'Is it about a bicycle?': Flann O'Brien in the Twenty-First Century*. A regular contributor to *The Dublin Review*, Taaffe was also the co-editor, with Edwina Keown, of *Irish Modernism: Origins, Contexts, Publics* (Peter Lang, 2010) and the co-organiser of the 2011 'Flann O'Brien Centenary Conference' in Trinity College Dublin.

DIRK VAN HULLE, Professor of English Literature at the University of Antwerp and director of the Centre for Manuscript Genetics, recently edited the new *Cambridge Companion to Samuel Beckett* (2015). With Mark Nixon, he is co-director of the Beckett Digital Manuscript Project (www.beckettarchive. org) and editor-in-chief of the *Journal of Beckett Studies*. His publications include *Textual Awareness* (2004), *Modern Manuscripts* (2014), *Samuel Beckett's Library* (2013, with Mark Nixon), *James Joyce's Work in Progress* (2016) and several genetic editions in the Beckett Digital Manuscript Project, including *Krapp's Last Tape/La Dernière Bande*, *L'Innommable/The Unnamable* (with Shane Weller) and the *Beckett Digital Library*.

Editors' introduction

Ruben Borg, Paul Fagan, John McCourt

The editorial that announces the arrival of Brian O'Nolan's surreal, anarchic and all too short-lived Dublin monthly magazine *Blather* (1934–35) strikes an openly rebellious pose.

> BLATHER is here.
>
> As we advance to make our bow, you will look in vain for signs of servility or for any evidence of a slavish desire to please. We are an arrogant and a depraved body of men. We are as proud as bantams and as vain as peacocks. **BLATHER doesn't care**. A sardonic laugh escapes us as we bow, cruel and cynical hounds that we are. It is a terrible laugh, the laugh of lost men. Do you get the smell of porter? [...]
>
> In regard to politics, all our rat-like cunning will be directed towards making Ireland fit for the depraved readers of BLATHER to live in. In the meantime, anything that distortion, misrepresentation and long-distance lying can do to injure and wreck the existing political parties, one and all, BLATHER will do it. [...] Every nerve will be strained towards the achievement of the BLATHER Revolution and the achievement of the BLATHER Dictatorship, followed by the inauguration of the BLATHER Communist Monarchy. Gunplay will be rife, the Motherland will be soaked in a bath of blood, Chinese Tong Wars will stalk the land. But we will win the day and the brutal military heel of BLATHER will crush the neck of its enemies. [...]
>
> **Anyhow, you have got a rough idea of the desperate class of man you are up against. Maybe you don't like us?...**
>
> **A lot we care for what you think.**[1]

Cast in the self-contradictory (*Blather* Communist Monarchy!) comic mode of youthful exuberance, this insurrectionist manifesto establishes many of the planks (and pranks) of the more mature writer's aesthetic platform. The tactics of 'distortion, misrepresentation and long-distance lying' inform O'Nolan, Niall Montgomery and Niall Sheridan's absurd correspondence to *The Irish Times* (under such spurious signatures as 'Whit Cassidy', 'Judy Clifford', 'Hilda Upshott', 'Jno. Ruddy', 'Velvet-Texture', 'Na2 Co3', 'CuSO4' and 'F. O'Brien') intended to challenge and poke fun at the then considerable cultural authority of Seán O'Faoláin, Frank O'Connor and Patrick Kavanagh. There are menacing echoes, too, in the 'cruel and cynical hounds' behind *Blather* of the 'arrogant and [...] depraved body of men' who roam The Parish of *The Third Policeman*, marshalling the slipperiness of language to claim an authority they would wield arbitrarily to 'crush the neck of [their] enemies'. And in the manifesto's talk of bending Ireland towards the vision of a group of 'depraved readers' there are hints of Myles na gCopaleen's ambiguously ironic swipes at The Plain People of Ireland and the savage satire of the Gaeilgeoir in *An Béal Bocht*.

Subtler still than the satirical send-off of institutions of knowledge and power – and the parody of cultural and scientific pretentions – foregrounded in this early period, is the sustained contemplation of the 'problem' of authority at issue in all acts of writing and reading. '*Aistear Pheadair Dhuibh*' [The Tale of Black Peter] (1933) registers, early in Brian O'Nolan's career, the writer's recurring motif of literary creation as an ethically problematic act that engenders violent protest. Frustrated with life in the barren, unfertile bog,[2] Peadar finally cracks, waking the local priest to demand 'WHO CREATED ME AND THIS MISERABLE COUNTRY?':

> 'God didn't create it', the priest answered. 'It was Parthalán Mac an Dubhdha, author, and Feidhlimídh Ó Casaidhe, poet – both natives of Dublin ...'
>
> Peter did not say another word, but grabbed a fine heavy double-barrelled shotgun [...] and departed without delay. [...] He was never heard from again, but it was said that there was some bad business done in Dublin. (*SF*, 44)

Yet if the death of Peadar's authors is to be understood as a liberating gesture, the story's closing paragraph suggests that the freedom gained is a compromised one, soon overtaken by the new bland despotism of consumerism: 'there are shops on the bog now, selling bus-tickets and cigarettes and the *Daily Mail*' (*SF*, 45).[3]

In 'Scenes in a Novel by Brother Barnabas (Probably Posthumous)' (1934), O'Nolan inverts this narrative situation to write from the perspective of an author 'engaged [...] in the composition of a posthumous article' with the certain knowledge that his own character, Caruthers McDaid, is coming to murder him (*SF*, 49).⁴ Upon sitting down to write Chapter Five, in which McDaid is 'required to rob a poor-box in a church', Barnabas finds himself embroiled in an agonistic debate with the character he has created:

> 'Sorry, old chap', [McDaid] said, 'but I absolutely can't do it'.
> 'What's this, Mac', said I 'getting squeamish in your old age?'
> 'Not squeamish exactly', he replied, 'but I bar the poor-boxes'. [...]
> 'Not another word', said I sternly, '[...] you burst the poor-box or it's anthrax in two days'.
> 'But, I say, old chap, that's a bit thick'.
> 'You think so? Well, I'm old-fashioned enough to believe that your opinions don't matter'
> We left it at that. Each of us firm, outwardly polite, perhaps, but determined to yield not one tittle of our inalienable rights. (*SF*, 50–51)

On the basis of this standoff between a creation striving for autonomy and a creator 'old-fashioned enough to believe that [his subject's] opinions don't matter', Barnabas's short confession is most often read as a parable in which 'metafiction becomes an antidote to the tyranny of traditionalist realist authorship'.⁵ But in fact, at the very moment in which it might have announced the birth of the reader at the expense of the death of the author, the scene suggests a strange impasse. The encounter is unresolved ('We left it at that') with each party 'determined to yield not one tittle of [its] inalienable rights'. As the murmurs of insurrection become louder, Barnabas starts to suspect all of his characters of plotting and colluding against him: 'The book is seething with conspiracy and there have been at least two whispered consultations between all the characters, including two who have not yet been officially created' (*SF*, 52). We are left with the paranoid image of the author, anticipating a treasonous rebellion whose execution must remain beyond the story's limits. Rather than offering a clean declaration of readers' and characters' rights to liberty – a *Common Sense* manifesto for fiction – the scene seems more engaged in comically testing the *problem* of the function and force of concepts such as 'independence' or 'authority' in the literary event.

This project to interrogate the problematic authority of authorship from a variety of narrative perspectives culminates in *At Swim-Two-Birds*, which constructs a *mise en abyme* structure that can contain both the perspective of the overworked and mishandled creation and that of the authoritarian creator charged with regulating chaos into order and narrative momentum. Suspicious of the other's intentions, each party endeavours to wrestle or maintain control. In the novel, clear lines of division between author and authored are effaced, with the narrator, Trellis and Orlick inhabiting both positions in increasingly mediated ways. The same slip from emancipatory revolution to authoritarianism that shapes the *Blather* manifesto is staged in the overthrow of the author Trellis by his creations and their subsequent turn to arbitrary rule. As Kimberly Bohman-Kalaja notes, if the trial of the author Trellis 'underscores the inseparability of aesthetic and ethical textual corruption', then the 'authorial crimes he is accused of [...] are not only his crimes, but the crimes of the authors who conspire to punish him as well'.[6] Intriguingly, Trellis is persecuted by his creations only for them to be consumed in a fire to effect the author's liberation.

If *At Swim-Two-Birds* offers the *dénouement* of O'Nolan's authorial antagonisms throughout the 1930s, the war years see him refocus his attention on the suspect authority of the reader. His standard narrative situation of the hostile encounter between the author and the authored is developed in 'John Duffy's Brother' to exhibit a peculiar hesitation about the reader's access to the narrative event. This reservation informs the story's refusal to name its subject or account for his strange transformation.[7] Indeed, as the opening lines suggest, the fact that the reader should come to know anything of Mr Duffy's plight means that some kind of ethical breach must have taken place:

> Strictly speaking, this story should not be written or told at all. To write it or to tell it is to spoil it. This is because the man who had the strange experience we are going to talk about never mentioned it to anybody, and the fact that he kept his secret and sealed it up completely in his memory is the whole point of the story. Thus we must admit that handicap at the beginning – that it is absurd for us to tell the story, absurd for anybody to listen to it, and unthinkable that anybody should believe it. (*SF*, 54)

The Third Policeman opens, comparably, with the de Selby scholar's nervous bid for the reader's attention: the awkward *incipit* 'Not everybody knows how I killed old Phillip Mathers' (*CN*, 223). From this curious gesture towards the narratorial privileges of omniscience and disclosure, the novel explores the dangers of monomaniacal reading (and misreading), the dubious authority of self-authenticated expertise and the inexorable turn towards murder embedded in 'the serious responsibility of any person who declined by mere reason of personal whim to give the [de Selby] "Index" to the world' (*CN*, 231).[8] The suggestion that the certainties of overzealous readers might be even more pernicious than the tyrannies of authorship informs, too, the attack on the cultural clout of the Gaeilgeoir in *An Béal Bocht*, in which it appears that the ideology and clichés of *'na dea-leabhair'* [the good books] (*ABB*, 56) play a determining role in the poverty-stricken conditions of Corca Dhorcha. This 'depravity' is unavoidable, 'Myles na gCopaleen' suggests in the 12 February 1943 *Cruiskeen Lawn* column, owing to 'The blind urge to read, the craving for print'.[9] In Myles's diagnosis of this pathology, 'The writer can be systematically discouraged, his "work" can be derided and if all else fails, we can (have recourse) to the modern remedy known as "liquidating the intellectuals". But what can you do with the passive print addict? Absolutely nothing'.

As he transitioned from 'Flann O'Brien' to 'Myles na gCopaleen' (and beyond to 'George Knowall' and 'John James Doe'[10]), O'Nolan's rebellions changed both in tone and in tactics. In the columns of *Cruiskeen Lawn*, O'Nolan takes up this riotous indignation with added vigour and focus, setting his sights on the (highly debatable) role of the 'artist' in society (particularly the spurious authorities of WAAMA and the 'corduroys'); those who would claim the expertise to delimit the value, function and potential of the Irish language (whether Dinneen's dictionary or anyone who feigns to have spoken Irish 'when it was neither popular nor profitable'); the clichés, bores and bureaucrats who squander the columnist's resources, time and attention. Yet there is a slow but noticeable turn, a levelling of temper and timbre from absurd flights to a (somewhat) more grounded focus on the local and the concretely political through the various forms of fakery foisted upon The Plain People of Ireland by state and local bodies. There are the increased engagements with the minutiae of the internal workings of the Irish government ('Home Rule is fine, but I am afraid you have not got yourselves quite … quite *right* yet') and swipes against the Central Bank (in a charge all too relevant to the country's recent predicaments, Myles condemns the bank's 'moist paternalism' as 'disgusting and scandalous').[11] There is also a broadening of horizons to take issue with geopolitical powers. On 13 May 1946, Myles notes that 'many decent Irish persons were horrified to read of the monstrous tidal wave that killed hundreds of people in Honolulu' during 'the atomic bomb experiments carried out by the Americans in the Pacific'.[12] At issue, once again, is less the specific form of destruction than the assumption of an unwarranted jurisdiction:

The Americans feel that they are in duty bound to destroy the earth by detonating terrestrial energy simply because they feel that a revival of 'German aggression' is inevitable and that the world market for U.S. automobiles, questionable films and shiny magazines will thus be menaced. [...] is it necessary for the Americans to bring about the end of the world? Contrary, probably, to their belief, they did not make it and the plan to destroy it savours of *lèse majesté*.

The late novels *The Hard Life* and *The Dalkey Archive* further exhibit Flann O'Brien's knack for dissecting the spurious authorities of institutions, be they religious (the Pope), patriarchal (Collopy), scientific (De Selby) or literary (James Joyce). Yet these interventions also take on an air of nuclear age resignation, suggesting that it is only a matter of time until technological advancement places into the hands of these institutions the means by which to draw the final curtain on the world (De Selby's DMP). This apocalyptic turn of mind also follows Myles's growing interest in more sacred targets: the writings of the church fathers, Augustine and Loyola, the scripts of tradition, philosophy, science.

Behind all the masks, the same anti-authoritarian temperament animates O'Nolan's comic drive. His writing mobilises a variety of conflicting authorial positions but remains poised between *avant-garde* and conservative approaches to the authorities of science, religion, politics, history and literary tradition. There is something Quixotic in the systematic targeting of civic institutions and something Kafkaesque in the identification of authority with public bureaus and faceless departments (Max Brod's memory of Kafka laughing uncontrollably while reading out excerpts from *The Trial* bolsters the comparison). On the one hand, an embittered critique of institutional power – ecclesiastic in *The Hard Life*, legal in *The Third Policeman*, academic in *At Swim-Two-Birds*; on the other, an unreserved and outspoken participation in municipal life that invests the politics of *Cruiskeen Lawn* with a practical, down-to-earth idealism. O'Nolan's keenest contribution to the counter-cultural politics of late modernism, then, may well be a compound literary persona, an odd poster boy for twentieth-century baditude – not the rebel without a cause, not the restless youth in a leather jacket, but the paranoid civil-servant 'everyman' in a brown suit, part Quixote, part Joseph K.

O'Nolan's status as an anti-authoritarian writer is inextricable from his place in the history of comic thought. From the court jester to the political satirist, comedians have been applauded for daring to speak truth to power. Yet this must remain a backhanded compliment, if it implies that making us laugh is not in and of itself a sufficiently noble calling. To a significant extent, the story of O'Nolan's own reception hinges upon the contrasting ways in which the political force and aesthetic merit of comedy has been conceptualised by his allies and adversaries in Irish and modernist contexts. For many of his contemporaries – and in particular for the post-independence realists Seán O'Faoláin, Sean O'Casey, Frank O'Connor, Liam O'Flaherty and Patrick Kavanagh – his anarchic comic spirit was a lower, even 'inauthentic' form of expression that failed to meet 'the predicament of the writer in this time and place, faced with the complex realities of political independence rather than the impending dream of the Republic'.[13]

The roots of this association of comic thought with the lowly and the unserious were already planted in Aristotle's definition in the *Poetics*:

> Poetry now diverged in two directions, according to the individual character of the writers. The graver spirits imitated noble actions, and the actions of good men. The more trivial sort imitated the actions of meaner persons [...] Comedy is, as we have said, an imitation of characters of a lower type – not, however, in the full sense of the word bad, the ludicrous being merely a subdivision of the ugly. It consists in some defect or ugliness which is not painful or destructive. To take an obvious example, the comic mask is ugly and distorted, but does not imply pain.
>
> The successive changes through which Tragedy passed, and the authors of these changes, are well known, whereas Comedy has had no history, because it was not at first treated seriously.[14]

From the outset, then, it is not the 'funny' but rather the lowbrow and the unserious that properly define a Comic spirit – a constitutive *inferiority* made eloquent and self-aware. Following these humble beginnings, comedy has often found itself in an antagonistic relation to authority – countering nobility with meanness, gravity with levity and, at its very best, blurring the distinction between the serious and the unserious. No surprise that insolence should have become a habit of comic performance, the funny man's political reflex. To the extent that it revels in the failures of inferior men and the celebration of the baser passions, comedy's strong suit has always been precisely the close-up on the ridiculous defect, the mean strike below the belt. It is fitting, then, and telling, that O'Nolan should open his comic account with a 'sardonic laugh' amid the company of an 'arrogant and a depraved body of men' at pains to let their readership know exactly how little they care for what they might think of them (*MBM*, 96–98). Even as we recognise the limitations of Aristotle's definition of the Comic spirit – its partiality, its reductiveness – we can scarcely do justice to O'Nolan's treatment of authority without taking the riotous comedic muse into serious account.

Focusing on the satirical and comedic energies invested in his style, *Flann O'Brien: Problems with Authority* highlights O'Nolan's clowning with bureaucratic, religious and scientific powers in the sites of the popular, the modern and the traditional in both national and international contexts. The theme opens onto a variety of characteristic Mylesian concerns: it resonates with the impertinent send-up of political and religious orthodoxies; it sustains satire and touches on the very nature of comedic inspiration. It tells us that O'Nolan's writing is always, in some way, a writing against the weight of received wisdoms, inherited sureties. Most pressingly, it compels us to consider the many ways in which this body of work brings into sharp relief the kinship between comic genius and an anti-authoritarian temperament.

On whose authority?

Since its inception, O'Nolan criticism has sought to situate the writer's work in opposition to a variety of literary, philosophical and political jurisdictions. For M. Keith Booker, for instance, O'Nolan's writing turns back to Menippean satire in order to tilt against the Enlightenment authorities of science, epistemology and humanism, while for Keith Hopper it looks forward to the post-modern turn in its hostile resistance to the author's potentially despotic authority.[15] More recently, Joseph Brooker and Carol Taaffe have positioned O'Nolan in his own time and place and found him subverting the cultural power of local authorities, movements and institutions.[16]

The current wave of O'Nolan studies, initiated by the establishment of the International Flann O'Brien Society and *The Parish Review* journal in 2011, has brought with it a series of shifts in the reception of the author's work, with a systematic critical reappraisal that has found in the writer's very marginality, liminality, slipperiness, even ephemerality a fruitful site in which to explore afresh questions of authorship, the politics of Irish cultural power and the variegated sites of modernist poetics. Three 2014 publications in particular have helped to push new ground. Julian Murphet, Rónán McDonald and Sascha Morrell's *Flann O'Brien & Modernism* reoriented the critical conversation away from the post-modernist emphasis of the 1990s to acknowledge that O'Nolan's variously innovative and populist writing troubles critical commonplaces about modernism itself by virtue of its ephemerality and parochial energies.[17] Maebh Long's *Assembling Flann O'Brien* read O'Nolan's *œuvre* against a wider tradition of twentieth-century thought, from Freud, Lacan and Žižek to Schlegel, Derrida and Agamben.[18] And Ruben Borg, Paul Fagan and Werner Huber's *Flann O'Brien: Contesting Legacies* undertook to demystify the clichés and myths still haunting O'Nolan studies by 'contesting all of the labels that have been attached to the author'.[19]

The present volume implicitly touches on each of these approaches in its focus on the theme of authority. As David Gunkel summarises, 'Authority figures [...] regulate semantic dissemination and dispersion, identify the place and proper limits of responsibility, and provide a standard metric for evaluation and judgment'.[20] The premise that O'Nolan's writing challenges diverse authority figures on several fronts thus presupposes that the author works to complicate or destabilise efforts to regulate meaning, draw limits and pass final verdict. Yet the question of *who* might 'provide a standard metric for evaluation and judgment' is particularly evocative of O'Nolan's battles with critical authorities, both in his own writing and his posthumous reception. In this respect, consideration of O'Nolan's 'problems with authority' also entails a careful interrogation of the *critical* orthodoxies that endeavour to capture a body of writing that is at once modernist and anti-modernist, that is satirical both of the Irish Revival and of its critics, that excoriates The Plain People of Ireland as it claims to be their one true defender. In the essays gathered here, among other strands, O'Nolan's reputation as a neglected modernist innovator in search of an audience is contested through his engagements with popular forms and writing for national broadcast; his standing as a lonely pioneer of postmodernist practice is recalibrated against new modernist and Revivalist coordinates; and his local notoriety as the Dublin character mocking current events in the profane site of the daily paper is complicated by his more scholarly reflections on the legacies of ancient philosophies, pre-Colonial Gaelic traditions, and diverse sacred texts. The purpose of challenging canonical definitions and recruitments of O'Nolan is not to replace old orthodoxies with new ones, but rather to make a pitch for a mode of inquiry more finely attuned to the multifacetedness and prodigality of the writer's riotous imagination in its own inveterate questioning of fixed positions and commonplaces.

At the same time, the publication in 2013 of *The Short Fiction of Flann O'Brien* and *Flann O'Brien: Plays and Teleplays* by Dalkey Archive Press compels us to reconsider, at least partially, the authority the major novels had previously held over our critical attentions to the neglect of once marginal titles in the author's canon.[21] Likewise, the vast collections of O'Nolan's correspondence, manuscripts and drafts housed in Illinois, Boston and Texas, as well as the *Irish Times* online digital archive, have given rise to genetic and cultural materialist approaches that seek to explore the borders of authorship and authority in O'Nolan's ever-expanding *œuvre*. *Flann O'Brien: Problems with Authority* participates in the ongoing bid to redraw the boundaries of the O'Nolan canon by paying overdue attention to the writing for *Blather*, the early (and still uncollected) Irish-language *Cruiskeen Lawn* columns, his casual pieces for *The Bell* ('Going to the Dogs!', 'The Trade in Dublin', 'The Dance Halls'), his writing for theatre (*Faustus Kelly*, *Rhapsody in Stephen's Green*), his short fiction ('John Duffy's Brother', 'Two in One') and his late teleplays for Telefís Éireann (*The Boy from Ballytearim*, *Flight*, *The Time Freddie Retired*, *The Dead Spit of Kelly*, *The Man with Four Legs*, *A Moving Tale*). Yet by reframing the key issues of this broadened canon through its concerns with the issues of power, law, control, government, influence, tradition and prestige, the essays in this collection are able to draw together disparate elements of the author's multi-genre work. And even as the volume finesses longer-running critical conversations about the ways in which O'Nolan's texts are shaped by towering twentieth-century figures such as Joyce and Beckett, the theme of authority allows each of the contributors to read O'Nolan in new, enlightening and often surprising comparative contexts, from Voltaire, James Stephens and Arthur Eddington to Luigi Pirandello, Saint Paul and Carlo Emilio Gadda. These readings are arranged into three broadly defined sections, which enact critical conversations that re-examine O'Nolan's 'problems with authority' through his encounters with his mass and *coterie* readerships, local and international literary peers and movements, and sacred texts in Irish, religious and modernist contexts.

'neither popular nor profitable': O'Nolan *vs.* The Plain People

While it expands upon the recent reorganisation of O'Nolan's work against the coordinates of Irish and European modernisms, *Flann O'Brien: Problems with Authority* also troubles this conversation by engaging O'Nolan's encounter with the popular, a previously under-analysed counter-current in the author's work. Myles's agonistic relationship with The Plain People of Ireland is well known, yet befitting the anti-ideological comic energies of his writing, it is often unclear where lines of sympathy are to be drawn. The ambivalence is central to O'Nolan's writerly persona; and that he himself saw it as such is made clear in a late filmed interview in which he drunkenly proclaims 'I'm one of The Plain People of Ireland; notwithstanding which, I've a giant intellect'.[22] In this spirit, *Flann O'Brien: Problems with Authority* opens by interrogating O'Nolan's often confrontational, even bellicose relationship with his readerships. In addressing his penchant for dissecting rehearsed attitudes and subverting expectations, the first section touches on some of the subtler notes in O'Nolan's treatment of authority, such as his subversions of genre, his simultaneous contempt for cliché and exploitation of the stereotype, his strategic division of audiences through his bilingual writing and his needling of scientific authority through covert engagements with popularisations.

In the collection's opening essay, Carol Taaffe refutes the commonplace assumption that as a neglected *coterie* writer, O'Nolan adopted a condescending stance towards the popular. Looking beyond the established novels to his writing for *Blather*, *The Irish Times* and *The Bell*, Taaffe rather finds a writer 'inclining towards popular culture, to the everyday world' (p. 33). By shifting emphasis to O'Nolan's writing for mass readerships and within popular forms (daily newspapers, comic journals, detective fiction, American adventure novels), Taaffe makes a compelling case to nuance our view of the totalising conservatism of 1930s' Ireland to make room for its idealism, populism and belief in cultural democracy. Building on her previous pioneering work uncovering O'Nolan's problems with the intellectual cachet of high or elite modernism, here Taaffe demonstrates that 'far from lacking readers, Brian O'Nolan always had them' (p. 24) and infers that claims to the contrary rather imply that 'he had the wrong kind of readers' (p. 25) for certain critical tastes.

This invitation to revise commonplaces concerning O'Nolan's relationship to sites of popular culture and mass readership is taken up in the remaining four contributions of the volume's first section. Tracing the evolution of O'Nolan's parodies and exploitations of national stereotypes across his early *Blather* and *Cruiskeen Lawn* articles, mid-career plays and late-era teleplays, Maebh Long addresses the writer's diverse clashes with the dubious authority of 'authentic' Irish identity. Long positions O'Nolan's 'sustained performance of the post-independence search for national identity' (p. 34) within a genealogy of vexed attempts to come to terms with the stereotypes, clichés and archetypes of the stage Irishman in his urban and rural manifestations. The essay finds that his performance occupies a liminal space in this tradition, situated 'between the parodic undercutting of stereotypes and their adoption' (p. 34). Most compellingly, Long breaks new ground by reevaluating O'Nolan's two Telefís Éireann sitcoms *O'Dea's Your Man* and *Th'Oul Lad of Kilsalaher* and finding that they propose a darkly satirical claim – namely, that the 'real' Ireland is itself, in O'Nolan's view, 'populated by inauthentic character types' and walking stereotypes (p. 53).

Maria Kager examines the bilingual (and often multilingual) columns of *Cruiskeen Lawn*'s early years and notes the creative, comic and combative stakes of Myles's repeated assertions of his 'linguistic authority as a bilingual' (p. 55) in speaking to, and for, the paper's diverse language readerships. Bringing neurolinguistic and psycholinguistic tools to bear upon these critically under-analysed early columns, Kager offers a different angle from Long regarding O'Nolan's depictions of Irish accents, clichés and localisms by tracing the connection between bilingual wordplay and comic creativity in his writing. Catherine Flynn picks up from Kager's explication of Myles's bilingual 'war campaign on bad language' (p. 70) to unearth his treatment of a very real war in these early *Cruiskeen Lawn* columns. In her recent article on the contested attribution to O'Nolan of letters to *The Irish Times* signed by 'Oscar Love' in support of the Spanish republican government, Ute Ana Mittermaier concludes that 'Further research will be necessary to establish to what extent O'Nolan [...] comment[ed] extensively on socio-political matters of international interest'.[23] Here, Flynn demonstrates Myles's employment of the Irish language as a veil behind which to write covertly about international politics – specifically, Japanese foreign policy. Uncovering the ways in which these Irish-language columns mobilise the Irish language towards creating a sly aesthetic of the 'half said', Flynn reveals that '*Cruiskeen Lawn*'s most intense engagements with the issue of Japan occur behind several veils: of the Irish language, of typographical play, of pun, of literary allusion, of translation' (p. 85). The essay closes by noting that 'If Japan features again after the Allied victory when Myles comments on the rudeness of dropping atomic bombs on the Japanese, that's another story' (p. 86).

While Keith Hopper has resisted previous readings of O'Nolan as a truly Einsteinian writer by noting that he 'nowhere says anything about relativity that could not have been gleaned from an adequate popularisation',[24] here Katherine Ebury intervenes to investigate the exact nature of the writer's encounters with the science popularisations of Arthur Eddington and Sir James Jeans. As these popularisations explained Einsteinian physics to their readers through literary analogies to the 'vulnerable, grotesque and distorted bodies' depicted in the works of Lewis Carroll and Jonathan Swift (p. 88), so Ebury interrogates O'Nolan's changing vision of the authority of science through a comparative approach to the bodily distortions of *The Third Policeman* and *The Dalkey Archive*. By addressing this gap in the critical conversation and historicising the encounters between literature and science writing, the essay provocatively reframes previous understandings of O'Nolan's problems with the authorities of science (including the calamitous effects of the atomic bomb) and faith. What emerges is a picture of O'Nolan, throughout his columns and novels, variously challenging and turning to good account the diverse engagements of these popularisations with the authorities of the observer and of the new physics itself.

Mixed inks: O'Nolan *vs.* his peers

Joseph Brooker's recent comparative reading of O'Nolan and Patrick Kavanagh calls for a more focused cultural contextual consideration of O'Nolan's clashes and collaborations with Dublin figures (many of whom, nevertheless, spent considerable spells outside of the country) such as Denis Devlin, Brian Coffey, Niall Sheridan, Niall Montgomery, R.M. Smyllie and Brendan Behan.[25] The essays of this volume's second section take up this mantle to contextualise and historicise O'Nolan's work in order to illuminate its responsiveness to or mediation by contemporary events and attitudes. In five interventions, the contributors here further advance and complicate conversations about O'Nolan's place in modernism and twentieth-century Irish writing by moving beyond the usual categories and comparative contexts to consider his models of cognition, his employment of the pseudonym, his engagements with modern economies of exchange, his modes of problematising the task of his future biographers, and his submerged collaborations with Irish forebears, family members and European contemporaries writing 'at the problematic tail-end of the modernist era' (p. 170).

Dirk Van Hulle usefully questions lines of division in literary history and chronology by considering the light that O'Nolan's writing sheds on critical debates about the continuum between cognitivist and postcognitivist modernisms. Summoning the current 'new modernist' turn in O'Nolan studies – in which O'Nolan is reconceptualised as a pivotal, rather than secondary or supplemental, author against whom to reevaluate modernism's authority – Van Hulle explores 'John Duffy's Brother' and *The Third Policeman* as key texts in rethinking high and late modernism's conceptualisations and representations of cognition. Reading the cognitive models offered in these texts in relation to those offered by Joyce ('A Painful Case', *Ulysses*) and Beckett (*Murphy*, *Watt*, *L'Innommable*, 'Stirrings Still'), Van Hulle traces 'a gradual development' in modernism 'away from Cartesian internalism in the direction of more "extensive" models of the mind' (p. 118). Against these coordinates, O'Nolan emerges as an '*Umwelt* researcher', in David Herman's term, exploring 'the lived, phenomenal worlds that emerge from, or are enacted through, the interplay between intelligent agents and their cultural as well as material circumstances'.[26] Thus reappraising the view that O'Nolan's writing distinguishes itself as a postmodern break from modernism, Van Hulle argues provocatively that 'With its focus on "widening out the mind" and with its liminal status between Joyce and Beckett, Brian O'Nolan's "*Umwelt* research" constitutes a significant site on this continuum between modernism and late modernism' (p. 118).

Ronan Crowley continues this trend of returning to history for the motivating contexts of O'Nolan's transformative art by locating the writer in the cultural field that formed his immediate intellectual inheritance: the Irish Literary Revival. By unearthing the dominant culture of pseudonymity operative in the movement, Crowley moves beyond standard rehearsals of O'Nolan's perceived points of departure from Literary Revivalism to stress that his writing offers continuities with and within it. Reframing the politics of coy misrepresentation at play in O'Nolan's many *noms de plume* within a Revivalist context, Crowley reorients our certainties away both from analyses of the Revival as insistently anti-modern and from O'Nolan's response to it as an unvariegated rejection on these terms. In the process the essay reveals a surprising kinship between O'Nolan and the Revivalists in their attempts to 'problematise notions of originality and authority, authorship and community' (p. 135).

Discerning a subtle contradiction in Carol Taaffe's dual claims that *The Third Policeman* is based on James Stephens's *The Crock of Gold* and constitutes an apolitical novel, R.W. Maslen reads O'Nolan's posthumous masterpiece as a 'radical reimagining' (p. 136) of Stephens's novel that corresponds with the new political shapes emerging in Ireland and Europe in the 1930s and 40s. If *The Third Policeman*'s many debts to, and resonances with, Stephens's maverick text suggest that an 'insurrectionary attitude'[27] lurks beneath its surface, then Maslen profitably teases out these political drives through a comparative reading of the novels' economic models and attitudes to state authority. Ultimately, the essay contends, O'Nolan reconceives Stephens's novel as an elaborate trap in which Ireland, its people and its countryside form an integral component of a general global movement towards self-destruction that has brought Europe to the brink of a war that threatens to dismantle humanity itself.

Ian Ó Caoimh takes the warning at the heart of *An Béal Bocht* of 'the need for vigilance when dealing with all forms of (auto)biographical portraiture'

(p. 153) as a launching point from which to contest a number of authorities in O'Nolan studies, most prominently that of the biographer. Contrasting Anthony Cronin's *No Laughing Matter: The Life and Times of Flann O'Brien* with Ciarán Ó Nualláin's earlier *Óige an Dearthár .i. Myles na gCopaleen*, Ó Caoimh unpacks in rich detail the ways in which the success of *An Béal Bocht* has prevented neither critic nor biographer from relapsing 'into a characterisation of the Gaeltacht that forces Brian and Ciarán's shrewd, carnivalesque representations' of Irish localities 'into a reductive binary between the "real" and the "idealised"' (pp. 153–154). By casting much-needed light on O'Nolan's writerly relation with his brothers Ciarán and Caoimhín and exploring the question of a family style, Ó Caoimh demonstrates that the most drawn-upon passages in Ciarán's biography have been fundamentally misinterpreted and conceal a subversive intent which not only bolsters the satire of *An Béal Bocht*, but also suggests parallels with the refashioning of mythological material in *At Swim-Two-Birds*.

John McCourt revisits O'Nolan's late career novel *The Hard Life* through a close reading of its chapters 'which cover the fatal, shambolic trip to Rome and the Vatican' undertaken by Collopy, Fahrt and Manus (p. 172). From this vantage point, McCourt finds a number of new textures and themes in the novel's study of squalor, reading it, at once, as a failed study in perfection (or a study in failed perfection), a play on the Christian concept of '*felix culpa*', a parody *both* of Joyce and Irish domestic realism, a (post-)modernist play with simulacra and imposture and a text rewarded by a comparative reading with Carlo Emilio Gadda's celebrated 1957 Italian novel *Quer pasticciaccio brutto de via Merulana*. All the while McCourt traces the novel's failures (intentional or otherwise), finding ultimately that it is significantly less than the confrontation with authority – clerical and lay – that the author sought to stage in its pages.

Gross impieties: O'Nolan *vs.* the sacred texts

Crucial to any evaluation of O'Nolan's anti-authoritarian impulses is his apparently hybrid status as an *avant-garde* writer who evinces a distinctly Catholic imagination; or, in Carlos Villar Flor's evocative formulation, as 'A Postmodernist Who Happens to Be a Thomist'.[28] Even as the radicalism and experimentalism of the author's output is beyond doubt, its innovativeness is often belied by the author's traditionalism or anti-modernist proclivities. To address this ambivalent relation to the authorities of tradition, the essays that comprise the collection's final section consider the lasting impact of

O'Nolan's oftentimes irreverent repackaging of inherited myths, sacred texts and formative canons, the Pauline dimensions of his anti-modernist rhetoric, his debts to Menippean satire and his refusal of literary and ideological closure.

Louis de Paor takes up this focus on O'Nolan's wrangling with past authorities by reevaluating the importance of the writer's college years to the development of his aesthetics. The essay draws attention to O'Nolan's scholarly engagement with a pre-colonial Gaelic tradition and examines the impact of his early studies – the sustained interest in early Irish language writing, the curriculum in Irish at UCD and the MA thesis on Nature Poetry in Irish – upon his bilingual sensibility. Emphasising the two different versions of Ó Nualláin's thesis, and revising previous estimations of their worth, de Paor also considers the extent of O'Nolan's debt to Standish Hayes O'Grady's *Silva Gadelica* and J.G. O'Keeffe's seminal 1913 translation of *Buile Suibhne*. In a final move that synthesises O'Nolan's simultaneous debts to Irish tradition and to modernist thought, de Paor provocatively suggests that the author's sustained interest in medieval Irish poetry and the 'incomplete bilingualism' of twentieth-century Irish letters is exactly the feature of his work that makes it so resonant with Roland Barthes's post-structuralist 'dream of an unalienated language' (p. 203).

Developing this theme, Alana Gillespie offers a detailed exploration of the deconstructions of cultural nationalism and Catholic tradition that inform the almost punkish attitude to authority found in *At Swim-Two-Birds* and *The Dalkey Archive*. Summoning Walter Benjamin's writing on the aura of tradition and Jacques Derrida's rejection of the notion of a pure, unmixed present, Gillespie traces the moves and strategies by which these novels draw attention to the gaps in (and thus the alternative histories of) the foundational texts and events of these movements and metanarratives. Reviewed by this light, O'Nolan's recycling and recontextualising of borrowed myths and scriptures (both canonical and apocryphal) has a profoundly transformative effect on authoritative texts and their receptions that at once challenges, destroys and rejuvenates tradition. As such, these acts of subterfuge reveal an ethical and political responsibility, shared by the reader and the author, to destabilise narratives that have been taken for granted – even if what we uncover 'may be unsettling' to our most cherished beliefs (p. 215).

Drawing together the section's theme of O'Nolan's ambivalently traditionalist and anti-modernist impulses, Ruben Borg reads O'Nolan's fiction in the context of a Pauline rhetoric of conversion. Focusing on the recurrent motif of *death-in-life* in *The Dalkey Archive*, 'Two in One' and the 'Sir Myles' fragments from *Cruiskeen Lawn*, Borg suggests that the chief appeal of Saint Paul's writing for O'Nolan is that it offers a model by which 'to characterise his own ambiguous status as an experimental modernist writer, and, simultaneously, a critic of modernist *avant-garde* pretentions' (p. 219) through its articulation of a paradoxical relation to the law – a *neither/ nor-but-both-at-once* logic of self-identification with a legal subject or a legal community.

Dieter Fuchs reads *The Dalkey Archive* in the tradition of Menippean satire, a philosophical literary mode that flouts all kinds of established authority by way of parody and carnivalesque inversion. Fuchs relocates from previous archetypal and topical analyses of O'Nolan's Menippean credentials,[29] to situate *The Dalkey Archive* more precisely within the Hellenistic and Roman Menippean traditions. Reading against these coordinates, Fuchs unearths the more precise debt owed in De Selby's seriocomic underwater colloquy with Saint Augustine to Lucian's *Dialogues of the Dead,* and places the tongue-in-cheek afterlife of the literary authority of Joyce within the Varronian tradition of the *Summa,* as echoed in the 'archive' of the novel's title. These traditions of Menippean rebellion against the authority of institutionalised knowledge and its representatives inform and frame Mick Shaughnessy's encounters with, and ultimate rejections of, the patriarchal authorities of executive state power, patristic theology, literature, philosophy, science and even the local policeman and his bicycle – and frame the novel itself as a self-ironic encyclopaedia of human knowledge.

Closing the collection's interrogations of O'Nolan's diverse stances against inherited textual authorities, Tamara Radak contemplates the role of hypertextuality in the 'branching text' of *The Third Policeman.* Aligning the novel's most striking formal feature, its accumulative and increasingly intrusive 'fictional footnotes', with its multiple temporalities, ontological hesitations and proliferation of 'possible worlds', Radak teases out the complex ways in which O'Nolan's posthumous novel tests and complicates the culturally dominant notions of time, space and narrative closure popularised by the tradition of the 'well-made novel'. Positioning *The Third Policeman* at the centre of a critical conversation between hypertext theory, possible worlds theory, Todorovian hesitation and Deleuzian incompossibility, Radak suggests these digressive and deliberately misdirecting hypertexts both deconstruct textual hierarchies and disturb reading processes and experiences. As the anonymous and unnameable author of the footnotes invites us to 'participate in the riotous carnival of reading',[30] Radak investigates the implications of this complex of footnotes and temporalities for the hallowed functions of authorial authority.

* * *

The increasingly international contexts in which O'Nolan is being read invite us to reconsider his profile as a satirist, a local comedian, a critic of provincial attitudes, a formal innovator and a powerful, inimitable voice in the twentieth-century *avant-garde*. As the boundaries of his canon continue to expand and to be redrawn, O'Nolan's writing appears to be constantly repositioning itself between local and international perspectives, displaying an uncanny knack for comic doubling and self-contradiction, embracing the innovative spirit of the times, yet unmasking its pretensions. Thirty years after the urban and absurdist *Blather* manifesto, we find the mature figure of 'George Knowall' writing in the decidedly local and conservative *Nationalist and Leinster Times*, Carlow, and reflecting upon the basics of humour. The definition he offers reveals that even as the sites and politics of O'Nolan's riotous art metamorphosed, its anti-authoritarian comic spirit remained constant: 'If you have a man who has a certain arrogance of manner and who is impeccably dressed, it is very funny to pour a bucket of dirty water over him, preferably from an upstair's [*sic*] window. *Should we not pity a person subjected to such a plight*? No, indeed. We roar laughing' (*MAD*, 107).

PART I

'neither popular nor profitable'

O'Nolan *vs.* The Plain People

I

'irreverence moving towards the blasphemous'

Brian O'Nolan, *Blather* and Irish popular culture

CAROL TAAFFE

In 1939, Brian O'Nolan was not a popular writer. He was even, perhaps, a notoriously unpopular writer – at least to those who would look back on his career knowing that his lack of commercial success may have contributed to his publisher's rejection of *The Third Policeman*. But he had more readers, and more readers in unexpected places, than the legend of his brilliant failure allows. There was Jorge Luis Borges, of course, who in 1939 reviewed *At Swim-Two-Birds* for *El Hogar* in Buenos Aires. It was a strange coincidence of talents, though even if O'Nolan had known how far his book travelled he could not have appreciated how well it had found its mark.[1] He himself would send it in more predictable directions: to James Joyce in Paris, who sent back his approving remarks, and to Ethel Mannin, who reacted less encouragingly.[2] But the book also made more unexpected journeys. At least two copies would turn up in Australia, one imported by the booksellers Ewins in Ballarat, a shop dealing in contemporary modernist literature, and another bought from the David Jones bookstore in Sydney to join the library of a Gallipoli veteran. No other copies of that doomed first edition are known to have reached Australia. It was lone readers who found this odd book, outliers in every sense. The reader in the goldmining city of Ballarat had also bought Samuel Beckett's *Murphy* in 1938; the buyer in Sydney was an artist versed in Cubism and Expressionism.[3] If *At Swim-Two-Birds* travelled much farther than its author might have reasonably expected, the evidence suggests that it reached only the cognoscenti.

It might seem ironic that *At Swim-Two-Birds*, a novel that mimics the blend of the esoteric and the everyday (though tilting in favour of the latter) found in Joyce's *Ulysses*, should begin its career as a *coterie* publication. Shortly before the publication of this strange novel, which married Joyce and T.S. Eliot with Gaelic sagas and middle Irish manuscripts, Niall Montgomery confided to a friend that he looked forward to seeing 'Frank Swinnerton and the other English critics in the soup properly',[4] as if it were really a private joke conducted at their expense. As *The Irish Times* noted, the novel was clearly a product of the 'National University tradition', with O'Nolan rehearsing the parodies and ideas he and his collaborators had first developed in the University College Dublin student magazine *Comhthrom Féinne*.[5] This observation presupposed a welcoming audience for *At Swim-Two-Birds*, albeit a limited one. Still, the newspaper's review of the novel on 25 March suggested that while it was 'all rather involved', *At Swim-Two-Birds* would present 'no difficulty to the average reader'.[6] The disjunction between a *coterie* literature and popular culture is of course one of the subjects of the novel itself, its humour often fuelled by the clash between different types of readers as much as between different literary styles. The novel, the student notes, is 'self-administered in private' (*CN*, 21); to write requires solitude and introspection, to retire – as he says – into the privacy of the mind. But if Sweeny is a model of the poet tortured in his isolation, much of the comic energy of O'Nolan's novel comes from Dublin's talkers and schemers. The modern, experimental novel might address itself to an educated minority, or to select avant-gardists, but in *At Swim-Two-Birds* that limited constituency is mocked as frequently as the readers who want only a 'nice simple story with plenty of the razor' (*CN*, 167).

Yet Colm Tóibín has ascribed to Brian O'Nolan – as to his near contemporaries Fernando Pessoa and Jorge Luis Borges – a sense of intellectual isolation that would become a constitutive element of his strange fiction: 'The sense that there was no one much to read the work these writers were producing ate its way into the tone and structure of the work itself'.[7] In other words, it was the lack of a suitable readership in Ireland that could make a novel like *At Swim-Two-Birds* possible:

> In a society where there is no body of readers, it is not easy to write with a reader in mind, a reader who wants a story in which time is represented in a straight line and in which characters are filled with

feelings and longings [...]. It is much easier to make a story or a novel in which the reader is already built-in and which wrong-foots or even usurps the idea of reading.[8]

So the novel becomes a form of shadowboxing, the author's dialogue with himself. Admittedly, Ireland in the early twentieth century might have been an island of writers but it was not, to all appearances, an island of readers.

A decade before *At Swim-Two-Birds* was published this conceived lack of Irish readership was taken up as a point of defence by those who objected to elements of the Censorship of Publications Act (1929). During a Dáil debate on the proposed legislation, the Cumann na nGaedheal TD Hugh Law argued that there was little real necessity to place controls on books entering the country:

> Go up and down the countryside and in how many provincial towns, even of a considerable size, will you find books? There must be tens of thousands of houses in this country in which no book is to be found, unless it be a prayer-book or possibly an old copy of *Knocknagow* or *Moore's Melodies*.[9]

The 1929 legislation was primarily intended to address publications advocating birth control and imports of British tabloid newspapers (particularly those publishing sensational accounts of crime) and so was concerned above all with the interests of a mass readership. The fact that it was later used to ban much contemporary literature was not anticipated either by its drafters or by the campaigners who had lobbied for legislation. Tellingly, the countrywide campaigns led by the Irish Vigilance Association in the 1910s and 1920s had typically persecuted newsagents rather than booksellers; the Association paid little attention to developments in literary fiction, reflecting the similar lack of interest on the part of the readers it targeted. By the time O'Nolan came to write *At Swim-Two-Birds* little had changed. In 1936 James Devane, a contributor to the short-lived literary magazine *Ireland Today*, complained of the low sales of fiction in Ireland; in his view, economic factors curtailed the development of a national literature:

> I have heard it costs three hundred pounds to publish a novel. Four thousand copies must be sold to pay costs, and of these four thousand, four hundred at most may be sold in Ireland. From this fact it is obvious that an Irish novel is not possible to-day. An English publisher decides the fate of the Irish novel. English critical standards measure its worth.[10]

As far as the publishing fate of *The Third Policeman* was concerned, that jeremiad would hold true. (It would be an astute English publisher, Timothy O'Keeffe, who would persuade O'Nolan to return to fiction in the 1960s and who oversaw the posthumous publication of that 'lost' novel.) But if the rejection of *The Third Policeman* is taken to have shaped O'Nolan's career – if the novelist in him was prematurely buried for lack of an appreciative readership – it is curious that the critical and commercial success of *An Béal Bocht* a year later did not have the reverse effect on its author.

The irony is that far from lacking readers, Brian O'Nolan always had them – far more, at least, than most of his contemporaries working in Ireland. Initially finding literary celebrity in the fishbowl of University College Dublin, the first months of his career as a novelist coincided with his invasion of the *Irish Times* letters page and his successful launch as a national newspaper columnist. In writing for *The Irish Times* for the next twenty-six years he had a broad platform, if not quite a popular one. When *Cruiskeen Lawn* first appeared in 1940 the newspaper might have been the journal of a social and intellectual minority, but its reach was still far greater than a literary novelist might expect to achieve. And so to that degree and in that sense, O'Nolan was a popular writer and positioned himself as such. Even in privately promoting *At Swim-Two-Birds* in 1939 he already wryly presented himself as a determinedly professional writer, more concerned with popular and financial success than with aesthetic achievement. The assertion might have been tongue-in-cheek but it became a prominent theme in *Cruiskeen Lawn*'s self-conscious mockery of Dublin's middle-class 'corduroys' and aesthetes, the excesses of modernist writers and their scholarly followers. In his newspaper column, O'Nolan continued to play the outsider to the rather exclusive worlds of scholarship and art that he had mocked so assiduously in *At Swim-Two-Birds* and *The Third Policeman*. The curiosity is that his turn to journalism has been so little considered as a choice in its own right, rather than as an accidental and regrettable consequence of the reception of his first two novels.

Like those novels, the ephemeral comic writing which dominated O'Nolan's writing career (at least in bulk) resists easy classification, even as journalism. As throwaway work it also subverts ideas of cultural value, and the scepticism towards art so frequently expressed in *Cruiskeen Lawn* is characteristic of its peculiar anti-aesthetic.[11] All these factors may have contributed to the relative critical neglect of the column and to the longstanding assumption that the tragedy of O'Nolan's career was that he lacked the readership and appreciation that would have encouraged his real talents to flourish. But he had readers, of course. The implication, perhaps, is that he had the wrong kind of readers.

In discussing the neglect of *Cruiskeen Lawn,* Jon Day astutely highlights the anxiety over the 'aesthetic status of journalism' that has been such a feature of its critical reception.[12] Admittedly, an important factor in dictating the paths of scholarly research on O'Nolan's work has been the limited availability of the columns outside the five published collections[13] – at least until the launch of the *Irish Times* digital archive in 2007. But that anxiety over the aesthetic status of journalism cannot be too easily discounted, and the lingering critical hesitation is worth exploring; O'Nolan's work as a columnist subverts certain cultural assumptions that are very slow to change. One of these is the presumed pre-eminence of the novel form, with much more critical attention paid to his weak later novels *The Hard Life* and *The Dalkey Archive* than to the comic journalism produced at his peak. Another is the classification of 'literature' itself: is this literature, or journalism, or something in between? And since *Cruiskeen Lawn* was published in a daily newspaper, alongside news reporting and the Dublin social diary, 'Bertie' Smyllie's editorial and the sports pages, it was also interestingly positioned at a crossroads between different reading communities.

With the growing interest in opening up O'Nolan's literary archive – looking away from the three great novels to also explore the short stories, the plays, the television scripts, the newspaper columns, and any amount of ephemeral journalism – his career might begin to take on a rather different appearance. In this broad retrospective, it becomes all the more clear that the vast majority of his writing was ephemeral, designed to be disposable. This part of his work also had a very different implied readership, and a different relation to its actual readers, to that of the early novels. And while the newspaper column displays many of the comic strategies that disrupted O'Nolan's fiction, in *Cruiskeen Lawn* these strategies are at work in a very different context. The habit of digressiveness, the narrative discontinuities, collaborative authorship, serialism, sharp juxtapositions and disjunctive styles might challenge the conventions of the novel but, as Stephen Young has pointed out, they are far more typical of the magazine or newspaper, which is where O'Nolan's comic writing had first taken shape.[14] If Myles na gCopaleen's parodies and uses of public rhetoric – court reports, political speeches, journalism, advertising – echo Joyce's *Ulysses,* an important difference between them is in their relationship to the public sphere. In

Cruiskeen Lawn, O'Nolan did not engage with such discursive writing from the distance of an experimental artwork. His work appeared in a daily newspaper and was responsive to a wider audience. It was the work of a civil servant and a newspaperman who was professionally attuned to writing as something that is socially performative, a dialogue in the world.

So that critical anxiety over the 'aesthetic status of journalism' is well placed. It is telling that *Cruiskeen Lawn* was self-consciously set apart from the literary world and its 'corduroys', and for many years hardly penetrated the canon of Irish writing, quite besides that of international modernism. The column's styles and modes were self-consciously embedded in Irish public discourse, playing out the tensions and contradictions of its time. As Andrew Gibson has written of Joyce, of *Cruiskeen Lawn* it might be possible to say that 'laughter negotiates rifts and divisions that are historical, cultural, and inward at once'.[15] Unlike *Ulysses* or *A Portrait of the Artist as a Young Man*, O'Nolan's newspaper work directly intervened in public discourse and operated in the sphere of popular culture. To O'Nolan and his contemporaries – readers who were less familiar with Joyce's journalistic endeavours than with his local caricature as an aesthete gone mad in his ivory tower – that intervention was surely a revealing gesture.[16]

Their attitude to Joyce echoed the values of contemporary Ireland, reflecting both its cultural conservatism and its anti-intellectualism. And indeed Myles na gCopaleen's commentary on Joyce could at times degenerate into a defensive philistinism. But the populist and anti-elitist values underpinning some of that criticism had their roots in a particular historical situation. Elsewhere in Europe, such a sceptical response to the idea, aesthetic and institutions of 'Art' became the stuff of the artistic *avant-garde*; in post-independence Ireland, the cynicism ran deeper. While Joyce's 'Work in Progress' was appearing in Parisian literary journals such as *Transatlantic Review* and *transition* throughout the 1930s, a generation schooled in the War of Independence had rejected his revolution of the word in favour of their own, very real, social revolution. The dominant Irish *avant-garde* of that decade was to comprise a body of social realists whose commitment to producing a critical image of the new Ireland reflected the documentary turn of the time. In his 1934 review of contemporary Irish poetry, Beckett might have famously framed Irish modernism as an oppositional aesthetic, but in the local context it could also appear socially and politically reactionary.[17] It was clear that W.B. Yeats's alienation from the conservative Catholic ethos of the young state, for example, went hand in hand with his revulsion at the cultural democracies of mass-market newspapers and modern education.[18]

The populist cultural values of the new Ireland could be regressive and conservative; they were also part of its democratic ethos and at times they were subversive of its *status quo*.

This subversive spirit is visible in one of O'Nolan's first ventures as a professional writer: the short-lived comic magazine *Blather*. Founded with his brother, the journalist Ciarán Ó Nualláin, and their friend Niall Sheridan, it ran for only five issues between August 1934 and January 1935.[19] This was a magazine without any apparent ambitions as a satirical journal, instead thriving on silliness and on travesty of its own form, with bombastic editorials, fake letters' pages and competitions, and a habit of haranguing its readers. But its humour also had a political colouring that would be largely absent from the later *Cruiskeen Lawn* – a shade closer to *Dublin Opinion* and the political bent of predecessors like *Zoz, Pat,* and *The Lepracaun*.[20] Published just before O'Nolan joined the civil service, *Blather* carnivalised Irish party politics in a manner that would soon be impossible for him to do. Equally notable, in this context, was *Blather*'s tendency to use Irish popular culture (and its Anglo-American influences) as a means of undercutting the dominant political and cultural narratives of the young Irish state.

As if answering the vigilance campaigns against 'evil literature' that had been directed at the popular British press, *Blather*'s first editorial announced the magazine as 'the King Rat of the Irish Press, the paper that will achieve entirely new levels in everything that is contemptible, despicable and unspeakable in contemporary journalism'.[21] It assumed the kind of boundless authority that Myles na gCopaleen would soon assert over The Plain People of Ireland, with the editors claiming to have 'de Valera and the entire Fianna Fáil Cabinet in our pocket'.[22] But any comic or satirical authority asserted in *Blather* was soon undercut. A central tool in its comic arsenal was the *non sequitur*, often used to amplify the comic incongruity of material that sits comfortably side-by-side in the daily press:

> Every nerve will be strained towards the achievement of the BLATHER Revolution and the establishment of the BLATHER Dictatorship, followed by the inauguration of the BLATHER Communist Monarchy. [...] we will win the day and the brutal military heel of BLATHER will crush the neck of its enemies. Write to us for the address of your nearest BLATHER Study Circle. Write to us for a free cut-out pattern of the BLATHER Patent Woollen Panties and say good-bye to colds. Write to us for our pamphlet, 'The BLATHER Attitude on Ping-Pong'.[23]

To a degree, much of the humour of *Blather* plays on these kinds of inconsistencies. But its comic incongruities, drawing together what normally stands apart, also exploited fault lines in contemporary Irish culture — particularly in its treatment of Anglo-Irish relations.

Unlike *Cruiskeen Lawn*, *Blather* paid relatively little attention to literary and critical affairs, Irish or otherwise. Instead it took its co-ordinates from the daily press: from the satirical magazine *Dublin Opinion*, *The Irish Independent*, the British *Daily Mail* or Éamon de Valera's *Irish Press* newspaper, even burlesquing press rivalry by finding comic nemeses in *The Irish Grocer* and *The Garda Review*. Admittedly, in *Blather* there were already Myles's familiar pot-shots at the folk aesthetic of the Irish Literary Revival, particularly the plays of John Millington Synge. An article on the government subsidy to the Abbey Theatre noted that with the arrival of the Abbey players in Boston, 'thousands of playgoers who turned their faces sadly to the emigrant ship early in the present century because of "Riders to the Sea" are now pouring back from the States in hordes'.[24] But the magazine's cultural co-ordinates were just as likely to be provided by the conventions of popular magazines or tabloid newspapers, the new Irish radio stations, Hollywood film, or popular fiction.

This was little more than a decade after independence and at the height of the state's Gaelicisation policy. The continued popularity of British newspapers like the *Daily Mail* had not only contributed to the passing of the Censorship of Publications Act; more recently, it had also led to the imposition of heavy taxes on press imports. *Blather*, like *At Swim-Two-Birds*, appeared to exploit deliberately these anxieties over popular reading tastes. Its material not only undermined the idea of cultural homogeneity that was central to the policy of Gaelicisation, but also the credibility of its populist appeal to a sense of national community. It was the Irish-language journalist Ciarán Ó Nualláin who introduced this element to *Blather*'s second issue in October 1934. 'The West's Awake! A Heart-Pounding Melodrama', which blends the wild wests of America and Gaelic Ireland, had first been published under his name in the UCD magazine, *Comhthrom Féinne*.[25] The potboiler element of that story continues with a Jimmy Cagney-style shoot-out in issue three, which in turn gives way to the English detective story in 'The Mystery of the Yellow Limousine', in which Sherlock Holmes wanders Dublin disguised as Éamon de Valera, a rat, a lost collar-stud, a disused lamp post and finally, a cigarette butt.[26]

The Anglo-Irish fusion reached its apogee in the penultimate issue of *Blather* with the story '*Eachtraí Shearluic*' [The Adventures of Sherlock]. It is written in a mode common to both Ciarán and Brian O'Nolan – and arguably attributable to either – veering as it does between pastiche of Conan Doyle and the Fianna tale:

> It was a morning late in the autumn of 1887 and the yellow fog which obliterated Baker Street and dulled its sounds, imparted to us a peculiar feeling of isolation in our chambers. *Bhí Searluc suidhte cois teineadh, a dhruim cromtha agus a chraig leathan lodartha líonta le na aghaidh fada fiadháin. Bhí súil amháin nimhneach ag stána, amach eadar dá mhéar ar an marbh-theinidh mhóna.* [Sherlock was sitting by the fire, his back bent and his broad, flabby hands supporting his long, savage face. One malignant eye was staring out between two fingers at the dying turf.][27]

When '*Bhatson*' rises from his '*Meenabeg Mercury*' and moves to the window (clearing the London fog as he goes) he sees no black hansom cabs, but rather a bog stretching westwards as far as the eye can see. The transposition of Sherlock Holmes to a Gaelic underworld is complete when Oisín of the Fianna arrives in search of his companions. '*Tabhair tuairisc dúinn ar Fhionn*', demands Holmes, in the formula of the Fianna stories, '... *agus aithris dúinn a mhian* and pray do not omit the smallest detail, because though apparently trivial to the layman, it often represents an invaluable clue to the trained investigator'. Holmes, suspecting Oisín to be Moriarty in cunning disguise, takes him to a Dublin psychiatric hospital on the back of a turf truck, where both are incarcerated together.

The confusion of the modern and the mythic here, the play between two languages and two cultures, would become key notes of *At Swim-Two-Birds*. And maybe in the formality of Conan Doyle's language, as in the intellectual character of Sherlock Holmes himself, it is possible to see trace elements of Myles na gCopaleen. In any case, this Anglo-Irish fusion of the Gaelic Sherlock Holmes exposes two sides of the Irish schoolboy's literary inheritance. Like many Irish writers of their generation, the O'Nolan brothers grew up as essentially Victorian readers. Frank O'Connor, a close contemporary, would admit that 'To have grown up in an Irish provincial town in the first quarter of the twentieth century was to have known the nineteenth-century novel as a contemporary art form'.[28] But rather than Turgenev or Tolstoy, the lodestars for the Cork writers O'Connor and O'Faoláin, the writers of *Blather* were fixed on popular adventure stories of empire, cowboy westerns and the omniscient powers of the detective as much as the mythic sagas that then dominated the Irish education system.

Such literary collisions are a mainstay of *At Swim-Two-Birds*, but in *Blather* they are allowed to carry clearer political implications. A comic hybrid like the *Meenabeg Mercury*, the paper that Watson is reading in this story, marries the metropolitan and the provincial — *The London Mercury* with the clumsily Anglicised *Meenabeg* — but in a story of Anglo-Irish cross-contamination the selection of that Irish source is quite pointed. '*Meenabeg*' echoes Muine Bheag, the name only recently given to the Carlow town of Bagenalstown, which like Kingstown and Queenstown was renamed after 1922. Founded in the early eighteenth century by Lord Walter Bagenal as a planned community modelled on Versailles, Bagenalstown was a reminder of the Anglo-Irish inheritance in an independent Ireland. Unlike Cobh or Dún Laoghaire, its renaming never wholly succeeded. Today it is still Bagenalstown to its residents and Muine Bheag to the Irish state. But 'Meenabeg' is the most confused of all, a re-Anglicisation of a Gaelic impostor, and its Anglo-Irish comedy carnivalises the contradictions and discontinuities in the political and cultural inheritance of the new state.

But the basis of this Gaelic Sherlock Holmes was not a fanciful invention by the writers of *Blather*. An Gúm, the Irish state publishing house, had published its own Sherlock Holmes story that year: *Cú na mBaskerville*, translated by Nioclás Tóibín. The Gaelic Sherlock Holmes joined Irish translations of books by Robert Louis Stevenson, Emily Brontë, Oliver Goldsmith and others, as An Gúm attempted to supply fiction in Irish for a growing readership in that language, given the introduction of compulsory Irish to the education system in 1922. The policy was partly a response to the limited original material available to the publishing house, and partly a means of infusing Irish writing with new techniques. As Philip O'Leary has pointed out, many progressives in the Revival movement viewed translation as a means of 'bringing Irish speakers out of the provincialism imposed on them by Anglicisation'[29] — counter-intuitively, Gaelicisation might have been a means of opening Ireland out to European culture. But in reality it was translations from English that dominated An Gúm's output, and translations as a whole dominated its publications list. By 1936, they accounted for 82 of the 100 novels published over its first decade.[30] Among its contributors was O'Nolan's uncle Fr Gearóid Ó Nualláin, who translated Tolstoy and Pushkin into Irish. The lists were also filled with Jack London, W.H. Davies, H. Rider Haggard, R.M. Ballantyne, Joseph Conrad and popular American adventure novels like Captain Mayne Reid's *Boy Hunters of the Mississippi*.[31] There might have been an element of reverse cultural appropriation at work in translating

English classics into Irish, but the numbers of mystery and adventure novels included – many with clearly imperialist subtexts – reflected the popular tastes of the Irish reading public. And that was perhaps a pragmatic gesture in a decade when among Ireland's bestselling publications, as Elizabeth Russell has shown, were the *Programme of the Coronation* in 1937 and the *Irish Independent Handbook on Emigration to England*.[32]

The discordant cultural energies of the new Ireland were similarly recognised in a *Blather* editorial claiming that the magazine had been banned in Germany for its 'stern and unrelenting attitude' on a proposed *Anschluss*.[33] Like the notorious 1898 editorial in which the *Skibbereen Eagle* had vowed to keep its eye on the Russian Tzar,[34] *Blather*'s joke projects an exaggerated sense of its own authority that far outreaches its status and influence – perhaps mimicking the outsider's perspective on the new Irish Free State itself. In continuing circulation in Germany after the ban, *Blather* claims, it first masqueraded as Lord Beaverbrook's *Daily Express*; next it will appear as the *Daily Mail*, then *Our Boys*, the children's weekly then published by the Irish Christian Brothers – a native counterpoint to the British *Boy's Own* magazine. The characteristically Mylesian theme of imposture is already in play here, with its reminder of textual unreliability. But in the confusions of a newly post-colonial culture, Irish masquerades as British and *vice versa*. The Catholic and nationalist ideology of *Our Boys* ironically only mimics the heroic imperialism of the original *Boy's Own*. The inclusion of *The Daily Express* in the joke reflects its recent notoriety for running a front-page headline reporting a Jewish boycott of German goods as an act of aggression ('Judea declares war on Germany'[35]). The uniting element, perhaps, is the strain of reactionary populism shared by all these publications, whether British or Irish. Overall, as a magazine *Blather* dissolved the attitudinising of the popular press in its characteristic silliness, but in such instances it also played on a certain continuing unease in the 1930s about the porous boundaries of Irish popular culture – an unease that was reflected in the cultural protectionism of the new state.

The more bizarre products of that tendency – the three decades of literary censorship, or the banning of jazz music and 'crooners' from the national airwaves – have given O'Nolan's Ireland the reputation of repressive and provincial monotony. The hell of *The Third Policeman*, Anthony Cronin noted, might really be Tullamore in the Irish midlands: its 'same unchanging sameness' (*CN*, 364) is everywhere in provincial Ireland.[36] In a slightly different sense, Seamus Deane's *Strange Country: Modernity and Nationhood in Irish Writing Since 1790* takes monotony as a constitutive element of the period's national narrative. The essentialism underpinning the contemporary sense of Irish cultural identity, Deane writes,

> is coercive because it always insists on the necessity of reconciling difference with sameness, discontinuity with continuity, arguing, for instance, that the same Irish spirit prevailed time and again [...]. It is productive of monotony, because it orders miscellaneous materials into repetitive, typifying narratives.[37]

And those 'repetitive, typifying' cultural narratives become cliché and stereotype in the end, the building blocks of so much of O'Nolan's satiric humour in *At Swim-Two-Birds* and *An Béal Bocht*. But reading this Ireland through *Blather* or *Cruiskeen Lawn* is also to be aware of its very real contradictions and discontinuities. If *Cruiskeen Lawn* is a monstrous caricature of Ireland in the mid-twentieth century, as Stephen Young has argued, then this caricature is achieved through myriad styles and voices, where close attention to the ordinary is productive of fantasy and oddity.[38] The very form of *Cruiskeen Lawn*, or *At Swim-Two-Birds*, is a counterpoint to those 'typifying' national narratives that Seamus Deane describes. Their ultimate expression might have been the 'ready-made' novel *Children of Destiny* that O'Nolan once planned to write with his university friends – a combination of Irish nationalist Whig narrative and literary cliché. That wry mode of humour was typical of Brian O'Nolan and his collaborators but it was also characteristic of their city, a place that generated an atmosphere of 'irreverence moving towards the blasphemous', as Colm Tóibín has put it.[39] To some degree the monotone, provincial Ireland of the post-independence years – the Ireland which killed off 'Flann O'Brien' – is itself a historical cliché, a 'repetitive, typifying' narrative of its own. Decades before cultural historians got there, *Cruiskeen Lawn* served as a warning to resist cliché, to resist the urge to order miscellaneous materials into neat narratives, to remain alert to the contradictory elements of the cultural data.

The path of Brian O'Nolan's own career is a case in point. In the same month that Myles na gCopaleen first appeared in *The Irish Times*, 'Flann O'Brien' contributed an essay to the first issue of *The Bell*. It was about dog tracks. In the next issue he wrote about public houses; a few months later it was dance halls.[40] These were observational pieces without too much of Flann O'Brien's flair about them. Perhaps they bored him – perhaps they bored his editor, Seán O'Faoláin – because he never contributed again. The style fit with the documentary ambitions of the new magazine, as if O'Nolan was composing an Irish version of J.B. Priestley's *English Journey* (a feat which O'Faoláin would complete that year with his own travelogue, *Irish Journey*). They now seem slightly out of place within O'Nolan's *œuvre*, reminiscent not of modernism or post-modernism but of another fashion of the 1930s: the taste for realism and documentary, for images of 'ordinary' life. Many of O'Faoláin's editorials from that early period of *The Bell* are certainly preoccupied with a thirties' ideal of cultural democracy: 'we have entered into a new phase of our history [...]. The social revolution here has invited the populace to come into the world of letters, of paintings, and of music, to enjoy and to create. The populace has not done that in Ireland for two hundred years'.[41] Myles na gCopaleen's commentary on the journal would cast it in quite a different light – as the plaything of aesthetes and self-indulgent critics – and certainly O'Faoláin was capable of frustrating his own democratic intentions in some of his more patrician editorials. But the choice of subject in those three articles, whether it is O'Nolan's or not, is suggestive of the populist mood of the time. That mood played within his experimental fiction too, in the dissonant and debunking voices of *At Swim-Two-Birds*, or the epistemological scepticism of *The Third Policeman*. It would contribute, among other factors, to the unusual shape of a career that moved from post-Joycean experimentalism to television comedy, advertising, and the exploitation of a literary brand. (Not only was 'Myles na gCopaleen' used to sell Odearest mattresses, but the multi-authored nature of *Cruiskeen Lawn* effectively created a franchise out of a literary style.[42]) Admittedly, *The Bell* pieces are not typical of Brian O'Nolan's work. In some ways they do not quite fit with it, or at least not in any significant way; in a packed and varied career they are easy to overlook. But like *Blather*, they show O'Nolan's interests inclining towards popular culture, to the everyday world. And in terms of his publishing career, that instinct to orientate himself towards the daily press rather than the world of the limited edition would place him in a unique position in Ireland as a writer of modernist credentials who, for nearly three decades, addressed a wide and responsive readership.[43] The curiosity, in the end, is that his posthumous reputation would often suggest quite the opposite.

2

'No more drunk, truculent, witty, celtic, dark, desperate, amorous paddies!'

Brian O'Nolan and the Irish stereotype

Maebh Long

As Myles na gCopaleen once declared, 'The stage Irishman is most un-dead'.[1] Haunting representations at home and abroad, stock characters created during colonial rule lived on post-independence, casting shadows of easy cheer and indulgent lamentation, guileless honesty and cunning duplicity, mangled logic and drunken bravado over depictions of national identity. Portrayals of the Irish self laboured under the constant threat of inauthenticity, negotiating between the extremes of an Irishness so recognisable as to be the revenant of the old cliché, and one so muted as to fail to be Irish at all. Written in the midst of this anxiety of influence, Brian O'Nolan's works are a sustained performance of the post-independence search for national identity. They engage, with varying degrees of sincerity and success, with the stereotypes and clichés imposed on and adopted by the Irish; aggressively rejecting their authority, satirically undermining their limitations, and operating in collusion with their appeal.

This essay looks at the ways in which O'Nolan's minor articles, plays and teleplays oscillate between the parodic undercutting of stereotypes and their adoption. Although the line between satirical destabilisation and complicit appropriation cannot be definitively established, as O'Nolan's career progressed and he engaged with performance-orientated formats, there was a tendency for the satire to be less focused, the references more prosaic, the humour less intricate, the politics less refined and the plots less convincing: all of which combine to suggest a growing dependency on cliché, rather than its attenuation. While O'Nolan was deeply interested in depictions of Irish accents and voices, and although these local elements were vitally important in allowing presentations of Ireland that legitimised difference from English grammatical and phonetic structures, I argue that O'Nolan's later plays and teleplays frequently allowed the vibrancy of his depictions of personas and speech patterns to stagnate into stage clichés. Two complications of this tendency are O'Nolan's television series for Telefís Éireann (the forerunner of RTÉ), *O'Dea's Your Man* (1963–64)[2] and *Th'Oul Lad of Kilsalaher* (1965), which can be seen to satirise identity and culture through the appropriation of stereotypical themes and characters. Commenting first on the relation between national images and stereotypes, this essay compares O'Nolan's early use of stage stereotypes in *Blather* and *Cruiskeen Lawn* with his later plays and teleplays.

'Ahone, ahone, ahone, a Cree!'[3]

When Tim Haffigan, G.B. Shaw's personification of the stage Irishman in *John Bull's Other Island* (1904), deceives the Englishman Tom Broadbent with his fawning, drinking and 'rollicking stage brogue',[4] the Irish expatriate Larry Doyle quickly disabuses Broadbent of his self-satisfied, imperial indulgence. Doyle argues that Haffigan's demeanour and dialect is no more than a useful mask that plays on English conventions of the Irish idiot:

> No Irishman ever talks like that in Ireland, or ever did, or ever will. But when a thoroughly worthless Irishman comes to England, and finds the whole place full of romantic duffers like you, who will let him loaf and drink and sponge and brag as long as he flatters your sense of moral superiority by playing the fool and degrading himself and his country, he soon learns the antics that take you in. He picks them up at the theatre or the music hall.[5]

Haffigan had a long tradition of Irish guises upon which to draw. The first dialect-speaking Irishman can be dated back to *The Famous History of the Life and Death of Captain Thomas Stukeley* (1596),[6] Ben Jonson's *Irish Masque at Court* (1613) has Irish servants speak of cramming their mouths 'phit shamrokes and butter',[7] and *Sir John Oldcastle* (1600) has a wheedling 'savage villain, this rude Irish slave'[8] cut his master's throat so that he could steal his gold, only quickly to be divested of it: 'Wee's me, saint Patrick! Ise kill me mester for chain and his ring, and nows be rob of all: mee's undoo'.[9]

As England's power in Ireland expanded, the Irish stock character became correspondingly lampooned, moving gradually from a figure of perplexing otherness to a reassuringly familiar fool. During the seventeenth century the stereotype was commonly featured 'Drinking, bragging in his cups, nursing his pride and forever taking up arms in defence of his "honour", hunting fortunes, murdering logic and the English language'.[10] The growing control of Ireland in the latter half of the eighteenth century saw the stage and cartoon Irishman portrayed as increasingly 'contemptible [...] a prime source of humour and a proverb for all that was inferior or ridiculous'.[11] By the mid-nineteenth century the figure was so ubiquitous on the English stage as to be worthy of immediate parody. Henry J. Byron's *Miss Eily O'Connor* (1861), a burlesque of Dion Boucicault's *The Colleen Bawn* (1860), has Miles na Coppaleen – 'a model Stage Irishman, in fact a perfect Pat'un'[12] – satirise stage conventions, noting the 'never failing recipe' of the Paddy's appearance, accent, clothing, attitudes and intelligence:

> MILES: Behold in me that happy, ragged rogue,
> The stock stage Irishman – without the brogue.
> To manufacture which, this will you'll see
> Turn out a never failing recipe.
> He must have lightish hair, extremely curly,
> His teeth must be particularly pearly,
> Because he shows them all whene'er he grins;
> Dilapidated hose must veil his shins;
> Not having shaved, he must be blackish muzzled,
> And this must be his attitude when puzzled.
> [*striking the stock attitude of the puzzled stage Paddy, with his right hand in his hair*]
> On symptoms of a row the most remote,
> He must insist on taking off his coat.
> The stock remark of a dramatic Pat
> Must be when vexed at all – 'Get out of that!'
> Though 'Arrah' must of all his observations
> The *arra* root be of his conversations.[13]

In opposition to this long history of the stage Irishman – which O'Nolan, writing as 'Myles', characterised as the Abbey players trinity of 'Shaun, the Shuler', 'Biddy, the travelling woman' and 'Teague, a tramp'[14] – Irish theatre (and later film and television) attempted to portray an authentic national identity not bound by alterity or the stereotypical. The stock character, however, cast a long shadow, and what was warmly welcomed as truly Irish was just as often roundly dismissed as utter fabrication. Promoted as a 'true history First told by an Irishman and now Dramatised by an Irishman',[15] Boucicault's *The Colleen Bawn* was intended to free Ireland from imposed, hackneyed conventions. Its announcement bill distanced Ireland, and Boucicault's play, from such misrepresentations by proclaiming that 'Irish dramas have hitherto been exaggerated farces, representing low life or scenes of abject servitude and suffering. Such is not a true picture of Irish society'.[16] Yet when W.B. Yeats and Lady Gregory created a national theatre, their rejection of Ireland's false depiction as 'the home of buffoonery and of easy sentiment'[17] was precisely a rejection of writers such as Boucicault.[18] In turn, when Yeats and Gregory attempted to position Ireland as 'the home of ancient idealism',[19] Frank Hugh O'Donnell condemned their efforts as 'constructing an impossible country'[20] falsely secured by a 'Celtic Past [which] never existed anywhere outside [their] own productions'.[21] O'Donnell denounced the new theatre in his pamphlet 'The Stage Irishman of Pseudo-Celtic Drama' (1904), arguing, with all the ire of Myles na gCopaleen, that 'the title of "The Irish National Theatre" was entirely correct, except that it was not Irish, it was not national, and it had very amateurish claims to be a theatre'.[22] Against the National Theatre's version of authenticity, O'Donnell presented his superior claim to legitimacy: 'I am a Gael of the Gaels, the son of Gaelic-speaking Gaels, cradled in the legends and traditions of my race, and I know how Mr Yeats's parodies of Ireland are [...] insolently un-Irish'.[23] Some forty years later this very formulation would be ridiculed in *An Béal Bocht* as ludicrously inauthentic.

While the innovations of one theatrical generation frequently become the wearisome conventionalities of the next, in the case of Ireland the anxiety of authenticity runs deeper than the rejection of preceding dramatic trends. Even after the end of Empire the colonised still have to struggle, domestically and internationally, for the authority to self-define, as their identity has long been bound up in the iteration of cliché and a power discourse aligned to their suppression. Declan Kiberd notes that J.M. Synge, on receiving O'Donnell's pamphlet, 'felt that men such as O'Donnell were so intent on avoiding any taint of Stage Irishness that they had ceased to be real – they had forgotten who they truly were in their endless campaign not to be somebody else'.[24] Domestic and international gazes cannot unsee a long history of conventions of representation, and stereotypes inevitably haunt new attempts at independent identity, be they on the stage, page or street.

A national identity suggests a collectivity, strengthening or creating unity by making visible shared conventions, heritage and vernacular. A stereotype comments upon collective difference, establishing the Other's deviancy and inferiority by measurement against standards extrinsic to the Other. When we explore the discourse of types – stereotypes, character types, national archetypes – we are effectively engaging with a discourse of metonymies and synecdoches. In the case of national archetypes, the presence of the 'type' (that is, the part) should enable collective membership of a vibrant, dynamic whole, as all citizens identify in some way with the metonymic representation, but are not subsumed by it. In the case of the stereotype, the dominance of the type masks the existence of a complex, diverse, heterogeneous whole, as the varied population of a nation is reduced to hackneyed clichés. Thus, while the national archetype is a metonym ideally enabling unity through difference by multiple relations to the type, the stereotype is a metonym that masks its metonymy, as it makes the type – the part – appear to *be* the whole and thereby suppresses difference. Of course, archetypes and stereotypes cannot always be so satisfyingly distinguished, as national identity can be as hegemonically imposed, reductive and stagnant as any cliché, but once it becomes an inevitability that obscures or obstructs diverse enactments of identity, be it domestically or internationally constructed, it finds itself in the realm of stereotype.

Walter Lippmann, whose *Public Opinion* (1921) is credited with coining the modern usage of the term 'stereotype', locates its entrapping argument in Aristotle's defence of slavery. In *Politics* Aristotle writes that 'He then is by nature formed a slave, who is fitted to become the chattel of another person, *and on that account is so*'.[25] As Lippmann interprets this formulation:

> All this really says is that whoever happens to be a slave is by nature intended to be one. [...] Each slave holder was to look upon his chattels as natural slaves. [...] This is the perfect stereotype. Its hallmark is that it precedes the use of reason; is a form of perception, imposes a certain character on the data of our senses before the data reaches the intelligence.[26]

The self-perpetuating illogic of the stereotype is performative and, as Homi Bhabha argues, protean in its work to stabilise power imbalances.

While the stereotype is usually criticised as a reduction or simplification, Bhabha complicates this position by arguing that the 'stereotype is not a simplification because it is a false representation of a given reality. It is a simplification because it is an arrested, fixated form of representation'.[27] The stereotype prevents alternate, singular representations that might engender empathy in the colonising nation or encourage rebellion in the colonised, and so heterogeneity is repressed by the insistent repetition of clichés: 'the *same old* stories of the Negro's animality, the Coolie's inscrutability or the stupidity of the Irish *must* be told (compulsively) again and afresh, and are differently gratifying and terrifying each time'.[28] The authority of the stereotype is founded on iteration and insistence, and its perceived legitimacy is established by this repetition and reinforcement.

Embedded in this restricted characterisation is the reinforcement of the coloniser's superior identity, presenting a fiction of firm yet wholly hierarchised origins in which the colonised has always been in need of guidance and the coloniser always capable of giving it. This narrative, deeply satisfying for the coloniser, is exemplified in the tone and condescension of Christopher Salvsen's London article on O'Nolan from 1968:

> Irish humour is not primarily witty, but elaborate, tortuous, inventive parody, like the Book of Kells, a mixture of verbal play and truculent fantasy: truculent because an Irishman can never be himself, locked as he is in the masks and antics of clowning, and just enough aware of his predicament to feel obscurely resentful.[29]

The colonial Other is considered to be ontologically or essentially different – therefore with a fixed identity – and yet its continued difference from a colonial power in flux must be retained through adjustments to its representation, as the purpose of the colonial Other is to underpin continually the dissimilarity between the stereotyped group and those in power. Hence the swings in the Irish stereotype from playful fool to dangerously irresponsible agitator, often represented in cartoons in British periodicals such as *Punch*, *Fun* and *Judy* with simian or suilline features, depending on the political climate and the actions of the English themselves. While the hierarchy is maintained it becomes paradoxical and overdetermined, as the stereotype is forced to carry the load of contradictory or mutually exclusive identities based on differing anxieties. The colonial subject is made radically other while being entirely knowable in each articulation. Each instance in which the stereotype is invoked results in the disavowal of alternative representations, thereby enabling the Other to be simultaneously bone-idle and desperate to work, excessively stupid and dangerously cunning, of a premodern collectivity when the colonial powers are based on individualism, and of an infantile egoism when the colonial powers are founded on community. The structure of the stereotype prevents cognitive dissonance by embedding all interactions with the colonial subject within this matrix of discounted inconsistency.

Recognising the persistent trace of the colonial stereotype and the potential for national identities to stagnate into clichés, how does one find an authentic voice that manages to be representative of a nation, while not descending into the death of individuality and singularity – a voice that avoids the partial presence of the ethnic stereotype and attempts to present an identity outside these hierarchies and power plays? The answer, simply, is that one does not, as there are no stable origins, uncontaminated trajectories or definitive histories. As soon as the culturally or nationally authentic is thought to imply a single, essential category we move from the metonymic plurality and potentiality of the national archetype to the metonymic subterfuge of the stereotype. The only authoritative formulation of national identity is one that brings together diverse elements of social, cultural, historical, geographical or ethnic traits in plural, adulterated and protean ways. As Gregory Castle puts it, 'the problem of authenticity is less one of finding the appropriate technique for unearthing cultural essences, and thereby arriving at what is authentic about culture, than it is one of coming to terms with the fact that authenticity is, in a sense, an impossible goal'.[30] As such, 'the representation of inauthenticity may in fact be the best way to arrive at an authentic expression of Irish national aspirations and the ambivalent process of Irish identity formation'.[31] A nation must find ways of speaking of itself, to itself, for itself in all its difference and impurity. It must have the right to discard the mantle of colonial or political Other and self-represent, while acknowledging that an authoritative depiction of any national or ethnic self is founded on complex, detailed adulteration.

Myles once berated Synge for creating a 'counterfeit bauble' of Irish life,[32] and he repeatedly attacked those who chose romantic idealisations of the state over acknowledgements of national inadequacies and inequalities. Yet, the consistencies of O'Nolan's attacks on inauthenticity are matched by the regularity with which the concept of 'real' Irish identity is questioned. His writing consistently works to avoid easy assumptions of an authentic national self. For his newspaper persona O'Nolan adapted the name of Boucicault's Myles na Coppaleen, thus positioning himself between stage cliché and innovative cultural commentator by embracing the brogue, *poitín* and easy cheer of Boucicault's Myles while simultaneously satirising and deriding him as a foolish fabrication. The contaminations between languages, histories and concepts of purity are performed in his spelling of Myles's surname: the correct eclipsis of 'gC' is undone by the inaccurate, Anglicised 'leen', and the authentic is seen to be inextricable from the inauthentic.

'May the brogue of ould Ireland niver forsake your tongue'[33]

In keeping with *Pat*, *The Leprechaun*, *Zozimus* and *The Jarvey*, comic weeklies published in Dublin in the late nineteenth to early twentieth century, O'Nolan's contributions to *Comhthrom Féinne* and his own short-lived Dublin monthly *Blather* explore the authoritative and the inauthentic in Irish identity through subversive uses of brogue and the stage Irishman.[34] His work in these publications frequently lacks the cutting satire of *An Béal Bocht* and lays no claim to subtle parody; and yet, the pieces' clear disruption of easy positions and tired clichés, as well as their genuine delight in hyperbole and the ridiculous, produces complicating, teasing representations of stock characters and scenes. O'Nolan's mock-dramatic sketch 'The Bog of Allen' (1933), for example, parodies the Literary Revival's home-grown stereotypes by saturating the set with the trappings of 'real' Ireland: drapes made from Irish poplin, an iron pike for insurrections, the woman of the house dressed in green and seated at her spinning wheel, the cow looking in through the half door and the hungry man home from cutting turf. As Allen and Maggie Bogg admire the 'rich purple of the Celtic Twilight [as it] falls over the Bog', their house sinks deeper and deeper into the ground while they croon clichés in the doorway:

> *Maggie*: Musha.
> *Allen*: Surely.
> *Maggie*: Wisha.
> *Allen*: Begorrah.
> *Maggie* (*her soul flooded with poetry*): Anish, now, musha.
> *Allen*: Surely. (*long pause*) Aye.... Musha.
> *Maggie*: Begorrah. (*MBM*, 42–43)

Underpinning O'Nolan's satire of the language of the Abbey Theatre is a sharp commentary on the illusory nature of authenticity and independence. Interspersed with the symbols of Irishness are hints of England: Wigan coal burning in the fire and a smell of fish and chips despite the fact that there's

'Bacon an' Cabbage an' Stirabout' for dinner. The stereotype is not merely mocked as a literary fabrication, but also condemned as one that masks political and economic dependencies.

In *Blather*, O'Nolan names Abbey English as the Received Pronunciation of Ireland and presents a theatrical example of the correct pronunciation and idiom of Hiberno-English:

> *Phelim*: [...] For last night, at the grey coming of the twilight, the redcoats seized a poor Croppy boy as he watered his stag in the glen. O, woe, woe, woe!
> *Peadar*: Alas, alas, poor Yorick.
> *Shaun*: The pity of it. The pitiful pity of it is heavy on my heart this day.
> *Peadar*: A bitter black curse on these Redcoats, surely. [...]
> *Shaun*: Och, och, ochone, alannah. Och, och, Ochone. (*MBM*, 158)

In this instance, stock historical references, parodies of literal translations from the Irish and familiar bursts of transliterated lamentation are joined by well-worn, if misquoted, lines from *Hamlet*, as O'Nolan can't resist the urge to follow his pattern of excessive lamentations by adding an extra 'alas'. Clichés, O'Nolan implies, can claim no authenticity other than themselves, and become consistent only with their own conventions. Stage Irish laments occupy the same plane of reality as overworked lines by the Prince of Denmark, as the theatre refers to the authenticities of the theatre and not beyond it. The implied danger is that if the dramatic works of the Abbey are allowed to become the standard dialect of Ireland, then the Irish voice will be founded on a simulacrum. In rejecting the notion of purity we do not render all impurities equal: for O'Nolan the Irish identity of the Abbey is a constructed inauthenticity too far.

In the following issue of *Blather* the editors propose that the annual government subsidy of £750 awarded to the Abbey Theatre should be sent directly to them, thereby preventing the company from restaging works perpetuating Irish clichés. But a 'government representative' explains that

> the money is paid on condition the Abbey Players go to America and remain there for nine months of the year. The idea is to prevent at all costs the further production in Dublin of *Riders to the Sea* and *Professor Tim*. [...] It is admitted that thousands of playgoers who turned their faces sadly to the emigrant ship early in the present century because of *Riders to the Sea* are now pouring back from the States in hordes. (*MBM*, 143)

Cruiskeen Lawn continues this mode of satirical engagement. Myles's proposed drama *The Four Green Fields*, for example, is presented as a 'good *genuine* Irish play', and features 'MYLES NA GOPALEEN with a keg of potheen on his shoulder and a shillelagh in his hand, off to Philadelphia in the morning'.[35] The proposed drama includes Mother Machree, love triangles between Danny Boy, Betty Martin and John Kelly, a weightlifting contest, returned emigrants, police raids, concealed identity, interludes of traditional music and dancing 'by a chorus of leprahauns [*sic*] and banshees'.

In many of O'Nolan's actual stage and television plays, however, the extravagances of these earlier, blatantly satirical sketches are lost, and tired parody supports, rather than subverts, cliché. This change is not only the result of a lack of riotous excess or nuance symptomatic of his difficulties in writing outside of a dominating discourse. It is, perhaps more importantly, a matter of ensuring that the audience is also able to shake off the traces of old, colonial representations and listen to regional accents without hearing the traces of stage brogue. While O'Nolan deliberately played on this confusion, he frequently fell afoul of it. Joseph Holloway, for example, described *Rhapsody in Stephen's Green* (1943) as a 'pointless burlesque in Irish dialect over-emphasised to the point of grotesque exaggeration', arguing that Myles had 'turned the play into Stage-Irish dialect, of many counties, and introduced far too many "bloodies" and "Ah gods" into his text. Much of the talk reminded [Holloway] of the good old red-nosed [word illegible] apelike music hall Irish cross-talkers of long ago'.[36] Similarly, the *Irish Times* review of *Faustus Kelly* (1943) argued that Kelly's colleagues tended to bring the drama 'down to the level of ordinary Abbey comedy, and to get laughs in the old-fashioned way' – by depending on cliché.[37] In a roguish acknowledgement of the difficulty that critics and audiences had with the brogue/accent tension, O'Nolan had an actor take his author's bow on the opening night of *Faustus Kelly* 'dressed as the traditional stage Irishman with pipe, caubeen and cutaway coat, who did a bit of a jig and then vanished'.[38] This parody – a mockery of the old stock representations of the Irish, a jeer at the Abbey Theatre for prolonging those representations and a self-directed taunt at O'Nolan's own complicity in staging work there – did little to undercut the reception of these 1943 works as tired and hackneyed. Nor is the fault wholly to be laid at the feet of a national anxiety of identity: the adoption of different regional inflections and intonations in these two pieces hovers awkwardly between a regressive use of dull personas and a progressive attempt to express multiplicity within Irish speech patterns, and thus national diversity, in a humorous way. Rather than finessing the line between 'real' regional accents and 'fake' stage brogue, these works are in danger of widening the stock type's repertoire.

O'Nolan's teleplay *The Boy from Ballytearim* (1962) is similarly troubled by the slippage between accent and brogue, individual and type.[39] A dramatisation of Moira O'Neill's poem of the same name, the plot remains largely unchanged: a son leaves impoverished Ireland to seek his fortune and returns years later as a rich man, eager to marry his sweetheart. However, she has died, and, heartbroken, he leaves his parents once again. But, as O'Nolan writes, '*the sentiment of Moira O'Neill's Poem has been turned upside-down and the pathos largely nullified. An attempt is made to achieve comedy by the exploitation of the regional accent, after the manner of O'Casey and the Dublin accent*' (*PT*, 287). O'Nolan labours to turn tragedy into comedy, but, never adept at engaging with the emotional, he cannot turn the loss described in O'Neill's work into farce, and the awkward remnants of sorrow in the final act undo the last vestiges of satire. To a series of dull discussions O'Nolan adds the 'cheerful and jaunty' Packy the tramp, whose entrance involves an immediate commentary on alcohol: 'Lord bliss us, that's not watter ye have' (*PT*, 304). There are visual jokes about the bad taste of *poitín*, and Peter and Annie discuss Parnell, drinking at the fair and the lack of anything in Ballytearim 'but work an' muck an' starvation' (*PT*, 297). On the surface the script plays so strongly on stock types that it cannot but be a mockery, yet as it lacks an incisive edge, it operates less as a rejection of than as a reliance on tired clichés, with little subversive humour or satirical point. More egregious, however, is O'Nolan's presumption that rural accents are innately comical, and that the simple use of local expressions and country concerns will inevitably render a banal domestic scene humorous:

> ANNIE: [...] God look down on us, there's enough trouble here. The praties bad, a pig with the gollops, a turkey hidin' her eggs, and then Hughie ....
> PETER: Ah now, please God, things'll turn out all right.
> ANNIE: Aye. If we don't forget to say wur prayers. Do ye want me to try to roast a few of these spuds for yer eggs? Do you want chalahaans with yer tea?
> PETER: Naw, Annie. Just make me a wee bit of boxty an' plenty of tea. Lord, I'm dyin' for a cup o' tea. (*PT*, 290–91)

In O'Nolan's 'exploitation of the regional accent' the rural becomes so strongly conjoined with old caricatures as to wholly assimilate country accents into brogue and equate country lives with unfunny stereotypes.

This gradual slippage in parody can be demonstrated through the evolution of O'Nolan's use of the *Seanbhean bhocht* avatar of Ireland. She first features in *Blather* as a firmly demythologised agony-aunt:

> This, as far as we can remember, is the Shan Van Vocht; we keep her in the office all day to give the place a homely atmosphere and to ensure that the boys won't ruin the carpet with their cigarette-ash. These Damn Scallions, she is saying to herself. What Made Me Eat Them? Do you want advice on Life from a Mature Person? Write to her about your troubles, if you must whine to somebody else about them. (*MBM*, 109)

In Yeats and Gregory's *Cathleen ni Houlihan* (1902), the *Seanbhean bhocht* seduces the groom-to-be into forsaking his fiancée and fighting for Ireland. In *Blather*, Mother Ireland's worries about strangers in the house and the loss of her four green fields are comically, if ruthlessly, reduced to domestic tribulations and stomach troubles. Far from inspiring the youth to fight for her, she becomes the recipient of their minor concerns. Thus her role of disrupting the homely for national glory is inverted: politics become forsaken for minor domestic checks and woes. While the association of the Celtic Twilight with digestive issues may not be subtle, its deliberately heavy-handed rejection of idealism is nonetheless effective.

Seven years later the *Seanbhean bhocht* makes an appearance in *Cruiskeen Lawn*, this time as a reworking of the song 'The Sean-bhean Bocht'. The ballad, which usually optimistically reflects on the hopes of the 1798 rebellion, is now set in contemporary Ireland, a place purposefully denied romance as 'The bread's not what it was', 'The fags are hard to buy' and 'The coal is mainly slack'. But these difficulties and the political realities of modern Ireland, it is cynically recognised, are effortlessly washed away with foreign beer and easy nationalist rhetoric:

> The porter's getting pale,
>   Says the Shan Van Vocht,
> Its strength's begun to fail,
>   Says the Shan Van Vocht,
> But the sea-divided Gael
> Can live on Spanish ale
> And Hurrah for Granuaile,
>   Says the Shan Van Vocht.[40]

Twenty-one years later when the *Seanbhean bhocht* reappears in *The Boy from Ballytearim*, again in the form of a song, the cynicism remains, as Peter sings the first verse to caution against trusting the French in the First World War by reminding Annie of their failure to help the Irish:

> The Frinch are in the bay,
> Says the Shan Van Vocht,
> They'll be here without delay,
> Says the Shan Van Vocht,
> They'll come in from the say,
> They'll anchor at the kay,
> And we'll have them here for tay,
> Says the Shan Van Vocht. (*PT*, 301)

What worked as a full six stanza parody – placed between reflections on the use of sand and one of Myles's literal translations of *An tOileánach* – within the fragmented, satirical structures of *Cruiskeen Lawn* falls flat as a single stanza within an already laboriously clichéd play. Wry commentary on the ease with which domestic comfort replaces political ideals is replaced with the banal domesticity that marks all of Annie and Peter's conversations. While the first stanza of the 1941 version rhymes 'say' and 'tay' with an unexpected 'eau-de-vay', this exotic phrase is replaced in 1962 with the disappointingly mundane 'kay' (*PT*, 301). Thus the political point, as well as the implication that Hughie, whose entrance follows the scene, will do as little good for his family as the French did for Ireland, is sorely reduced. While acknowledging that humour and its effects are enmeshed within subjective understandings of style and taste, an interpretation of *The Boy from Ballytearim* must also concede that the play lacks the absurdism, pedantry, stylistic innovation, sardonic quotation, cultural commentary or exuberant glee that mark O'Nolan's more formally complex, or deliberately simple, works. In O'Nolan's attempt to turn tragedy into comic farce not only does he reveal nothing new, he presents a work more uninterestingly dependent on hackneyed tropes than the original. Joseph Brooker describes O'Nolan, and Patrick Kavanagh, as 'ferociously critical of any self-conscious performance of nationality', as they understood the role of the writer to expose 'enthusiastic manifestations' of Irishness as 'demeaning delusion'.[41] While this claim is true of many of his earlier works, as an aging O'Nolan's ferociousness gave way to cantankerousness and laboured humour, the demeaning delusion began to supplant its critique.

Much of the difficulty of *The Boy from Ballytearim*, *Faustus Kelly* and *Rhapsody in Stephen's Green* is tied to the tension between urban and rural accents, and between the perceived neutrality of 'educated' pronunciation against the stronger inflections of the working classes. As the traditional stage character tended to be rural rather than urban, and usually impoverished, the cliché haunts representations of rural life more potently than it does representations of the metropolitan, with middle-class Dublin particularly removed. Hence *The Man with Four Legs* (1962), *The Time Freddie Retired* (1962), with its involvement of kangaroos in Dublin zoo, and *The Dead Spit of Kelly* (1962), with its nonspecific urban associations – it is set in *'Dublin, though it could be any city or big town'* (*PT*, 387) – fail to evoke the cliché or cause anxieties of representation. But once the scene moves from a middle-class urban lifestyle to either the rural or the working class, the stage persona becomes discernible. The Agent in *A Moving Tale* (1962), for example, is described as *'An appalling savage with the flattest of Dublin accents, a depraved gurrier'* (*PT*, 267) and is a drunken, duplicitous cheat who alternates between working-class Dublin phrases and the allusions of the old stock character: 'Well now, begob! Are ya married to her or is this another graw-machree-mo-colleen-dhas business?' (*PT*, 276). While so much of *Cruiskeen Lawn* worked to ridicule the concept of hackneyed language use and to play on the different voices of contemporary Ireland, O'Nolan's interest in the accents, idioms and dialogue of less educated members of society made it difficult to avoid the shadow of the stage cliché, which, Yeats argues, turns 'an irresponsible type, found oftenest among boatmen, carmen, and gentlemen's servants, into the type of a whole nation, and [thus creates] the stage Irishman'.[42] This tension of representation – in which apprehensions about education, income and old senses of national difference are exacerbated by the anxious tendency to look through the gaze of the dominant power – renders depictions of the rural or the working class fraught for the writer, actor and audience.

The teleplay *Flight* (1962) is exemplary of this problem. Presenting a vignette on an Aer Lingus plane, like *The Boy from Ballytearim* its humour focuses on the characters' accents and personas – Dublin, Northern Irish and English – and on escalating Anglo-Irish tensions on board. The Englishman, a caricature of the indignant, self-entitled Londoner, drawls a laconic 'I don't like the Irish, actually' (*PT*, 351) and in his dislike insists on seeing the stage Irishman everywhere. When a sudden movement of the plane causes the captain to land in a female passenger's lap, he laments the amorous tendencies of the Irish. When he mishears the captain, thinking he said that they might have to 'Land on the sea', he calls the expression's prepositional inaccuracy 'Terribly Irish' (*PT*, 353). Similarly, the Northerner tells the 'mild old lady' who hits the Englishman over the head with her umbrella that she is behaving

worse than those in the 'wilds of Conamawra' (*PT*, 352). But while those
from the United Kingdom – with the exception of the *'magnificent blonde'*
(*PT*, 345) Englishwoman – see the Irish as stereotypically wild, lascivious and
ignorant, the Irish passengers are already old, hackneyed types – sensitive and
aggressive drunkards, quick with recourse to colonial grievances and eager
to sing 'The Wild Colonial Boy' as the plane descends. While the punch line
attempts to laugh at the Englishman as the plane has landed in Wexford rather
than London, the real joke is at the expense of individuality.

Shaw directly addressed the confusion of accent and brogue in *John Bull's
Other Island*, where the wheedling Haffigan was authentic from Broadbent's
perspective because his accent and demeanour matched the Irish characters
Broadbent had seen on stage – Haffigan thus fit comfortably into the clichéd
category of 'Irishman'. But Broadbent's ability to recognise a 'Paddy' means
that he cannot identify a Corkman or a Clarewoman, as the category of stage
Irishman obfuscates and denies regional differences, and the variety of Irish
accents are subsumed under the encapsulating, restrictive label of 'brogue':

> BROADBENT (*still incredulous*). But his brogue!
> DOYLE. His brogue! A fat lot you know about brogues! I've heard
> you call a Dublin accent that you could hang your hat on, a brogue.
> Heaven help you! You don't know the difference between Connemara
> and Rathmines. (*With violent irritation.*)[43]

O'Nolan encourages his audience to be able, unlike Broadbent, to distinguish
between the accents of the west and the Pale. However, rather than undoing
the stage caricature, these differences just add local specificity to its repertoire.
To the single stock Irishman, and woman, we can now add regional flavours,
but little more. The plane's crash landing sets us down back in the realms of
cliché.

'What ish my nation?'[44]

One might, however, attempt to temper these accusations of stereotype-
adoption through recourse to Myles's caustic pronouncement that he has
'personally met in the streets of Ireland persons who are clearly out of
Synge's plays. They talk and dress like that, and damn the drink they'll swally
but the mug of porter in the long nights after Samhain'.[45] That is, it is not
that O'Nolan misrepresents the real through the prism of the stereotype, nor

that people are becoming stereotypes, but rather that the stereotype has so long interacted with national and international senses of Irish identity that the real was always contaminated, and O'Nolan is authentically representing the already inauthentic. While this refinement is unconvincing for the works engaged with above, it resonates with the cultural confusion performed in O'Nolan's two television series, *O'Dea's Your Man* and *Th'Oul Lad of Kilsalaher*. Both play on a favourite character type of O'Nolan's, the poorly educated urban dweller popularised in The Brother sketches and The Plain People of Ireland, and while they lack the wit and skill one would expect of O'Nolan, they do perform, with differing degrees of insight, the complications of Irish selfhood during the beginnings of a new medium: television.

The 1960 Broadcasting Authority Act stated that 'the Authority shall bear constantly in mind the national aims of restoring the Irish language and preserving and developing the national culture and shall endeavour to promote the attainment of those aims'.[46] The government hoped that a national television service would promote 'an official Catholic, Gaelic-inflected culture'[47] as 'an Irish perspective, rooted in Irish popular culture, would counteract any feared negative cultural influence from the old imperial centre'.[48] Television was co-opted to the presentation of an Irish identity that eschewed foreign stereotype, but in so doing it ran the danger of homogenising Irish life into a state-approved cliché. When understood in relation to this agenda, the subversive elements of *O'Dea's Your Man* and *Th'Oul Lad of Kilsalaher* come into focus. While they clearly work to establish a lower-middle-class Irish identity, they also strongly satirise the actual degree of investment, knowledge and commitment much of the country had in the official view of Ireland. Both series comprise short sketches exploring different topics and as such contain much in common with *Cruiskeen Lawn* – fragmented bursts of humorous reflections, often marked by malapropisms, misunderstandings and illogical positions. *O'Dea's Your Man* is set in 'an old-fashioned (no electric nonsense here) railway signal box' (*PT*, 417), which is designed to evoke a pub setting, and primarily consists of dialogue between Jimmy O'Dea and Ignatius (David Kelly). *Th'Oul Lad of Kilsalaher* takes place in a 'comic kitchen' containing a Saint Brigid's cross, a picture of J.F. Kennedy, a fiddle, a shotgun and a television/radio (*PT*, 427–28). Marie-Thérèse, whose nickname is 'Puddiner', and her uncle Hughie (named Andy in early episodes) are from Dublin, although the stage directions note that 'they are exiles in the country. Country customs and situations obtrude' (*PT*, 427). As such, *Th'Oul Lad of Kilsalaher* presents dialogues between male and female, young and old, urban and rural, national and international, Irish and English languages, and both series together perform the confusions and impurities of national culture, thereby subtly revealing the naiveties of the Broadcasting Authority Act.

The first episode of *O'Dea's Your Man* is littered with Irish clichés: an alcoholic colleague Rafferty is described as a 'walkin bucket of pison' (*PT*, 418),[49] while the virtues of whiskey are extolled as a grain-based nourishment that 'loosens up th'arteries, smoothes down the nairves, and gives the party takin it a luvly complexion. It does the heart good, if ya know what I mane' (*PT*, 420).[50] A meal of fresh mushrooms is described as 'a breakfast fit for the King of the Great Blasket Island' (*PT*, 418),[51] a man who consumed poisonous fungus is described as 'sweatin like a trooper in Vinegar Hill' (*PT*, 418),[52] while the episode ends with a joke about the Dublin Fusiliers – 'Dubalin Fusialeers' – as fuelled by Fusel oil; that is, Fusel alcohol (*PT*, 421–22). However, this tirade of Irish allusions is complicated by a later episode disparaging 'all that Irish jazz when it comes to names', as 'There's far too many Shauns in this country. Ireland's crawling with Shauns'.[53] The same destabilisation is found in the depiction of Irish sporting triumphs. The victory of Tipperary Tim at the 1928 Aintree Grand National at odds of 100/1 is presented as an example of Irish triumph: 'Look how often we've shown the whole world the way home in the Grand National at Aintree in the days that're gone ... Shaun Spadach [*sic* – Spadah], Tipperary Tim'.[54] Yet this achievement is implicitly derided, as Tipperary Tim's success came only because every other horse fell, and while Tipperary Tim and Shaun Spadah, the 1921 winner, were bred in Ireland, their jockeys, trainers and owners were all British.[55] This irony is compounded by Jimmy's pronouncement that the success of the Irish is due to Ireland's limestone base, making the Irish 'limeys'. In this manner *O'Dea's Your Man* works through a range of identity questions and politics, presenting an authentically inauthentic sense of identity as familiar stage and street clichés are mixed and naïve assumptions are interspersed with unexpected references: when Jimmy is asked what he's reading he says, 'It's not *Fanny Hill* anyway, Ignatius'.[56]

Th'oul Lad of Kilsalaher self-consciously calls attention to stage Irish farce when Puddiner says that her nickname 'is low vulgarity the like of which you'd oney hear in the Queen's Theatre in Dublin'.[57] O'Nolan adds a sly dig at both Puddiner and Hughie (named Andy in this early episode) as they both envisage the Abbey Theatre as the pinnacle of sophistication. Puddiner says that Shamus is going to take her to the 'Dress Cercle of th'Abbey [...] T'improve me mind for meself', and her uncle waxes lyrical about 'Sally [*sic* – Sara] Allgood and Shaun O'Casey, and *Riders to the Sea*. They were a great crowd, th'oul crowd'.[58] In a later episode, Puddiner suggests that in as much as dignitaries in London are buried in Westminster Abbey, important actors in Ireland should be buried (although with rather more ritual than Beckett's Murphy had requested) in the Abbey Theatre.[59] In this scene of urban attendees 'bettering' themselves by watching rural Abbey characters, O'Nolan offers a wry, contaminated sense of reality and fiction, as viewers watch urban television characters who are watching rural stage characters created by watching a mix of 'real' and stage peasants.

Both *O'Dea's Your Man* and *Th'oul Lad of Kilsalaher* present national concerns about the Irish language, depicting even the older generation of Gaelic Leaguers – Jimmy and Hughie in each series – as speaking heavily accented, limited Irish. In 'The Language Question' Jimmy and Ignatius discuss compulsory Irish in governmental departments. While Ignatius is unsure about the idea, Jimmy insists that people know more Irish than they use: 'The whole lot of us knows Irish oney we don't speak it. Amn't I slavin' here for CÓLUCIIT UMPAR ERIN [*sic* – Córas Iompair Éireann, Irish Transport System, CIÉ]?'[60] Over the course of the episode Jimmy suggests Irish alternatives for English words, but the words tend to be single nouns or short phrases, and with the exception of *cólucht*, a misquotation of *córas*, these words are transliterated into English phonemes. Speaking Irish becomes equated with performing Irish cultural acts like dancing to 'a grand helter-skelter of lovely Irish tunes',[61] and when Jimmy sings 'Cruiskeen Lawn', Ignatius says that 'There's a lilt to that. That's real Irish. That's what you'd hear from the old crowd'.[62] 'Real Irish' identity and heritage is understood as speaking a few words in Irish and eschewing foreign dances. This tendency, reminiscent of the uncle's committee in *At Swim-Two-Birds*, figures in the same way in *Th'oul Lad of Kilsalaher*, where the Irishness of John McCormack is quietly derided as a pale substitute: 'THE GARDEN WHERE THE PRATIES GROW. Now there was a ballad for you, Puddiner. And MOTHER MACHREE. Aaaaaaah … God love you and keep you Mother Macree. Do you know, Puddiner it was all real Irish'.[63]

In 'Beirt Eile', Puddiner's ignorance as to the very location of Ireland leads to speculation on Irish language classes. Hughie waxes lyrical about his time in the 'Gyayltucht in Dunny Goal be the name of Cloghsneely',[64] where it rains on the bogs and boulders and 'little white cottages with dripping thatch' on two-acre plots.[65] Evocative of the cultural divide of *An Béal Bocht*, this episode plays on a strong urban/rural dichotomy, and the Gaeltacht is described as though it were in a foreign country. Puddiner aptly describes her generation as 'confused', since 'I speak English, uncle, because I never learnt it, and I don't speak Irish because it was taught to me at school'. Here O'Nolan balances parody and a potential point of empathy between Puddiner and her audience, whose attitudes to and aptitude in Irish, O'Nolan assumes, would be quite similar. In the preceding Halloween episode O'Nolan felt obliged to insist in the stage directions that '*It is for the Producer to see to it that the Irish words* Samhain, Sahmna*, are pronounced correctly*'.[66] Clearly his lack of confidence in Irish language abilities was not restricted to the audience.

In 'Hughie for Pres!' Hughie says that he would be happy to let people become violent over political differences outside Áras an Uachtaráin, as 'You have the Royal Family across the water watchin horse racin at Ascot with half of the nags staggerin about, half-gone from all the dope that's in their blood, fommin and frothin at the mouth, and giving buck-leps to throw th'unfortunate jockeys'. To this Puddiner replies, 'Aw, that's civilisation. But a free-for-all, that's too … too Irish. Two parties bashin hell out of each other is undignified'.[67] This assimilation of, and anxiety about, the cliché of the wild Irish – not helped by Hughie's repeated threats of the 'business end of his blackthorn stick' – is presented even more cuttingly in *O'Dea's Your Man*, when Ignatius hints that the death of the Irish language is linked to the absence of a colonising force, because without resistance there is no reason to preserve the language: 'You'll never see times like that again. Let Erin remember the days of old when the Saxon foe betrayed her'.[68] But Jimmy adds that those days aren't gone, as 'Isn't Kathaleen Nee Houlihan there, with the stranger still in her green fields? Remember to speak all the Irish you know and the battle is won'.[69] Resistance is insisted upon while reduced to a comfortable pint ordered in Irish. And if the publican tells you to stop singing 'real Irish' songs, Jimmy says, then you ask yourself, what would Robert Emmet say?

> Ignatius – Well … I suppose he'd say no man has the right to put a stop to the onward march of a nation.
> Jimmy – He'd say nothing of the kind. He'd first give your man a look of withering scorn and then he'd say BEEDAHUSHT AGUS NAWBOCKLESH.
> Ignatius – Ah yiss, I suppose he would. Bould Robert Emmet, the darlint of Erin.[70]

In giving to Emmet lines attributed to Parnell, O'Nolan calls to an extensive history of colonisation and resistance, but one whose legacy is suppressed by a contemporary confusion of historical detail. This inheritance is further undermined when Emmet's political contribution to Irish independence is reduced to a drinker insisting on singing nationalist songs in English and using limited Irish – a cutting reference not only to contemporary linguistic and political engagement, but a sly allusion to the fact that the most famous leaders of rebellions were protestant and native English speakers.

Irish identity, as performed in *O'Dea's Your Man* and *Th'oul Lad of Kilsalaher*, is marked by pseudo-Irishisms – drinking, dancing, singing, arguing and loudly proclaiming independence while supporting it with little linguistic, historical, geographical, political or cultural knowledge. This contradiction makes a darkly satirical claim: 'real' Ireland is populated by inauthentic character types, as many of these clichés are, to various degrees, lived realities. However, the types occupy a space between the metonymic openness of national archetypes and the closure of the stereotype, and identity is recognised as a constant process of self-formation, self-understanding and self-representation. The series' comedy opens the characters' accents, cultural signifiers and idioms up to audience identification or rejection, and thus, at the very least, to domestic debate. From this perspective *O'Dea's Your Man* and *Th'oul Lad of Kilsalaher* successfully inhabit a liminal space between authenticity and inauthenticity, archetype and stereotype, pride and disappointment, and in this undecidable space perform the ambiguities and ambivalences of national identity. This liminality enables them to move beyond both straight mockery of and reliance on old stock characters to present the – inevitable – impurity of Irish identity. Thus, while their interrogations of Irish selfhood took place within sometimes disappointing plots and dialogues, and although many of them exhibit a tendency for overdependence on the old stock character, O'Nolan's plays and teleplays demonstrate a performance of the anxiety of identity in the face of deep-rooted yet protean cultural clichés and offer an important insight into the inauthenticity of self and nationhood.

3

Lamhd láftar and bad language
bilingual cognition in *Cruiskeen Lawn*

MARIA KAGER

Bilingual writers there are many. Yet, writers who are bilingual *as writers* – that is, who write and publish in two different languages simultaneously – are scarce.[1] As is the case with bilinguals in general, each bilingual writer presents 'a special case'.[2] Isaac Bashevis Singer and Czesław Miłosz wrote exclusively in their first languages, while Eva Hoffman and Richard Rodriguez changed language dominance in childhood and wrote in their second, then dominant language. Ágota Kristóf, Emine Sevgi Özdamar and Józef Teodor Konrad Korzeniowski (*aka* Joseph Conrad) wrote in a second, or even third, language they acquired as an adult. Elsa Triolet, Samuel Beckett and Vladimir Nabokov started their careers as writers in one language and then switched to write in another.[3] Brian O'Nolan/Brian Ó Nualláin is the rare bilingual writer who started his writing career *as* a bilingual writer: from the moment he entered the Irish literary scene, he wrote both in English and in Irish. And where other bilingual writers who write in two languages, such as Beckett and Nabokov, start out writing in one language and only later became bilingual as writers, O'Nolan followed the opposite trajectory: he started out as a bilingual writer, yet gradually ceased writing in Irish and eventually wrote only in English.

In spite of a recent surge of academic interest in bilingual writing, the works of Brian O'Nolan/Brian Ó Nualláin have remained largely unilluminated by the light of bilingualism studies. O'Nolan's critics have recognised the importance of the writer's bilingualism, yet here attention has focused predominantly on treatments of his gradual abandonment of writing in Irish in light of the 'ideological freight' the language had come to have in the Irish Free State and of O'Nolan's 'increasing identification of revivalist ideals with a xenophobic nationalism'.[4] The significance of the ideological and political burden of Irish for O'Nolan's writing is undeniable, yet in the present essay I would like to approach the writer's bilingualism from a different angle. Using recent neurolinguistic and psycholinguistic research that has shown active bilingualism to enhance metalinguistic awareness – the ability to reflect on and manipulate structural properties of language independent of meaning – I trace the creative tension that results from O'Nolan's writing with more than one language in hand.

This tension becomes visible especially in the *Cruiskeen Lawn* columns, where it is given shape through a revealing focus on the symbiotic relationship between linguistic misuse and creativity. In the columns, Myles na gCopaleen repeatedly asserts his linguistic authority as a bilingual and campaigns against the use of 'bad language': of slovenly speech and incorrect pronunciation in both English and Irish. Yet the excessive attention that this 'bad language' receives also reveals the irresistible attraction it holds for its 'tireless reporter' Myles, who seems both repulsed by and obsessed with the linguistic sins he documents for posterity.

Brian between Irish and English

In his introduction to the translation of Brian Merriman's *Cúirt An Mheán Oíche* [*The Midnight Court*] from Irish into English, the Belfast poet Ciaran Carson writes:

> I hesitate to call myself a native speaker: true, Irish is, or was, my first language, but I learned it from parents for whom it was a second language; and it has been a long time since it was the first language in which I think, or express myself, although I sometimes dream in it. Compared with my English, my Irish is impoverished. Yet I can remember a time when English was foreign to me.[5]

It is hard to say in which language Brian O'Nolan thought and dreamed, and his writing in Irish was certainly not 'impoverished', but otherwise Carson's insight into the linguistic background and complexities of his childhood might have been written by O'Nolan himself. O'Nolan grew up speaking Irish at home and did not hear much English spoken during the first years of his life.[6] Although Irish was his first language, he learned it from parents for whom it was not native. Inspired by the ideology of the Gaelic revival, Brian's father – born Michael Victor Nolan but later transliterating his name to Micheál Victor Ó Nualláin – had resolved to bring up his children in Irish. His mother Agnes [*née* Gormley]'s knowledge of the language was not as thorough as her husband's, so although Irish was Brian's mother tongue it was not his mother's tongue.[7] However, Agnes's Irish was sufficient to ensure that there was no necessity to speak English in the home. Thus, even though his first language was Irish, Brian O'Nolan cannot exactly be called a native speaker in the common understanding of the term. In her excellent *Ireland Through the Looking-Glass: Flann O'Brien, Myles na gCopaleen and Irish Cultural Debate*, Carol Taaffe notes that 'it is curious that though O'Nolan and his siblings were fluent in Irish, this fluency had its provenance in a *learned* language, not largely supported by contact with native speakers'.[8]

Careful to protect his children's Irish and without any Irish schooling in the vicinity, Micheál educated his children at home until Brian was eleven years old. By that time, Brian had gradually learned English from books, from English-speaking relatives and from neighbours. Anthony Cronin records that Brian and his brothers would spend hours in the local shop listening to the talk of the customers, which 'they found the more fascinating precisely because English was unfamiliar to them'.[9] The anecdote suggests that O'Nolan had an early curiosity about language, as does the following story from his childhood, also related by Cronin. Hearing some people in the street speak in 'flat Offaly accents' from a window one day, Brian began to mimic them. When his father warned him, *as Gaeilge*, to be quiet for fear they might hear him, Brian responded *as Béarla*: 'And as for you, sir, […] if you do not conduct yourself I will do you a mischief'.[10] This ear for accents and taste for eavesdropping and linguistic mimicry would become central features of the Myles persona.

When Brian and his siblings attended the Christian Brothers School in Dublin they began speaking English more frequently outside the home. English was the language of instruction in school and many of their friends hardly spoke Irish. Cronin comments that 'Although the assumption was that [Irish] was still the O'Nolans' main language of converse, from now on it was increasingly less so'.[11] After finishing school, Brian studied Irish and German at University College Dublin (UCD) and was an honours student in Modern Irish. He returned for a master's degree and wrote a thesis on *Nádúir-fhilíocht na Gaedhilge*, Irish nature poetry. While a student at UCD, O'Nolan also contributed stories and short fictional pieces to a number of publications, most notably *The Irish Press*, *Inisfail*, the student journal *Comhthrom Féinne* and *Blather*, a magazine he co-founded with his brother Ciarán and Niall Sheridan in 1934. Many of these items were written in Irish, or a bilingual mix of Irish and English, and several demonstrate the same playful concern with language matters as his later writings. The short stories '*Díoghaltais ar Ghallaibh 'sa Bhliain 2032!*' (1932) and '*Teacht Agus Imtheacht Sheáin Bhuidhe*' (1932), for instance, not only engage with the language question thematically, but also display the same mix of Gaelic uncial and Roman font that we see in many of the later *Cruiskeen Lawn* columns.[12] Although he might have been speaking Irish less than he used to, O'Nolan ensured his continued active bilingualism by both studying the language and writing in it creatively.

While his posthumous international reputation has hinged upon his English-language novels, during his own lifetime O'Nolan was most famous for his daily bilingual newspaper column in *The Irish Times*, the *Cruiskeen Lawn* (from the Irish '*an crúiscín lán*', 'the little full jug'), which he wrote from 1940 until his death in 1966. The column appeared mainly in Irish for the first year, then Irish and English alternated until 1943, and after 1943 it appeared almost exclusively in English. Yet even as O'Nolan gradually ceased publishing in Irish, Taaffe cites a number of his diary entries from 1943 which were written in Irish. Assuming that one usually writes one's diary in the language that feels most natural, these entries suggest that Irish continued to take up that position for O'Nolan, even as he wrote increasingly in English in his professional and creative capacities. (Intriguingly, the brief but striking entry regarding the poor reception of his play *Faustus Kelly* is bilingual: '*Droch-léirmheastaí ar* Faustus Kelly. Fuck' [Bad reviews of *Faustus Kelly*. Fuck].[13]) Yet whatever their dominant language, the *Irish Times* columns created a 'polytonal' discourse through multilingual wordplay and observations on the (im)possibilities of translations between Irish and English that displays a linguistic complexity which would have been inconceivable had O'Nolan not been bilingual himself.

Bilingualism and metalinguistic awareness

Bilinguals speak two languages and monolinguals speak one – this is a seemingly unambiguous and indisputable statement of fact. Yet the number of languages spoken is not the only disparity between bilinguals and monolinguals. Current studies from the fields of neurolinguistics and psycholinguistics suggest that bilinguals such as O'Nolan differ from monolinguals beyond the overt difference of being fluent in a second language. Recent neurolinguistic research demonstrates, for instance, that bilingualism increases cognitive capabilities. Speaking more than one language appears to change the way the brain is organised for language both on a functional and an anatomical level. Bilingualism affects language functioning and, consequently, 'linguistic expressions of bilinguals and multilinguals differ from those of monolinguals'.[14]

An important recent discovery is that bilingual speakers can never entirely 'turn off' one of their languages. As a consequence, when a bilingual is speaking in one of his or her languages, both languages are active – in linguistics this co-activation is called 'language non-selective lexical access'.[15] The psycholinguist Annette de Groot explains:

> when bilinguals are conversing with their interlocutors in one of their languages the mental system that stores the other language is not completely at rest. A bilingual linguistic system is noisier than the language system of monolingual language users because, during both language comprehension and language production, linguistic elements of both linguistic subsystems are activated.[16]

Experiments have shown, for instance, that when bilingual speakers of French and English read the word 'coin', both the English meaning 'piece of money' and the French meaning 'corner' are activated, independent of the language in which they are speaking at that moment.[17] Kroll and Hermans suggest that this phenomenon means that

> the language system itself is fundamentally open, with interactions that reshape language use and carry domain-general cognitive consequences for the ability to resolve competing alternatives. Even proficient bilinguals appear to be unable to selectively switch off the language not in use when they hear, read or speak one language alone.[18]

In other words, 'fluent bilinguals show some measure of activation of both languages and some interaction between them at all times, even in contexts that are entirely driven by only one of the languages'.[19]

Because a bilingual's two languages are always active, the bilingual brain appears to refine a number of specific cognitive skills. The brain of a bilingual has to use mental resources to control the extent to which each language is activated. Having constantly to exert inhibitory control, suppressing or ignoring one language in order to be able to speak the other, bilingual people become better at what in neurolinguistics is called 'control of selective attention',[20] also known as the 'executive control function': the system responsible for attention selection, inhibition, shifting and flexibility that are 'at the center of all higher thought'.[21] Bialystok *et al.* explain: 'lifelong experience in managing attention to two languages reorganizes specific brain networks, creating a more effective basis for executive control and sustaining better cognitive performance throughout the lifespan'.[22] Since bilinguals use this executive control system more it becomes more efficient, creating a cognitive system with 'an increased ability to attend to important information and ignore the less important'.[23] Thus, bilingualism re-wires the language system in such a way that bilinguals are different from monolinguals. Their experience with two languages leads to the development of new connections and neural pathways in the brain, causing bilinguals to have a different brain anatomy than monolinguals.

For example, bilinguals tend to have a larger auditory cortex – a brain area heavily involved in the perception and production of speech sounds – which allows them to distinguish, perceive and produce speech sounds more easily.[24] As we will see, this is an interesting discovery with regard to O'Nolan's writings, especially concerning Myles's recordings of Dublin speech and his purported offence with 'bad language', with people who lack his 'superior' linguistic abilities.

Another important aspect of the different cognitive functioning in bilinguals with regard to my consideration of O'Nolan as a bilingual writer is an increased metalinguistic awareness. Metalinguistic awareness is the conscious understanding of the structural properties of one's language. More precisely, it is 'the ability to reflect on and manipulate the structural features of language independent of meaning',[25] or 'the awareness of language itself, independent of the message it is conveying'.[26] Bilingualism promotes metalinguistic awareness because the dual linguistic environment of bilinguals leads them to notice, compare and analyse the structural aspects of language in more advanced ways.[27] Bilingualism not only 'boosts word awareness', writes de Groot, but 'particularly, the awareness that a word's form and its meaning are not inseparable entities but have become associated merely through convention'.[28] As a consequence, bilinguals are more readily aware 'that the relation between a word's sound and meaning is arbitrary, that a particular thing (or living being or abstract concept) remains this very same thing if its name were to be changed into a completely different one'.[29] In short, it is easier for bilinguals to disregard the established meanings of words, 'to see through the meaning of language to its underlying structure',[30] and to perceive and reproduce speech in a distinct way.

A number of recent studies suggest that the cognitive advantages fostered by bilingualism can promote creative thinking. Having two linguistic systems, two words for one and the same concept provides bilinguals with the ability to see the world from different points of view and to switch between these different perspectives. Anatoliy Kharkurin, for instance, explores research that suggests that bilinguals outperform monolinguals on a number of creativity tasks – tests that, for instance, require subjects to come up with uncommon uses for common objects. This is, Kharkurin claims, because these kinds of tests require the same kind of suppression of irrelevant information that bilinguals use on a daily basis as they navigate their two language systems: 'The inhibition of irrelevant information that is more efficient in individuals with great command of their languages seems to facilitate the extraction of an original solution and assist in focusing attention on the unconventional, atypical solutions to creative problems'.[31] Ellen Bialystok too finds that 'creativity may indeed be an indirect beneficiary of bilingualism, at least in the way it is assessed on psychological tests',[32] and Li Wei writes that bilinguals are 'able to extend the range of meanings, associations and images, and to think more flexibly and creatively'.[33]

So, bilinguals have a brain that is wired differently from that of monolinguals; they perceive and produce linguistic sound in a distinct way and they possess a metalinguistic awareness that gives them a more sophisticated understanding of the structures of language as well as a sensitivity with regard to its sounds and creative possibilities. If the linguistic expressions of bilinguals are indeed different from those of monolinguals in these significant ways, it should follow that the linguistic expressions of bilingual writers manifest these unique capacities, insights and perspectives. That this is the case with Brian O'Nolan's writing becomes most clear from his *Cruiskeen Lawn* columns, which teem with multilingual puns and deliberate mistranslations alongside dissections of the differences between Irish and English, bad translations from the Irish and the confusing creativity of Dinneen's dictionary.

Molotoff bread-baskets

O'Nolan's obsession with language and translation becomes apparent from the very first *Cruiskeen Lawn* column, which appeared on 4 October 1940

under the byline 'From a Correspondent' and signed '*An Broc*' [The Badger].
The item was bilingual, framing in English a comic dialogue in Irish between
a mother and her son Shawn Beg,[34] who, reading *The Irish Times*, refuses to
finish his porridge until she provides him with an adequate Irish translation
for the war term 'Molotoff bread-basket'.[35] The scene was a reaction against a
28 September article in the paper, which had questioned the possibility and, in
fact, the desirability, of reviving the use of Irish in everyday life. The writer
of the piece had claimed that this task, which 'would be hard enough, even
in normal years, unless conversation could be limited to requests for food and
drink', becomes almost impossible in these wartime years, 'when children all
over the world are trying to keep pace with an influx of new words as a result
of war news bulletins'.[36] The correspondent continues: 'Parents who confine
the family meal-time discussions to conversations in Irish must find it very
difficult to explain such words as air-raid warden, incendiary bomb, non-
aggression pact, decontamination, and Molotoff bread-basket'.[37]

O'Nolan has a field day with this. The mother in *An Broc*'s column refuses
to give her son an Irish translation for Molotoff bread-basket. The son,
exasperated, exclaims '*Cad chuige nach dtig linn Béarla a labhairt sa teach seo?*'
[Why can't we just speak English in this house?], upon which utterance his
mother, 'leading with her right', boxes his ears and says: '*Bhéarfad-sa* Molotoff
bread-basket *duit, a thaisce, a aingilin bhig léigheanta*' [There's your Molotoff
bread-basket, my treasure, my little learned angel]. '*An Broc*' adds dryly:

> Of course, there is no necessity for such scenes, because the Irish for
> Molotoff bread-basket is easy. One can say it several ways –
>> *Cliabh aráin an duine-uasail Uí Mhuilitíbh.*
>> *Manna Rúiseach.*
>> *Rúiskeen Lawn.*
>> *Feirín ó Stailín.*
>> *Brad-bhascaod Mhalatábh.*[38]

These translations are all wonderful but none of them provide the type of
translation one might expect to encounter in a news item about the war (nor,
of course, is that the purpose). The first is a more or less literal translation,
'the bread basket of mister Molotoff'; the second means 'Russian manna'; the
third is a play on 'Crúiskeen' and 'Russky', thus, in a way, Russianising the
title of the column; the fourth means 'gift from Stalin' rendered in the form
of a typical Irish name; and the last suggestion transliterates the phrase using
the rules of Irish lenition, consequently 'translating' it into Irish.[39]

Although Myles was critical of those who suggested the modern world could not be 'translated' into Irish, he was equally critical of those who endeavoured to translate Irish into English and make it available to the modern world. Bad translations were ubiquitous, in Myles's view, and they were all offensive in their own unique way. The translation that most often suffered from Myles's caustic condemnation was *The Islandman*, Robin Flower's 1934 English translation of Tomás Ó Criomhthain's autobiographical *An tOileánach* (1929), later parodied by O'Nolan in *An Béal Bocht* (1941). Anne Clissmann suggests that it was, 'probably, the literalness of [Flower's] translation which annoyed him'.[40] Under the heading 'Literally from the Irish', a number of *Cruiskeen Lawn* columns mimic the style of Flower's translation by exaggerating their literalness and creating an all but incomprehensible English: 'I was a day in Dingle and Paddy James, my sister's man, in company with me and us in the direction of each other in the running of the day' (*BM*, 275).

The authority of Dinneen's dictionary was another frequent butt of Myles's jokes. An tAthair Pádraig Ó Duinnín (Father Patrick Dinneen) had assembled his Irish–English dictionary, *Foclóir Gaedhilge agus Béarla* (1904), from Irish poetry rather than from spoken language. The resulting discrepancies between language as it was used by Irish speakers such as O'Nolan and the definitions found in the dictionary were an endless source of fun:

> THE Irish lexicographer Dinneen, considered *in vacuo* is, heaven knows, funny enough. He just keeps standing on his head, denying stoutly that *piléar* means bullet and asserting that it means 'an inert thing or person'. Nothing stumps him. He will promise the sun moon and stars to anybody who will catch him out. And well he may. Just *take* the sun, moon and stars for a moment. Sun, you say, is *grian*. Not at all. Dinneen shouts that *grian* means 'the bottom (of a lake, well)'. You are a bit nettled and mutter that, anyway, *gealach* means moon. Wrong again. *Gealach* means 'the white circle in a slice of a half-boiled potato, turnip, etc'. In a bored voice he adds that *réalta* (of course) means 'a mark on the forehead of a beast'. Most remarkable man. Eclectic I think is the word.[41]

Dinneen's tendency to yield a profusion of definitions for a single word receives a similarly ironic treatment:

> There is scarcely a single word in the Irish (barring, possibly, *Sasanach* [English person]) that is simple and explicit. [...] Here is an example

copied from Dineen [*sic*] and from more authentic sources known only
to my little self:

Cur, *g.* curtha and cuirthe, *m.*, act of putting, sending, sowing,
raining, discussing, burying, vomiting, hammering into the ground,
throwing through the air, rejecting, shooting, the setting or clamp
in a rick of turf, selling, addressing, the crown of cast-iron buttons
which have been made bright by contact with cliff-faces, the stench of
congealing badger's suet, the luminance of glue-lice, a noise made in an
empty house by an unauthorised person, a heron's boil, a leprachaun's
[*sic*] denture, a sheep-biscuit, the act of inflating hare's offal with a bicycle
pump, a leak in a spirit-level, the whine of a sewage farm windmill, a
corncrake's clapper, the scum on the eye of a senile ram, a dustman's
dumpling, a beetle's faggot, the act of loading every rift with ore, a
dumb man's curse, a blasket, a 'kur', a fiddler's occupational disease, a
fairy godmother's father, a hawk's vertigo, the art of predicting past
events, a wooden coat, a custard-mincer, a blue-bottle's 'farm', a gravy
flask, a timber-mine, a toy craw, a porridge-mill, a fair-day donnybrook
with nothing barred, a stoat's stomach-pump, a broken ———

But what is the use? One could go on and on without reaching
anywhere in particular.[42]

In O'Nolan's hands 'Dinneen's dictionary became a weapon of mass
befuddlement',[43] confusing any poor soul who attempts to speak or translate
Irish but who is not, like Myles and his creator, fluent enough to do so
without the aid of a dictionary – note Myles's reference to 'more authentic
sources known only to my little self'. This stance points towards an interesting
inconsistency. On the one hand, O'Nolan, through Myles, was invested in
demonstrating that Irish was an imaginative and flexible language, suitable
for the needs of the modern world. On the other hand, he lampooned anyone
who tried to engage with the language in a way that differed from his own
native and creative way of using and interacting with Irish. It seems as if his
bilingual linguistic sensitivity to language – expressed in both a desire for the
'correct' use of language and a claim to the authority to determine what *was*
the 'correct' use – is engaged in an internal war with his wish for Irish to
flourish. In the columns this war is externalised in the form of an incessant
concern with pronunciation – especially with bad pronunciation – and with
linguistic clichés.

Myles's war on bad language

O'Nolan's concern with pronunciation often takes the form of a play on the different orthographic regulations of Irish and English. Writing English according to Irish phonetics and spelling rules is a favourite game of O'Nolan's and one he plays frequently in the Myles columns. Here, for instance:

> *Aigh nó a mean thú ios só léasaigh sat thí slips in this clós, bhears a bíord, and dos not smóc bíocós obh de trobal obh straigeing a meaits. It is só long sins thi did an anasth dea's bhorc dat thí thinks 'manuil leabear' is de neim obh a Portuguis arditeitear.* (BM, 263)

These lines, when spoken aloud according to standard Irish pronunciation, approximate phonetically to the following 'English' words:

> I know a man who is so lazy that he sleeps in his clothes, wears a beard and does not smoke because of the trouble of striking a match. It is so long since he did an honest day's work that he thinks 'manual labour' is the name of a Portuguese agitator.

In recognition of Myles's virtuoso bilingual performance, this little episode is followed by '[*Lamhd láftar*]' – or, 'loud laughter'.

Often these hybrid 'English/Irish' strings of text occur in the middle of an otherwise Irish narrative, resulting in a hilarious simultaneity of contrasting languages. In another Irish sketch we read: '*Pearsain I láthair: Sur Tharbhaigh Baigineal, an óifisear obh de Cbhín, in ful réidiméinteals*' [Characters present: Sir Harvey Bagenal, an officer of the Queen, in full regimentals] (BM, 274). These instances, where English is written orthographically as though it were Irish, give us English as it would sound to an Irish ear unaccustomed to the English language. The opposite occurs as well: Irish written as though it were English. The most common offender is the early recurring character of Taidhgín Slánabhaile, who will say, for instance, 'Kod ay soh'[44] for '*cad é seo?*' [What is this?] or 'Tigim. Guramahagut'[45] for '*Tuigim. Go raibh maith agat*' [I understand. Thank you]. Here we not only get Irish rendered the way it would sound to an unaccustomed English ear, but also *bad* Irish the way it would sound to a native Irish ear – and a sly joke on phony Gaeilgeoirí. This metalinguistic play with the phonetics and orthographies of Irish and English shows a keen interest in the audio and visual surfaces of language, which is another, less obvious, marker of O'Nolan's bilingualism: a locus where we can see the traces that a bilingual brain may leave in literary language and where O'Nolan's metalinguistic awareness of the arbitrariness of language and his sensitivity to its sounds and forms become most visible.

Joseph Brooker describes O'Nolan's interest in listening to his audio environment – to the Dublin and rural Irish speech patterns from different classes and walks of life that surrounded him daily – and suggests that the 'recording of voice, and its creative recreation, is among the most highly developed skills that he displays'.[46] For Brooker, O'Nolan's work 'drew on the speech he heard around him; and it testifies that one can dedicate oneself to faithfully transcribing that soundtrack'.[47] I agree, and would suggest that this 'highly developed' skill in O'Nolan's work is a direct consequence of his bilingualism. Discussing *The Hard Life*, a novel he described as 'simply a study in the Dublin way of speaking', O'Nolan wrote that he had 'set [the dialogues] down in absolutely accurate Dublinese' and reflected that he had 'made a bit of a fetish of the natural way of speaking in Dublin', something that was all the more important because it was typically 'botched' by people who 'don't know how to listen'.[48] O'Nolan does know how to listen, and the recorded conversations in *Cruiskeen Lawn* are as much a 'study in the Dublin way of speaking' as are those in *The Hard Life*.

In the column Myles pays meticulous attention to the peculiarities of people's speech and records them with a linguistic precision that would befit a linguistic anthropologist. Here, for instance, a 'Dublin Man' and a visitor from England try – and fail – to hold a conversation:

> VISITOR: I pick up Auden.
> DUBLIN MAN: Pairdin?
> I pick up Auden. Jew now wear I get a 17 bus?
> Pairdin?
> Jew now wear the 17 bus stops I mean?
> I beg yer pairdin?
> I want to get to Witehall. Jew now wear Witehall is I mean?
> Sairtintly I do. Do you know Westminster?
> I pick up Auden?
> You'll see the Houses of Parliamint there. You don't go across the river but you turn sharp left.
> Wot you mean?
> Pairdin?
> Wot I wanted to know is wear do I get a 17 bus I mean.

A 17 bus? Shure yer croobs is on the very spot.

I pick up Auden?

Pairdin?

Wot I want to now is——

Gob here's a seventeen! If it's Drumcondra or Collins's Avenue or Whitehall you're goin to, this is your man.

I say, I mean——

O.K. Cheers now!

As the Dublin Man 'Departs to Whitehall in a 17 bus, pleased that he has shown courtesy to a stranger', the Visitor 'stops another man, who happens to be a NORTHERN VISITOR' and the confusion escalates:

I say, I pick up Auden …

Hullo there!

Aoh … Hellaoh, I mean …

At's a graun day the day.

Pod in? Jew now wear the buses stop I mean to say?

What was that?

Witehall. I want to get to Witehall.

Wheighthaul? At's a brave dastance to thon place.

Pod in?

What's that? Eye don't know what yer sayin.[49]

Although the first visitor tries to adapt to the local speech (using 'Pod in', his rendition of the Dublin Man's 'Pairdin', instead of his own 'I pick up Auden') he never manages to locate his bus, and instead finds an untimely death in Dublin's traffic: 'Jew now wot I think of the Irish? I say – helloah! *TEXI!* (*Rushes into road to hail passing taxi. Fails to see approaching Whitehall bus, which kills him.*)'. It is his linguistic ineptitude that causes the visitor's untimely demise at the author's hand. The difference between 'good' and 'bad' language is here literally a matter of life and death.

In another column, 'taken down' in a 'well-known Dublin restaurant', a diner and a waiter struggle with the correct pronunciation of French dishes:

DINER: Have you a me and you?

WAITER: Pairdin?

DINER: Is there no me and you in the place?

WAITER: Oh sairtintly sir. (*Hands over card.*)

D (*musing*): I wonder what we'll have today at all. I think we'll try the horse dovers.

W: Sairtintly sir.

D: Hould your horses now for a minit. What's all *this* about?

W: That sir? That's what we call the hoofs poesh benedicteen, a very tasty dish sir. Eggs. […]

D: Have you any tamata soup at al?

W: Sairtintly we have.

D: Hould your horses for a minit now. Wait till we see what we're going to have […]. Powl. Pow let rotty. What's this thing down here. Powlet.

W: I wouldn't recommend that at all sir. It's supposed to be chicken. I seen some of it.

D: I see. Fair enough. Hold your horses now. Horses dovers for a start. Then a drop of the tamata. Is the rolls fresh?

W: Made this morning sir. […]

D: I'd give me eyes for bacon and cabbage.

W: Pairdin?

D: Be the gob I would.

W: I see. If you look down here you will find that we have a jambone de pay ose epinard. (*FC*, 46–47)

This exchange goes on in the same manner for a good while, with the waiter and the diner bestowing their Dublin pronunciation on *saumon grillé* ('saumon grillee'; 'Fish again? There's more fish on this card than in the say if you ask me'), *steak bordelaise* ('steak borderlays'), *légumes* ('Will you have any lay gooms sir?' 'Pairdin?') and *petit pois* ('petty poys') (*FC*, 48).

In each of these columns the energy of the tales that are told, or rather the conversations that are reported, rests almost exclusively with the detail and texture of the language. In the first column this energy centres on the misunderstanding that results from the different pronunciations of English that the Dublin man, the English man and the Northerner have. In the second, the comedy resides with the mispronunciation of French and with the contrast between the Dublinised French terms and the men's regular Dublin talk. Their garbled French constitutes a contrast with the linguistic abilities of the recorder Myles na gCopaleen, who has demonstrated on more than one occasion in these columns that he also knows French 'pairfectly' (*FC*, 39) and marks his linguistic superiority by casually littering his own musings with correctly rendered French expressions: 'To change the subject (*plus ça change*, one fears)' (*FC*, 112); 'raison-d'être' (*AW*, 37); '(qu'importe en effet, *tout cela?)' (BM,* 373); *'Ça…ça…c'est tout à fait égal. V'savez' (AW,* 128) *– et ainsi de suite.*

Above all, these columns show the precision with which O'Nolan records language: the smallest differences in pronunciation are rendered with care. This minute attention to speech is visible throughout the columns. 'Certainly', for instance, can take the form of the 'sairtintly' of the 'Dublin Man' from the first piece and the waiter from the second, but can also be pronounced as 'certaintly' *(AW,* 77) and The Brother's assertion that in 'a sairten city be the name of Liverpool' there is a 'sairten big hospital' *(FC,* 18) suggests that there are even more possible variations – it just takes a keen ear to hear them. The same is true for Dublin, which can sound like 'Dubalin' *(FC,* 33), 'Dubbalin' or 'Dubballinn' *(FC,* 40) – as in 'I'm an ordinary Dubballinn maaan me parents was all in this city when the crowd of whippersnappers that's going nowadays wasn't even thought of' *(FC,* 41).

Again and again, these recorded conversations emphasise phonetic fidelity to the unique peculiarities of speech: 'The Man Who Is Not Such A Fool As To Consult Doctors About His Ailments' can be heard to say, 'Is it put meself into the hands of your men when I have the bread knife below on the dhresser if I want to do meself in. […] *Docthors,* is it?' *(FC,* 68–69); the aforementioned 'Dubballinn maaan' exclaims: 'Ah but shure listen you don't know the half of it. Me dear man luckit here' *(FC,* 40); 'The Plain People of Ireland', discussing the perils of 'dirty sinful foreign literature' declare, 'Aisy now, aisy there! Did you not see be the papers where there's goin' to be an end once and for all to that class of rascality […] Will you whist man, before you shame us all' *(AW,* 83); an 'unidentified' person in the Scotch House: 'Now listen here to me like a good man. Do you know what I'm going to tell you. That crowd has the whole lot of us destroyed. Do you know what I'm telling you? Shure we're not men at all nor half men' *(FC,* 37); and one Mick, overheard on the phone in a public house by the column's 'tireless reporter' *(FC,* 30) has some great lines too: 'Well do you know by gob I was thinking about you yesterday what am I talking about it was this morning when his nabs and the young wan with him down in Ussher's Island' *(FC,* 26).

The stakes of Myles's relentless, almost obsessive detailed attention to the variances of pronunciation are borne out directly in a column that is worth quoting at length:

> The language problem again – I *am* sorry but we must, you know. First, pronunciation; this is very important. Carelessness in the formation of

vowels and consonants, when it is accompanied by improper breathing, bad phrasing and the forcing of the voice, leads inevitably to slovenly speech. Nothing produces so bad an impression on a stranger; you cannot give too much attention to this matter – with it is bound up the whole question of national prestige. Dublin people are perhaps the worst offenders in this respect. One thinks immediately of the words: 'Cow', 'Man', 'Office', 'Foreign', 'It', 'This', 'Carry', 'Dog', readers can finish the list (themselves). You know how they come out: 'Keahaouw', 'Mhaaanh', 'Uffuss', 'Phurren', 'Ihh', 'Dis', 'Korry', 'Dawg'… It is simply not good enough, that is all. (*FC*, 95)

This quote shows, I think, the creative tension borne of O'Nolan's bilingualism that is apparent throughout *Cruiskeen Lawn*: the assertion from authority that the language recorded is 'slovenly', 'bad', 'simply not good enough' and that those who speak in this way are 'offenders' seems to be contradicted by the amount of detailed attention that is given to this offensive way of speaking and by the delight in the recorded language that seeps through the descriptions.

Myles, who protests he is 'no eavesdropper, no Paul Pry' (but who is obviously exactly that), makes a point of distinguishing his own sophisticated language from that of the offending eavesdropped and emphasises how distasteful the overheard conversations are to him (*FC*, 25). It is the resulting contrast in styles that provides these columns with their energy. One exchange 'carefully overheard by the present writer in, more betoken his own place, the Scotch House' and presented to the reader as a 'verbatim note' is concluded with, 'Exit of pained eavesdropper' (*FC*, 34).[50] Another conversation, recorded 'for the information of posterity', ends after one last 'Do you know what I'm going to tell you…?' with '(I went home at this stage. Too damn well I knew what he was going to tell his companion and me)' (*FC*, 37).

These instances illustrate the offence that the 'pained eavesdropper' claims to experience as a consequence of all the slovenly language he overhears. There is, indeed, a *sairten* belligerence in Myles's recordings of Dublin speech, an assertion of linguistic authority over all these sinners against *dacent* pronunciation. In one column, when '*Mise*' [me] fulminates 'bitterly' against the habit of English-language newspapers of writing in Irish on Saint Patrick's Day, beslobbering the language 'with laudatory mucus', '*Voices*' respond: 'But is this all we're going to have – a tirade, violent denunciations' (*AW*, 24–25).

One might be tempted to make the same evaluation of the critical recordings of Dublin speech in the *Cruiskeen Lawn* columns and see them as a tirade against slovenly speech, a war campaign on bad language.

This view is supported by the column's renowned recurring feature, The Catechism of Cliché. Myles's tirade against the clichés that he finds 'polluting millions of conversations' (*FC*, 67) almost literally takes on the form of a war in as much as cliché users are recurringly 'put to death' on Myles's 'orders' in the same way that betrayers of the fatherland are executed without trial in times of war: 'Early morning workers passing by my lodgings on Monday probably heard two volleys. Actually I had my firing squad at work in my yard' (*FC*, 66). The two 'base types' who met their last end in the columnist's garden – and are now 'in their graves' as 'a warning to others' – were users of the clichés 'It's a Disease, You Know' and 'But if we all did that' (*FC*, 66–67). In another instance of The Catechism of Cliché, we read:

> Do what I do. Carry a small grey American automatic and make sure that it is always stuffed with bullets. Then when some bleating fish-gilled bags opens up and says –
>   'Of course, backing horses is a mug's game'
> – just empty the gun into his low-grade jungle forehead. (*BM*, 209)

What is bothering Myles about the clichés is that they are dead language, '*Bearla Marbh*' [dead English]: 'A cliché is a phrase that has become fossilized, its component words deprived of their intrinsic light and meaning by incessant usage' (*BM*, 227). And those who use dead language deserve to die themselves.

Yet the many instances of recorded 'slovenly' speech, of the (mis) pronunciations of the various Dublin men Myles notes down are anything but dead. On the contrary, they are alive, they are lively, and they endow the columns with the energy that keeps you reading even when nothing is being said, really.[51] O'Nolan, as Myles, appears to take immense pleasure in the Dublin speech he records. Although he professes not to, the care with which he records the expressions of Dubliners seems to belie his objections. The linguistic tension that arises from the writer's bilingualism and runs through the columns is actually its driving force, and what seems a war on bad language is, in effect, a tribute to its energy and literary potential.

4

'the half-said thing'

Cruiskeen Lawn, Japan and the Second World War

CATHERINE FLYNN

On 27 September 1940, Japan signed the Tripartite Pact with Germany and Italy. Japan would not enter into war with the United States and Britain until the attack on Pearl Harbour in December 1941, but the nation had been at war with China for three years by 1940, conquering huge tracts of territory and displacing millions of Chinese. The *Irish Times* editorial from 11 October, one week after the first instalment of *Cruiskeen Lawn*, discusses the art of diplomacy amid shifting geopolitics. The editorial announces an unprecedented understanding between the United States and Britain, brought about by the new, threatening alliance. Yet the editorial, titled 'Common Cause', also draws attention to Japan's declarations of a desire to cooperate with the United States:

> Japan made her recent pact with Germany and Italy. There is a general belief in the United States that this agreement was directed openly against America, although, according to Mr Matsuoka, the Japanese Foreign Minister, it actually was designed to help, rather than to embarrass, President Roosevelt's Government.[1]

The notion that Japan's signing of the Tripartite Pact would help the United States is a paraphrase of the Pact itself, which declares the 'desire of the three Governments to extend cooperation to nations in other spheres of the world'; it fails to mention, however, the euphemistic condition that those nations must be 'inclined to direct their efforts along lines similar to [the three Governments'] own for the purpose of realizing their ultimate object, world peace'.² The *Irish Times* editorial praises Japanese verbal tactics amidst tense international relations: 'For sheer subtlety, the Japanese have no superiors in the art of diplomacy. They know how to fish in troubled waters with unequalled skill'.³ The metaphor of fishing in troubled waters has a literal referent in Japan's fulfilment of its need for resources amidst a strained international situation, while the reference to Japan's 'sheer subtlety' invokes the country's reputation as a centre of aesthetic sophistication and refinement, and its perceived emphasis on cultivated ritual rather than authentic spontaneity.

In a series of Irish-language *Cruiskeen Lawn* instalments over the next months, Brian O'Nolan points to unexpected political and linguistic similarities between Ireland and Japan. In these early instalments, *Cruiskeen Lawn* exceeds *Irish Times* editor R.M. Smyllie's brief of countering the 'chauvinism and hypocrisy' associated with contemporary promoters of the Irish language.⁴ The instalments on Japan engage polyglot writing, literary allusion and complex rhetorical effects to lead readers to consider the position of Ireland in world politics, while offering oblique commentary on the Irish state's own territorial policies, all the while evading strict wartime press censorship.⁵ Far from illustrating Hugh Kenner's claim that the wartime *Cruiskeen Lawn* offers a retreat into an 'Irish solipsism',⁶ these instalments show O'Nolan inventing, in order to engage with the issues of the war, an aesthetics of the half-said.

In the *Irish Times* editorial, the territory desired by the Japanese is referred to with a term borrowed from the foreign policy of the German National Socialist Party: 'the Washington authorities seem to be convinced that Japan is preparing a further *coup* in the Far East, with a view, *inter alia*, to the removal of American influence from what is regarded in Tokyo as Japanese *Lebensraum*'.⁷ Japan in fact had its own term for territorial expansion, *hakkō ichiu*. The term forms the exclamatory byline of a report in *Cruiskeen Lawn* of 28 October on its public adoption by Matsuoka. The *Daily Express* report comes as a bracing surprise in the instalment, following Myles's depiction of Irish inebriation and camaraderie – a surreal segment on John Ruskin, or '*Rúiscín Lán*' [drunken Ruskin] as he is rendered by his new friend Charles Parnell – and ironically rave reviews of new Irish-language books by Seosamh Mac Grianna and Liam Ó Rinn, titled *Mo Bhealach Féin* [*My Way*] and *Mo Chara Stiofán* [*My Friend Stephen*].

HAKKO ICHIU!
Mr Matsuoka said that Japan recognised the principle of 'Hakko Ichiu'
('the eight corners of the universe under one roof', or 'the whole world
one family'). We would be glad to welcome any other Powers ... if they
should desire to join us in the spirit of 'Hakko Ichiu'. However, we are
determined to eliminate any nation that may obstruct 'Hakko Ichiu'.
                                                            —*Daily Express*.[8]

A two-and-a-half-thousand-year-old notion, *hakkō ichiu* was revived in the
twentieth century and popularised by Prime Minister Fumimaro Konoe as
meaning that Japanese imperial domination of the entire globe was a matter of
divine will. The conceit of divine sanction is echoed in Matsuoka's statement
that Japan recognises the principle of *hakkō ichiu*, rather than chooses it to
name a programme of political action. We can understand *hakkō ichiu* as the
articulation in Japanese terms of the spirit of the Tripartite Pact, and it was
surely presented as such in public pronouncements, yet the two terms present
competing universalities.[9] The Japanese slogan is a piece of rhetoric that
facilitates a broader cooperation – most notably between Japan, Germany and
Italy – while masking a fundamental opposition.[10] While the Tripartite Pact
assigns to Japan the specific territory of 'Greater East Asia' in the new world
order, *hakkō ichiu* precedes the Tripartite Pact historically, even as it aspires to
supersede it with the ultimate dismantling of the two other signatory nations.

In his rapid alternation between warmth and coldness, invitation and
threat, Matsuoka's speech displays the kind of rhetorical skill ascribed to
the Japanese in the *Irish Times* editorial. His determined reiterations of the
slogan present it as the inevitable outcome of any situation, whether the
happy conglomeration of like-minded countries or the massive destruction
of opposition. The *Cruiskeen Lawn* response also switches between opposites.
Following the *Daily Express* quote on '*Hakko Ichiu*', the instalment reverts to
Irish, with a comic return to the amicable: '*Cuir Gaedhilg ar "Hakko Ichiu",
a Pheadair*' [Put 'Hakko Ichiu' into Irish, Peadar]. This request, made by
O'Nolan's Myles na gCopaleen persona, meets Matsuoka's intention of
world domination with a local and even insular language. Indeed, Peadar, a
recurring character in the column's conversations about the Irish language in
the autumn of 1940, begins by translating *hakkō ichiu* as the opposite of *Sinn
Fein*, which he associates with local unity and cooperation – before entirely
switching course:

Cuir Gaedhilg ar 'Hakko Ichiu', *a Pheadair.*

    Tamall oshoin, nuair bhí aiséirghe poilitíochta ar siubhal againn agus muinighin againn as oileánachas, aondacht agus cur-le-chéile, sé sluagh-ghairm a cheapamar ná 'Sinn Féin'. Do réir deallraimh tá an smaoineamh contráilte ag an duine-uasal Matsuóca agus ar an adhbhar san d'fhéádfaí 'Daoine Eile' a chur mar aistriú ar 'Hakko Ichiu'.

    Acht de bhrígh go bhfuilmíd ag iarraidh na Sé Conndachthe do bhreith slán tharnais agus ocht beanna na hÉireann do chur arís faoi aon dhíon rialtais amháin, is follus go bhfuil ár 'ndaoine-eileachas' féin ar siubhal againn.

    Ach sin scéal eile.[11]

[Put '*Hakko Ichiu*' into Irish, Peadar.

    A while ago, when we had political uprisings going on and hope in island-life, unity and supporting one another we thought of the slogan 'We Ourselves' [*Sinn Féin*]. By all appearances, the respected gentleman Matsuoka [*Matsuóca*] has the opposite thought and so '*Hakko Ichiu*' would have to be translated as 'Other People' [*Daoine Eile*].

    But as we are trying to get the Six Counties back safe again and to put the eight peaks of Ireland under the roof of one government again, it's clear that we have our own 'Other-Peopleness' going on.

    But that's another story.]

Peadar's provocatively shifting translation plays on the Irish word for 'other' [*eile*], as he uses it to construct the neologistic phrase '*ár "ndaoine-eileachas" féin*' [our own 'Other-Peopleness'], evoking the old word for 'alien' [*eileachadh*]. Proclaiming both the foreignness and localness of *hakkō ichiu*, Peadar swiftly deflects, immediately disavowing the idea that the Irish nation's aim to reunify the island of Ireland resembles the Japanese aim of global domination. This deflection, however, has the connotation of a news item waiting to be published, '*Ach sin scéal eile*' [But that's another story].

    In drawing attention to a shared Japanese and Irish desire for territorial expansion, *Cruiskeen Lawn* pushes its role in a newly 'liberal' *Irish Times* to an extreme: its resistance to Irish parochialism begins with a consideration of world politics through the Irish language, yet extends to denying the difference between Irish national republicanism and imperialism. O'Nolan's resistance to 'chauvinism and hypocrisy' is both absurd and pointed. Likening the young nation to an imperial aggressor, the column enacts its own policy of expansion, depending on the capacity of the Irish language to contend with contemporary issues and on O'Nolan's own virtuosity. At this moment of subversion of values held sacred by many and enshrined in the Irish Constitution, the column gains a broader sphere of impact and a more sophisticated mode of expression through visible self-censorship: code-switching, false piety and theatrical deflection.

A week later, on 8 November, Myles apologises. After another capitalised exclamation of *HAKKŌ ICHIU*, he declares that he issues his apology under fear of death not at the hands of Irish republicans but of the Japanese:

[HAKKO ICHIU!
Excuse me. I have a cold.

A little while ago I made a statement about *Hakko Ichiu*, that Japanese principle that wants the human race to be one big family [*mar chonnlán mór amháin*], without strife or dispute between them henceforth.[12] I compared that proposal to *Sinn Féin*, but I'm sorry that I did. It seems that I didn't understand exactly what I was saying. There is an obituary of me taken out by the editor in last Sunday's '*Nichi Nichi Shimbun*' [*Tokyo Daily News*]. This is what he said:

[*Text in Japanese kanji*]

I am ashamed. If I had known that that would be the story, I wouldn't have spoken as I did.]

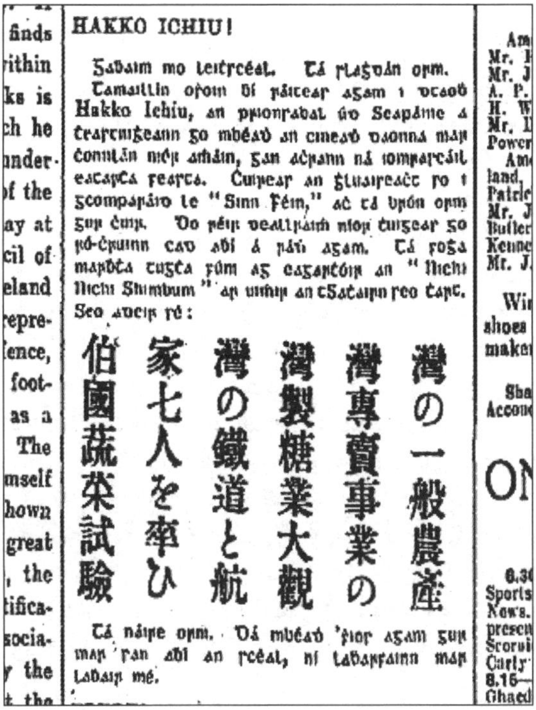

Fig. 4.1 *CL*, 8 November 1940, p. 4.

The tone of this section is clearly comic, beginning as it does by treating *hakkō ichiu* as the sound of sneezing. No reader would believe that Myles could be anything but incorrigible. The death threat is clearly a dodge: why the editor of the *Tokyo Daily News* would be incensed by the views of a columnist on a remote neutral island is a question that hardly bears being asked. Clearly, the opposite party in the comparison is the sensitive one: the Irish nationalists who are angered at being compared with belligerent imperialists. If Myles is to be put to death by the Japanese, the column implies, then the Irish might smile and leave him to his fate.

The graphic impact of this grovelling apology has the opposite effect: combining Irish uncial font with gloriously foreign Japanese *kanji* produces a visually stunning *Cruiskeen Lawn* instalment. The obituary from the *Tokyo Daily News* invades the *Irish Times* column like an advance guard of the Japanese army, its vertical ranks of logograms as foreign in appearance as its occupying soldiers might be. The inscrutability of the Japanese characters for the majority of the *Irish Times* readership facilitates their function as an alibi for Myles. But there is one more twist. On translation, the characters yield something quite different from an obituary:

> The agricultural products of the bay in general.
> Among the specific business of the bay.
> The overview of the sugar-producing industry.
> The railroad and shipping of the bay.
> The departure [i.e. death] of seven members of a household.
> The testing of vegetables from Brazil.[13]

While O'Nolan may have excerpted a random Japanese text, it is hard to imagine that he would not have deliberately used as an obituary a list of topics of the kind he dealt with every day in his work as a civil servant. (The list perhaps announces his death by another cause, the boredom of bureaucratic reportage.) The items easily belong in an Irish context and while the final reference to Brazil might mark the list as pertaining to Japan, it is conceivable that Ireland, another island nation, would import food from Latin America. Despite the stark visual contrast, the Japanese text is not a statement of radical antagonism but rather evidence of the two countries' shared everyday realities and practical concerns. Ironically, this moment of aesthetic sophistication enacts an affirmation of the mundane, a half-said assertion of Japanese-Irish commonalities in the everyday work of sustenance. This is perhaps the closest

O'Nolan comes to a sincere avowal – made in impersonal terms, hidden to most readers in foreign script and surrounded by profuse apologies.

A week later, the 16 November *Cruiskeen Lawn* turns to classic Irish literature to establish a sense of connection between the two countries:

THE SUN OF HEAVEN
'Anois teacht an arthraigh beidh an lá dul chun síneadh'.
Sin adubhairt na Seapáinaig le goirid nuair shroicheadar Gaillimh insa scríb 'na baile soir. Bíonn an ghrian i gcomhnuidhe ag éirghe 'na dtír féin agus do réir mar ghluaisid chuici ar bhord luinge, beidh an lá dul chun síneadh. Rud eile, chuaidh siad siar ar a mbealach soir, ach ní fiú trácht ar san.
Seán Buidhe a bheirim féin ar aon fhear Seapánach a líonann radharc mo shúile agus mé amuigh ag siubhal mo siubhail.[14]

THE SUN OF HEAVEN
'Now with the coming of the ship, the day will be getting longer'.
That is what the Japanese said shortly after they reached Galway, in the writing of their eastern home. The sun is always rising in their own country and, as one moves towards it on a boat, the day is getting longer [*dul chun síneadh*]. Another thing, they went west [*siar*] on their way east, but it isn't worth commenting on that. *Seán Buidhe* [Yellow John] is what I myself would call any Japanese man who would fill the sight of my eyes and I out walking my walk.

The opening quote '*Anois teacht an arthraigh beidh an lá dul chun síneadh*' is a distortion of the first line of the famous poem 'Cill Aodáin' by the wandering bard Antoine Ó Raifteirí (1779–1835): '*Anois teacht an earraigh beidh an lá dúl chun síneadh*'. Frank O'Connor translates the first lines of Raifteirí's poem as follows:

Now with the springtime the days will grow longer,
And after St Bride's Day my sail I'll let go;
I put my mind to it and I never will linger
Till I find myself back in the County Mayo.[15]

Changing *earraigh* to *arthraigh*, the *Cruiskeen Lawn* section begins: '"Now with the coming of the ship, the day will grow longer". That is what the Japanese said shortly after they reached Galway, in the writing of their eastern home'.

Contemporary readers must have responded with amusement to this twisting of the famous line to refer to the 1940 repatriation of Japanese civilians, routed by the Red Cross from Europe to Japan through Galway Bay. As this Irish literary enshrinement of nostalgia for native locality is distorted, the eighty miles from Galway to Ó Raifteirí's native Killedan in County Mayo is rendered tiny in contrast with the six-thousand-mile journey that faces the Japanese. This increased distance amplifies the poetic allusion's power as a vehicle for empathy with a people far from home; at the same time, the allusion presents the internationally organised expulsion of foreigners.

In Myles's next comment, this ambivalence is joined by suspicion towards those who wander: 'The sun is always rising in their own country and, as one moves towards it on a boat, the day is getting longer'. As the brightening days of spring are associated with the Land of the Rising Sun, they conjure up imperial conquest, figured by the rising sun of the Japanese flag. China may in fact be the intended destination of the Japanese, as suggested in Myles's punning of '*dul chun síneadh*' [growing longer or extending] with *dul go dtí an tSín* [going to China]. When Myles declares that he would call any Japanese man walking on Irish land *Seán Buidhe* [literally 'Yellow John'], he invokes the traditional Irish name for 'John Bull', the personification of England. This English connotation is amplified by the description of Japan's supposed uniqueness – 'the sun is always rising in their own country' – which recalls the British Empire, on which the sun never sets. A sense of sly opposition emerges in Myles's presentation of the Japanese journey home: '*chuaidh siad siar ar a mbealach soir*' [they went back on their way east]. As '*siar*' means 'west' as well as 'back', the observation can suggest either confused wandering or intentional invasion of land that lies to the west of their country, as China does from Japan and Ireland does from England. In another instance of avowal and deflection, Myles dismisses this notion immediately upon raising it: '*ach ní fiú trácht ar san*' [but it isn't worth commenting on that].

The section's title, 'The Sun of Heaven', also suggests its homonym, 'The *Son* of Heaven', which was the appellation given to the Emperors of Japan and China. This implied 'Son of Heaven' might refer to the unknown Japanese man who 'fills the sight of my eyes and I out walking my walk', an expression that identifies sight with occupied space. This wordplay suggests another collapse of terms: as 'John Bull' becomes *Seán Buidhe* [Yellow John], the 'Son of Heaven' is not an Emperor, far less Christ, the Western Son of Heaven, but rather *any* Japanese man. Yet it also works the other way: *any* Japanese man is himself 'Yellow John', 'John Bull', the Emperor of Japan and, possibly, the 'Son of God'. We might also apply this title to all Christians, who also see

themselves as children, if lesser ones, of God. If the line from Ó Raifteirí is
altered to house both Irish and Japanese longing for home, a traditional title
is adapted to accommodate one and all. O'Nolan superimposes notions of the
common and the great, the local and the universal, as he creates a writing that
wavers between opposites.

This wavering has several effects. It advances *Cruiskeen Lawn* through
virtuosity and comic devilment. It reveals the arbitrary and even ridiculous
nature of markers of power and belonging, a project of heightened importance
in 1940.[16] These aims of writerly ambition and political intervention are
joined in *Cruiskeen Lawn*'s purposeful confusion of space. The *kanji* of the
8 November column are foreign invaders that conceal surprisingly familiar
and local concerns; the Irish poetry of the 16 November column conveys
an alien homesickness. This complexity of location is also to be seen in the
column itself: linguistically and programmatically apart from the rest of
the paper, the format of *Cruiskeen Lawn* suggests a space of play rather than
reportage or advertisement. Yet this peripheral status allows the column to
evade the official legal limits put on wartime commentary. Using quotation,
translation, allusion and pun to engage with events officially under the
purview of the main newspaper, the column becomes an increasingly active
part of *The Irish Times*, offering a more incisive and provocative engagement
with contemporary events than the editorials or articles. *Cruiskeen Lawn*'s
undoing of its own marginality is accompanied by its insertion of Ireland into
world politics, achieved through suggestion rather than direct statement. In
this geographical repositioning, as in the case of the undoing of markers of
identity, the elliptical nature of each phrase is crucial as it offers a pretext for
further signification that cannot be made concrete.

The paired tendencies of ellipsis and connection are pushed to an extreme
in an instalment on 28 November. It begins, almost ritually at this point, with
the slogan *hakkō ichiu* and presents a conversation in Irish between Myles and
Yosuke Matsuoka, now on such intimate terms that they can read each other's
minds:

[HAKKO ICHIU!
I had a conversation yesterday on the long-distance telephone with the
respected gentleman Matsuoka [*Matsúoca*] who is engaged in foreign
affairs in Japan. We were talking about *Hakko Ichiu*, the state of the Irish
[*stáid na Gaedhilge*] and the language question. This is what we said:
  Me: Are you about to . . . . . ?
  Him: No, but in a month's time . . . . .

Me: But Roosevelt [*Rúisbheilt*] said . . . . .
Him: I know, but if there is a fall of the second . . . . .
Me: There was a red-haired woman . . . . .
Him: And the king's yellow shirt . . . . . .
Me: Without mentioning my own turf-cutting, there was . . . . .
Him: I would go happily were it not . . . . .
Me: But—

And so on. You don't understand the conversation? If you do not, I don't think there's much to be said about the education you received. The respected gentleman *Kuno Meyer* understood the likes of me; he wrote the following:

> *'Like the Japanese, the Celts were always quick to take an artistic hint; they avoid the obvious and the common-place; to them the half-said thing is the dearest'*.]

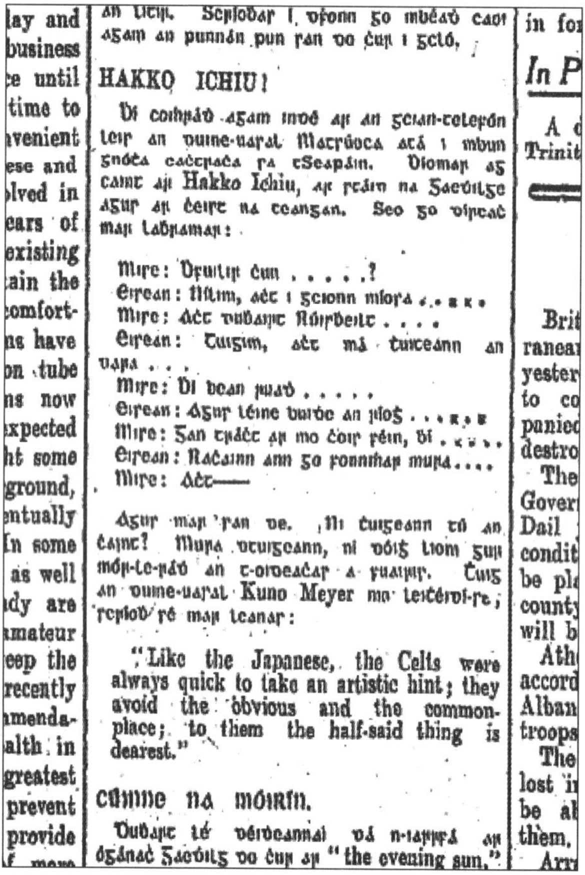

HAKKO ICHIU!

"Like the Japanese, the Celts were always quick to take an artistic hint; they avoid the obvious and the common-place; to them the half-said thing is dearest."

Fig. 4.2 *CL*, 28 November 1940, p. 4.

The comedy of this cosy scenario is increased by the absorption of the names of globally consequential figures into Irish, in the transliterations *Matsúoca* and *Rúisbheilt*. Much of the humour lies in the obscurity of their half-sayings. Myles's 'There was a red-haired woman ...' and Matsuoka's 'And the king's yellow shirt ...' have at first glance the delightful absurdity of spy-speak, an effect amplified by the strange accretions on the dots of the ellipses which resemble a combination of Morse code and covert symbols (see Fig. 4.2). Yet the elliptical comments nonetheless have referents in Ireland, in its poetic female personification, and in Southeast Asia: the Thai throne is associated with the colour yellow and yellow shirts are worn in honour of the king. A fuller context can be ventured: Matsuoka's imminent strategising as he calculates on the defeat of a second country after France's surrender in June 1940. On 15 November 1940 *The Irish Times* reports on tensions between Thailand and Indo-China – the takeover of command of the Thai army by the Premier in order to prevent a *coup*, the massing of Thai troops on the banks of the Mekong River, and a Thai attack on a Chinese village on 16 November – and speculates that the situation will afford Japan 'a pretext for the landing of troops and the "restoration of order"'.[17] The article presents the global interconnectedness of this situation by citing a Reuters excerpt from the Chinese newspaper *Central Daily News*:

> Remarking that Prince Konoye and Mr Matsuoka prefer to watch the attitude of the United States and Russia, the writer says: 'If the United States is ready to resist Japan's southward expansion with force, and if Soviet Russia is prepared to put obstacles in the way of Japan's ambitions, we believe that she will temporarily postpone her action [...] We believe that Japan is still adopting a wait and see policy before attacking Singapore and the Dutch East Indies in view of China's strong resistance and the re-election of Mr Roosevelt'.[18]

Like Thailand, Ireland experienced both territorial ambition and vulnerability during the Second World War: the desire for reunification on the one hand and, on the other, the threat of invasion for logistical purposes by a larger power. Dublin was in covert negotiations with both Germany and Britain at this point.[19] Yet, Myles's role as covert Irish representative is as comic as his familiarity with Matsuoka's thoughts. The conversation reveals the limits of a minor nation angling for advantage in the shifting situation by attempting to connect itself with major powers. If Ireland's location is of strategic importance for both Germany and Britain, it is very far away from

Japanese concerns. Myles's global manoeuvres fail as he tentatively attempts to include Japan in Irish affairs. 'Without mentioning my own turf-cutting, there was …' is followed by Matsuoka's ellipsis, a delicately expressed refusal to enter into Irish territory: 'I would go there happily were it not …'. Myles's last contribution to the exchange, 'But—', is a curtailed objection rather than a knowing intimation.

Myles distracts us from this distressed and inarticulate note by quoting German philologist Kuno Meyer's assertion of the deep and essential sympathies between the Irish and the Japanese.[20] The English citation stands out in an otherwise Irish uncial instalment, offering an unqualified truth to readers who cannot access the Irish and who see only the names of the interlocutors in association with *hakkō ichiu*. The pronouncement by a German authority that the Irish and the Japanese share a readiness for subtle communication underlines this sense of a conspiracy conducted in the Irish language. In defining Myles's conversation with Matsuoka in terms of the 'half-said thing', Meyer's words make explicit *Cruiskeen Lawn*'s own strategy of implication and ellipsis.

This moment emphasises the difference between territorial and linguistic expansion. If calculating double-speak enables Matsuoka politically, Myles's use of the strategy of covert and incomplete communication fails to elicit Japanese involvement in Irish territory. Yet, proceeding under the banner of 'HAKKO ICHIU!', the *Cruiskeen Lawn* instalment renders the whole world under one roof linguistically and imaginatively, as it represents Matsuoka in conversation, long distance, in the Irish language. As *hakkō ichiu* overtly cooperates with and secretly opposes *Lebensraum*, *Cruiskeen Lawn* has a deeply ambivalent relationship to *hakkō ichiu*. The long-distance phone conversation follows a section in which Myles complains bitterly of the tediousness of the traditional songs performed at the house of '*Pilib Ó Pilibín*', including old standards greeting the returning exile such as '*Óró Sé Do Bheatha Abhaile*' [Oh, you're welcome home]. His Irish-language exchange with Matsuoka performs a contrasting gesture: its iconoclastic ellipses reach outward to complex contemporary global politics and issue an invitation to a foreign power to enter Irish soil.

The *Cruiskeen Lawn*'s strategy of 'half-saying' progressively trains its readers to search for connections between the column and the articles which surround it, prompting them to question the significance and reference of even the most Irish of scenarios. Two months after the elliptical dialogue with Matsuoka, *Cruiskeen Lawn*'s aesthetic of suggestion becomes even less explicit. On 21 January 1941, the column abuts a Reuters report on

Matsuoka's restatement of Japan's policy of *hakkō ichiu*, 'Japan to Implement Three-Power Pact: "New Order in Greater East-Asia"'. Immediately adjacent is Myles's report on his project to 'construct an Irish-speaking factory in Country Antrim to make silk purses out of sows' ears' [*monarcha Gaedhlach a chur ar siubhal i gconndae Aontruime le spáráin a dhéanamh as cluasa cráin-muice*] and a dialogue which presents the vain attempts of an Irish speaker to purchase some tweed.

Fig. 4.3 *CL*,
21 January 1941, p. 6.

On the page and in the global arena, Ireland might be perceived as separate from world politics; the articles present one country straining towards ever-increasing dominion and another absorbed in local pursuits and tokens of the past. However, the contiguity of these neighbouring articles suggests a deeper identity between Japanese and Irish 'ideals'. Myles's founding of a silk factory emulates a quintessentially Japanese industry and his Irish-speaking operation in County Antrim, one of the six counties of Northern Ireland, extends Irish cultural territory in a way that mimics Japanese expansionism. This implicit commonality is reinforced as both the Reuters report and the neighbouring *Cruiskeen Lawn* column present unrest as an unexplained impediment to salutary economic progress. Matsuoka speaks of his desire to establish 'a sphere of common prosperity throughout Greater East Asia', as Japan leads all peoples to 'conciliation and co-operation [...] thereby setting an example of universal concord', and he represents China as resisting this prosperous amity: 'The Chiang Kai-shek *regime*, however, is riddled with internal disruption and friction, which are rapidly growing acute, while the masses under its control are suffering from high prices, a dearth of commodities and other severe tribulations'.[21] Myles's foreign venture is marked by similar tensions. Efforts to sink a well to service the factory fail mysteriously, amidst growing friction: '*Bhí an lucht oibre díomhaoin le linn an ama so agus chonacthas domh taréis scathaimh go raibh easaontas ag iomarscal ag éirghe eatartha — troid, ciapáil agus achrann go deo aca*' [The workers were idle during that time and it appeared to me after a spell that discord and contention were arising between them – unrelenting conflict, strife, and confrontation].[22] Myles's factory manager suspects sabotage, observing, somewhat vaguely, '*Sílim go bhfuil daoine éigin ag iarraidh na monarchan so do lot. Tá obair éigin ar siubhal nach dtuigim*' [I think that someone is trying to ruin the factory. There is some work going on that I don't understand]. Nonetheless, Myles and his manager sink a pipe, find water and proceed with the pig- and purse-production. '*Ba chuma liom go deo dá mbéadh an scéal gan innsint*' [I never cared if a story is without news], Myles remarks in conclusion. His comment acknowledges the absence of political commentary in his story, as he and his manager blithely disregard the conflict among their 'workers' just as Matsuoka fails to link Chinese 'internal disruption and friction' to the country's having been invaded by Japan. Half about Ireland, half about Japan, part nationalist wish-image, part allegorical satire, Myles's story refuses a single meaning or place of reference. It is its juxtaposition with the Reuters report which activates the content of the column.

Following Myles's story of the silk purse factory is an Irish-English dialogue in which an Irish-language speaker fails in his efforts to purchase a piece of tweed for a suit. That the man is a relic of a former generation is suggested by the section's heading, which literally means 'Interview with Senior Citizens'. Yet '*Agallamh na Seanórach*' is also the title of a twelfth-century Middle Irish narrative in which Oisín and Caoilte Mac Rónáin recount the exploits of the Fianna to Saint Patrick. Instead of being listened to attentively, this elderly man is treated as an incomprehensible alien, referred to as a 'furren gennilman' and sent away from the establishment: 'I am afraid you will have to speak in English, my man [...] You had better be off'. The shop owner displays his 1902 Gaelic League certificate of fluency in Irish, declaring in English, with smatterings of mispronounced Irish commonplaces, the risks he ran to speak the language: 'As you can see, I was learning Irish at a time when it was neither popular nor profitable [...] Much as your life was worth to speak your native tongue'. This fiction of authenticity amidst hostility accompanies the present scenario of aggression towards actual speakers of Irish. The senior citizen might as well be speaking Japanese; Matsuoka understands Irish better than Irish shop attendants do. The column's staging of the 'chauvinism and hypocrisy' associated with contemporary promoters of Irish follows its previous image of the ancient language thriving on foreign soil, associated with the technology of silk factories rather than with traditional tweed.

Japan disappears from *Cruiskeen Lawn* until 1942 when, on 18 February in a section on journalistic mishaps, Myles directs readers' attention to the following report:

> And look at this.
>
> 'Admiral of the Fleet Sir Roger Keyes said at Faversham, Kent, that thanks to possessing sea power which could not be challenged in Far Eastern waters, Japan's ability to transport and maintain large army and air forces was due solely to her unchallengeable sea power'.—*Irish Independent*. That's pretty clear, isn't it?[23]

Myles presents for his readers' amusement a sentence with circular reasoning which explains Japan's 'unchallengeable sea power' as based on its 'possessing sea power that could not be challenged'. The muddled statement suggests the confusion of British war strategists, yet its circularity also indicates the threat that Japan's fleet poses by portraying it as omnipresent and ineluctable. For a reader limited to English, the column appears to be preoccupied with mocking imprecise language, yet to the reader familiar with the Irish instalments of *Cruiskeen Lawn*, the column implicitly presents the principle of *hakkō ichiu* in action, in Japanese domination of both East Asia and the minds of English admirals. Bound by law from directly commenting on the future of the war, the instalment implies rather than states a ruinous prospect. If linguistic precision is the ostensible ideal, the column mobilises linguistic concerns not to retreat from the war but rather to engage with the experience and the logic of contemporary global conflict.

Cruiskeen Lawn's most intense engagements with the issue of Japan occur behind several veils: of the Irish language, of typographical play, of pun, of literary allusion, of translation. Through these complex effects, the column enacts a strategy of half-saying which allows a series of overlapping identifications: between Irish and Japanese, Japanese and British, Irish and modern, local and foreign, nationalist and imperial. The column creates for itself a paradoxical role, both conservative and experimental, as it displays the polyvalent power of the traditional Irish language while undermining any identity associated with it. Its instalments on Japan speak to an Irish readership, yet its various strategies of half-saying develop that readership's rhetorical skill and its awareness of the implication of Ireland in world events. Instead of 'chauvinism and hypocrisy', *Cruiskeen Lawn*'s aesthetics of the half-said engages the Irish language to entertain international connections and critical thinking. If Japan features again after the Allied victory when Myles comments on the rudeness of dropping atomic bombs on the Japanese,[24] that's another story.

5

Physical comedy and the comedy of physics

in *The Third Policeman, The Dalkey Archive* and *Cruiskeen Lawn*

KATHERINE EBURY

In the opening pages of *The ABC of Relativity* (1925), Bertrand Russell tries to help his readers to understand the new physics by asking us to reimagine our bodies:

> If we were not much larger than an electron, we should not have this impression of stability, which is only due to the grossness of our senses. [...] If – to take the opposite extreme – we were as large as the sun and lived as long, [...] you would again find a higgledy-piggledy universe without permanence.[1]

Arthur Eddington, another key populariser of Einstein, also wrote strikingly about the relationship between the body and the world:

> I am standing on the threshold about to enter a room. It is a complicated business. In the first place I must shove against an atmosphere pressing with a force of fourteen pounds on every square inch of my body. I must make sure of landing on a plank travelling at least twenty miles a second round the sun [...]. I must do this whilst hanging from a round planet head outward into space, and with a wind of aether blowing at no one knows how many miles a second through every interstice of my body.[2]

In fact, the new physics was explained through reference to vulnerable, grotesque and distorted bodies, as part of disproving positivist ideas about the rational authority of the observer. In popularisations, the observer's body was frequently made strange as part of thought experiments to prove the strangeness of matter on both the quantum level and at the level of the whole cosmos. An important reference point for this uncanny body, at least for Eddington, was the transforming body of Alice in Lewis Carroll's novels *Alice in Wonderland* and *Through the Looking-Glass* and also the body of Lemuel Gulliver in Jonathan Swift's *Gulliver's Travels*.

This essay will discuss Brian O'Nolan's changing vision of the authority of science through a comparative approach to the representation of the human body in *The Third Policeman* and *The Dalkey Archive* and in relevant moments from the *Cruiskeen Lawn* columns. While Charles Kemnitz (1985), Keith Booker (1991), Andrew Spenser (1995) and most recently Samuel Whybrow (2011) and Jack Fennell (2014) have approached *The Third Policeman* as a response to Einsteinian physics,[3] much of the evidence for this critical tradition comes, instead, from O'Nolan's explanation of his method in *The Dalkey Archive*. O'Nolan explained to his publisher the influence of J.W. Dunne and Einstein on that novel:

> The idea is that time is as a great flat motionless sea. Time does not pass; it is we who pass. With this concept as basic, fantastic but coherent situations can easily be devised, and in effect the whole universe torn up in a monstrous comic debauch.[4]

The essay will bring a new focus to the question of the influence of physics on O'Nolan through a discussion of how his portrayal of the 'fantastic', 'monstrous' and 'debauched' body in the novels is indebted to the concepts and style of popular science. My discussion of O'Nolan's intertextuality will initially be grounded in his response to science in *Cruiskeen Lawn*. While we might think that O'Nolan uses the body to ground and satirise scientific speculation, I will argue that his portrayal of absurd bodies, such as the Atomic Theory in *The Third Policeman* or the physical and temporal effects of the braincurdling gas DMP in *The Dalkey Archive*, tends in the same direction as the scientific popularisations that he must have used to plan these novels; to dethrone the observer while empowering imaginative responses to the cosmos.

Popularisation

Keith Hopper argues that O'Nolan 'nowhere says anything about relativity that could not have been gleaned from an adequate popularisation'[5]; and yet, though detailed readings of O'Nolan's texts in relation to the new physics have been undertaken, little attention has been paid to the sources of his knowledge in popularisations. Some exceptions to this critical gap are Mary A. O'Toole (1988), Mark O'Connell (2009) and Alana Gillespie (2014).[6] In particular, O'Connell's recent work on O'Nolan, Dunne and Jorge Luis Borges shows a good attention to sources and intertexts in relation to style, arguing that 'Dunne's ideas had a conspicuous impact on [...] the literary fiction of the fantastic'.[7] Discussions of the influence of scientific ideas on O'Nolan's work are of course relevant, but still tend to flatten the texture of his engagement with the language and metaphors of science. Hopper's statement implies a dismissal of O'Nolan's scientific interests, but it is worth questioning how an 'adequate popularisation' might have influenced not just O'Nolan's ideas, but also his style.

And popularisations of the new physics certainly had a style of their own, not unlike that which O'Connell identifies in Dunne: on 'frequent occasions', he suggests, Dunne's 'façade of sober scientific enquiry gives way to the giddy thrill of de Selbean metaphysics'.[8] In fact, although Dunne's esoteric speculations are very different to popularisations by Sir James Jeans and Arthur Eddington in terms of their perceived scientific value, their writing styles possess notable similarities. Moreover, the 'giddy thrill' of metaphysics is there even in the comparatively 'sober' popularisations of Jeans and Eddington, who both attempted to argue that relativity was conducive to an idealist philosophy of nature and to a Christian God. Gillian Beer offers us a model for how literary critics might approach influential scientific popularisations of relativity and quantum theory in relation to modernism through the 'giddy thrill' of their flights of fancy: for example, she writes that Eddington's style is dependent on 'storied sequences, but these sequences are not like nineteenth-century narratives [...]. Abduction is only part of the pleasure. As prominent is dissolution, false endings, wayward connections, and simultaneities'.[9] In many ways, Beer's description makes Eddington sound like Flann O'Brien.

We cannot be sure exactly which popularisations O'Nolan read, lacking a record of the detailed scientific note-taking which we find in James Joyce's or Samuel Beckett's archives. Still, in the columns of *Cruiskeen Lawn*, O'Nolan, as Myles na gCopaleen, refers to the popularising work of both Jeans and

Eddington. In one column, 'the brother' has taken a job in the new Dublin Institute for Advanced Studies (DIAS) founded by Éamon de Valera in Merrion Square and is reading 'Sir James Johns' (read Jeans):

> WELL do you know the brother's taken to the books again.
>
> **You do not say so.**
>
> Comes home to the digs wan day a month ago with a big blue one under d'arm. Up to the bedroom with it and doesn't stir out all night. The brother was above havin a screw at the book for five hours non-stop. The door locked, of course. That's a quare one.
>
> **Odd behaviour without a doubt. [...]**
>
> The brother was readin a book about quateernyuns be Sir James Johns.
>
> **A most remarkable personality, your relative.**[10]

This column was originally published in 1943, the centenary of the Irish mathematician William Rowan Hamilton's discovery of quaternions ['quateernyuns'], which was marked and celebrated by the DIAS and de Valera-sponsored public events. There is a complex irony in the scene: no book exists by Jeans about quaternions. Does Myles invent this book to make quaternions appear more important, in a (likely parodic) show of conformity with the State's push to commemorate the centenary? Or, given both the way Hamilton's science appeared sidelined outside Ireland and the hostile mispronunciation of Jeans's name, does Myles implicitly accuse the new physics of forgetting its roots in quaternions? The joke does not seem to be on Hamilton. Quaternions are certainly a playful shorthand for difficult science in the columns in this period,[11] but, unlike the DIAS, they are just as often imagined positively: in fact, Myles regularly implies that it was Sir Myles (the da), or some other na gCopaleen family member, who actually discovered quaternions.[12]

The column continues by moving from Jeans to contemporary astronomy, implying that this science too might have its roots in Hamilton's work:

> But I'll tell you another good one. The brother does be up in the night-time peepin at the moon.
>
> **I see.**
>
> What do I see wan night and me comin home at two in the morning from me meetin of the Knights only your man pokin the head out of the window with the nightshirt on him. Starin out of him at the stars.

A practice beloved of all philosophers throughout the centuries.
Well I'll tell you this, mister-me-friend: you won't find yours truly losing sleep over a book be Sir James Johns. Damn the fear of me been up peepin out of the window in the night-time.[13]

Eddington, like Jeans, is satirised in the columns. In a 1944 column, Myles uses Eddington as a starting point for a riff on higher mathematics: 'A note in my diary says: "Ten to the power of seventy-nine. Write on this joke"'. He continues:

But here is what I am really getting at – the uniquely prolonged sneer that Eddington embodied in the paper he read to us at the Royal Society in the fateful autumn of '33.

'In the maze of connection of physical constants' he said, 'there remains just one pure number——(Ho-ho-ho, I cannot help interjecting)——'which is known only by observation and has no theoretical explanation. It is a very large number, about 10 (to the power of 79), and the present theory indicates that it is the number of particles in the universe. It may seem to you odd——'(Not at all, not at all, one murmurs)——'that this number should come into the various constants such as the constants of gravitation. You may say, how on earth can the number of particles in remote parts of the universe affect the Cavendish experiment on the attraction of metal spheres in a laboratory? I do not think they affect it at all. But the Cavendish and other experiments having given the result they did, we can deduce that space will go on and on, curving according to the mass contained in it until only a small opening remains and that the 10 (to the power of 79)th particle will be the last particle to be admitted through the last small opening and will shut the door after it'.

Bye-bye 10 (to the power of 79).
Mind that step![14]

Myles seems to have sourced his Eddington from an article published in *The Observer* on 12 November 1933, entitled 'Infinitesimal and Infinite: Sir A. Eddington Finds the Link' as the article ends with the same lengthy quotation (*sans* Mylesian interjections).[15] In fact, this particular *Cruiskeen Lawn* column appears to be a straightforward pastiche of *The Observer* article, as it also highlights Eddington's concept of a 'comparison aether' and the equation ($10m-136mm+m^2 = O$) mentioned in the previous paragraph of his column, while also playing with the tone of excessive deference used in relation to Eddington ('The most vital proof of Sir Arthur Eddington's brilliance…'). However, it seems very likely that O'Nolan had gone more deeply into Eddington's popularisations – if not for the thought experiments and intertextual references to Carroll and Swift which I will later discuss, then for the critique of science which Myles provides, which I suspect is straightforwardly (and somewhat ironically) borrowed from Jeans's and Eddington's popularisations.

In the 10 March 1947 column Myles offers a five-point critique of the science of the new physics. Here are the first three points:

> The following statements are statements of fact *ex authoritatis natura*, having been made by me:
>
> 1. The 'science of theoretical physics' is not a science at all but a department of speculation. Its speculative materials are incomplete and fallacious: incomplete because elements incapable of human observation are excluded; fallacious because the limited observation possible is undertaken by humans. Insofar as it purports to be concerned with investigating the causation of life according to rational criteria, it is sinful.
>
> 2. Its procedure is the observation of what appear to be natural 'laws' and the deduction therefrom of other 'laws' and 'facts'. A serious fallacy derives from this obsession with order. All science is meaningless unless referable to the human race. Physicists are deluded by the apparent orderliness of the universe. They do not realise that the forces of disorder – being energies residing in the human brain – are immensely more powerful than those of order and are such as to reduce planetary and other examples of order to inconsequence […].
>
> 3. All major 'scientific discoveries' do not add to what is already known but merely push farther back the horizon of human ignorance (i.e., the only sort of ignorance that exists): *Example.–* Before the atom bomb existed researchers were addressing the finite and soluble problem of making the bomb. […] But the instant the bomb was made and used, there was created a limitless ignorance as to how a defence against the bomb could be devised.[16]

I would have us compare:

> — *point 1.* with Eddington in *The Nature of the Physical World* (1929): 'We must not regard any of the foregoing speculations or conclusions as

in any way final or established. Indeed, science is only just entering upon its latest and most comprehensive problem, the study of the universe as a single entity, and it would be folly to treat the first tentative results as final'[17];

— *point 2.* with Eddington in *Space, Time and Gravitation* (1920): 'we have found that where science has progressed the farthest, the mind has but regained from nature that which the mind has put into nature'[18];

— *point 3.* with Eddington's statement on quantum theory from *The Nature of the Physical World*: 'An addition to knowledge is won at the expense of an addition to ignorance. It is hard to empty the well of truth with a leaky bucket'.[19]

In fact, the scientists and popularisers of the new physics were extremely aware of its provisional status. In *Einstein's Wake* (2001), Michael Whitworth argues that 'the new physics was attractive because it simultaneously carried the authority of science, but seemed to undermine some of that authority'.[20] In the columns of *Cruiskeen Lawn*, Myles projects claims to authority onto the scientists who disclaimed it (he uses, for example, the word 'sneer' to characterise lectures given by both Eddington and Einstein) and then borrows critiques of the new physics from self-questioning popularisations such as those of Jeans and Eddington. Myles's own playful claim to authority in this example ('The following statements are statements of fact *ex authoritatis natura*, having been made by me') is also problematised and opens the column up to self-reflexive irony, especially for a contemporary readership who would have known Eddington's approachable public persona better than we do.

Alana Gillespie's recent essay on '*Cruiskeen Lawn* and the Role of Science in Independent Ireland' implicitly suggests that Myles's practice here is borrowed from the Catholic apologist Alfred J. O'Rahilly, who argued that 'science [...] is essentially aristocratic and exclusive', while Christianity is intended for everyone.[21] Gillespie also cites a more sneering moment from Eddington: 'There are less than a thousand people in the world who really understand the Einstein theory of relativity, and less than a hundred people who can discuss it intelligently'.[22] Still, in this moment Eddington and Myles are quite close in perspective, as Gillespie shows: Myles uses Eddington's statement in a 3 August 1942 column to critique the Irish education system.[23] And Samuel Whybrow has argued further that *Cruiskeen Lawn* columns which attack contemporary science are, in fact, 'directed not at the science per se but at the preponderance of people who simply cannot use it'.[24] Another compelling explanation for these critical columns is the comic potential of scientific intertextuality, as with *The Observer* article which Myles pastiches: intertextuality can certainly be usefully added to the dialogic, open-minded model of investigation that Gillespie proposes Myles employs in the columns.[25]

At other times in the columns, Myles alludes, often scathingly, to the presence of Erwin Schrödinger in Ireland, who had left Nazi Germany for the DIAS because of his political views.[26] Though Schrödinger's critique of the First Cause went down famously badly with Myles,[27] Peter Bowler has pointed out that Jeans's and Eddington's popularisations were deliberately open to religious faith:

> Publishers and authors – including scientists – usually hoped to make money from popular science literature, but most of the authors also had deeper motivations. Some scientists felt that it was important that the public was informed about science by people who knew what was really going on. But there was often a wider agenda underlying the ostensible contents of the books and articles. Arthur Eddington and James Jeans wrote about the latest developments on cosmology and physics, but did so to make a point about the relationship between science and religion.[28]

Val Nolan has recently highlighted the mixture of science and religion in *The Dalkey Archive*, where De Selby is 'a physicist […] a theologian also', arguing that De Selby's scheme is eschatological, the 'ultimate Roman Catholic fantasy'.[29] Jack Fennell argues similarly that 'O'Nolan expended a lot of energy trying to recapture the state of non-contradiction between science and religion that had notionally existed between Catholicism and Newtonian physics, but with little hope of success'.[30] Here, though, Fennell seems to exaggerate the difference between Newtonian and Einsteinian perspectives on religion and to ignore much of the real texture of the popularisations with which O'Nolan was familiar in order to explain the author's pessimism in *The Dalkey Archive*.[31] At the end of this novel, Fennell argues, somewhat hyperbolically: 'The ideological conflict between science and religion is over. All that remains is for science to sweep away the traces of a defeated god'.[32] But it is important for us to acknowledge the extent to which O'Nolan's pessimism was willed. He deliberately rejected optimistic efforts by popularisers to continue 'the state of non-contradiction' which he too was seeking: a vast gulf exists between Jeans and Eddington and an anti-theistic contemporary figure such as Richard Dawkins. It may well be that O'Nolan's response to Jeans's and Eddington's efforts to reconcile science and faith was primarily satirical, especially after the Second World War, when he was more justly angry about the misuse of science to create the atomic bomb. However, the scientists' efforts might nonetheless explain why he was drawn to them in the first place, and their efforts certainly chime with his.

Bodies, texts, intertexts

There has been a longstanding critical tradition of framing *The Third Policeman* as nonsense writing, with a key reference point being a comparison with Carroll's *Alice in Wonderland*.[33] Sometimes Swift is added as an influence, as in Bernard O'Donoghue's 1982 essay 'Humour and Verbal Logic' in *Critical Quarterly*.[34] My focus on contemporary popular science is intended as a contribution to this critical conversation. We can take from Myles's references in *Cruiskeen Lawn* that O'Nolan was familiar with at least the works of Jeans and Eddington and the strategies that they used to convey the radically changed worldview created by the new physics, including intertextual references to nonsense literature and thought experiments which sought to undo the reader's common sense view of nature. Crucial in that process was the use of intertextuality. Here is a typical sample of the 'quotations' section of the index of Eddington's scientific popularisations:

> *The Nature of the Physical World*
> Boswell, 326
> Rupert Brooke, 317
> *Carroll, 28, 291, 344*
> W. K. Clifford, 278
> Dickens, 32
> Einstein, 294
> Hegel, 147
> Huxley, 173
> Kronecker, 246
> Lamb, 316
> Milton, 167
> Newton, 111
> *Nursery Rhymes, 64, 70, 262*
> Omar Khayyam, 64, 293
> O'Shaughnessy, 325

Russell, 160, 278
Shakespeare, 21, 39, 83, 292, 330
Swift, 341
Whitehead, 145 [my emphasis][35]

This selection from Eddington's index, with references to nonsense literature italicised for emphasis, shows us the kind of intertextual literary and scientific support that he required for his explanations. Katy Price has commented on the '*Alice in Wonderland* spirit of Eddington's expository style',[36] so it is significant that authors such as Carroll and Swift as well as other nonsense writings such as nursery rhymes appear prominently in these lists.[37] In fact, both O'Nolan critics and popular scientists have sought to explain the absurd effect of language or mathematics that radically changes the reader's or observer's worldview through analogy with the epistemological challenge that Alice undergoes.

In one example, part of a much longer passage, Eddington contrasts *Alice in Wonderland* and *Gulliver's Travels* in relation to relativity theory.

> Let us compare two well-known books, which might be described as elementary treatises on relativity, *Alice in Wonderland* and *Gulliver's Travels*. Alice was continually changing size, sometimes growing, sometimes on the point of vanishing altogether. Gulliver remained the same size, but on one occasion he encountered a race of men of minute size with everything in proportion, and on another voyage a land where everything was gigantic. It does not require much reflection to see that both authors are describing the same phenomenon – a relative change of observer and observed.[38]

Both texts are used as examples of changes of scale and their effect on the observer. Eddington imaginatively positions himself in the perspective of Alice and Gulliver in order to demonstrate that the authors 'are describing the same phenomenon'.[39] And yet at the same time, his tone is close to the storybook quality that Price has identified. Earlier, Eddington gives a more typically scientific example of a thought experiment, but is unable to resist giving Gulliver again as a reference point:

> Suppose that by development in the powers of aviation, a man flies past us at the rate of 161,000 miles a second. [...] If we could catch an instantaneous glimpse as he passed, we should see a figure about three feet high, but with the breadth and girth of a normal human being. And

the strange thing is that he would be sublimely unconscious of his own undignified appearance. [...] But when he looks down on us, he sees a strange race of men who have apparently gone through some flattening-out process [...].

It is the reciprocity of these appearances – that each party should think the other has contracted – that is so difficult to realise. Here is a paradox beyond even the imagination of Dean Swift. Gulliver regarded the Lilliputians as a race of dwarfs; and the Lilliputians regarded Gulliver as a giant. That is natural. If the Lilliputians had appeared dwarfs to Gulliver, and Gulliver had appeared a dwarf to the Lilliputians – but no! that is too absurd for fiction, and is an idea only to be found in the sober pages of science.[40]

Eddington gives a further use of Gulliver in *The Expanding Universe*: 'Intrinsically Lilliput and Brobdingnag were just the same; that indeed was the principle on which Swift worked out his story. It needed an intruding Gulliver – an extraneous standard of length – to create a difference'.[41]

Gulliver's body in these examples, as with Alice's body in the previous one, are primarily imagined as standards of measurement. Eddington's intertextual use of nonsense literature aims to convey to the reader of his popularisations the counterintuitive, fantastic world ushered in by the new physics by specifically targeting the reader's body and compelling us to reimagine ourselves. The troubling of the observer's body in order to discover an 'unfamiliar world' common to contemporary popularisations of the new physics, including Jeans and Russell as well as Eddington, is relevant for O'Nolan's portrayals of fantastic, uncanny bodies that cannot be viewed from a stable perspective. Bodies characterised by some form of distortion are particularly notable in *The Third Policeman*, but this is also a feature of *The Dalkey Archive*. From Sergeant Pluck's body, which gives an 'impression of unnaturalness, amounting almost to what was horrible and monstrous' (*CN*, 267); the narrator's wooden leg which occasionally seems to have sensation (*CN*, 324); the eyes of Mathers (*CN*, 239) and Finnucane (*CN*, 256); the DMP which in *The Dalkey Archive* both alters the physical weight of Mick and Hackett and removes their time (*CN*, 626); and the Atomic Theory that threatens the integrity of all bodies in both novels – seeing other bodies and inhabiting one's own is a particularly fraught, absurd and subjective affair in O'Nolan's universes.

Whybrow has touched on O'Nolan's portrayal of the body in arguing for a reading of *The Third Policeman* as a science fiction novel, since 'the disgusting body is a familiar sci-fi trope'.[42] Both Nolan and Whybrow have briefly highlighted moments from *Cruiskeen Lawn* which powerfully link the human body and science. For example, Nolan cites a 'Keats and Chapman' column on the atomic bomb: 'The dread instrument produced a number of freak effects, the most noteworthy of which was to blow the backs off several human beings, leaving them alive, conscious and otherwise intact'.[43] Whybrow references a piece on dentistry, which concludes that in a dental extraction, 'there has been a violent and irrevocable interference with the personal integrity of the patient and this proportionately with the balance of the entire universe, of which he is for himself the sole preceptor, sensuant and interpreter'.[44] Whybrow's passage is emphatically about the observer; I would suggest that a more specific context for these moments and for the portrayal of the body in O'Nolan's novels is an intertextual relationship with popular science.

The opening of Jeans's *The New Background of Science*, perhaps the very book that Myles imagined 'the brother' reading, explains why making the human body strange is a necessary part of the new physics: 'The physicist who can discard his human spectacles, and can see clearly in the strange new light which then assails his eyes, finds himself living in an unfamiliar world'.[45] Jeans goes on to compare our entrapment within our bodies and their perceptions with 'a prisoner in the cell', which is relevant considering the narrator's criminal status and vexed relationship with his body in *The Third Policeman*. And yet the observer's body, flawed though it is, remains necessary: Eddington argues that 'the observer's body can be regarded as part of his laboratory equipment' and 'Our bodies are to be regarded as scientific instruments used to survey the world'.[46] In Eddington's *The Nature of the Physical World* these examples become more specifically linked to concepts of the new physics: 'The atom is as porous as a solar system. If we eliminated all the unfilled space in a man's body and collected his protons and electrons into one mass, the man would be reduced to a speck just visible with a magnifying glass'.[47] Eddington's 'speck' and 'magnifying glass' might make us think of MacCruiskeen's ever-diminishing chests:

> When he felt my look he came over to me and gave me an enormous magnifying-glass which looked like a basin fixed to a handle. [...] through the agency of the glass I was in a position to report that he had two more [chests] out beside the last ones, the smallest of all being nearly half a size smaller than ordinary invisibility. (*CN*, 285)

Eddington and Jeans both use the observer's body as a measure not just of size, as mentioned earlier in the Alice and Gulliver examples, but also of time. Eddington asks us to imagine one person remaining on earth and another person travelling at great speed:

> Thus so far as bodily processes are concerned the fast-moving traveller lives more slowly. His cycle of digestion and fatigue; the rate of muscular response to stimulus; the development of his body from youth to age. [...] If the speed of travel is very great we may find that, while the stay-at-home individual has aged 70 years, the traveller has aged one year.[48]

It seems clear that a version of this thought experiment has influenced the portrayal of time and eternity in *The Third Policeman*, where the absence of time in the space of eternity is measured in the stasis of the observer's body.

> 'It is simple', the Sergeant said. 'The beard does not grow and if you are fed you do not get hungry and if you are hungry you don't get hungrier. Your pipe will smoke all day and will still be full and a glass of whiskey will still be there no matter how much of it you drink and it does not matter in any case because it will not make you drunker than your own sobriety'. (*CN*, 341)

Similarly, *The Dalkey Archive*'s Mick Shaughnessy attempts to prove time and relationships of cause and effect through bodily change: 'For instance, if you permit me to drink enough of this whiskey, by which I mean too much, I'm certain to undergo unmistakeable temporal punishment. My stomach, liver and nervous system will be wrecked in the morning' (*CN*, 620). In *The Third Policeman*, while metaphysical or supernatural explanations are customary for the narrator's return home to find John Divney aged by many years, 'enormously fat and [...] quite bald' (*CN*, 400), this critical reflex obscures an equally important source: Eddington's discussion of the effect of great speed on the body of the traveller compared to a companion who remains at home.[49]

Further, looking at popularisations of the new physics can make the effect of the Atomic Theory/Mollycule Theory on the body, which is mentioned in both texts, seem less fantastical and more realistic. Though Eddington uses nonsense literature and humorous thought experiments to explain his difficult mathematics, he is assertive in his rejection of a 'commonsense view' that would seek to reduce the value of these new ideas:

However successful the theory of a four-dimensional world may be, it is difficult to ignore a voice inside us which whispers 'At the back of your mind, you know that a fourth dimension is all nonsense'. [...] What nonsense to say that this solid table on which I am writing is a collection of electrons moving with prodigious speeds in empty spaces, which relatively to electronic dimensions are as wide as the spaces between the planets of the solar system! What nonsense to say that the thin air is trying to crush my body with a load of 14 lbs. to the square inch! [...] Let us not be beguiled by this voice. It is discredited.[50]

Eddington's 'solid table', like Sergeant Fottrell's bicycle or Pluck's sheep, is only molecules: 'What is a sheep only millions of little bits of sheepness whirling around doing intricate convulsions inside the baste' (*CN*, 678, 294). Eddington further reminds us that our experience of gravity is an 'atomic experience': 'we never feel the force of the earth's gravitation; what we do feel is the bombardment of the soles of our boots by the molecules of the ground, and the consequent impulses spreading upwards through the body'.[51] It is the effect of these 'impulses' on the body that Fottrell and Pluck are anxious about in their respective novels: 'people who spend most of their natural lives riding iron bicycles over the rocky roadsteads of this parish get their personalities mixed up with the personalities of their bicycle as a result of the interchanging of the atoms' (*CN*, 296). In an example even closer to Eddington's point about gravitation, the Atomic Theory does not just apply to bicycles: 'But walking too far too often too quickly is not safe at all. The continual cracking of your feet on the road makes a certain quantity of road come up into you' (*CN*, 300). At heart, the Atomic Theory or Mollycule Theory expresses an anxiety about the observer's relationship with the world.

Our unnamed first person narrator in *The Third Policeman* stands in the place of the observer in scientific popularisations. (Mick serves a similar, though less effective, function in *The Dalkey Archive*.) The narrator's body responds with fear and trembling to the phenomena that he observes and narrates – the uncanny bodies of Mathers and the policemen; the fantastic creations of MacCruiskeen; eternity: for example, 'my heart [...] working on again with slow heavy hammer-blows which seemed to make my whole frame shudder' (*CN*, 241). Similarly, his body responds involuntarily when warned about the Atomic Theory: 'After he had finished speaking I found myself walking nimbly and lightly on my toes in order to prolong my life' (*CN*, 300). The world of *The Third Policeman* is built to prove the limitations of the narrator-observer's mind and body to cope with the world around him.

At the same time, he is unable to ever admit this, using the language of rationality in a way that is entirely performative: confronted by the spectre of Mathers, he responds, 'I knew that I would go mad unless I got up from the floor and moved and talked and behaved in as ordinary a way as possible' (*CN*, 240). Crucial to many of these discussions of the fantastic aspect of the narrator's world is the language of 'framing', 'magnitude' and 'perspective' used in scientific popularisations. For example, he responds to the police station: 'the whole morning and the whole world seemed to have no purpose at all save to *frame* it and give it *some magnitude and position* so that I could find it with my simple senses and pretend to myself that I understood it' [my emphasis] (*CN*, 266). He uses similar language of MacCruiskeen's vanishing chests: 'Queerly enough they looked to me as if they were all the same size but invested with *some crazy perspective*' [my emphasis] (*CN*, 284). Much later, when finally unobserved in a dreamlike moment he surrenders this notion of himself as rational observer and with it the language of observation ('definition, position and magnitude'):

> Every inch of my person gained weight with every second until the total burden on the bed was approximately five hundred thousand tons. This was evenly distributed on the four wooden legs of the bed, which had by now become an integral part of the universe. My eyelids, each weighing no less than four tons, slewed ponderously across my eyeballs. [...] United with the bed I became momentous and planetary. Far away from the bed I could see the outside night framed neatly in the window as if it were a picture on the wall. There was a bright star in one corner with other smaller stars elsewhere littered about in sublime profusion. [...] Robbing me of the reassurance of my eyesight, it was disintegrating my bodily personality into a flux of colour, smell, recollection, desire – all the strange uncounted essences of terrestrial and spiritual existence. I was deprived of *definition, position and magnitude* and my significance was considerably diminished'. [my emphasis] (*CN*, 324–27)

In truth, the de Selby scholar seems far more likely to learn something about the cosmos now that he has removed his 'human spectacles', as Jeans puts it, and yet his transformed and distorted body, which has reference points in popular science, Jonathan Swift and Lewis Carroll, offers him no great revelation. As we have seen, Jeans compares our entrapment within our bodies and their perceptions with 'a prisoner in the cell' before proceeding to explore how mathematics could allow us to understand our subjectivity and vulnerability so that by comparing viewpoints we might arrive at something like knowledge of the external world.

Alice and Gulliver experience a profound alteration of their worldview through the nonsensical transformations and confusions of scale that their bodies and selves undergo. Despite the connection between physical comedy and the comedy of physics made throughout *The Third Policeman*, O'Nolan's narrator is unable to accept the counsel that the new physics gives about the necessity of accepting our human limitations in order to understand the cosmos. The famous circularity of the novel conveys not just eternal punishment, but also the failure of his version of rational sense-making. Less compelling because even less transformative, Mick's journey in *The Dalkey Archive* is not even an attempt to make sense of the unfamiliar, but rather to return it to the everyday, hence his fitting entrapment in bourgeois domesticity at the end of the novel.

As we have seen, O'Nolan was fully aware of the way the science of the new physics undermined both its own authority (seen primarily in the *Cruiskeen Lawn* columns) and the authority of the observer (visible in connections between thought experiments from popularisations and the novels). O'Nolan treats self-critique by Jeans and Eddington, and equally their attempts to reconcile science and faith, as material for satire, and throughout both novels de Selby/De Selby is portrayed as a mad or hubristic scientist. However, De Selby's apparent self-abnegation at the end of *The Dalkey Archive* – 'I will make a most unambiguous retraction of my error' (*CN*, 748) – suggests that he has been compelled to acknowledge these problems with scientific authority, as has O'Nolan's readership.

PART II

MIXED INKS

O'Nolan *vs.* his peers

6

'widening out the mind'

Flann O'Brien's 'wide mind' between Joyce's 'mental life' and Beckett's 'deep within'

DIRK VAN HULLE

As Susan Stanford Friedman noted in her 2001 article 'Definitional Excursions: The Meanings of Modern/Modernity/Modernism', the semantics of the term 'modernism' changed from signifying 'rebellion' and 'rupture' in the 1960s to 'elitism' and 'the Establishment' in the 1990s. Thus 'modernism' became the authority with which emancipatory postmodernism had problems: 'Modernism was the supreme fiction, the master narrative, the great white hope. To its po-mo descendants, modernism is the enemy'.[1] That was the moment when Flann O'Brien, given his many 'problems with authority', was often seen as a typical exponent of postmodernism. A monograph that marked the critical consensus in this period is Keith Hopper's important study *Flann O'Brien: A Portrait of the Artist as a Young Post-Modernist* (1995).[2]

In the same decade, referring to John Barth's term 'late-modernism', Brian McHale suggested in *Constructing Postmodernism* (1992) that 'Beckett qualifies for membership in the late-modernist category', whereas Flann O'Brien's *At Swim-Two-Birds* was mentioned as an example of 'postmodernist "Chinese-box" texts' and *The Third Policeman* as 'postmodernist fiction', characterised by labyrinthine 'interior spaces'.[3] With reference to Beckett, McHale indicated a border between modernism and postmodernism that was marked by 'the distinction between the cognitivist and the postcognitivist Beckett'.[4] The terms cognitivism and postcognitivism were indirectly defined by means of McHale's distinction between an early Beckett and a later Beckett; that is, 'the Beckett who is still preoccupied with modernist issues of reliability and unreliability of narrators, radical subjectivity, and multiplicity of perspectives, as in *Watt* and *Molloy*' and 'the Beckett who focuses instead on the status of fictional worlds, the power (and impotence) of language to make and unmake worlds, and the relationship between fictional being and elusive "real" being, as in *Malone Dies*, *The Unnamable*, and many of the later short texts'.[5]

In the meantime, postmodernism 'has receded into the historical past', as Wang Ning puts it in 'Historicizing Postmodernist Fiction', the introduction to a recent special issue of *Narrative*.[6] It is remarkable that while postmodernism is in the process of being 'historicised', the revival of modernism has led to what is now sometimes called the 'new modernist studies', which 'resist singular ideas of modernism'.[7] And whereas McHale categorised Flann O'Brien as postmodernist (and Beckett as perhaps more of a late modernist), Rónán McDonald and Julian Murphet refer to Tyrus Miller's notion of late modernism[8] in their endeavour to

> reorient the study of O'Brien away from a waning, if not yet obsolescent critical paradigm, and towards the extraordinary reinvention of modernism taking place today, a paradigm to which it could well be argued he always and already belonged as a reluctant second-generation black sheep.[9]

In the recent revival of Brian O'Nolan studies, the author's status has been one of the issues at stake, especially his status between Joyce and Beckett. He had been sandwiched between them for far too long, and it is the merit of this new and vibrant field of study that O'Nolan's work is now being recognised as more than worthy of study in its own right. Yet, rather than examining whether or to what extent he has become an 'authority' of his own, I propose to regard O'Nolan's liminal status between Joyce and Beckett anew in relation to modernism, late modernism and postmodernism. This liminal status will be explored as a significant site in which to investigate what from a 'postcognitivist' or 'post-Cartesian' perspective can be seen as a continuum between modernism and late modernism. In the meantime, the term 'postcognitivism' has taken on different meanings. In 1992, notions such as the 'extended mind' and 'enactivism' – which are now considered part of a postcognitivist paradigm[10] – had either not yet been coined or had not yet gained currency. This essay traces a gradual transition from modernism to late modernism in terms of the respective attitudes to cognition presented in the writings of James Joyce, Brian O'Nolan and Samuel Beckett.

Umwelt researchers

In 'Re-Minding Modernism', David Herman suggests that while the so-called 'inward turn' of modernism is a critical commonplace, modernist authors did not necessarily evoke the minds of their characters in terms of an 'inside' in opposition to an 'outside', but rather in terms of an interaction with an environment, a nexus between intelligent agents and their material and cultural circumstances.[11] Herman refers to the biologist Jakob von Uexküll's notion of '*Umwelt*' to denote the surroundings as *perceived* by an individual organism, suggesting that modernist authors can be called '*Umwelt* researchers'.[12] Von Uexküll's notion of '*Umwelt*' designates an organism's model of the world, based on the aspects in its environment that are meaningful to this organism (for instance water, food or shelter).[13] Similarly, many modernist authors investigated human organisms' *Umwelten* according to a model in which mind and world are inseparable.

This view on modernism's preoccupation with the mind in terms of '*Umwelt* research' accords with some recent paradigms in cognitive philosophy. According to the 'extended mind' thesis proposed by Andy Clark and David Chalmers (1998), the mind is not necessarily confined to the head, as held in the standard internalist picture of the mind. O'Nolan often seems to poke fun at the internalist model of the mind; for instance in *The Third Policeman* when he makes the Sergeant insist three times on the internal aspect of his mind, as he asks MacCruiskeen for 'the readings' in order that he can 'make mental comparisons *inside* the *interior* of [his] *inner* head' [my emphasis] (*CN*, 312).[14] The 'extended mind' thesis has affinities with enactivism, according to which the mind should be understood primarily in terms of the interactions of persons with their environments. This enactive interaction includes the manipulation of tools; 'tools are us', according to Lambros Malafouris: 'Material signs do not represent; they enact. They do not stand for reality; they bring forth reality'.[15]

With reference to modernist literature, Herman's enactive reading of Joyce's *A Portrait of the Artist as a Young Man* and Virginia Woolf's *Mrs Dalloway* is a convincing argument to stop regarding literary modernism as an 'inward turn', but it is hard to bring Herman's reading in line with some of the modernists' own statements. Woolf was one of the modernists who most fiercely proclaimed a radical break from (late) realists such as Arnold Bennett, H.G. Wells and John Galsworthy by stating that, in contrast to them, her generation's approach was to 'Look within'.[16] As for Joyce, Herman's suggestion may even apply to his earlier work. I suggest that Joyce increasingly presented his characters' minds in terms of cognition in context, a sort of 'extended mind' hypothesis *avant la lettre*, and that early manifestations of this trend are already noticeable in *Dubliners*. O'Nolan and Beckett, as second-generation modernists or late modernists, further explored the possibility of cognition in context and 'widening out the mind', often *per negativum*, by demonstrating the untenability of Cartesian internalism. To investigate this process in cognitive approaches to literature, I focus on elements of proto-enactivism – aspects of fictional evocations of the mind that presage enactivism before this concept had been coined in philosophy – in three short works of fiction from three periods in twentieth-century literature: 'A Painful Case' (written in 1905, published in 1914) by James Joyce, 'John Duffy's Brother' (1940) by Flann O'Brien and 'Stirrings Still' (1989) by Samuel Beckett.

James Joyce, 'A Painful Case'

In the opening paragraph of 'A Painful Case', Mr James Duffy is characterised by means of his surroundings, starting from the place where he lives, Chapelizod, 'because he wished to live as far as possible from the city of which he was a citizen and because he found all the other suburbs of Dublin mean, modern and pretentious'.[17] In ever smaller concentric circles, the description zooms in on the 'lofty walls' that surround him in his 'uncarpeted room'; then on his bookcase ('The books on the white wooden shelves were arranged from below upwards according to bulk. A complete Wordsworth stood at one end of the lowest shelf and a copy of the *Maynooth Catechism*, sewn into the cloth cover of a notebook, stood at one end of the top shelf'); then on his desk, where writing tools are at the ready; and eventually *into* his desk:

> Writing materials were always on the desk. In the desk lay a manuscript translation of Hauptmann's *Michael Kramer*, the stage directions of which were written in purple ink, and a little sheaf of papers held together by a brass pin. In these sheets a sentence was inscribed from time to time and, in an ironical moment, the headline of an advertisement for *Bile Beans* had been pasted on the first sheet.[18]

Apart from the autobiographical element of the Gerhart Hauptmann translation,[19] the little sheaf of papers and the pasting of the headline are interesting in that they suggest that Mr Duffy's 'saturnine' nature is not only a psychological state attributed to the influence of bodily fluids (caused by an excess of bile according to medieval medicine). This mental characteristic also manifests itself in 'extensions' of the mind. In the last sentence of the first paragraph, Joyce does not so much 'look within' his character's mind (to use Woolf's term), as open up the 'internalism' of his character's melancholy nature by 'lifting the lid of the desk' and describing the inside in sensory terms: the 'faint' fragrance that escapes ranges from the smell of 'new' pencils to that of an 'over-ripe' apple. The faintness of this fragrance is significant in itself, as will be discussed presently in connection with O'Nolan and Beckett. Here, in the context of Joyce's early aesthetics, the 'over-ripe' apple already prefigures a disturbance of Mr Duffy's mind, for the next sentence unequivocally characterises him as someone who 'abhorred anything which betokened physical or mental disorder'.[20]

This particular emphasis on the mind is characteristic of a more general modernist concern, not just with the world but with the *world-as-perceived*, or in von Uexküll's terms: not just with the *Umgebung* (environment) but with the *Umwelt* (the organism's model of the world). The story's starting point seems to be a Cartesian model of the mind, stressing the mind/body dualism: 'He lived at a little distance from his *body* [...]. He had an odd autobiographical habit which led him to compose in his *mind* from time to time a short sentence about himself containing a subject in the third person and a predicate in the past tense' [my emphasis].[21] When Duffy starts meeting Mrs Sinico, the emphasis is almost exclusively on the mental connection: 'he entangled his thoughts with hers [...] provided her with ideas, shared his intellectual life with her'.[22] When she asks him why he does not write out his thoughts, he suggests with (careful) scorn that writing down one's thoughts is for 'phrasemongers, incapable of thinking consecutively for sixty seconds'.[23] Mr Duffy's separation of mind and body is apparently so strict that he does not even allow himself the use of writing tools as an extension of the mind.

This use of writing tools is one of the key examples of Andy Clark and David Chalmers's foundational article on 'the extended mind'. Their example is the notebook of a fictitious Alzheimer's patient ('Otto'), who uses this simple tool as an extension of his memory. And other cognitive philosophers have elaborated on the theme of 'Otto's notebook', suggesting that not only Alzheimer's patients but almost any human being 'thinks on paper' once in a while. Richard Menary speaks of 'Thinking as Writing' (2007), and 'radical enactivists' such as Daniel Hutto and Erik Myin (2013) argue that 'the extended mind' concept is still too limited as it implies a spatial model of an inside versus an outside – an 'inside' that is extended only in exceptional cases. Instead, they suggest that these extensions are not exceptions, but the rule, and that the mind is not just 'extended' but 'extensive'.

Against this cognitive philosophical background, Mrs Sinico's impact on Mr Duffy is quite remarkable. The effect of her companionship is described in botanical terms and compared to 'a warm soil about an exotic'; it is said to emotionalise his 'mental life'.[24] But as soon as contact between body and mind is established ('Mrs Sinico caught up his hand passionately and pressed it to her cheek'), the 'orderliness of his mind' is disturbed and needs to be restored by 'break[ing] off their intercourse'.[25] The word 'intercourse' in this context has more connotations than its more limited meaning in the next paragraph ('friendship between man and woman is impossible because there must be sexual intercourse').[26] The agreement to 'break off their intercourse' has philosophical ramifications if the intercourse between Mrs Sinico and Mr Duffy is read as the connection between body and mind. The term 'intercourse' is similarly employed to imply a connection between body and mind in O'Nolan's works.[27] And in Beckett's *Murphy*, this connection is also described by means of the word 'intercourse' in the famous Chapter 6, on 'Murphy's mind': 'Thus Murphy felt himself split in two, a body and a mind. They had intercourse apparently, otherwise he could not have known that they had anything in common. But he felt his mind to be bodytight'.[28]

'Bodytight' is an apt description of Mr Duffy's mind and its 'orderliness'.[29] After the announcement of Mrs Sinico's death ('knocked down by the engine of the ten o'clock slow train from Kingstown'), he *thinks* she 'touches' him on different occasions: 'he thought her hand touched his' and 'he seemed to feel her voice touch his ear'.[30] In the penultimate paragraph, it is striking how Joyce focuses on Mr Duffy's sensory experiences: 'He *looked* down the slope [...] he *saw* some human figures [...] he *felt* that he had been outcast from life's feast [...] he *heard* in his ears the laborious drone of the engine' [my emphasis].[31] And then, in the last paragraph, when the mental presence of Mrs Sinico fades, the absence is still expressed in terms of sensory experiences, albeit *per negativum*: 'He could not feel her near him [...] nor her voice touch his ear. He waited for some minutes listening. He could hear nothing [...] He listened again: perfectly silent. He felt that he was alone'.[32] The sensory experience of silence also marks the end of the second story under scrutiny.

Flann O'Brien, 'John Duffy's Brother'

The experience of silence in 'John Duffy's Brother' is conveyed in the story's closing scene – in which John Duffy's brother comes to no longer be 'possessed of the strange idea that he was a train' (*SF*, 56) – through an allusion to John Keats:

> It was a complete cure. Never once did the strange malady return. But to this day John Duffy's brother starts at the rumble of a train in the Liffey tunnel and stands rooted to the road when he comes suddenly on a level-crossing – silent, so to speak, upon a peak in Darien. (*SF*, 58)

The reference to Keats's 'On First Looking into Chapman's Homer' suggests an ironic reading of the lines, evoking the epiphanic moment of 'stout Cortez' (actually Vasco Núñez de Balboa) and his crew, staring at the Pacific, 'Silent, upon a peak in Darien'.[33] When one reads Keats's poem as a statement of faith in literature's capacity to evoke such an epiphany, O'Nolan's echo ('silent, so to speak, upon a peak in Darien') questions the whole notion of art's capacity to provoke an epiphany. In Joyce's story, Mr Duffy's 'mental life' was to be awakened, amid the sensory experience of silence, by the epiphanic realisation of his paralytic loneliness; in O'Nolan's story, the mental life of John Duffy's brother is seriously disturbed, but if there is any spiritual manifestation or realisation at the end of the story, it is neither sudden nor epiphanic. It is more like a repeated reminder of the frailty of human cognition.

From a cognitive perspective, the protagonist's temporary mental metamorphosis – when 'John Duffy's brother was certain that he *was* a train' (*SF*, 56) – can be read as a thought experiment in extreme empathy. In this regard, the experiment is comparable with Leopold Bloom's attempt to figure out what it must be like to '*be*' his cat, and how his cat must see him, on the opening page of Chapter 4 in Joyce's *Ulysses*: 'Wonder what I look like to her. Height of a tower? No, she can jump me'.[34] Here, both Joyce and O'Nolan come very close to David Herman's definition of modernist writers as '*Umwelt* researchers in von Uexküll's sense – explorers of the lived, phenomenal worlds that emerge from, or are enacted through, the interplay between intelligent agents and their cultural as well as material circumstances'.[35] As Joyce tried to find out what Mr Duffy's or Leopold Bloom's *world-as-experienced* looked like, so O'Nolan examined the *Umwelt* of John Duffy's brother. But O'Nolan goes a step further than Joyce. Whereas Chapter 4 of *Ulysses* is a pretty harmless experiment in empathy or the capacity to put oneself in

another organism's place, Mr Duffy's total identification with the train in
'John Duffy's Brother' transgresses a border of what is socially considered to
be 'sane'. This transgression is only temporary, and the silence, 'so to speak',
in the presence of the train at the end of the story is less the silence of the
sublime and limitless view of the Pacific, than the painful confrontation with
the proximity of sanity's edges.

The sublime silence evoked in Keats's poem is the kind that Charles Darwin
experienced on one of his expeditions across the Andes during the voyage of
the *Beagle*. When he reached the first pass, Darwin noted in his field notebook
how the view made him speechless: 'Never shall forget the grandeur of the
view from first pass' and '(view from the 1st ridge) something inexpressibly
grand: would not speak'.[36] There is a tension between the silence evoked in
Darwin's field notebook or in Keats's poem and John Duffy's brother's silence
at the end of the story. In O'Nolan studies, this tension has been expressed by
means of a contrast between horizontal vastness and vertical infinity, as in Sue
Asbee's choice of metaphors: '*new horizons* are opened for the explorer, for
the poet Keats and for John Duffy's brother, the inoffensive, quiet citizen of
Inchicore who would have preferred *the unfathomable depths* of his mind to have
remained undiscovered' [my emphasis].[37] The image of 'unfathomable depths'
perpetuates the internalist model of the mind, which the narrator in Beckett's
L'Innommable [*The Unnamable*] criticises as a '*Stupide hantise de la profondeur*'
[Stupid obsession with depth].[38] Instead, O'Nolan suggests a metaphor of
horizontal extension by referring to Keats's evocation of the panoramic view
of the Pacific, thus deliberately employing the same metaphor for *both* the
sublime and the painful silence.

This type of vista, combining desolation and sublimity, is evoked in Myles
na gCopaleen's description of traversing bogland by train in a *Cruiskeen Lawn*
column: 'The unrelieved bogland scenery on such a journey would be a
bit tedious to the eye, but *telescopes* could be supplied for viewing the more
distant *vistas*' [my emphasis] (*BM*, 114–15). The mental 'vista' which John
Duffy's brother views 'with his father's spyglass' (*SF*, 54) shows the limits
of his *Umwelt*. Mr Duffy surveys the valley's inhabitants 'with an eagle eye'
(*SF*, 54), but as Paul Fagan notes, he is also portrayed as 'a *mis*reader'.[39] Apart
from mistaking a walking stick for a shotgun, Mr Duffy also watches people
without seeing or knowing the social connections disclosed by the omniscient
narrator. He watches 'Martin Smullen' but 'Mr Duffy did not know his name',
let alone the name of Mr Smullen's sister, for 'Mr Duffy had never even heard
of her' (*SF*, 55). The exploration of both these narrative limits and the limits
of the protagonist's *Umwelt* is explicitly presented as 'modern writing', which

'it is hoped, has passed the stage when simple events are stated in the void without any clue as to the psychological and hereditary forces working in the background to produce them' (*SF*, 56).

Mr Duffy's spyglass used to be the prosthetic eye of his father, 'late of the Mercantile Marine', who would be familiar with vistas like the one described by Keats; who would often spend his sea-leave 'thumbing a book of Homer'; and who one day 'took leave of his senses in the dining-room' (*SF*, 55). If 'tools are us', as Malafouris contends, the spyglass plays a role in enactive cognition, but this telescopically extended mind is just as fragile as the Cartesian mind. The voyeur in Mr Duffy Jr is also well aware of the possibility of being watched himself: not just he himself but also his uncanny *doppelgänger* 'Mr Train' (*SF*, 57). The realisation that 'one is neither oneself nor *one* self' is directly linked to Duffy's fear of being discovered and his anxiety to renounce what Fagan refers to as the 'secret inner self' and to conceal it from 'the authority of normative readers'.¹⁰

The Third Policeman, L'Innommable **and the Cartesian model of mind**

The exploration of these edges of 'mental life' recurs in other works of the 1930s and 1940s, for instance in the Magdalen Mental Mercyseat in Beckett's *Murphy* or the asylum in *Watt*. In Flann O'Brien's *The Third Policeman*, another edge of 'mental life' is explored, not just the border zone between life and death, but also the infinitesimal infinity of introspection – the complete opposite 'so to speak' of the view of the Pacific upon a peak in Darien. The first-person narrator in *The Third Policeman* pictures Joe (his 'secret inner self') as

> A body with another body inside it in turn, thousands of such bodies within each other like the skins of an onion, receding to some unimaginable ultimatum[.] Was I in turn merely a link in a vast sequence of imponderable beings, the world I knew merely the interior of the being whose inner voice I myself was? (*CN*, 327)

This is how his mind pictures itself to be, possibly based on a description by J.W. Dunne in *An Experiment with Time* (1927):

> How would you define rationally a '*self-conscious*' observer [...] – he must be able to say: This is *my*-'self'. And that means that he must be

aware of *a 'self' owning the 'self' first considered*. Recognition of this second 'self' involves, for similar reasons, knowledge of a third 'self' – and so on *ad infinitum*.[41]

This regression *ad infinitum* is what critics of the Cartesian view of the mind refer to as the homunculus model: the idea that one's sensory experiences are processed by a small homunculus inside the head implies that this homunculus' experiences in turn need to be processed by an even smaller homunculus in his head, and so on. The image of MacCruiskeen's chests within chests or boxes within boxes ('What is happening to this box we are in?' *CN*, 283–85, 337) corresponds remarkably well with this homunculus model. It also accords with Beckett's parenthesis in a letter to Georges Duthuit: '(odd how I always see things in terms of boxes)'.[42] The letter was written on 2 March 1949, just before Beckett started writing *L'Innommable*, in which the idea of a 'homunculus' inside a head is made thematic. The manuscript even visualises it in the shape of a *matryoshka*-doll-like drawing.[43]

If these regressions *ad infinitum* in *The Third Policeman* and in *L'Innommable* can be interpreted as pushing the Cartesian model of the mind to extremes, thus demonstrating its untenability, the question is whether these texts suggest any alternative model of the mind. The Sergeant in *The Third Policeman*, for instance, is in favour of 'widening out the mind': '"It does a man no harm", the Sergeant remarked pleasantly, "to move around a bit and see things. It is a great thing for widening out the mind. A wide mind is a grand thing, it nearly always leads to farseeing inventions"' (*CN*, 338). In the opening chapter the narrator relates: 'I did not go home direct from school. I spent some months in other places broadening my mind' (*CN*, 225). And as if to push the Cartesian body–mind split to extremes, this broadening of the mind is immediately confronted with the imperfections of the body: 'In one of the places where I was broadening my mind I met one night with a bad accident. I broke my left leg (or, if you like, it was broken for me) in six places' (*CN*, 225).

The problem with the Cartesian model is that it posits a dichotomy between inside and outside. A week after the letter mentioning his seeing things in terms of boxes, Beckett wrote again to Duthuit, this time doing away with the inside/outside dichotomy and suggesting they are 'one and the same': 'the break with the outside world entails the break with the inside world, that there are no replacement relations for naïve relations, that *what are called outside and inside are one and the same*'.[44] In *L'Innommable*, Beckett seems to be looking for a more adequate metaphor to express this idea.

Although the inside and outside are still presented as opposites, divided by a 'tympanum', the vibration of this tympanum takes into account the notion of 'interaction' as an increasingly important element in his model of the mind or consciousness:

> perhaps that's what I feel, an outside and an inside and me in the middle, perhaps that's what I am, the thing that divides the world in two, on the one side the outside, on the other the inside, that can be as thin as foil, I'm neither one side nor the other, I'm in the middle, I'm the partition, I've two surfaces and no thickness, perhaps that's what I feel, myself vibrating, I'm the tympanum, on the one hand the mind, on the other the world, I don't belong to either.[45]

In *The Third Policeman*, the narrator experiences a similar erasure of self and bodily integrity, leading to an ontological confusion of inside and outside.[46] The question is whether, expanding on Joyce's project and O'Nolan's development thereof, Beckett managed to dissolve the inside/outside dichotomy in his later works.

Samuel Beckett, *Stirrings Still*

In Beckett's penultimate text, the tympanum is still stirring. The protagonist of *Stirrings Still* is an old man, sitting 'at his table head on hands' and while he is sitting he sees himself rise and go. It seems impossible to separate outside from inside, for this sensory experience (seeing) is simultaneously outward-looking and introspective – if we try to maintain the obsolete spatial metaphor. Inside and outside are perhaps not quite 'one and the same', but almost: 'For when his own light went out he was not left in the dark. Light of a kind came then from the one high window'.[47] He seems to be closing off his senses to the outside ('There had been a time he would sometimes lift his head enough to see his hands', but this time seems to be gone by).

Then, in the second section of the short text, 'he began to wonder if he was in his right mind'. Apparently, he still is in his right mind, 'For could one not in his right mind be reasonably said to wonder if he was in his right mind and bring what is more his remains of reason to bear on this perplexity in the way he must be said to do if he is to be said at all?'[48] Without knowing how, he eventually manages to emerge into the outer world 'in the guise of a more or less reasonable being'.[49] He hears clocks and cries and tries to figure out their 'whenceabouts'. He therefore brings to bear 'on all this his remains of reason'; he wonders whether his 'memory of indoors' and later whether his 'memory of outdoors' was perhaps at fault, but he 'found it of none'. The text focuses on his sensory (especially aural and visual) experiences. He is 'all ears' until he ceases 'if not to hear to listen'; then he sets out to 'look about him'; he is 'all eyes' until he ceases 'if not to see to look' and sets out to 'take thought', sinking his head 'as one deep in meditation'.[50] But after vainly delving in his remains of reason, he moves on.

'So on' is how the third and last section opens. Instead of the combination of visual and aural experiences in section 2, section 3 concentrates on the aural sense: he hears a sentence, not from outside, but 'from deep within'. What he hears is: 'oh how […] it were to end where never till then'.[51] The ellipsis is filled with the note 'and here a word he could not catch'. The text suggests that the word might be 'sad' or 'bad'. Depending on the word he cannot catch, it might be a good or a bad idea to put an end to it.[52] Since he cannot hear it, he cannot make up his mind.[53] The manuscript[54] shows how intimately this word was connected in Beckett's mind to the first canto of 'Inferno' in Dante's *Divina Commedia*, more specifically the moment Virgil appears for the first time and is described as '*per lungo silenzio* […] *fioco*', 'hoarse from long silence' – an aural impression. At the same time, '*fioco*' can also relate to the 'faint' visual appearance of Virgil. During the writing process, Beckett hesitated between the translations 'hoarse' and 'faint'; that is, between the aural and the visual experience. This is a rather significant detail in a text that deals with 'the hubbub in his mind so-called'.[55] The word he is looking for is important, as it determines whether life is still worth living in his situation, or whether it is better to put an end to it, 'stir no more'.[56]

The 'still' in the title *Stirrings Still* has the same 'negative capability' as the word 'still' in the middle of Keats's 'Ode on a Grecian Urn': at the very centre of this poem, in the middle of the third of its five stanzas, the enormous tension between dynamism and stasis, between the depicted action of dancing figures on the urn and the stillness of their fixation in a work of art is expressed most concisely in this monosyllabic 'still':

> For ever warm and *still* to be enjoy'd,
> For ever panting, and for ever young.[57] [my emphasis]

Similarly, the tension between the heard music of the depicted musicians and the 'unheard' music of the beholder's imagination is evoked in the sentence from 'deep within' in Beckett's *Stirrings Still*. The sentence is not spoken aloud, and yet there is only one word that the protagonist cannot hear. The reason why he cannot 'catch' it is because it is said to be too 'faint': 'then again faint from deep within oh how and here that missing word again it were to end where never till then'.[58] Not unlike Keats's use of the word 'still', the equally monosyllabic adjective 'faint' captures the simultaneous experience of aural (heard/unheard) and visual (stirring/still) experiences, a synesthetic experience with roots that went back more than fifty years in Beckett's life as a writer, as far back as his student years, when he studied Dante's *Divina Commedia* with his teacher Bianca Esposito. The open variant underneath Beckett's note in the manuscript (hesitating between 'faint' and 'hoarse from long silence' as translations for the word 'fioco') shows Beckett's appreciation of the full ambiguity of the word '*fioco*' and Dante's capacity of 'living in uncertainties' to use Keats's definition of 'negative capability'. For when Virgil appears for the first time in 'Inferno' he has not yet spoken, so he cannot be 'hoarse from long silence'; and if the figure of Virgil is 'faint' when it first appears to Dante, it is remarkable that this visual impression is followed by an aural explanation, '*per lungo silenzio*' [from long silence].

This long silence – 'so to speak, upon a peak in Darien' – and the 'faintness' of the word that cannot be caught constitute a motif in the three stories discussed in this essay, spanning almost 100 years of Irish literature. The word 'faint' in Beckett's 1989 text is just as much concerned with the senses as it is in Joyce's 'A Painful Case', written in 1905.[59] In Beckett's case, it relates to an aural and visual experience, in Joyce's case the sensory experience is olfactory – the 'faint fragrance' of the over-ripe apple in the desk of Mr Duffy. What is interesting about this adjective is that it serves as a metaphor of 'internalised' mental life that draws attention to the mind's extensiveness: even the most radical attempt to shut one's mind off from the environment (like the old man sitting with his head on his hands) ends up referring to the senses, suggesting that the human mind is an interaction, rather than a space inside a skull. And even if, in the case of 'John Duffy's Brother', 'Mr Train' is to be interpreted as 'a secret *inner* self' [my emphasis],[60] the literary *exploration* of this secret self is a form of *Umwelt* research, investigating the way the organism or intelligent agent enacts an environment that is inseparable from its own structure and actions.

'silent, so to speak'

Against the background of the categorisation of twentieth-century literature with labels such as modernism, late modernism or postmodernism, it seems useful to also try and discern patterns that form a continuum. In terms of evocations of the fictional mind, it is possible to trace a gradual development, away from Cartesian internalism in the direction of more 'extensive' models of the mind, even though each of the texts under discussion precedes the publication of Clark and Chalmers's essay 'The Extended Mind' (1998). In the case of Brian O'Nolan's work, this post-Cartesian model, as explored in 'John Duffy's Brother', can be of help in framing the 'modernism' debate in O'Nolan studies.

Two decades after Keith Hopper's portrait of Flann O'Brien as a 'post-modernist', the notion of postmodernism still has currency, but it is interesting that Hopper himself nuances this categorisation. In his 2014 essay 'Coming Off the Rails: The Strange Case of "John Duffy's Brother"', Hopper describes the story's 'open-ended text, which invites the reader to participate in the construction of meaning but which resists any single or absolute interpretation' as 'a hallmark of […] literary post-modernism'.[61] But he immediately adds that 'this concept can be traced at least as far back as the Romantic period', notably to Keats's 'negative capability'.[62] Given this affinity between periods, it is surprising that Hopper (referring to a 1969 publication by Nathan A. Scott) tries to re-establish a break by regarding this notion of negative capability as a 'key distinguishing feature that differentiates post-modernism from modernism'.[63] Perhaps this capability of being in uncertainties could just as well be seen as part of a continuum between modernism and late modernism; not a break between what McHale (referring to Higgins) called cognitivism and postcognitivism, but a gradual exploration of 'postcognitivist' or (proto)enactivist models of the mind. With its focus on 'widening out the mind' and with its liminal status between Joyce and Beckett, Brian O'Nolan's '*Umwelt* research' constitutes a significant site on this continuum between modernism and late modernism.

7

Phwat's in a nam?

Brian O'Nolan as a Late Revivalist*

Ronan Crowley

Irish Pseudonyms.—I have been for years collecting information of Irish signatures (pseudonyms, initials, etc.), and have obtained some thousands of solutions. Every delver in Irish book-lore has met some time or other with books giving the clue to certain pseudonyms, and I would be glad to have direct, or through the I.B.L. [*Irish Book Lover*], any lists any reader may have formed in this department. It is not uncommon to find written on titles or otherwise conveyed, the name of the real author of pseudonymous books. Any help that can be given me on the subject will be gratefully received and properly acknowledged.

—D.J. O'Donoghue (1910).[1]

Second-generation Mylesians rightly contested the culture of anecdote and insider reminiscence that had coalesced around Brian O'Nolan in the early years of his reception. This was the home-grown variant of 'two broad strands' of criticism anatomised by Keith Hopper in *Flann O'Brien: A Portrait of the Artist as a Young Post-Modernist* (1995): 'The indigenous school of Irish criticism', by contrast to the internationalist perspective, was 'invariably folksy and anecdotal, and often lacking in critical acumen'; the 'insular tone' of its scholarship, with some notable exceptions, 'would have made [O'Nolan] blush'.[2] One of the primary contentions of this essay is that the frequency with which we reiterate O'Nolan's recourse to pseudonymity, singling out his practice as though it were novel or unique, represents the last vestige of that soft-focus engagement, a critical myopia born of our underexamined and under-historicised appreciation for *noms de plume* in the Irish literary field.[3] Recuperating some of the intricate and intimate ecologies in which the pseudonym flourished in the decades surrounding O'Nolan's emergence reveals his penchant for pseudonymity as less a wayward, idiosyncratic point of departure than a decision consistent with a well-established and widely practised strategy of self-presentation and calculated misrepresentation.

Dollying out from O'Nolan, then, to adopt the terminology of the cameraman, widens the critical perspective from one lone actor (however plurally characterised) to the broader literary field that grants breadth and depth to his practice. To admit into the frame fellow practitioners who adopted pseudonyms or cultural mediators who, like D.J. O'Donoghue, sought to decode them is to show that the slippery authority of the proper name was a consistent and constituent element of the Irish literary field, long preceding the advent of O'Nolan. Such a focus on system over cell is what Pierre Bourdieu terms 'relationality' or 'relational thinking'.[4] To be sure, 'the glorification of "great individuals"' as Bourdieu writes – 'unique creators irreducible to any condition or conditioning'[5] – is a persistent feature of commentary on the arts in general and on matters Irish in particular. But addressing the wider system of social relations and signification that sustains pseudonymity is to follow through on the logic of the practice. For what could be more counterintuitive than localising its functions of displacement and multiplicity to a single actor? A tight shot framing O'Nolan, as it were, paradoxically serves to reassert his authority as masterful renunciate and threatens to fix in place a singular, authoritative locus of meaning.

The mid-century furnishes a great deal of evidence for what Timothy Dalrymple calls 'the subterfuge of pseudonymity'.[6] Nonetheless, the device enjoys a long, august history, one commensurate with the emergence of authorship itself. In carving out a more nuanced reception for O'Nolan, however, second-generation Mylesians went in the opposite direction, plumping for the prolepsis of the artist as 'young post-modernist', in Hopper's able formulation.[7] At that time, the mid-1990s, modernism was 'the enemy', as Susan Stanford Friedman recalls: castigated for a perceived elitism and sniffy disregard for mass culture, roundly condemned for its dodgy politics.[8] But an ongoing critical rehabilitation, largely synonymous with the new modernist studies inaugurated at the turn of the millennium, has divested the field of these stigmas and, moreover, annexed much of what was formerly termed the 'postmodern' to modernism's disciplinary hinterland.[9] As far as criticism of O'Nolan is concerned, such redefinition underwrites the collection *Flann O'Brien & Modernism* (2014), which reassesses the writer as a modernist or late modernist or, in Stephen Abblitt's felicitous pairing, even as a 'reluctant modernist'.[10]

Under the rubric of modernism, O'Nolan might profitably be put in dialogue with such pseudonymous writers as, *inter alia*, Guillaume Apollinaire (*né* Wilhelm de Kostrowitzky), Ford Madox Ford (Ford Hermann Hueffer), Jean Rhys (Ella Gwendolyn Rees Williams) or Rebecca West (Cicely Isabel Fairfield). One might cite the self-described 'neutral pseudonym of "Joseph Conrad"' adopted by Józef Korzeniowski or invoke Gordon Craig, who had such an impact on W.B. Yeats's theatrical sensibility and who contributed most of the writing to *The Mask* (1908–29) under some sixty-five pseudonyms.[11] In truth, however, such is the range of modernist engagements with the practice and possibilities of pseudonymity that Paul Valéry's characterisation of Stendhal, who 'gave himself a hundred pseudonyms, less to hide behind than to feel himself live in several versions',[12] might reasonably be applied to the entire modernist enterprise. But whereas, for Stendhal, 'writing is synonymous with being pseudonymous', in Ralph Schoolcraft's phrase,[13] what distinguishes later responses to the practice is the widespread disbelief, commensurate with modernism, in the very unity or coherence of the self in putative control of its textual doubles.

Fernando Pessoa, for example, whose use of pseudonyms has been put in productive apposition with O'Nolan's, confesses in *The Book of Disquiet* to being 'the empty stage where various actors act out various plays'.[14] Well-known for 'liv[ing] in several versions', he put forward the concept of the 'heteronym' to articulate a distinctly modernist take on pseudonymity and amassed over seventy major and minor creative surrogates, writing variously as Alberto Caeiro, bucolic poet, Ricardo Reis, amateur Latinist, or Álvaro de Campos, naval engineer. For Pessoa, heteronymity differs from pseudonymity insofar as heteronyms connote not simply false or fictitious names but also distinguish a series of alternative authorial personae, each of whom is invested with a distinct creative sensibility and individuated biography. This species of involvedness Adrian Oțoiu wittily hyphenates as 'alter-native identities'.[15]

Theorists of the pseudonym will look in vain for a comparable justification in O'Nolan's writing. As Myles na gCopaleen in *Cruiskeen Lawn*, he took a catholic line on the 'eccentric feat' of 'masquerading under a pseudonym'.[16] If 'Saorstát Éireann' could be a 'pseudonym' for Ireland, Myles was equally content to out '"Lady" Gregory' as the 'pen name of the famous traveller Denis Johnston'.[17] He even claimed the names of real people as his own pseudonyms – or, more properly, 'allonyms' – drawing Austin Clarke, the rugby great W.E. Crawford and '"Pluto" (or "Plato", was it?)', among others, into an orbit of fanciful association.[18] The degree to which O'Nolan's grab-bag of recognised pseudonyms constitutes a set of heteronyms is uncertain. Myles and Brother Barnabas, for example, enjoy such full and fantastical biographies that they might be said to represent the heteronym *par excellence*. On the other hand, for all the paucity of information about Flann O'Brien's background, O'Nolan evidently thought that this authorial persona was sufficiently distinct that he declined Anthony Cronin's suggestion to revive the pen name in the 1950s by replying, 'I don't know that fellow any longer'.[19]

To go the route of deracinated internationalism is to ignore a context considerably closer to home and one which formed O'Nolan's more immediate intellectual inheritance. For all the pleasing continuities with Pessoa, a figure like T.C. Murray, the Abbey dramatist, offers a more versatile metric for understanding Irish attitudes to pseudonymity. Not averse to using pen names over his published work, Murray even shifted between different pseudonyms in manuscript as he drafted and redrafted the play that would become *The Serf* (1920).[20] The work's anticlericalism was such that he submitted it to the Abbey 'under pen-name', as Yeats informed Lady Gregory, and the detachment of pseudonymity allowed Murray to applaud his own work 'heartily' during its first run, according to Joseph Holloway.[21] But to ascribe a work to different hands in the relative privacy of the literary workshop indicates a strategic use of pseudonymity for creative or aesthetic compartmentalisation, not unlike the affordances of the heteronym. Such 'introversion' also highlights the ways in which adopting or refining a *nom de plume*, much like the process of drafting a literary work, consciously and unconsciously implicates the author within a set of wider relations – these range from expectations about genre and gender to the agreed-on concerns and coordinates of a national literature.

Regrettably, no comprehensive resource or database exists to chart the multitudinous lives of the Irish pseudonym. The epigraph that heads this essay flags an earlier attempt, contemporary with the Revival, to pin down the rich history of the practice as it had flourished in the eighteenth and nineteenth centuries. O'Donoghue's projected guide never actually appeared, however, the endeavour being cut short by his death in 1917.[22] But a database could extend his focus through the present day, thereby ranging from Charles Maturin, whose early Gothic novels were published under the pseudonym 'Dennis Jasper Murphy', to Oscar Wilde, whose assumed name 'Sebastian Melmoth' was lifted, in part, from the title character of his granduncle's *Melmoth the Wanderer* (1820), and on, more recently, to the likes of Jean Fisher (*née* Medbh McGuckian) or Benjamin Black (John Banville).

A database would provide 'solutions', to adopt O'Donoghue's term, for such apparent one-offs as Andrew Belis (Samuel Beckett), Michael Ireland (Darrell Figgis) or Sirius (Edward Martyn). The pseudonym 'Richard Sheridan', by contrast, was something of a family affair; the stage name of Thomas MacDonagh during the heyday of the Irish Theatre Company, it was revived by his brother John MacDonagh after the revolutionary's execution. A database would also ventilate the thinking that made George Moore adopt the pointed pseudonym 'Paul Ruttledge' for an article in *Dana* attacking the Irish National Theatre or which caused Tim Healy to publish an anti-Parnellite screed under the pen name 'Gutter Sparrow'. Moreover, it would name writers who exploited the ambiguities of pseudonymity to comment on or to praise their own work in public. Pseudonymity allowed Ernest A. Boyd, for example, to boost his own anti-conscription pamphlet, *The Sacred Egoism of Sinn Féin* (1918), as a 'provocative work' in the New York *Dial*.[23] It was also turned to good account by Brinsley MacNamara who favourably reviewed *The Irishman* (1920) by 'Oliver Blythe' for the *Irish Independent*.[24] These examples help to contextualise O'Nolan's modest dabbling in this self-propelled form of log-rolling. As Myles na gCopaleen, he expressed delight in *Cruiskeen Lawn* at 'the reception given to my book', *An Béal Bocht*; as Myles na Gopaleen twenty-four years later, he implored 'let me say a word about that book *The Dalkey Archive*'.[25]

More pressingly, a national inflection places O'Nolan, whom 'Almost everybody' knew as 'Myles',[26] in the company of fellow Irish writers whose pseudonyms largely displaced their personal names in public and private life. Figures such as Æ (George William Russell), MacNamara (John Weldon) and Seamus O'Sullivan (James Sullivan Starkey) as well as those whose pseudonyms we no longer even recognise as concealing different birth-names – *inter alia*, Sean O'Casey (John Casey), Desmond FitzGerald (Thomas Joseph Fitzgerald)[27] and Padraic Colum (Patrick Collumb) – all put their literary personae in everyday correlation with the lived self. Hailed in the street or addressed in correspondence by their pseudonyms, they drew up contracts and signed legal documents with assumed names. One might dub this community, after Oţoiu, the 'alter natives'. But inasmuch as such embodiment reorients the individual writer back towards Yeats's 'bundle of accident and incoherence that sits down to breakfast',[28] the peculiar state of Irish play also suggests a conception of pseudonymity that is altogether more radical – and yet much more pervasive – than the private drama of Pessoa's heteronyms. In this respect, the realignment of O'Nolan's pseudonymity with that of his immediate Irish literary forebears and contemporaries underscores a crucial point of overlap between modernism and its traditional counter, the Irish Literary Revival.

The Revival: from revilement to reveille

Irish literary historiography has long written off the Revival's set of interlocking coteries and causes as a monolithic formation, more *bête noire* for modernist precocity than the crucible in which certain actors and agents fused the striking contradictions at the heart of metrocolonial Ireland to produce its finest literature.[29] Accordingly, the reorientation proposed by this essay requires a fresh look at Revivalism as a prerequisite to exploring O'Nolan's debts to and place within its manifold. The dominant critical account of the period still proceeds by cordoning off a small subset of principals from the general body of practitioners – typically singling out Yeats, Synge and Gregory – to condemn the movement outright for the triple offence that is a singular offence: Protestant Anglo-Irish landlordism. Violence to history, creed and class notwithstanding, thus are denigrated the 'Irish and not Irish'.[30]

Such condemnation enjoyed traction at the turn of the century, when it was employed as a cogent vehicle of delegitimation. D.P. Moran and the programme of Irish Ireland is perhaps the classic case here.[31] For Terence Brown writing in 1980, however, accounting for the curious fact of a generation of writers from Protestant Ireland who wrote 'in a national mode' was a recent critical turn, one that involved close examination of 'the history of the Anglo-Irish as a colonial class faced by a nascent Catholic nationalism in the late nineteenth and early twentieth centuries'.[32] Though it was not a thesis he advocated, such claims proceeded by identifying a cabal of writers, who were 'conscious of the insecurity of Anglo-Ireland's social and political position, and possessed to greater or lesser extents by racial guilt', and thus sought to redeem their tribal failures by contributing to the national cause.[33] At stake, however, was nothing less than the establishment of an Irish cultural identity irreducible to the rising Catholic nationalist majority.

Since about 2000, the 'old accusations' of Anglo-Irish dominance in the literary field have been countered and softened by a generation of new scholarship.[34] What Edna Longley termed 'a new academic vogue' emerged at the time, with millennial calls for reappraisal quickly ushering forth a number of special issues, edited collections and monographs.[35] For Margaret Kelleher, editor of the *Irish University Review*'s special issue on 'New Perspectives on the Irish Literary Revival', the landscape of Revivalism was 'richly and provocatively expanded' by a pointed rejection of 'a traditionally author-centred criticism that continues to be obsessed with the canon and which has lingered in the context of Revival writing long after its dismissal elsewhere'.[36]

In step with this expansive tendency, the prevailing sense of the "'Anglo-Irish" in the narrow sense', in Vivian Mercier's phrase – 'members of the peerage or landed gentry and of English protestant ancestry' – has come in for sustained critique.[37] Clare Hutton has variegated the heretofore monochrome image of Anglo-Ireland through deft analysis of the backgrounds of middle-class Protestant writers.[38] Recovery scholarship trained on, among others, the Gore-Booths means that Protestant aristos of a revolutionary or creative bent can no longer simply be dismissed as naïve outriders in the throes of bad faith or as *declassés* striving for relevance.[39]

Quite why the notion of a '(mostly Ascendancy) Irish Literary Revival' – in a revealing parenthetical from James M. Cahalan[40] – remains so biddable and is so frequently reiterated becomes clear once such rehearsals are read in context. A recent high-profile volume, for example, deploys the trope in perhaps its bluntest form: 'Joyce considered Irish nationalism a provincial fantasy. The writers of the Irish Renaissance themselves (Lady Gregory, William Butler Yeats, John Synge, Sean O'Casey, George Russell, George Moore) were all wealthy Anglo-Irish Protestants mining Irish peasant themes'.[41] Inasmuch as this denunciation applies to perhaps one person on the list – and only when her body of work is ruthlessly thinned of its richness and variety – such comparisons are made to set an anointed literary practitioner off to advantage. Similar presumptions underlie Flore Coulouma's charge that 'Flann O'Brien's satire targets Irish revivalists as middle-class snobs cut off from the linguistic reality of 20th century Ireland'.[42] The lesson of recent scholarship, however, is that the old models, prejudices and pieties no longer offer an adequate account of the creative ferment to which O'Nolan belonged and responded.

In advancing O'Nolan as a putative late Revivalist, there is more at stake than the sort of laboured re-periodisation satirised so ably by Paul K. Saint-Amour in his witty 'Interlude' for *English Literature in Transition*: 'We Have Never Been Modernists', he maintains.[43] His point is that the professional categories and compartmentalisation of literary criticism tend to hinder cross-period scholarship, blinkering the critic to the solemnities and shibboleths of her own field and misrepresenting contiguous or overlapping periods. Insisting on the Revival as modernism's contrary or converse, as the older critical orthodoxy held, or even as an incubatory moment for Irish modernism, as more recent assessments have conceded, relegates figures like O'Nolan to a disciplinary no man's land, chaffing against the strictures of Irish cultural nationalism yet ultimately too stay-at-home to qualify for modernist cosmopolitanism.

This double bind is as much a creation of our 'movement categories', in Kristin Bluemel's phrase,[44] as it is representative of the post-independence Irish literary field. In the case of O'Nolan, it finds expression in Hopper's contention that 'the two towers' confronting the writer were 'the twin legacies of Joyce's modernism and Yeats's celtic revival – and he was nervously uncomfortable with both'.[45] Not only does such polarisation overlook the vast middle ground of literary practitioners and cultural intermediaries who operated in the period, but also missing are Yeats's and Joyce's own frequent migrations between these two apparently incommensurate positions. David Holdeman, for example, has provocatively antedated Yeats's modernism to 1903 and the Dun Emer Press *In the Seven Woods*.[46] Moreover, we tend nowadays to understand the early Joyce as part of rather than simply opposed to the Revival – even as something of a 'revivalist manqué'.[47] As the contradistinction of Revivalism from Irish modernism becomes increasingly less tenable, the crucial takeaway for O'Nolan studies is that the coordinates by which critics assign O'Nolan his place in the literary field are themselves shifting. In fine, we are compelled to re-evaluate the writer and his *œuvre* on new terms.

'what's this his name is?'[48]: Revivalist pseudonymity

It is surely curious that the Revival, a broad cultural platform routinely criticised for its perceived essentialism, should have such frequent recourse to pseudonym usage. Typical is Richard Ellmann's eye-rolling dismissal of Revivalist renaming, localised in *James Joyce* (1959) to 'Samuel Chenevix Trench, a member of an old Anglo-Irish family' and the model for Haines in *Ulysses*:

> Trench [...] had embraced the Irish revival so passionately, and to Joyce so offensively, that he called himself Dermot Trench and had his new name confirmed by deed poll in 1905. He was just back from a canoeing trip through the country, and felt that he now knew what Ireland was really like.[49]

While Trench's recourse to legal process to cement his name change may have been unusual, Ellmann's pooh-poohing fails to recognise the capacity for individual and collective reinvention, the spirit of play and political activism synonymous with the *nom de guerre*. Roy Foster, by contrast, observes that for the Irish revolutionary generation 'Renaming was a powerfully symbolic act, often taking the form not merely of finding the nearest Irish version to one's

English name but of adopting a queenly or mythic identification such as Emer (Helena Molony) or Lasairfhíona (Elizabeth Somers)'.⁵⁰ More mundanely, perhaps, Kathleen Cruise O'Brien (*née* Katherine Sheehy) used her husband Francis's connections with *The Irish Statesman* and *The Freeman's Journal* to place her short stories but opted to publish them under the unattached pen name 'Fand O'Grady'. Gender-neutral or masculine pen-names, on the other hand, allowed Irish women writers to craft authorial personae distinct from their gender. In this vein, Sydney Gifford wrote for *Sinn Féin* as 'John Brennan'; Iseult Gonne published as 'Maurice Gonne' in the little magazines *Aengus* and *Tomorrow*; and Rosamond Jacob elided her gender outright as 'F. Winthrop'. Moving in the opposite direction, Séamus Ó Grianna wrote as 'Máire' and Roger Casement penned journalism under the names 'Shan Van Vocht' and 'The Poor Old Woman'.

Rónán McDonald and Julian Murphet have linked O'Nolan's reliance on pseudonyms to 'a modernist notion of subjectivity that thwarts singular or positivistic ideas of a coherent, self-contained individual', but they qualify this welcome repudiation of essentialism by insisting on the practice's 'precursors in an Irish tradition of self-concealment or self-invention'.⁵¹ Yet Irishness could itself be the mode of concealment. The literary field at the turn of the century was sufficiently flexible and accommodating to admit the London-born Alfred Willmore in the guise of 'Micheál macLiammóir', an Irish-speaking Corkonian. Progressively Hibernicising his name as 'Micheál Wilmore', then 'Miceál MacUallmoir', he illustrated book covers for the Talbot Press a full decade before partnering with Hilton Edwards to found the Dublin Gate Theatre Studio.⁵² Arnold Bax, south Londoner, became in Ireland 'Dermod McDermott' and, more enduringly, 'Dermot O'Byrne'.

Among those whose Irish identities were more complicated, Douglas Hyde was Gaelicising his name as 'Dubhglas de hÍde' by the late 1870s. He adopted the pseudonym 'An Craoibhin Aoibhinn' – glossed in *Ulysses* as 'the graceful pseudonym of the Little Sweet Branch' – as a 'deliberate act of discretion', in the words of Janet and Gareth Dunleavy.⁵³ The pen name not only immunised Hyde from the ire of his family for expressing alleged 'Fenian sentiments',⁵⁴ it also allowed him to concoct a lyric 'I' and implied author distinct from his Church of Ireland origins. In his first published poem, 'Shiubhal mé lá go tuirseach trom' [I walk today wearily, with heavy step] (1879), Hyde took on the persona of a bereft and homeless old man, a conceit well received by readers who, as Hutton argues, 'did not realise that the writer [...] was not an ageing native speaker, but actually an anglophone teenage Protestant who had no experience of the Famine'.⁵⁵ Similarly, for

Eamonn Hughes, O'Nolan's use of the 'Myles na gCopaleen' pseudonym makes a pitch for the conservative, unionist leanings of the *Irish Times* readership at the same time that it connects back to the Irish literary tradition through the name's antecedents in Dion Boucicault's *The Colleen Bawn* and Gerald Griffin's *The Collegians*.[56] Radical or reactionary, then, pseudonymity can equally mark a break with orthodoxy or advance a relationship to the establishment.

A less charitable view of self-refashioning would stress the pseudonym as commodity, given the marketability or sale value of an Irish pen name. In Joyce's 'A Little Cloud', for example, Thomas Chandler imagines the reception of his unwritten volume of verse along precisely these lines: 'It was a pity his name was not more Irish looking. Perhaps it would be better to insert his mother's name before the surname: Thomas Malone Chandler, or better still: T. Malone Chandler'.[57] This fusion of impostorship and opportunism is complicated by Joyce's own venture into pseudonymity. Declan Kiberd follows Ellmann in contending that 'so ashamed' was Joyce of the venue in which his earliest short stories were to appear, *The Irish Homestead*, that he sought to 'conceal the embarrassing connection' behind the distinctly un-Irish byline 'Stephen Dædalus'.[58] But by the time 'The Sisters' appeared in print on 13 August 1904, Joyce had already been using the pseudonym for over two months. The earliest of five surviving letters signed 'Stephen Daedalus' is one to Oliver St John Gogarty of 3 June 1904,[59] which predates Russell's commissioning letter by a full month. 'Stephen Daedalus' – without the ligature – is also the name that heads the manuscripts of the *Dubliners* stories composed before the summer of 1905. Indeed, by the time of Russell's July invitation, Joyce was already some several hundred pages into *Stephen Hero* with its eponymous protagonist closely modelled on himself (much more so than the Stephen of *A Portrait of the Artist as a Young Man*). As late as September 1924, Joyce was still using the pseudonym, however playfully, when he inscribed a copy of the American edition of *A Portrait* to his patron, Harriet Shaw Weaver.[60]

One might imagine that, in turn-of-the-century Dublin, explicit linkage of character to pseudonymous creator would have been accessible only to intimates and correspondents of the writer. Yet so confident was Austin Clarke of the association that he entitled his personal account of meeting Joyce in Paris in late 1920 '"Stephen Dedalus": The Author of *Ulysses*'.[61] The name 'Joyce' does not appear in the *New Statesman* write-up once. Decades later, Maurice Devane, the protagonist of Clarke's own *Mnemosyne Lay in Dust* (1966), was named for the pseudonym that the poet had used over book reviews in O'Sullivan's *Dublin Magazine*. Toing and froing between thin self-fictionalisation and the embrace of a pseudonym was thus far from unique to Joyce. Gogarty's own *Tumbling in the Hay* (1939) and *Going Native* (1940), for example, are narrated by Gideon Ouseley, two 'joyous dactyls'[62] that are only a single character away from 'Gideon Ousley', the pseudonym that appears over Gogarty's Abbey plays 'A Serious Thing' (1919) and 'The Enchanted Trousers' (1919). Thomas Weldon, the protagonist of MacNamara's 'The Smiling Faces' (1929), not only shares his author's own birth surname, but is also the pseudonym under which MacNamara published an early poem, 'The Haunted House', in *The Irish Weekly Independent* for 3 April 1915. More convoluted still is the case of Oswald Brannigan, the protagonist of MacNamara's 1919 short story 'Dr Oswald Brannigan'. The medical officer is an author manqué who 'wished he could write; write like this Dostoieffsky or like Ibsen, or like Strindberg. He would have something to say. But he had really no leisure for writing'.[63] After an outburst at a committee meeting costs him his job, he thinks ruefully, 'Oh, yes, he would have to write now'.[64] Three years later, MacNamara's own story 'The Encourager', a lethal send-up of Joseph Holloway, appeared in the Dublin literary magazine *Banba* ascribed to one 'Oswald Brannigan'. Such playfulness and sheer involutedness, when encountered in O'Nolan's writing, is typically weighted to argue his precedency to postmodernist fiction, but clearly the practice has its own antecedent in the Revival.

The objection might reasonably be raised that what distinguishes O'Nolan from his Revivalist precursors is a quantitative if not qualitative difference. He simply used so many more pseudonyms. Yet James Stephens published and performed under at least five different variations on his personal name: James Esse, Stephen James, Seumas James, Samuel James and Shemus Beg.[65] As 'James Esse', he even conducted 'An Interview with Mr James Stephens' for *The Irish Statesman* in 1923, providing a witty statement on the tensions between individual and communal authorship that prefigures O'Nolan's own oft-quoted statement on the interchangeability of literary characters (*CN*, 21).[66] The plurality of O'Casey's self-presentation in his six volumes of autobiography as, successively, Johnny Casside, Sean Casside, Sean O'Casside and Sean O'Casey is matched only by the range of pseudonyms under which he wrote: An Gall Fada, Green Searchlight, P. O Cathasaigh, Sean O'Cathasaigh and Craobh na nDealg (the last translates as 'The Thorny Branch', a parody of Hyde's pen name). Even the three 'alter natives' previously mentioned as examples of Revivalists more typically known by their pseudonyms, Æ, MacNamara and O'Sullivan, all employed a plurality of pen names. Russell used the alphabetical disguises 'O.L.S.', 'G.A.L.' and 'Y.O.' and the names 'Pan' and 'Querist', even admitting 'there may be others that I forget'.[67] In addition to Weldon and Brannigan, MacNamara also published as 'Oliver Blythe' and, very occasionally, under his given name. In 1910 and 1937, O'Sullivan published two collections that were billed as selections from the notebooks of the late J.H. Orwell,[68] reducing his own creative role to that of editor and writer of forewords in much the same way that Myles was credited as '*The Editor*' and foreword writer of Bónapárt Ó Cúnasa's authentic memoir *An Béal Bocht* (*CN*, 409).

The extensive run of pseudonyms adopted and discarded by Arthur Griffith, it must be conceded, leaves O'Nolan in the ha'penny place. In *The United Irishman*, the firebrand journalist usually wrote under the byline 'Cuguan' which, although 'It had a kind of Gaelic look' to Padraic Colum,[69] came freighted with colonialist inequalities reckoned on a transnational scale. For the name meant 'dove' in the pidgin language that served as a lingua franca in the South African mines where Griffith's club-foot disability lent him an uneven, rolling gait.[70] His rewriting of Synge's 'In the Shadow of the Glen' as 'In a Real Wicklow Glen' in *The United Irishman* was signed 'Conn', by contrast, but as each of his editorial ventures was suppressed – or in the case of *The United Irishman* prosecuted for libel – Griffith transferred his activities to a new nameplate and a fresh battery of pseudonyms.[71] Virginia E. Glandon has determined that, over the years of *Sinn Féin* alone (1906–14), the Dubliner ran through such names as 'Calma, Shanganagh, Ier, Lugh, Rathcoole, Mise, Nationalist, Old Fogey, Mafosta, Joseph Smith, Cloakey, Rover, Jap and Hop and Go One'.[72] In the same vein, P.J. Mathews identifies 'at least eleven pseudonyms' used by William Rooney for *The United Irishman*: '"Fear na Muintire", "Hi Fiachra" and "Criadhaire" in his poetry; "Shel Martin", "Sliabh Ruadh", "Glenn an Smoil", "Knocksedan", "Killeste", "Feltrim", "Ballinascorney" and "Baltrasna" in his prose'.[73] Casement, when not donning the drag of Ireland personified, wrote as 'X' around the turn of the twentieth century; as 'Irishman', 'X.X.X.' and 'Mars Ultor' in *Irish Freedom* in 1912–14; as 'Henry Bower', 'Diplomaticus', 'John Quincy Emerson LLD, an American citizen', 'One Who Knows' and 'Will E. Wagtail' in the pro-German *Continental Times*; and as 'An Irish American' and 'Batha MacCrainn' in *The Irish Review*.[74] Such tallies begin to resemble the long roster of Gaeilgeoirí lampooned in Chapter 4 of *An Béal Bocht* (*CN*, 438–39) but, incredibly, each set enumerated above represents the pseudonymic ranging of a single individual.

A crucial distinction between the comedy of *An Béal Bocht* and these examples lies in the motivation for adopting pen names. In a vicious dig for

The American Mercury, Boyd outlines some of the incentives offered by *noms de plume* in his caricature of 1930s' Marxist intellectuals: the 'literary Comrade' is 'a chameleon-like creature whose resources are such that he is not afraid, on occasion, to conceal his name under a pseudonym, in order the more safely to attack his opponents and to placate the friends from whom he draws his salary'.[75] But not every practitioner was quite so mercenary or Machiavellian. Pseudonymity lent a degree of immunity or protection to political activists and agitators when the forums in which they published were suppressed for sedition, prosecuted for libel or otherwise fell foul of the law. Likewise, physical force republicanism produced an altogether more urgent need for *noms de guerre*.

Pseudonyms denote names conferred by others as much as the pen names that a writer might assume for herself. A persistent aspect of Revivalist pseudonymity that, nonetheless, has received scant critical attention is the substitution of an alias for the real name of an historical person in the process of her fictionalising incorporation into a literary work. The inclusion of Niall Sheridan and Niall Montgomery as Brinsley and Kerrigan in *At Swim-Two-Birds*, for example, are consistent with this well-established practice. Mention has already been made of Trench as the basis for Haines in *Ulysses* (the likeness was apparently a poor one),[76] and Gogarty is often remembered solely as the model for Buck Mulligan in *Ulysses*. All the same, a half-dozen other pseudonyms were bestowed on the latter by friends and enemies alike as they worked him into their fictions. Norah Hoult even names Gogarty's stand-in 'Buck Mulligan' in her *Coming from the Fair* (1937).[77] Wider examples in this vein are legion. Perhaps representative are the various aliases that Francis Stuart gives to Iseult Gonne in his novels: she is fictionalised as Nancy in *Redemption* (1949); Veronique in *The Pilgrimage* (1955); Lenore in *Victors and Vanquished* (1958); Iseult in *Black List, Section H* (1971); and Lydia in *Faillandia* (1985). Pseudonymising the real people in one's circle allied to the associated genre of the *roman à clef* offered a way for new entrants to the Irish literary field – O'Nolan among them – to pinion rivals and exalt allies as they jockeyed for cultural capital, position and prominence.

'Gael Pen Name Cloys'[78]: O'Nolan's pseudonymity

Is O'Nolan, that employer of 'a myriad of pseudonymous personalities in the interest of pure destruction',[79] any different from his Revival precursors and contemporaries? While Oțoiu argues that O'Nolan's pseudonyms constitute an 'elaborate identity game [...] meant to problematize authorship',[80] the evidence from the period shows that his identity was rarely in question for readers or critics alike. In the 1939 'Time's Pocket' controversy in *The Irish Times*, for example, Seán O'Faoláin had pinioned 'Flann O'Brien' as an 'appropriately anachronistic pseudonym'; shortly thereafter the Corkman explicitly outed O'Nolan as its bearer in a review of *At Swim-Two-Birds* for *John O'London's Weekly*.[81] And, in January 1940, *The Irish Times* reported that the Trustees of the A.E. Memorial Award, despite bestowing the £100 prize upon Patrick Kavanagh, had given 'favourable consideration to the work of Mr Brian O'Nolan (Flann O'Brien)'.[82]

In 1943, no less a publication than *TIME* magazine identified 'the favourite Irish newspaper columnist' as 'Brian O'Nolan' in its pen portrait, and *The Irish Times* reported a *New York Herald Tribune* piece which had lauded 'a civil servant, named Brian O'Nolan, who writes under the names of "Flann O'Brien" and "Myles na gCopaleen"'.[83] To the *Irish Times* readership of 1947, it was apparently an 'open secret for many years that Flann O'Brien was the early *nom de guerre* of the gentleman who has since acquired a national, and extra-national reputation as "Myles na gCopaleen"'.[84] Indeed, when 'The Martyr's Crown' was published in *Envoy* in 1950, the clarification went in the opposite direction; an asterisked footnote glossed the 'Brian Nolan' by-line as 'Myles na gCopaleen'.[85] But the expository trend was independent of new publications requiring such glosses. The *Irish Times* coverage of the centenary of the Literary and Historical Society in 1955 noted that Vivion de Valera had defeated 'Brian Ua Nuallain, *alias* Flann O'Brien, *alias* Myles na Gopaleen' for the auditorship of the society in 1933.[86] Brendan Behan even contributed a Mylesian 'Catechism' in this vein as part of his *Irish Times* review of the reissued *At Swim-Two-Birds* in 1960:

CATECHISM

Q. Who is Flann O'Brien?
A. Brian Nolan.
Q. Who is Brian Nolan?
A. Myles na Gopaleen.[87]

In later years, the newspaper went on to poke fun at its own explicatory tendencies. The write-up of Hugh Leonard's *When the Saints Go Cycling In* credited the play's source material, *The Dalkey Archive*, to 'Flann O'Brien (alias, etc.)'.[88] With such periodic reminders interlinking O'Nolan's pseudonyms put before the public, it is difficult to agree with Rüdiger Imhof's early assessment that the 'plethora of pen-names protected his privacy and gained him immunity from possible retaliatory attack'.[89] One need hardly be an insider of the mid-century Dublin literary scene if the readers of *TIME* magazine were privy to such information.

However much we might be surprised at the speed and frequency with which O'Nolan's predominant authorial personae were publicly aired, such transparency ought to be read in the context of the vibrant culture of pseudonym usage operative at *The Irish Times*, the preferred venue for the writer's most prolific pen name. R.M. Smyllie, for instance, who as editor had given O'Nolan his start on the column, adopted the byline 'Nichevo' as early as 1921 and continued to employ it right up to August 1954, a few weeks shy of his death.[90] Of the Earlsfort Terrace set, Sheridan contributed a regular column as 'Birdcatcher', a racing tipster, for over a decade, and Montgomery went under the cross-dressed colours of 'Rosemary Lane' for the twice-monthly column 'The Liberties', which ran from January to December 1964.[91]

The contributions of O'Nolan's compères to *Cruiskeen Lawn* have been convincingly documented by Carol Taaffe, but 'An Irishman's Diary' – frequently the butt of Myles's attacks – was itself, in the words of Tony Gray, 'a contributed column to which any staff member could contribute'.[92] Gray declared himself 'Class of 1948–49', but by that time the 'Quidnunc' byline had already masked a long, illustrious succession of contributors. W.A. Newman inaugurated the inquisitive or nosy persona in late 1927 and was followed by Patrick Campbell in the mid-1940s, before Brian Inglis took over as 'Pro-Quidnunc'.[93] After Gray's departure, Seamus Kelly wrote the Diary as 'Quidnunc' for the better part of thirty years. Alluding to this plurality in *Cruiskeen Lawn* for 13 December 1950, Myles wondered if Denis Guiney, the owner of Clerys department store on Dublin's O'Connell Street, might be convinced to 'put all the Quidnuncs of the last fifteen years into one of his windows for the Christmas?'[94] Quidnunc, for all Myles's quarrel with him, was thus closer to the 'textual facades' that Joseph Brooker sees behind the collective-writing policies of *Comhthrom Féinne* and *Blather*.[95]

In this light, O'Nolan's 'De Me', a short contribution made late in life to the *New Ireland* annual for 1964, becomes complicated as straightforward self-portraiture. However shot through the piece may be with Myles's wordplay and irreverence, Cronin takes it largely at face value, mining what he terms a 'rare essay in autobiography' for *No Laughing Matter* (1989).[96] But the essay's oft-quoted second half adopts a distinctly avuncular tone:

Apart from a thorough education of the widest kind, a contender in
this field [of writing] must have an equable yet versatile temperament,
and the compartmentation of his personality for the purpose of literary
utterance ensures that the fundamental individual will not be credited
with a certain way of thinking, fixed attitudes, irreversible technique of
expression. No author should write under his own name nor under one
permanent pen-name; a male writer should include in his impostures a
female pen-name, and possibly vice versa.[97]

As familiar as the sentiment about the benefits of pseudonymity may be,
what O'Nolan elaborates is, in fact, not a personal conceit but a general
programme for distancing author from flesh-and-blood writer. 'De Me' is, at
this juncture, thus less descriptive – less self-description – than prescriptive.
Critics tend to reproduce the piece in light of O'Nolan's own recourse to
pseudonyms but, restored to context, it is clear that what he offers instead is
advice to aspiring writers. In a paragraph not reproduced by Cronin, the self-
styled 'brief discourse' maintains its instructional ethos:

A literary agent (there are probably 50 firms in London alone) is essential
for the financial realisation of a writer's worth, particularly for the
dissemination of his works abroad in translation, but the practitioner
of the literary craft who is crafty will have several agents unknown to
each other, each dealing with him under a particular pen-name which
is not disclosed to the agent to be a pen-name. There is method in this
apparent perversity, as will be clear to all who equate poverty, lust, ill
health and revenue commissioners as the prime afflictions of mankind.[98]

O'Nolan adumbrates an entire field of cultural production, one with
London at its heart, in which circulation abroad and in translation must be
countenanced, and in which both the artistic work and the pseudonymous
practitioner alike need to be situated within the social conditions of their
production and consumption. Far from an individual conceit or personal tic,
then, recourse to pseudonymity multiplies, complicates and further entangles
Bourdieusian relationality – the space of positions and position-takings that
constitutes the Irish literary field.

O'Nolan, long seen as extraneous to the Revival, if not outwardly hostile
to it, was instead deeply engaged with its themes and methodologies: and not
simply in a polemical fashion. Rather than the mugging of the funny-man, his
practice of employing pseudonyms should be recognised as part of a dialectic

internal to the broader Revival – if we understand the movement as a broad, multifaceted platform that worked ceaselessly to question and problematise notions of originality and authority, authorship and community. Isolated from this context, his pseudonymising has repeatedly been misread as a private game. Once understood against a vibrant backdrop of related cultural activity, the pseudonym's politics of representation and coy misrepresentation and its role in the struggle internal to the cultural field come urgently to the fore.

8

Fantastic economies
Flann O'Brien and James Stephens

R. W. Maslen

In this essay I shall argue that Brian O'Nolan's *The Third Policeman* is (among other things) a radical reimagining of one of the best-loved Irish novels of the twentieth century, James Stephens's *The Crock of Gold*. In reworking Stephens's quirky nationalist fantasy for a later generation, O'Nolan arranges elements of the earlier novel into strange new forms adapted to the grim new social and political realities of the 1930s. Stephens conceived his book as an imaginative act of resistance against the unholy alliance of the church and the British state: pitting mutually supportive poverty against the reactionary self-interest of the middle classes, setting the passionate body into conflict with the cultural and religious authorities who sought to suppress it, and predicting a brilliant future for an independent, egalitarian and quasi-pagan Irish nation. O'Nolan reconceives Stephens's novel as an elaborate trap, in which Ireland, its people and its landscape wholeheartedly participate in the worldwide trend towards totalitarian authoritarianism and its inevitable outcome: self-destruction. The chief components of both novels are a pastoral, often lyric vision of the Irish countryside, a clutch of self-educated philosophers, a man condemned to death and some eccentric but threatening policemen. How and why such similar elements should have been recombined to produce such radically different texts, each of which issues an equally scathing assessment of the condition of Ireland at its own particular point in history, is the subject of this essay.

O'Nolan's debt to Stephens has often been noted. In 1966 an anonymous essayist argued in the *Times Literary Supplement* that O'Nolan owed more to the 'tradition of modern Irish fantasy and romance in which the definitive figure is James Stephens' than to Joycean modernism (though there seems no good reason to choose between these debts, since Joyce and Stephens were friends).[1] Thirty years later, Keith Hopper pointed out that *The Third Policeman*'s Sergeant Pluck is 'a fictional composition of [...] features borrowed from other texts (most notably James Stephens's policemen in *The Crock of Gold*)'.[2] Carol Taaffe has recently contended that the 'nearest predecessor to O'Nolan's fantasy was James Stephens's *The Crock of Gold*'.[3] None of these commentators took their perceptions much further, but the sheer frequency with which O'Nolan's debt to Stephens has been affirmed suggests that a close comparison is overdue. Taaffe's comments in particular open up a number of fruitful avenues of inquiry.

For Taaffe, *The Third Policeman* is a 'resolutely *apolitical* piece of nonsense' [my emphasis], which reflects O'Nolan's ambiguous attitude to Éamon de Valera's Ireland, caught between anger at and complicity with its oppressive paternalism towards its citizens.[4] It seems to me, though, that O'Nolan's evident fascination with *The Crock of Gold* can be read as the key to a decidedly *political* reading of *The Third Policeman*, which reinforces Shelly Brivic's contention that an 'insurrectionary attitude' lurks beneath the surface of O'Nolan's masterpiece.[5] Neither *The Crock of Gold* nor James Stephens could be described as in any sense 'apolitical', embroiled as they were in the ferment of nationalist activism that preceded the outbreak of the First World War.[6] O'Nolan's decision, then, to redraft Stephens's book in the context of the nationalist ferment that preceded the Second World War can itself be seen as a political act. That the political outlooks in question are so different can be ascribed to the different class backgrounds of the two writers, as well as to the times in which they wrote. And these differences emerge most clearly in the contrasting imaginative economies of their novels.

Stephens saw himself as having been shaped by the economic conditions of his upbringing. In a fragment of autobiography he represents his early life in terms of a series of transitions from one social *milieu* to another:

> The Dublin I was born to was poor and Protestant and athletic. While very young I extended my range and entered a Dublin that was poor and Catholic and Gaelic – a very wonderworld. Then as a young writer I further extended to a Dublin that was poor and artistic and political. Then I made a Dublin for myself, my Dublin.[7]

The recurrent note throughout these transitions is poverty. Stephens was educated at the Meath Industrial School for Protestant Boys, for which he qualified by getting himself arrested for begging at the age of six.[8] He left school at sixteen to work for a pittance as a solicitor's clerk, a life from which he was precariously set free by the success of his writing. Brian O'Nolan, by contrast, came from a Catholic middle-class background, took a master's degree in Irish literature at University College Dublin and followed his father into the civil service.[9] His father's early death left O'Nolan to support eleven siblings, but thanks to his salary the family never experienced poverty. At the same time, as a native Irish speaker O'Nolan was conscious of the quasi-mythical link that had been forged by scholars and patriots between economic deprivation and the Irish language. The association formed the basis of his satirical novel *An Béal Bocht*, in which the purest Irish is spoken by starving peasants who are kept artificially segregated from modernity, by government decree, in a fantastic Gaeltacht. Stephens and O'Nolan, then, had radically different experiences of poverty, but shared an intense awareness of the economic basis of relations between classes, between nations, between an author and his readers; and this awareness manifests itself on every page of their strangely linked masterpieces.

The dominant economy of *The Crock of Gold* is a romanticised version of the economics of the working classes, underpinned by the custom of gift exchange among the travellers who throng its rural highways. Men and women in Stephens's Ireland are always sharing bread, as well as advice and information, with random strangers they meet on the road. At one point the protagonist, an elderly philosopher, generously shares his one small cake with seven large labourers, male and female, and is rewarded with the 'larger part' of a food parcel belonging to one of them.[10] Later, when he is hungry again, he meets a young boy who tells him, 'I am bringing you your dinner' and spontaneously hands over another food parcel.[11] The generosity of strangers extends to the courtesies they exchange: verbal equivalents of the material gifts that sustain them on their travels. Having finished the meal donated to him by the boy the Philosopher tells his benefactor, 'I want nothing more in the world [...] except to talk with you', and the two quickly discover there is 'not so much difference' between a child and an old man.[12] Each of these chance encounters – with the boy and with the labourers – concludes with the Philosopher giving the strangers important messages from the Irish god Angus Óg, which serve to bind together the community of the poor in a single purpose: the democratisation of the reawakened Irish nation.

The Third Policeman, by contrast, is dominated by the economics of the middle classes, based on individual self-advancement, a paranoid concern to protect what they take to be their private property (though in this book, property is for the most part theft and the concept of ownership problematic), and a penchant for aggressive competition in all their dealings. The verbal courtesies they exchange are as elaborate as those of Stephens's travellers, but serve the function of a robber's mask as they seek to con conversationalists out of their possessions and even their lives. When the unnamed first person narrator meets a 'poorly dressed' stranger on the road his first reaction is to check that his wallet is safe, after which he decides 'to talk to him genially and civilly' in the hope of coaxing information out of him (*CN*, 256–57). The stranger's courteous replies to the narrator's civility ('More power to yourself') lead inexorably to a threat of murder ('Even if you have no money […] I will take your little life'), which is only averted by the discovery that both men possess an unusual feature in common – each has a wooden left leg (*CN*, 257–60). Shortly afterwards, the friendly welcome the narrator receives at the local police station quickly degenerates into another death threat, when he is arrested and condemned to be hanged for a crime of which there is no evidence that he is guilty.

In O'Nolan's world, too, information is guarded jealously as a source of power, not shared as it is in Stephens's Ireland. Policeman Pluck's second and third rules of wisdom – the only rules he follows that have nothing to do with bicycles – are 'Always ask any questions that are to be asked and never answer any' and 'Turn everything you hear to your own advantage' (*CN*, 272). Meanwhile the driving motive for the narrator's journey is a quest for gold to finance his pet project: the private printing of his otherwise unpublishable book on the unhinged philosopher de Selby, containing information of no conceivable value to anyone but a few scholarly authorities on the man himself, and to its author, of course, who hopes to join their exalted ranks by virtue of his volume. O'Nolan's inversion of Stephens's economy could not be more complete. The competition between individuals and social classes that underpins O'Nolan's novel – in contrast to the communal interests that dominate *The Crock of Gold* – can be summed up in the narrator's contempt, as a would-be scholar, for the intellects of the men he meets ('I decided now that he was a simple man and that I would have no difficulty in dealing with him exactly as I desired'; *CN*, 268), as he kills and lies his way towards the cashbox he requires to fund his project.

Stephens composed *The Crock of Gold* in a ferment of political and personal optimism. The year of its publication, 1912, saw the publication of the other two books that made his name: a quasi-realist novel, *The Charwoman's Daughter*, and the poetry collection that cemented his reputation as one of the finest Irish poets of his generation, *The Hill of Vision*. The immediate success of these volumes prompted Stephens to give up his job as a clerk, acquire an agent, and set off to seek his fortune in Paris.[13] His plans for the future, as the title of his poetry collection suggests, were ambitious. Stephens shared the vision of an independent socialist Ireland with his friends and fellow poets Thomas MacDonagh and Patrick Pearse, both of whom died in the Easter Rising. He dreamed of giving a suitable literary form to this vision by writing a multi-volume epic based on the Ulster Cycle, a work worthy of the richly creative and egalitarian society he expected Ireland to become. But the Free State turned out very different from the Ireland Stephens had imagined, and he completed only fragments of this project. It is therefore his two celebrated prose works of 1912, along with his early lyrics, that best articulate his youthful ambitions for his country.

O'Nolan seems to have been thinking about Stephens a good deal around the time when he was writing *The Third Policeman*. In 1938 he wrote to the older novelist asking permission to translate *The Crock of Gold* into Irish. As Taaffe points out, if this permission had been forthcoming the translation 'would have been his next project after *At Swim-Two-Birds*' – would have taken the place, in fact, of *The Third Policeman* in the chronology of O'Nolan's major works.[14] Stephens's refusal denied twentieth-century Irish literature what might have been one of its collaborative masterpieces; but it also enabled his fiction to undergo some unexpected mutations in the crucible of O'Nolan's imagination. In 1941, for instance, *The Crock of Gold* cropped up in *Cruiskeen Lawn* as one of the prized items on offer to wealthy customers of the Myles na gCopaleen 'book handling' service. In the *de luxe* version of this service, Myles's team of so-called 'master handlers' undertake to upgrade subscribers' private book collections (for a suitable fee) by padding them out with classic volumes, their title pages inscribed with 'forged messages of affection and gratitude from the author of each work', including an expression of esteem from 'Your old friend, James Stephens' (*BM*, 17–24). Stephens's influence may also be detected 'in the erudite dialogues of the Pooka and the Good Fairy' in *At Swim-Two-Birds*, as Taaffe points out, which recall the dialogues between the Philosopher and his brother in *The Crock of Gold*[15]; and in the many bar-room rhetoricians of *Cruiskeen Lawn*, who resemble the sponging old gentleman-philosopher in Stephens's story collection *Here Are Ladies* (1913).[16] It can be traced in O'Nolan's description of Sergeant Pluck, whose 'violent red moustache [...] shot out from his skin far into the air like the antennae of some unusual animal' (*CN*, 267), evoking the red moustache of the equally huge policeman in *The Charwoman's Daughter*, which 'stood out above his lip like wire' so that 'One expected it to crackle when he touched it'.[17] Even the multiple personae O'Nolan adopted might remind us of Stephens's many pen-names, from Tiny Tim to the Leprechaun, James Esse, Jacques and Seumas Beg.

In 1940, O'Nolan accomplished his most extended act of 'translation' from the work of Stephens: *The Third Policeman*, which translates *The Crock of Gold* into terms directly applicable to the global situation at the beginning of a second Great War and at the end of the depression. The fact that this *is* a translation of a sort emerges most clearly in the plot of each novel, which links capitalist economics to the crime of murder. In both books the desire for capital leads to violence; but the route from cash to aggression is quite different in each case, and the relationship between capital, violence and Ireland differs too, in ways that summarise the different worlds in which the authors found themselves.

The plot of *The Crock of Gold* involves a stock of money, the crock of the title; but the coins it contains play only a marginal role in the lives of their owners. The Leprechauns of Gort na Cloca Mora have accumulated the cash as insurance against the greed of mortal men. As one of them explains, 'a Leprecaun [*sic*] has to have a crock of gold so that if he's captured by men folk he may be able to ransom himself'.[18] Their traditional work as shoemakers, by contrast, participates in a non-monetary economy: it is remunerated in kind by mortals through the strict preservation of certain customs, such as leaving out a pan of milk for them on Tuesdays, removing one's hat when faced with a dust-twirl, and observing a pact of non-aggression against their special bird, the robin redbreast. The Leprechauns, then, inhabit a world where one economy is pitted against another, where the competitive thirst for accumulated capital which makes the crock necessary is set against a strategy of mutual cooperation within the working-class community; and the climax of the novel sees an escalation of the conflict between these two economies, with very nearly fatal consequences for Stephens's Philosopher.

The representatives of the capitalist economy in the novel are the policemen, called in by the Leprechauns in the course of a feud with one of their neighbours, Meehawl MacMurrachu, who stole their crock of gold on the Philosopher's advice. In revenge, the Leprechauns frame the Philosopher for the murder of his brother; and the men who come to arrest him bring with them an alien set of values, characterised by a rigid sense of hierarchy and a propensity for violence. Where the rural people in the book's community — mortals, gods and fairies alike — portion out their food and drink with scrupulous fairness, the policemen divide what they have according to rank, with the Sergeant drinking whiskey and his subordinates milk.[19] Where the Philosopher bases his wisdom on the behaviour of birds, beasts and insects on the assumption that all creatures were created equal – an attitude the book endorses by recording the thoughts of donkeys, cows and spiders – the policemen treat dumb animals with brutality, as if to confirm the brutal nature of their own social function. We hear of a policeman's pet jackdaw whose tongue was split with a coin to make it talk and which was accidentally trampled to death by its owner's mother[20]; of a dog that got kicked for counting too long[21]; and of a cat that ate her kittens, about which Policeman Shawn informs us: 'I killed it myself one day with a hammer for I couldn't stand the smell it made, so I couldn't'.[22] Soon after saying this, Policeman Shawn treats one of the Leprechauns with equal aggression. 'Tell me where the money is or I'll twist your neck off', he warns, driven half mad by his lust for fairy gold; and later, 'Tell me where the money is or I'll kill you'.[23] The brutality of Stephens's policemen is connected with money in an endless cycle of cause and effect. And when the Philosopher arrives at their barracks he discovers that the citizens they police, as represented by the prisoners in the cell, have been trapped in a similar cycle, body and mind.

Both prisoners were driven to crime by unfair dismissal from jobs in the city. The first was sacked for non-attendance owing to illness, the second summarily dismissed because of his age. Both men experience unemployment as a brutalising loss of identity, expressed in their exclusion from the system of verbal exchanges that define a community. When the Philosopher first enters the cell, neither man returns his greeting – the only time in the book when a courteous gesture is not reciprocated. The prisoners tell their stories in the dark without giving their names, so it is unclear which man is speaking. And the stories they tell identify inarticulacy as the first symptom of their exclusion from social and economic significance. The sickness of one prisoner manifests itself in an inability to write out words (like Stephens, he is a clerk): 'The end of a word seemed [...] like the conclusion of an event – it was a surprising, isolated, individual thing, having no reference to anything else in the world'.[24] Here, the loss of a coherent written language is the cause of his dismissal from his job, while its effect is that speech too fails him. He stops talking to his wife, and eventually leaves his family without a word of explanation or farewell. For the second prisoner, too, the loss of his job is quickly followed by a loss of articulacy: 'I did not allow my mind to think, but now and again a word swooped from immense distances through my brain, swinging like a comet across a sky and jarring terribly when it struck: "Sacked" was one word, "Old" was another word'.[25] When their income is taken away, each prisoner suffers the concomitant removal of the verbal grammar that binds one term to another and of the social grammar that links one man to his neighbour or to his sense of his own identity in the past.

In the end, it is the improbable intervention of the fairies, gods and heroes of old Ireland that frees these prisoners from the cycle of economic and social exclusion to which they have been condemned. The hosts of the Shee rise up under the leadership of Angus Óg to liberate the Irish workers in a pagan insurrection. And the most striking characteristic of the insurrectionists is their unity-in-diversity, their ability to reconcile individualism with collectivism, exuberance with organisation, as expressed in a universal language:

> For these people, though many, were one. Each spoke to the other as to himself, without reservation or subterfuge. They moved freely each in his personal whim, and they moved also with the unity of one being: for when they shouted to the Mother of the gods they shouted with one voice, and they bowed to her as one man bows. Through the many minds there went also one mind, correcting, commanding, so that in a moment the interchangeable and fluid became locked, and organic with a simultaneous understanding, a collective action – which was freedom.[26]

Stephens here represents the host of Angus Óg as practising a form of instantaneous communication, whereby they understand each other completely without discarding what makes them distinctive: precisely the obverse of the prisoners' isolation and anonymity. And this language aspires to be uttered beyond the confines of Stephens's narrative. The chapter in which the insurrection takes place is the only one with its own title, 'The Happy March', as if to ensure that its contents can be detached from the novel and deployed as the imaginative blueprint, or at least the incidental music, for an actual Irish insurrection of the kind that took place in 1916. Stephens's book, in other words, opens up at the end, offering its contents as common currency to the Irish people in a generously inclusive gesture of the kind with which it is filled, in an attempt to liberate them by example from the prison of their colonised minds.[27]

O'Nolan's novel, by contrast, affirms the continued entrapment of the Irish people. It reverses the class positions of the police and the novel's protagonist, forcing the reader to take the point of view of a *petit bourgeois* social climber instead of that selfless (if somewhat arrogant) servant of the community, Stephens's Philosopher. In contrast to the courteous and curious

Philosopher, O'Nolan's narrator feels only disdain for those he thinks of as his social inferiors – including the police. He too is a philosopher, but a parasitic one who seeks to accumulate cultural capital by publishing a wholly derivative volume, an index to the works of the incoherent *savant* de Selby. And de Selby himself is the polar opposite of Stephens's genial pedant: a solipsist who refuses to engage in dialogue with other thinkers, and who sees human existence not as a single organic entity but as a series of disconnected moments – 'a succession of static experiences each infinitely brief' (*CN*, 263) – each as detached from adjacent moments as he is from the rest of the human species. Where Stephens's Philosopher draws on the collective wisdom of beasts, children and ordinary people to develop his theories, de Selby rejects any form of consensus: he 'would question the most obvious realities and object even to things scientifically demonstrated' (*CN*, 265). And his works conduct their readers not to enlightenment but bloodshed. In the last of many footnotes on de Selby in the novel we see one of his commentators set out with bombs and guns to kill his German rival because they disagree on how the great man's writings are to be interpreted (*CN*, 373–76, n. 1). The link between this philosophy of exclusivity and obfuscation and the rise of Nazism is confirmed in an earlier footnote, where de Selby claims to be able to 'state the physiological "group" of any person merely from a brief study of the letters of his name' and avers that 'Certain "groups" [are] universally "repugnant" to other "groups"' (*CN*, 254, n. 3). One race or family, then, gets segregated from another in de Selby's thinking, just as one moment in time gets divorced from the next; so it is hardly surprising if the narrator of O'Nolan's novel, as the great man's acolyte, finds himself increasingly alienated from other people in the course of the narrative, baffled by their discourse, convinced that his private interests are opposed to theirs and prepared to kill to assert his own intellectual and economic superiority over those around him.[28]

Where Stephens locates his genial Philosopher in a gift exchange economy, O'Nolan ensures that his narrator-philosopher is acutely conscious that he lives in a cutthroat capitalist environment. He knows (as does the reader) exactly how his research on de Selby is funded – through the farm and the failing pub he inherits from his parents – and how the income from these combined resources is not enough to fund the publication of his Index. He imagines the contents of the cashbox for which he kills old Mathers not as gold but as 'Ten thousand pounds' worth of negotiable securities' such as stocks and bonds (*CN*, 251), so that for all his claim to be absorbed in matters of the mind he knows the market intimately. And he plans to use these assets not for some collective benefit but to enhance his financial and social worth as an individual, despite the fact that neither the cashbox nor the book he has written is his own: the cashbox belongs to Mathers and the book is made up of quotations from other writers, since in it 'the views of all known commentators on every aspect of the savant and his work had been collated' (*CN*, 229). The only forms of interaction with the community he undertakes, in fact, are competitive, and even his conversation entails a constant jockeying for position, a quest for the upper hand that merely sinks him deeper and deeper into a self-imposed confinement of body and mind.

In O'Nolan's novel, as in Stephens's, philosophers set out on journeys across an unspecified Irish landscape made up of rolling hills and bogland and populated by labourers, policemen, beasts and fantastical beings. But where Stephens's Philosopher, true to his convictions, travels in order to put right the wrong he did when he gave poor advice to Meehawl MacMurrachu, O'Nolan's travels for personal profit. Where Stephens's Philosopher encounters many women on his journey and engages in conversations with them about male–female companionship, O'Nolan's encounters only men, the closest he comes to female companionship being with an exquisitely proportioned bicycle (designed for a man, with a crossbar), which he thinks of as utterly compliant – a common sexist male fantasy.[29] Where Stephens's Philosopher draws abundant conclusions from his experiences on his travels, changing his opinions on many subjects as he walks, O'Nolan's narrator constantly fantasises about people and objects and has a tendency to forget everything that has just happened. 'If that watch of mine were found you would be welcome to it', he tells his departing soul at one point, to which his soul answers dryly, '*But you have no watch*' (*CN*, 368). This forgetfulness means he is incapable of reaping enlightenment from his adventures. In any case, with every step he moves further into a world powered by strange machines whose fabrication and functions defy analysis – such as the light boxes constructed by Policeman MacCruiskeen or the mysterious engines tended by the police beneath the ground – and which therefore fail to illustrate any universal laws.

On his journey to put right his mistake in misadvising Meehawl, Stephens's Philosopher makes his way into caves where gods dwell. In the first cave he encounters the Greek god Pan, in the second Angus Óg, the Celtic god of youth; and each deity presents him with something of value. Pan gives him a pleasure in his senses, Angus makes him his messenger to mortals, investing him with a sociability he did not possess before, a consciousness of and a keen interest in his place in the wider community. O'Nolan's philosopher, too, enters spaces like caves: an underground 'eternity' and a secret policeman's barracks in a house's walls; but in each he finds only policemen, personifications of an inescapable authority which is repudiated by the gods of Stephens, who ask only that mortals choose between them. Stephens's Philosopher has to negotiate terrifying darkness and discomfort to reach Angus's cave: 'He could not see an inch in front, and so he went with his hands outstretched like a blind man who stumbles painfully along'.[30] O'Nolan's narrator is similarly afflicted as he approaches the entrance to the underground eternity: 'I [...] followed the noisy Sergeant with blind faith till my strength was nearly gone, so that I reeled forward instead of walking and was defenceless against the brutality of the boughs' (*CN*, 335). But in each of the cave-like spaces the narrator enters, the underground 'eternity' and the secret barracks, he discovers truths about himself which he never acknowledges – in marked contrast to Stephens's protagonist, who not only recognises the worth of what the gods show him but also seeks to share this recognition with strangers on his way home.

What O'Nolan's narrator discovers in his two 'caves' is his own anonymity, which arises from his myopic obsession with accumulating financial and cultural capital. When he enters eternity in the wake of Sergeant Pluck he converts everything he sees into financial terms – in contrast with Stephens's Philosopher, who converts what he sees into topics of conversation and quirky aphorisms. For the narrator, eternity is a giant cashbox full of 'safe-deposits such as banks have', 'expensive-looking cabinets' and 'American cash registers' (*CN*, 339–40). When he finds he can get what he wants there, he can think only of ordering a 'solid block of gold weighing half a ton', which he afterwards exchanges for a more practical quantity of valuables: 'fifty cubes of solid gold each weighing one pound' and 'precious stones to the value of £200,000' (*CN*, 343–44). As he warms to the task of exploiting his miraculous environment, the narrator acquires the accessories of the ultimate capitalist icon, a futuristic Hollywood gangster robbing a bank vault. Along with the valuables he orders a blue serge suit and a weapon capable of killing 'any man or any million men who try at any time to take my life', thus transforming himself into a feeble imitation of James Cagney – its feebleness confirmed by the fact that he forgets to ask for a bag to hold his loot (Sergeant Pluck obligingly gets him one 'worth at least fifty guineas in the open market') (*CN*, 344–45). This excursion into cinematic fantasy confirms the link between his capitalist values and an early death; Cagney always dies young in his 1930s' gangster movies (as in *The Public Enemy*, *Angels with Dirty Faces* and *The Roaring Twenties*). The cinematic fantasy confirms too the groundlessness of the narrator's sense of superiority to the rustic police. No Hollywood gangster of the 1930s or 1940s was permitted to profit from his crimes, and it comes as no surprise when the policemen spring their trap, informing him that he cannot take any of his precious commodities back to the world above. And it also links him, almost incidentally, to the atrocities of global conflict. The weapon he orders can kill a million men as easily as one. The narrator's glib way with numbers, in other words, permits him to gloss mass murder as self-preservation, yoking the capitalist mentality he represents to the outbreak of the Second World War.

The second point in the novel at which the narrator shows his true *petit bourgeois* colours comes at the end, when he finally meets the mysterious third policeman of the title. On learning that the cashbox he is looking for contains the substance omnium – the building material from which anything and everything in the universe may be constructed – and on finding that Policeman Fox has confirmed his ownership of the box, the narrator launches into an extended series of fantasies about what he will do with its contents. While dismissing the pettiness of Policeman Fox's deployment of the omnium (he uses it to make strawberry jam and to improve the décor of his barracks), the narrator dreams of exploiting it to resolve the various more or less petty problems that have arisen in his own narrative, as related in the novel. And while each of his plans begins by sounding benevolent – giving John Divney 'ten million pounds' to make him go away, presenting 'every poor labourer in the world' with a golden bicycle – when he turns to thoughts of revenge on Sergeant Pluck his dreams mutate into nightmares (*CN*, 394–95). Once again his thoughts revert to the underground eternity, where his hopes of enriching himself were raised and dashed, and he proceeds to convert this mysterious space in his imagination from an Aladdin's cave to a sadist's cellar, with 'millions of diseased and decayed monsters clawing the inside latches of the ovens to open them and escape' and 'rats with horns walking upside down along the ceiling pipes trailing their leprous tails on the policemen's heads' (*CN*, 396). His grandiose projects are as limited as Policeman Fox's little ones, and infinitely more damaging, since they are dedicated only to arranging time and space to his own private satisfaction.

Ironically, the narrator's desire to differentiate himself from the other characters serves only to render him more anonymous – a tissue of financial and filmic clichés of the kind Myles na gCopaleen mocked in *Cruiskeen Lawn*. Many of Stephens's characters, too, are anonymous, in that they are nameless. But while the namelessness of his two prisoners confirms their exclusion from social discourse, the namelessness of other characters in *The Crock of*

Gold (the Philosopher, the Thin Woman, the Leprechauns, the women, men and children met on the road) identifies them as *representative*: quasi-allegorical symbols of a vibrant nation that is moving towards a new collective identity. The namelessness of the narrator in *The Third Policeman* confirms instead his biddable nature, his tendency to mutate into the person with whom he is currently in conversation, effectively losing himself in the process, to disastrous effect. When working on de Selby the narrator imbibes the selfish, irascible and amoral personality traits of his subject – with the result that he becomes capable of murder. So, too, he becomes indistinguishable from his devious friend John Divney, locked together with him in a horrifying pastiche of Ciceronian amity whereby each is the other's self, sharing bed and board while steadily winding each other up into an intense mutual hatred.[31] When speaking to Martin Finnucane, the narrator becomes the sworn brother of this one-legged murderer, without noticing or caring for the moral implications of their casual bonding. And when conversing with Sergeant Pluck and Policeman MacCruiskeen, he adopts their stylistic eccentricities in his narrative as well as in his conversation. Helplessly driven by the impulses of his chameleon disposition, the narrator mingles his personality with those of everyone else he meets, as if to confirm the tendency of Ireland and Europe in the 1930s to follow disastrous models and totalitarian authorities, large and small, with slavish admiration.

The narrator's namelessness, then, is that of Stephens's prisoners rather than his representative types. Unlike the prisoners, he is not excluded from conversation; but his most honest and satisfactory conversations are with himself, or rather with his soul, who has a name, Joe, and who is always on the verge of leaving him. Joe's disembodied voice, speaking to the narrator in the gloom of old Mathers's house as the narrator confronts the ghost of the man he murdered, might remind us of the disembodied voices of the prisoners who speak to the Philosopher out of the dark of the cell. In that episode the Philosopher, too, found himself unsure of his identity for the first time in his experience as the boundaries of his mind began to dissolve: 'The creatures of the dark invaded him, fantastic terrors were thronging on every side: they came from the darkness into his eyes and beyond into himself, so that his mind as well as his fancy was captured, and he knew he was, indeed, in gaol'.[32] This sense of the encroaching dissolution or erasure of the self resonates throughout *The Third Policeman*, especially in moments of darkness: the stormy dawn before the narrator's hanging, for example, or the terrible moment when he wakes from sleep to find himself blind, before recalling that his eyes were bound by Policeman MacCruiskeen before he nodded off.

The flip side of the narrator's desire to distinguish himself from others is the fear of losing his identity altogether; a fear substantiated on the last page of the novel, where he finds himself recommencing all his adventures – having forgotten them first, as is his wont[33] – in the company of one of his many doubles in the narrative, John Divney, as if there were no difference between him and his friend.

Most striking of O'Nolan's inversions of *The Crock of Gold* is what he does to the body. As an athlete – he was a gymnast – Stephens sought in all his work to liberate the body from the constraints imposed on it by the churches, Catholic and Protestant alike. Meehawl MacMurrachu's daughter Caitilin spends most of the novel in a state of Edenic nakedness, and although the Philosopher begins by disapproving he quickly reasons himself into acquiescence with her choice. 'If a person does not desire to be [...] protected who will quarrel with an honourable liberty?' he asks himself; 'Decency is not clothing but Mind'.[34] Soon afterwards he finds himself exulting for the first time in the energy of his own body: 'Years had toppled from his shoulders. He left one pound of solid matter behind at every stride. His very skin grew flexuous, and he found a pleasure in taking long steps such as he could not have accounted for by thought'.[35] O'Nolan's characters, too, are defined by their bodies; but in the policemen's case these are grotesquely, massively physical, always on the verge of heart attacks or seizures, brought on by their relentless consumption of candy and jam as well as excessive quantities of the stirabout that sustained the rural poor in *The Crock of Gold*. The narrator, on the other hand, is small and skinny, like the Philosopher; but where the Philosopher's emaciated frame testified to his hunger – the quality that brings the working classes together in solidarity when they share their meals[36] – the narrator's thinness and feeble appetite demonstrates his radical disconnection from people and things. The policemen's delight in food serves only to awake his snobbish disgust, whether at the effect their greed has on their monstrous bodies or at their inability to extend their imaginations beyond the narrow confines of the relative merits of different sweeties, the tastiness of stirabout, or the possibility of making strawberry jam out of the most powerful substance in the universe.

All of O'Nolan's bodies are ill-constructed machines, whose capacity to harbour sympathy or affection has been compromised by the discoveries of science. Sergeant Pluck's atomic theory depicts the world as a concatenation of samenesses, an arrangement of particles which merely get rearranged when a person dies, so that executing an acquaintance is no more problematic than devouring a bowlful of porridge (*CN*, 293ff). The narrator's leg is a symptom of this loss of affect in O'Nolan's universe. At one point he is afraid its woodenness is spreading through his torso, just as the atoms of bicycles spread into the bottoms of their riders. In *The Crock of Gold*, the goat-god Pan's half-bestial body insists on the animal sensuality which is part of our heritage as human beings and which enjoins us to delight in the sentient donkeys, cows and flies with whom the Philosopher comes in contact. But in *The Third Policeman*, John Divney's innocent, cow-like eyes conceal a vicious disposition,[37] and human beings have more in common with machines than animals. The Parish policed by Sergeant Pluck is populated with half-human, half-bicycle cyborgs, though none of these hybrids are as bereft of fellow-feeling as the narrator, who has become fused with de Selby's books, his mind stocked, like de Selby's pages, with useless inventions of no conceivable benefit to anyone but the ego of the inventor and his adoring commentators. As a result of this fusion, the narrator's substantial funds of pity are reserved for himself, and he sheds abundant tears over his own predicament. The only close relationship he forges (if one discounts his friendship with Joe, who is an aspect of himself) is with a bicycle, which he converts into a fantasy of female acquiescence, a willing, voiceless servant that mechanically submits to his every whim. Stephens's collaborative Ireland has been left far behind, a vision that has been outpaced by the speed of scientific and technological progress, hurtling the world towards conflict.

Nowhere is the difference between the books more evident than in their endings. O'Nolan's version of Stephens's 'The Happy March' involves an apparent liberation, in which the nameless narrator sails off into the night astride the Sergeant's bicycle, a *dea ex machina* (so to speak) in total harmony with her environment: 'all the time she was under me in a flawless racing onwards, touching the road with the lightest touches, surefooted, straight and faultless, each of her metal bars like spear-shafts superbly cast by angels' (*CN*, 380). Together man and bicycle liberate themselves first from Sergeant Pluck's barracks, then from the smaller police station presided over by Policeman Fox; and in the final section they even free Divney from the constraints of his grotesque mortal body, as if in imitation of Angus Óg's liberation of the Irish workers in *The Crock of Gold* ('Come away! come away! from the loom and the desk, from the shop where the carcasses are hung, from the place where raiment is sold and the place where it is sewn in darkness').[38] But this chain of liberations is an illusion. Unlike the Philosopher, the narrator and John Divney are guilty of their crimes, and both are undead rather than exuberantly alive by the end of the novel, trapped for all time in the cyclical jail of their forward momentum. As a result, where Stephens ends his book not so much with a march – happy or otherwise – as with a dance ('they returned again, dancing and singing, to the country of the gods'),[39] *The Third Policeman* ends with the narrator and Divney 'marching' in unison into Sergeant Pluck's police station – the place from which the narrator 'escaped' only pages before. Their mechanical, quasi-military return to the barracks aligns the novel as a whole with those 'adventure books' mentioned by the narrator in his conversations with Policeman Fox 'in which every extravagance was mechanical and lethal and solely concerned with bringing about somebody's death in the most elaborate way imaginable' (*CN*, 395). It would hardly have escaped O'Nolan's readers that Europe in 1940 could have been described in similar terms.

The comparison of the 'metal bars' of Sergeant Pluck's winsome bicycle to the 'spear-shafts superbly cast by angels' recalls the spears flung down by stars in William Blake's revolutionary poem *The Tyger*, from *Songs of Innocence and of Experience*. James Stephens was a self-professed Blakean visionary,[40] who sought in his poetry to adapt the Londoner's proto-socialist vision to the needs of an Irish insurrection (*Insurrections* was the title of Stephens's first collection of verse, in 1909, and his book on the 1916 Easter Rising was titled *The Insurrection in Dublin*). Brian O'Nolan, on the other hand, was a Swiftian satirist, for whom experience had long blotted out the possibility of recapturing or even celebrating innocence (as captured in titles such as *An Béal Bocht* and *The Hard Life*). But it is the memory of innocence, I would like to suggest – the beautifully crafted innocence of *The Crock of Gold* – that gives *The Third Policeman* its astonishing vitality and poignancy. The two books should be read in tandem.

9

The ideal and the ironic

incongruous Irelands in *An Béal Bocht, No Laughing Matter* and Ciarán Ó Nualláin's *Óige an Dearthár*

Ian Ó Caoimh

Among the papers of the composer Seán Ó Riada in the library of University College Cork there is a typescript dramatisation of Myles na gCopaleen's *An Béal Bocht*,[1] probably the script of the version which was taken off after the opening night at the Peacock Theatre, Dublin on 18 July 1967.[2] There are few notes on the script, but a handwritten line has been inserted in the middle of Bónapárt's opening speech: 'CHORUS: *Ní bheidh ár leithéidí arís ann*' [Our likes will not exist again].[3] However tantalising the idea of an unrealised musical version of *An Béal Bocht* by one of Ireland's foremost composers, the concept of the chorus is fitting for a phrase which continues in Irish life, in sites ranging from respectful codas to newspaper obituaries to knowingly self-referential t-shirt slogans. Discussing *An Béal Bocht* as regional literature, Máirín Nic Eoin recasts the phrase to ask whether the likes of Corca Dhorcha itself 'will ever be there again'. Nic Eoin points to the failure of Myles's parodic novel to influence the content or the continued output of the very type of autobiography it satirised, citing a lack of interest in *An Béal Bocht*, a shortage of literary ability and a narrow regionalism among the reasons for this failure.[4] For all of Bónapárt Ó Cúnasa's catalogue of endangered uniquenesses in Gaelic life, it seems, there subsequently proved to be no shortage of same.

For others, the achievement of *An Béal Bocht* lies not in its (apparently unavailing) influence on future writers of Irish autobiography, but rather in its influence on future readers of the genre. To read Bónapárt's *faux* autobiography is to participate in the application of dramatic irony and derive satisfaction as a third, minor party in a sophisticated exercise of subterfuge. Yet, once we have got the point and enjoyed the humour, we must be wary of categorising the text in ways that confine it to its own contextual sphere or linguistic medium and thus limit its potential satirical reach or discourage readers from revisiting it from new perspectives. For if the novel's achievement as a satire of Irish autobiographies and 'bad faith' *Gaeilgeoirí* seems secure, an attendant risk of submitting to the authority of such inherited readings and certainties, as with the inhabitants of Corca Dhorca and '*na dea-leabhair*' [the good books] (*ABB*, 56), may be to overlook its wider warning of the need for vigilance when dealing with all forms of (auto)biographical portraiture, including those of the author himself.

In line with *An Béal Bocht*'s lesson that received wisdom must be questioned not once and for all but as an ongoing concern, in this essay I want to re-evaluate the authority of biography and autobiography in Ó Nualláin studies and consider how the lessons of *An Béal Bocht* might continue to apply to the processes of Brian Ó Nualláin criticism itself. To these ends, I contrast Ciarán Ó Nualláin's oft-overlooked biography of his brother, *Óige an Dearthár .i. Myles na gCopaleen* (1973), with Anthony Cronin's more commonly cited *No Laughing Matter: The Life and Times of Flann O'Brien* (1989). Exploring the question of a family style between the Ó Nualláin brothers and casting light in particular on the cross-referential, at times collaborative relationship between Brian and Ciarán's writing, I demonstrate that some of the most drawn-upon passages in Ciarán's biography concerning his and Brian's youthful trips to the Gaeltacht have been fundamentally misinterpreted by Cronin and others. Against charges that Ciarán is idealising his subject, I argue that his stance rather suggests parallels with the refashioning of mythological material in *At Swim-Two-Birds* and carries a subversive intent which evokes and bolsters the satire of *An Béal Bocht*. In contesting not only their validity but also the authority such readings claim when they wrap themselves in the mantle of 'biography', I will suggest that the success of *An Béal Bocht* has not prevented Ó Nualláin's own biographers and critics from presuming themselves at times to be immune from the satirical objective of Myles's novel. Specifically, I will point to a number of key passages in which Ó Nualláin's later biographers and critics relapse into a characterisation of the Gaeltacht that forces Brian and

Ciarán's shrewd, carnivalesque representations of that liminal cultural and linguistic space into a reductive binary between the 'real' and the 'idealised'.

Am I my brothers' collaborator?

Ciarán Ó Nualláin was born in 1910, one year before Brian, whom he outlived by almost twenty years. In the same year in which *At Swim-Two-Birds* appeared, Ciarán published his own novel, *Oidhche i nGleann na nGealt* [*A Night in Madmen's Glen*] (1939), featuring a Holmesian hero named Parthalán Mac Mórna. Alan Titley writes that as one of the first of its type in Irish, *Oidhche i nGleann na nGealt* was a satisfactory example of the detective novel ('*Tús thar a bheith sásúil sa Ghaeilge ar an bhfoirm a shaothrú ba ea* Oidhche i nGleann na nGealt'). However, typically of the standing of most detective fiction, Titley does not rank it among what he calls the '*úrscéalta láidre fiúntacha*' [strong, worthwhile novels][5] also emanating from the state publisher An Gúm.[6] The *Oxford Companion to Irish Literature* makes stronger claims for *Amaidí* [Nonsense], Ciarán's columns from *Inniu*, the Irish-language weekly newspaper which he co-founded in 1943 and edited until 1979, contending that they 'rival his brother in wit'.[7] Of Micheál Victor Ó Nualláin, the siblings' father, the editors of the biographical series *Beathaisnéis* acknowledge '*gur beag fear eile a thóg beirt mhac a d'iompódh amach ina máistrí ar phrós na Gaeilge a scríobh*' [that few other men raised two sons who would turn out to be master-writers of Irish prose].[8]

The closeness of Brian and Ciarán's aesthetics may be seen in '*Cúrsaí Báis!*' [Matters of Death!], which Ciarán published in *The New Irish Magazine/An Sgeulaidhe Nuadh* around the time of *Blather*.[9] Anticipating the language of *An Béal Bocht* in places, Ciarán's mischievous short story brings together and sends up some of the formulaic techniques of oral literature and personages of Irish folklore, including the intermingling of fiction and folklore found in An tAthair Peadar Ua Laoghaire's *Séadna*, a text which would be explicitly referenced in *An Béal Bocht*'s satire of '*na dea-leabhair*'. Echoing the metafictionality of Brian's early Brother Barnabas pieces, the reader is also at one point addressed directly in a knowing mixture of flattery and invitation: '*Agus anois a léightheóir chóir, cuir ort do hata agus do chóta mór, óir caithfidh muid bualadh amach faoi doineann na h-oidhche ar feadh bómaite, go bhfeicfidh muid cé seo tá ag teacht aniar an bóthar chugainn. Féach romhat – creidim go bhfuil radharc géar agat – agus innis damh cé tchí tú*' [And now dear reader, put on your hat and overcoat for we must set off into the stormy night for a minute, to see who approaches us on the road from the west. Look ahead of you – I believe you are sharp-sighted – and tell me whom you see].[10]

Beyond the comparative aspect of their literary outputs, the collaborative dimension of the brothers' creative projects remains to be fully considered. Joseph Brooker has examined the anarchic, surreal spirit of Ciarán and Brian's byline-swopping close cooperation in the 1930s' college magazine *Comhthrom Féinne* and its graduate successor *Blather*,[11] – but their collaboration began before, and extended well beyond, these subversive Dadaesque publishing enterprises. Louis de Paor has raised the possibility that Ciarán's involvement in the late 1930s and early 1940s with the precursor to the fascist *Ailtirí na hAiséirghe* [Architects of the Resurrection] movement[12] may have damaged the brothers' relationship and influenced Brian's later decision to write only in English, particularly given *Ailtirí na hAiséirghe*'s association of the Irish language with its objective of fascist rule in Ireland and Myles na gCopaleen's criticisms of the movement's racist public speeches in *Cruiskeen Lawn*.[13] However, by the 1950s Brian could be found writing for *Inniu* under Ciarán's editorship, and Ciarán attempting a Keats and Chapman sketch in Irish in the paper, titled 'Keatman and Chaps', which he admitted was substandard.[14]

There was a third Ó Nualláin son who was also a writer of Irish prose, though much less prolifically so than his brothers: Caoimhín Ó Nualláin (Kevin O'Nolan), a folklorist and lecturer in Classics at University College Dublin and the editor of *The Best of Myles* (1968), *Further Cuttings from Cruiskeen Lawn* (1976) and *The Hair of the Dogma: A Further Selection from 'Cruiskeen Lawn'* (1977). Between the mid-1940s and the early 1950s, Caoimhín published a handful of pieces in the monthly magazine *Comhar* under the title 'Nuacht ón Ghealtacht'. These pieces also show some distinct similarities to Ciarán's *Amaidí* essays and Brian's *Cruiskeen Lawn* and *An Béal Bocht*, including elements of metafiction and surreality; elaborate puns; genre fiction parodies; intermingled languages, dialects and registers; Irish-language *bricolages* which demonstrate the cut-and-paste aesthetic of *At Swim-Two-Birds*; courtroom settings; and the near-obligatory reference to *Séadna*.[15] Even though Caoimhín's time as a columnist with *Comhar* was brief, the cross-sibling referential aesthetic appears to have been intact as late as 1987 in an article he published explaining how a storyteller's audience placed more value on long formulaic runs in folktales if they contained an element of mystery or obscurity. Caoimhín notes that the act of borrowing 'passages from a higher tradition led directly to corruptions which once received were impossible to alter and hence lack of comprehension led to admiration for the *crua-Ghaeilg*, the "hard Irish" of the storyteller'[16] – a formulation which brings to mind the scholar who visits Corca Dhorcha to record obscure dialect samples, for he understands *'go mbíonn an dea-Ghaeilge deacair agus an Ghaeilge is fearr beagnach dothuigthe'* [that good Irish is hard and the best Irish almost incomprehensible] (*ABB*, 36).[17]

These echoes and cross-references point to a key affinity in the three brothers' aesthetics: namely, the representation of Irish-speaking localities, both real and imagined, as places apart where the figurative is taken literally and the surreal implications explored. In the standard construct of the Gaeltacht we find a particularly Irish locale for Rousseau's eighteenth-century concept of the 'noble savage',[18] or rather a locus where that contrivance is superimposed onto the less palatable reality beneath. Since the beginning of the Revival period in the late nineteenth century, the topography, dialects and conditions of the coastal Gaeltacht regions had become newly emblematic. In the period of approximately fifty years since the end of the famine, the interest European philologists had been taking in Celtic studies began feeding into the domestic tradition, coming from an interest in the same language which in the popular mind was now predominantly a reminder of an impoverished past, a millstone to be shed in favour of the social mobility which English might forcibly provide. While this scholarly interest had some undoubtedly positive effects, it is its aspic-antiquarian strain, which perceives these districts as no more than repositories of peasant purity, that is satirised so successfully in the composite, distorted Gaeltacht of *An Béal Bocht*, in which the utopian totem of the island manifests itself repeatedly. We see it in the geographically impossible visibility from Corca Dhorcha of the three main Gaeltacht regions – whose main representative islands (the Blasket, Aran and Tory) are shown on the putative map that accompanies the text – and in the illustration of the *Cat Mara*, which is of course just a slightly tweaked map of Ireland rotated.[19] Yet this is a theme common to all three brothers' writing. Place names signal the uncanny particularity of these localities: as the action of *An Béal Bocht* takes place in the strange double of the Gaeltacht that is Corca Dhorcha,[20] so many of Ciarán's *Amaidí* adventures unfold in a place called Muileann na Mire [literally, Mill of Madness]. Reference is also made to Droim Dorcha, which shares the 'dark' element of *An Béal Bocht*'s topography, and to a place called Achadh Dhá Nóinín [The Field of Two Daisies], surely a deflationary echo of Brian's *Snámh Dá Éan*/Swim-Two-Birds. Furthermore, the title of Caoimhín's column, *'Nuacht ón Ghealtacht'*, is a pun on the word *Gaeltacht*, 'Irish-speaking area', which in a visual sleight of hand becomes *Gealt-acht*, an 'area of madness'.[21] In each of these liminal spaces, what is implicit but overlooked in the conventions of the 'real world' – and in the careless use of language, in particular – is followed through by the strict application of the logic of ironic doubling and carnivalesque reversal. As a consequence, the reader (like the scholar who visits Corca Dhorcha) is always at risk of, and must remain vigilant against, uncritically accepting the ways in which the subject is mediated in these ostensible '(auto)biographies'. This risk is particularly pronounced in the case of readers imbued with the cultural authority to summarise and refract the text's meaning: in particular, translators, biographers and critics.

The scope for such readerly lapses regarding his brothers' work was noted by Caoimhín in his response to Patrick C. Power's translation of *An Béal Bocht* as *The Poor Mouth: A Bad Story about the Hard Life* in 1973. Drawing on archival correspondence housed in Boston College, Maebh Long has shown that Caoimhín was among those dissatisfied with Power's version, finding it 'a little too easy going. It is not always faithful in detail and though this may not always matter there is danger of overlooking small points'.[22] The 'danger of overlooking small points' is of great thematic importance in the work of Brian, Ciarán and Caoimhín, whether operating singly or jointly, and this theme is continually revived beyond and between the borders of the brothers' texts when subsequent translations, biographies and critical readings intervene in their collaborative aesthetic yet fail to account fully for the ironised double-exposure of their representations of the Gaeltacht.

Self impressions

Even as critical studies of Brian Ó Nualláin multiply, the authoritative book-length biography remains Anthony Cronin's *No Laughing Matter: The Life and Times of Flann O'Brien* (1989).[23] Given this air of authority, Cronin's study has often crowded out Ciarán Ó Nualláin's earlier *Óige an Dearthár .i. Myles na gCopaleen* (1973), a collection of occasional (auto)biographical articles on the author's brother Brian, originally published in *Inniu*. Until recently, and notwithstanding an English translation by Ciarán's sister Róisín Ní Nualláin as *The Early Years of Brian O'Nolan/Flann O'Brien/Myles na gCopaleen* (1998),[24] *Óige an Dearthár* has been seen mostly as a quirky complement to Cronin's biographical monolith. Increasingly, the significance of its insights is being recognised, however here I want to argue more narrowly that its conceived shortcomings as biography, as articulated most forcefully by Anthony Cronin, John Cronin and Louis de Paor, are due to the fact that its sense of the (auto) biographical is more in tune with that of *An Béal Bocht* and the objects of that book's satire than these later critics acknowledge or perceive.

In his study *Self Impression: Life-Writing, Autobiografiction, and the Forms of Modern Literature*, Max Saunders refers to 'the ways in which these categories of autobiography, biography, fiction, and criticism begin to interact, combining and disrupting each other in new ways, from the late nineteenth century to the early twentieth'.[25] Saunders highlights 'the inevitable overlappings of genres, since genres are not pure entities' and sets out as his main argument that 'from the 1870s to the 1930s autobiography increasingly aspires to the condition of fiction'.[26] This overlapping of 'autobiography, biography, fiction, and criticism' captures perfectly the hybrid genre of *An Béal Bocht*, itself a fictionalised parody of the Gaeltacht autobiography genre, replete with supposed critical paratexts by its 'editor' Myles na gCopaleen. Notwithstanding Saunders's analysis, it is an adherence to a convention of blending truth and fiction that makes the Gaeltacht autobiographies distinctive. For Cathal Ó Háinle, the seeming discrepancies between historical facts and the accounts in some Irish autobiographies originate in the authors' perception of themselves as emanating from the *seanchas* genre ('lore' or popular tradition) of oral literature.[27] Accordingly, they see themselves having not only a licence but also an obligation to embellish their stories so as to improve the version of events they give; to do otherwise would be a disservice to the audience. In light of this reading, the exaggeration and sentimentality of the works parodied in *An Béal Bocht* – and, as we shall see, echoed in *Óige an Dearthár* – may not seem entirely unselfaware. Among the various fates which Brian claimed had befallen the rejected manuscript of *The Third Policeman* – with its own unusual liminal space in the form of The Parish – was a 'fanciful story about it being blown page by page out of the boot of a car during a trip' to the Donegal Gaeltacht.[28] The specific location of this tall tale in the Gaeltacht region most familiar to the brothers suggests an intriguing overlap between the speculative and the autobiographical in the Ó Nualláin family style.

While not an autobiography *per se*, *Óige an Dearthár* is primarily biographical and contains much that is autobiographical. And yet, critics have noted a certain evasiveness in its descriptions. Brendan Duffin's review of the English translation of *Óige an Dearthár* in 1999 called the book a 'quaint curio' which 'reveals more by what it does not say', yet which ultimately fails to produce any evidence to support Ciarán's claim that the impulse that gave rise to *An Béal Bocht*[29] was the outward expression of innate ability: '*Sé an fáth ar scríobhadh* An Béal Bocht *gur mhothaigh fear óg go raibh bua grinn ar leith aige a bhí ag tonnadh aníos agus go gcaithfeadh sé a ligean amach nó pléascadh'* [The reason *An Béal Bocht* was written was because a young man felt he had a particular talent for humour which was welling up and which he had to release or explode].[30] In the closing chapter of *Óige an Dearthár*, John Cronin summarises, Ciarán 'rounds on readers who describe [*An Béal Bocht*] as a satire and *rather naively* asserts that, since Brian enjoyed his boyhood visits to the Donegal Gaeltacht, he would have been unlikely to satirize the place and its people' [my emphasis].[31] I want to challenge this charge of naiveté in Ciarán's response to *An Béal Bocht*, by highlighting the ways in which *Óige an Dearthár* evinces the genre-overlapping described by Saunders and in places deploys this generic strategy to further the satirical goals of *An Béal Bocht* in deconstructing the idealising impulse of the coastal, westward, purifying, nostalgic thrust of Romanticism and Utopianism. It is true that the irony and cynicism of the brothers' representations of the coastal Gaeltacht regions were shot through with a familiarity with, and affection for, the area's geography, people and dialect, as evidenced in Ciarán's later claim that Brian's parodies of Tomás Ó Criomhthain's *An tOileánach* in *An Béal Bocht* came from 'exuberance, not malice'.[32] However, more significantly, their shared awareness of its socio-economic conditions enabled a more considered exploration of the region's surreal aspects, both in reality and in the public imagination shaped by literary and (auto)biographical accounts.

Alternative Ulsters

In *Óige an Dearthár*, Ciarán emphasises the occasion on which he, Brian and another brother, Gearóid, took their first trip to the Donegal Gaeltacht: '*Creidim gur chomh luath leis an bhliain 1927 a thug Brian, Gearóid agus mise ár gcéad chuairt ar Ghaeltacht Thír Chonaill, ar Chloch Cheannaola. Bhíomar fós ar scoil i mBaile Átha Cliath san am*' [I believe it was as early as 1927 that Brian, Gearóid and myself made our first visit to the Donegal Gaeltacht, to Cloughaneely. We were still in school in Dublin at the time].[33] He also refers to a separate visit he and Brian made with friends around 1929:

> *Timpeall na bliana 1929* [...] *chuireamar romhainn turas rothaíochta agus campála a dhéanamh go Gaeltacht Thír Chonaill, agus coicís nó mar sin a chaitheamh faoi chanbhás ann. Cúigear againn a chuaigh ar an turas seo* [...]. *Ar Ghort an Choirce i gCloich Cheannaola a bhí ár dtriall. Ba sin an cearn den Ghaeltacht ab fhearr aithne againn air. Ba í a gcéad chuairt ar an Ghaeltacht ag an triúr eile í.*[34]

[Around the year 1929 [...] we planned to take a cycling and camping trip to the Donegal *Gaeltacht*, and spend a fortnight or so under canvas there. There were five of us on this journey [...]. To Gortahork in Cloughaneely we were headed. That was the part of the *Gaeltacht* we knew best. It was their first visit to the *Gaeltacht* for the other three.]

In *No Laughing Matter*, Cronin's characterisation of Brian's early years draws on these and other passages from *Óige an Dearthár* that recount this period, crediting the source and specifying that the translations are Cronin's own. The short closing paragraph of Cronin's first chapter emphasises what he perceives to be Ciarán's idealised view of the Gaeltacht:

Ciarán's account of their arrival in the Gaeltacht tells us something of his almost mystical attitude to the Irish language: 'At that time when I would be approaching the Gaeltacht', he says, 'my heart would rise and I would be looking around me, grinning foolishly and trying to guess was I in the Gaeltacht yet, where the women would be more comely, the men more manly, the houses more beautiful, the apples redder and the countryside nicer than the countryside in any other place'.[35]

By way of comparison, Ciarán's original Irish text reads:

An uair sin nuair a bhínnse ag teacht ar chríocha na Gaeltachta d'éiríodh mo chroí agus bhínn ag féachaint timpeall go grinnshúileach ag iarraidh a chinntiú an sa Ghaeltacht a bhí me go fóill, ionann agus gur chóir go mbeadh na mná níos áille, na fir níos fearúla, tithe níos gleoite, úlla níos deirge agus bánta níos glaise sa tír sin ná in aon áit eile.[36]

Allowing for the selectivity that is an inevitable by-product of translation and re-contextualisation, what we have here is not so much synopsis as compression: an instance of mistranslation which amounts to mis-representation. Under the translator's cloak of invisibility, both interpolation and omission are being carried out. The subtlety and ironic self-awareness of Ciarán's source account have been effaced.

Firstly, while Ciarán does indeed say that his heart would rise approaching the Gaeltacht and that he did look around so as to be certain he had reached his destination, there is no use of any term which could be translated as 'grinning', let alone 'grinning foolishly'. To the act of looking about Ciarán attaches the adverb *go grinnshúileach*, meaning 'with a keen eye'.[37] We are left to conclude that Cronin's only basis for rendering the adjective *grinn* as the unrelated verb 'grinning' is the use of homoeophony. Furthermore, where the wording in *No Laughing Matter* has Ciarán making the Gaeltacht a place 'where the women would be more comely, the men more manly, the houses more beautiful, the apples redder and the countryside nicer', a modest but crucial qualifier has been silently omitted. The account in *Óige an Dearthár* reads: '*as if* the women *should be* more beautiful, the men more manly' [my emphasis] ('*ionann agus gur chóir go mbeadh*').[38] This distinction shows a degree of objectivity in the retrospective account which Ciarán as narrator implies may have been lacking in his younger self. Cronin merges the two personae, thereby giving both the same underdeveloped, idealised expectation.

Clearly, Cronin's translations from Ciarán's Irish source tend towards the baroque: for example, in referring to *Óige an Dearthár* as 'The Youth of the Brethren'[39] – and even allowing for his having confused the standard genitive singular with a variant genitive plural of *deartháir* – the choice of 'brethren' unnecessarily connotes religious and nationalistic coordinates not signalled by the original. To give Cronin his due, he does render the phrase '*na fir níos fearúla*' as the undeniably Flann-sounding 'men more manly' (which evokes, for example, the tautological texture of 'naked nudity' in *At Swim-Two-Birds*; *CN*, 61). Yet, it would be more accurate to translate '*na mná níos áille*' as 'the women more beautiful', rather than Cronin's 'more comely'. Given Cronin's sense that Ciarán is idealising his surroundings in his representation, it appears that the later translator and biographer has allowed the spirit of Éamon de Valera's oft-referenced 1943 Saint Patrick's Day radio broadcast to come whispering to his mind. In that speech de Valera notoriously summoned 'the laughter of comely maidens' as being among the characteristics of 'The Ireland we have dreamed of'.[40] According to Joseph Lee and Gearóid Ó Tuathaigh, de Valera's speech constructed a vision of an 'idealised Ireland' through what they term a 'bucolic *aisling*' (a poetic genre in which Ireland, personified as a beautiful woman, appears in vision form to the poet).[41] The generative nature of this idealising tendency can be seen in the frequently misquoted expansion of de Valera's phrase as 'comely maidens dancing at the crossroads': a desire to adjust the image of de Valera so as to display more idealism and sentimentality than he actually evinced on the occasion in question. The irony of this 'correction' of de Valera's speech – as de Valera was insufficiently de Valeraesque for retrospectively reinterpreting authorities – shows the contagious and partially successful nature of a wider receptivity among commentators and public alike to certain modes of historical rewriting. If we discern the same or similar processes at work in Cronin's refractions of Ciarán's ambivalent memoirs, we should remain mindful that it is exactly this tendency to yield uncritically to the idealising impulse that is deconstructed to such satirical effect in *An Béal Bocht* – and subsequently in *Óige an Dearthár*.

If one were to look for evidence more sympathetic to the inferences drawn by Cronin, there is some to be found on the same page of *Óige an Dearthár*, though Cronin does not make explicit use of this: '*Tá súil agam go dtiocfadh iarracht den mhothú sin orm go fóill; agus duine ar bith atá ábalta triall thar an chrích dofheicthe sin sa talamh chomh réchúiseach agus a thrasnódh sé an líne deighilte idir dhá chontae, ní mór mo mheas air*' [I hope that I might still experience something of that feeling; and anyone who is able to cross that invisible boundary in the ground as readily as he would the dividing line between two counties, I don't respect much].[42] However, Ciarán deflates this idea in his next sentence, admitting that the only way to be certain one is in the Gaeltacht is to address somebody along the way. He further flattens the sentiment two chapters later by confessing to the failing he would find so undesirable in others: '*D'fhéadfainn tiomáint i ngluaisteán trí Ghort an Choirce inniu gan é aithint thar bhaile eile – agus rinne mé sin. Tá sé athraithe ar fad*' [I could drive through Gortahork in a car today and not be able to distinguish it from another town – and I have done. It is completely changed].[43] In setting up the expectation to 'experience something of that feeling' again for the purpose of undermining it, we have here a sleight of hand. The more mature narrator of *Óige an Dearthár*, drawing on his experience over time, is better able than his younger self to delineate the boundaries between the real and the expected. His acknowledgement of the reality of change in the Gaeltacht makes it easier for him to move back and forth over the 'invisible' dividing lines between actual and idealised, though the reader (whether translator, biographer, or critic) may not be able to track these movements as easily, leading to a blurring of boundaries.

'Even the kangaroo has two legs!'

Probably the most referenced scene in *Óige an Dearthár* is Ciarán's account of his and Brian's encounter with the one-legged Máire Ní Ghallchóir. The local woman lives with her brother in what Cronin describes as a small thatched 'mud cabin' in the middle of the bog. Intriguingly, a phrase that Brian deleted from the manuscript of *An Béal Bocht* before submitting it to the publisher, in which the Seanduine Liath describes the house of Jams O'Donnell in the Rosses in Donegal to Bónapárt as '*cró beag leath-bhriste abhí saithte sa phortach*' [a half-broken little hovel stuck in the bog], is very close to Ciarán's description of Máire Ní Ghallchóir's dwelling.[44] And yet, in Ciarán's account, while the 'hovel' is old and thatched, it is described as being of 'yellow stone' (*'seanchró clochbhuí ceanntuí'*[45]) and not 'mud', as Cronin translates it. This distinction is telling, especially as there are other details in Ciarán's unflinching account which Cronin might have utilised instead for the desired effect: for example, Ciarán indicates the inadequacy of the structure that functions as a house and of the opening that is its door by putting both *'teach'* and *'doras'* in scare quotes.[46] Altogether, Ciarán's account of the encounter with this one-legged woman is significantly more detailed, varied and nuanced than those elements selected by Cronin for the Flann O'Brien biography.[47]

Cronin is not alone in his view that Ciarán is romanticising the representation of his and Brian's encounter with Máire Ní Ghallchóir. Louis de Paor allows for some *'osréadúlacht áibhéalta'* [exaggerated surrealism] in the intent of *Óige an Dearthár* by linking it with *An Béal Bocht*, but still claims Ciarán's mind has for more than forty years been in the grip of *'na deuleabhair'* [the good books] (*ABB*, 56), as Bónapárt Ó Cúnasa describes a certain type of Gaeltacht autobiography.[48] For de Paor, there is a tension between the Gaeltacht ideal which Ciarán has taken from those books and the very real deprivation he sees for himself in the actual Gaeltacht; yet, ultimately de Paor accuses Ciarán of 'piety' and of forcing an idealised viewpoint onto the one-legged woman's story so as to soften the horror of life and to rearrange the unpleasant material reality: *'Leis an gclabhsúr cráifeach a chuirtear siar ar scéal na mná braitear fráma solúbtha an idéil á shíneadh chun uafás an tsaoil a shéimhiú agus gné mhíthaitneamhach den bhfírinne nithiúil a bhí ag teacht lasmuigh de a thabhairt laistigh dá riar'* [With the pious conclusion which is forced on the woman's story the ideal's flexible frame is felt to stretch so as to attenuate life's horror and to bring an unpleasant aspect of the concrete truth which had come outside it, under its control].[49] Although informed to some extent by *No Laughing Matter* – a reminder of the extent of the biography's authority and influence – de Paor's claims are more serious, as he draws on and quotes directly from *Óige an Dearthár*. Nonetheless, in my view de Paor does not attach enough weight to the retrospective nature of the reminiscence, nor to the work Ciarán puts into subtly ironising his own pronouncements even as he formulates them. By giving various examples of the deprivation encountered, the reader's attention becomes focused primarily in one direction, so that when details appear which run counter to the accumulating account, these unexpected elements go unnoticed or are unconsciously censored. Both Cronin and de Paor overlook crucial, albeit camouflaged, elements which allow for a very different reading of the scenario.

Reminding us that both brothers witnessed this scene, one early reviewer of *Óige an Dearthár* posits the one-legged woman as the raw material for the ominous fourteen one-legged men of *The Third Policeman* pooling their resources to redeploy themselves as seven complete specimens.[50] However, Ciarán's detail that Máire Ní Ghallchóir gets around, even making a weekly two-mile journey to Mass, by 'executing giant hops', always without the aid of a crutch and in all kinds of weather,[51] draws on contextual referents that align it more closely with *At Swim-Two-Birds*, being related to two archetypes of Irish tradition: the *bean chaointe* [keening woman] and the *geilt* [madman]. The keening woman is typically barefoot (though not bare-legged) and described as giving three leaps. Though neither the keening woman nor the *geilt* are missing limbs, the latter is usually depicted as being in disarray and giving great leaps, as with *Buile Shuibhne* and Flann O'Brien's Sweeny.[52] (Another *At Swim-Two-Birds* personage, Moling, also gives three leaps in *Buile Shuibhne*.) An even more immediate resonance is the mill-hag in *Buile Shuibhne*, as Ciarán describes Máire Ní Ghallchóir as having an old face, '*aghaidh chaillí, chóir a bheith*' [the face of a hag, almost].[53] The mill-hag's leaping contest with Sweeny is re-enacted in *At Swim-Two-Birds*, where she also dies in the act of leaping, falling over a cliff while attempting to emulate Sweeny.

Most tellingly, in the middle of the paragraph in which Ciarán describes the woman's one leg and the shocking manner in which she is obliged to go from one place to another, we have this statement: '*Dhá chois atá ag an changarú féin!*' [Even the kangaroo has two legs!].[54] In evoking marsupial imagery, Ciarán may well be slyly alluding to the colloquy between the Pooka (from *púca*, another Irish folk figure, which sometimes takes the form of a small horse, or *capaillín*, appropriately[55]) and the Good Fairy in *At Swim-Two-Birds*. When the Pooka argues that the pocket existed long before the invention of trousers ('the quiver for arrows is one example and the pouch of the kangaroo is another'), the Good Fairy 'disincline[s] to think that kangaroos are human', arguing that 'to admit a kangaroo unreservedly to be a man would inevitably involve one in a number of distressing implications, the kangaroolity of women and your wife beside you being one example' (*CN*, 103–04). The Pooka retorts that he would not be surprised if his wife were indeed revealed to be a kangaroo, 'for any hypothesis would be more tenable than the assumption that she is a woman' (*CN*, 104). In his description of Máire Ní Ghallchóir, Ciarán amplifies this sense of hybridity through the visual and aural incongruity of the Gaelicised loanword *cangarú*, and the comical image it evokes is further emphasised by the thoroughgoing application of lenition in Irish, [*ag an*] *changarú*, making the human-animal contrast so out of place as to be disrespectful (if we take the scenario at face value).[56] The comparison of the old woman with a *cangarú*, combined with the allusions to the bathetic, preposterous colloquy of *At Swim-Two-Birds*, speaks to a collaborative, intertextual method that both ironises and complicates the surface piety and idealism of Ciarán's Gaeltacht scenes and implies the thin border where the bestial and human are overlaid, creating a double exposure of the Gaeltacht as a 'place apart'.

The conflation of human and animal in this mock-philosophical colloquy is a carnivalesque proposal – a case of the figurative being taken literally – that also functions to turn the natural order upside-down throughout *An Béal Bocht*. The human-animal cohabitation of that novel is recalled when Ciarán declares one would be reluctant to put a valued animal in the old woman's dwelling ('*a mbeadh scrupall ag duine beathach a ba luachmhar leis a chur ann*').[57] A further echo of inter-species confusion, mediated through the indistinctness of animal sounds and human language to a non-local, is found in the description of Sitric's sordid dwelling in *An Béal Bocht*: '*Daoine iasachta a bheadh ag gabháil thar bráid, cheapadh siad gur broc a bhí i dtalamh nuair a bhraithidís an anáil throm ag teacht ó thóin an phoill, agus dreach fiáin ar an áitreabh agus ar gach ní go hiomlán*' [Outsiders who would be going past used to think there was a badger in the ground when they would sense the heavy breath coming from the bottom of the hole, and the wild appearance of the dwelling and things in general] (*ABB*, 78). Maebh Long sees the blurred distinction between man and beast played out in *An Béal Bocht* as typified in an outsider preconception of the Irish language, so strong that it remains unchanged by encountering the reality of the situation:

> An inhuman language, [Irish] is spoken by those indistinguishable from animals. If these people who speak Irish resemble pigs, and the language they speak [is] confused with the grunting of pigs, how can it truly be a language at all, but simply the sounds, spoken by one on the border between animal and human?[58]

These bathetic intertextual echoes with his brother's novels destabilise the 'idealised' portraiture of the leaping woman in Ciarán's *Óige an Dearthár*: clear distinctions between alien perspectives and local realities are blurred, and there is a too-sudden drop in tone, a too-ready change of register before resuming the details of the startling scene for there not to be another intent at work. The scenario is now compromised, as a degree of doubt and even the possibility of artifice has been implied and an unpredictable or unstable potential introduced.

De Paor's characterisation of Ciarán's description of the one-legged woman's plight as '*cráifeach*' [pious] refers specifically to the final paragraph of the chapter of *Óige an Dearthár* under discussion. Here, Ciarán says he never discovered how the woman had lost her leg, or where, how or when she died. He speculates that she died mid-jump, when her heart finally refused its 'awful exertion' ('[*don*] *mhasla uafásach*'): '*Má sea, cé déarfadh nach cóir go dtabharfadh an léim dheireanach sin thar na taibhlí síoraí isteach i gCathair na Glóire í?*' [If so, who is to say that it wouldn't be proper for that last leap to take her over the eternal battlements into the City of Glory?].[59] Following the previous bathetic drop in tone, the register seems now to have been ramped up a notch too high. Combined with the cinematic nature of the climactic freeze-frame in the narrator's imaginings, the oratory appears to be teetering on ridicule. Taken in the context of the sense of doubt introduced by Ciarán elsewhere, these seemingly erratic swerves show not a lack of control, but a deceptively light hand on the wheel. The impression, then, is of a narrative presented too unreliably to be taken solely at face value, one at odds with de Paor's accusation of piety and Cronin's of near-mysticism.

A difficulty with such refined ironising, as Vivian Mercier has underlined, is that 'irony often defeats itself, and the better sustained the irony is, the more difficult it is to identify'.[60] Thus Allan Rodway's realignment of the ironic structure might supply a definition more apposite to the Ó Nualláin collective: that irony 'is not merely a matter of seeing a "true" meaning beneath a "false", but of seeing a double exposure (in both senses of the word) on one plate'.[61] Looking back on his own younger self, Cronin has written in *Dead as Doornails* (1999) of how the distancing that comes with the passage of time can bring a clearer perspective: 'I used occasionally be driven to fill up the pages of *The Bell* with portentous rubbish which, I am afraid, at the time I took all too seriously. I had failed to develop any ironic devices or protections of my own'.[62] As Cronin relates, the friend who intervened to advise him on this ironised approach was the author of *An Béal Bocht* and subject of *Óige an Dearthár*. Yet in missing or ignoring Ciarán Ó Nualláin's secret signage in the passages in *Óige an Dearthár*, there is a falling back into the trap set so successfully by *An Béal Bocht* in the first place. If the early twentieth-century professional scholars and enthusiastic amateurs who descend on Corca Dhorcha in *An Béal Bocht* are so eager to experience linguistic nobility that they ignore material savagery, *Óige an Dearthár*'s re-dressing of the Corca Dhorcha stage where their foregone conclusions were first played out shows this liminal, ironic mode still has the power to expose blind spots fifty years and more after his brother's novel began doing so.

Our likes will not exist again (and again and again)

As a figure in Dublin's journalistic and literary circles in the early 1970s, Ciarán was admired in certain circles for his lifelong dedication to demonstrating by example that the Irish language could be a medium to match English; yet he was also somewhat under-appreciated, writing partly in his brother's shadow, and had suffered materially for his chosen career path. The publication of the pieces first appearing in *Inniu* as *Óige an Dearthár* was, in these ways, a quiet act of solidarity with a deceased sibling, both personally and creatively. The full title, *Óige an Dearthár .i. Myles na gCopaleen* [The Brother's Youth i.e. Myles na gCopaleen], maps out the work's misleading mix-and-match of the autobiographical and the figurative, as it moves from implying the author's familial connection with his subject to complicating this association by linking the clarifying 'i.e.' not with the 'real' figure of Brian Ó Nualláin, or Brian O'Nolan, but with another of that brother's literary creations, Myles na gCopaleen. This overlap between the speculative and the autobiographical in the Ó Nualláin family style is further echoed in a claim Ciarán is reported to have made to an acquaintance that in fact *he* was The Brother to whom Myles was referring in his *Cruiskeen Lawn* columns,[63] despite there being no obvious point of comparison. In *Óige an Dearthár*, Ciarán gleefully points to the confusion inherent to the Ó Nualláins' identity-fragmentation and participatory solidarity that had been evident since their early collaborations in *Blather*, and its tendency to mislead unaware readers and critics: '*Ba mhór an sult liom údar Meiriceánach dhá phíosa de mo chuidse i* Blather *a chur i leith Bhriain agus brí mhór a bhaint astu mar léiriú ar na tréithe a bhí le bláthú ina dhiaidh sin ina chuid leabhar!*' [It was a great pleasure to me to have an American author attribute two pieces of mine in *Blather* to Brian and draw huge conclusions from them as indicative of the characteristics which would later blossom in his books!].[64] Yet there is a deeper insight in this confusion, as Ciarán's biography reveals a collaborative, indeed a conspiratorial, method that was a constant throughout the brothers' careers, even where the respective strands diverged. Through Ciarán's *a la carte* re-use of the subject matter and techniques of his brother's *At Swim-Two-Birds* and *An Béal Bocht*, familial intertextuality is deployed in detail by one brother to revisit and reinforce the concerns of the other, including, among others, the attempt to tinge a re-emerging idealism with a renewed irony.

A significant strand of *Óige an Dearthár*, then, functions as a follow-up spot-check on the audience of *An Béal Bocht* and finds that audience wanting. Moreover it goes a radical step further than *An Béal Bocht*. While the dramatic irony of Myles's novel gives the reader an opportunity to side with the author against the self-serving cultural asset-stripping visitors to the Gaeltacht, his brother's biography employs the same device practically on a meta-level, turning the focus 180 degrees, outward, to scrutinise no less a target than his own reader. John Cronin says of Brian Ó Nualláin that he 'constantly frustrated the activities of naïve interviewers and literal-minded biographers'.[65] He was not the only Ó Nualláin to do so.

10

More 'gravid' than gravitas

Collopy, Fahrt and the Pope in Rome

JOHN McCOURT

A lifelong Catholic, Brian O'Nolan would have found it hard to credit that in 2013 a conference in his honour would be held in Rome and that a Jesuit, Francis, would be seated on the throne of Peter. And yet O'Nolan has as much of a connection with the Eternal City as he does with any other city outside Ireland. This essay will focus chiefly on the irreverent and error-filled depictions of Rome and of the ecclesiastical seat of the Roman Catholic Church in *The Hard Life*. A burlesque of the novel's stated themes of perfectionism and squalor, this rare trip beyond Irish borders – the only such international journey depicted in O'Nolan's completed novels – casts further light on the author's ambivalent views of patriarchal authority (as exercised through the Irish State, the Catholic Church, and the literary and cultural milieus to which he belonged) in his declining years.

Critics have noted in particular *The Hard Life*'s uncertain and equivocal satire of ecclesiastical authority: Keith Hopper posits 'that it is meant to be a critique of the Irish Catholic experience, but one that fails through coyness, reticence and the disorganisation of resources',[1] while Joseph Brooker concludes that 'It is hard to say that the Pope loses any authority from his appearance here. And that is finally true of Catholicism itself'.[2] While my intention is not to attempt to resolve or recast this debate, I would like to suggest that the Roman (and Roman Catholic) intertexts and allusions in this novel can introduce new comparative contexts to this conversation and to O'Nolan studies more broadly. By widening the frames within which the novel may be viewed, we can consider its peculiarly belated (and deflated) engagements with realism and modernism, with some of the standard authorities of the Irish literary tradition (Swift, Sterne, Shaw, Joyce, O'Faoláin, *et al.*) but also with Italian contemporaries and predecessors, such as Alberto Moravia and Carlo Emilio Gadda. Benefits may be accrued from following O'Nolan out of Ireland and reading him, cheek by jowl, with those European contemporaries with whom he has much in common, and who are, like him, unhappy at the idea of writing within the limits of realism and struggling to find satisfactory modes of narration at the problematic tail-end of the modernist era.

Although initially greeted enthusiastically by reviewers delighted to see 'Flann O'Brien' finally back in print in book form, on balance the response to *The Hard Life* has mostly ranged from neutral to negative. Hopper sees in it 'a dramatic and regressive shift to an uncomfortable brand of comic realism, mixed in with a tentative and confused satire of post-colonial Irish society'.[3] The 'primary narrative', in Hopper's view, is 'a bleak and sordid comedy', a 'rather drab and long-winded satire', the overall effect of which 'remains starkly limited in its horizons, sadly unfunny, and seemingly devoid of any coherent focus'.[4] More recently, Carol Taaffe dismisses its 'pallid humour' and 'bland but marketable comic realism' which seem to be the work of 'an ineffectual ghostwriter'.[5] She laments that the 'haphazard comic performances which characterise his first novel are shoehorned here into a conventional linear narrative, which is restrained almost to the point of dullness'.[6] Jennika Baines argues, on the other hand, that the relationships between Collopy, Finbarr and Manus 'show the novel to be a more significant work than its well-documented shortcomings might have it', in so far as they reveal it to be 'an insecure, imperfect' travesty of the *Künstlerroman* in the Joycean mode, in which 'Rather than growing into his vocation as a writer' the protagonist Finbarr 'loses command over his own story' and 'becomes less capable of expressing his world or guiding the plot towards its completion'.[7] This feature is certainly borne out by close inspection of the handling of local geographical and cultural detail in the unusual Roman/Vatican interlude which is both subplot and climactic moment. While not wishing to claim that *The Hard Life* is a neglected masterpiece, despite (or perhaps because of) its many regurgitations of O'Nolan's earlier writings, the novel has its merits and its moments, some of which the author himself understood when he claimed that it was 'very funny. Its apparently pedestrian style is delusive'.[8] He was probably less correct in his claim that it was 'a very important book', although knowing the author and his tormented relationship with his own output, this was almost certainly a tongue-in-cheek comment. In his own words: 'it's a poor crow who isn't proud of its own dirt'.[9]

To a large extent it is true that in *The Hard Life* O'Nolan is fighting old battles from earlier times. The work reads today as it probably already read in Sean Lemass's rapidly changing Ireland – as tame and even whimsical. It was, as O'Nolan put it, little more than 'old, elegant, nostalgic piss',[10] somewhat undermining his decision to set the novel sixty years earlier, in an Ireland contemporary with Joyce's. Later, in 1964, after the postponement of the German translation of *The Hard Life*, O'Nolan, discussing the difficulties of translating the novel, stressed its local qualities and connected it with Joyce: 'Whatever about its merits, the book is concerned with matters of local idiom and idiosyncrasy, and the thing simply cannot be done in another language. I nearly died laughing 25 years ago when I got my hands on a French version of *Ulysses*'.[11]

If, as some claim, O'Nolan's underlying concern in his later years was to write more commercial works that could travel through translation, there is little in this text to suggest that he intended *The Hard Life* as part of any such plan. Its battles, as he acknowledged, were local but even if he flags his novel's antagonistic stance in the hope of having it banned in Ireland the reality is that its confrontation with authority – clerical and lay – is underpowered. That said, however, in showing all authority in Ireland to be placed in exclusively male hands, the novel, perhaps inadvertently, gestures towards a discussion of such patriarchy as a – or rather *the* – model of authority. It reflects its times in portraying an almost exclusively man's world but this reality of course should in no way exonerate O'Nolan from his often objectionable attitudes towards women. Hopper underlines the 'decidedly misogynistic' 'language and imagery' that O'Nolan uses 'to represent women'.[12] Taaffe emphasises that 'the only role for a woman in this novel is that of a cartoon grotesque who harbours a threat of sexual degradation, if not outright disease'.[13] Maebh Long captures this feature of O'Nolan's writing well when arguing that 'the women and domestic spaces within O'Nolan's works are highly problematic, exhibiting a sustained, misogynistic distaste, escalating in *The Hard Life* to palpable disgust'.[14]

Collopy's attempts to argue for women's public conveniences in Dublin see him appeal to a series of all-male authorities and are made without any recourse to hearing the opinions of those same women that might actually use such facilities. The ultimate authority to whom he makes recourse is of course the Pope. And yet, it is striking that the novel in its marginalisation of female characters seems, by omission, to challenge and destabilise the entirely male constructions of the Ireland that it describes. Despite Keith Donohue's contention that *The Hard Life* is 'a rather mild attack on [...] an already vanishing social order',[15] in the fifties Ireland still looked to Rome and the pre-Vatican II Catholic Church as the final arbiter in all sexual questions, in all matters regarding women's bodies. (We need only cite the political crisis of The Mother and Child Scheme in the early 1950s.) It is not a stretch to read the novel as an oblique (if somewhat hedged) critique of that recurring dynamic and of Rome's haughty disinterest in and judgement of such Irish matters.

However, the focus here is not to pass judgement on the novel but rather to focus on the chapters which cover the fatal, shambolic trip to Rome and the Vatican for what they, more narrowly, might add to this critical conversation. This section of the novel, although obviously different in setting to the rest of the work, remains in thematic and formal harmony with the novel as a whole. In order to relate the novel's Italian elements – its use of the Italian language and its choice of Roman settings, contexts and backgrounds, all seen through the work's deliberate and consistent 'pedestrian style' – as well as its staged clashes with patriarchal and church authority (and with the competing authorities of Irish realism and continental modernism), a brief reflection on the title is necessary.

On 10 February 1953, Myles na Gopaleen announced in his *Cruiskeen Lawn* column that he had begun the composition of a new novel in order to rectify the issue that 'no novel expressive of our agues had been posted c/o Posterity'.[16] Myles considers and summarily dismisses each of the candidates for such a designation: '*The Small Mark, Dan* [i.e. *The Small Dark Man*], by Maurice Walsh? No, too sentimental. O'Faolain's *A Curse of Paupers* [i.e. *A Purse of Coppers*]? No, no, no—too much pessichism [*sic*] in that unfortunate man's head'. In the end, the columnist determines that 'If the job done to be was, I would have to do it myself (as usual)'. Getting out his typewriter, Myles works out the title and a new pseudonym (if little else) for this new expressive novel, and announces that *The Hard Life: A Study in Perfectionism* would be published under the pen-name 'Felix Kulpa'. The eventually discarded title and pseudonym demand an attempt at elucidation, as they would have fitted the final work very well. As a wordsmith like O'Nolan would have known, the idea of perfectionism derives from the Latin *perficere* (to complete) and is commonly defined as a propensity for being displeased with anything that is not perfect. However, as Flann's favourite Jesuit, Father Kurt Fahrt SJ, would doubtless have enjoyed explaining, the term is also used to describe a Christian belief (often associated with John Wesley) that moral or spiritual perfection can be achieved *before* the soul has passed into the afterlife. Given O'Nolan's noted familiarity with Aquinas and Thomist teachings more generally,[17] he would also certainly have been well versed in Aquinas's argument that 'all substances seek their own perfection' or *telos*[18] and the theologian's writing on the hierarchy of possible levels of perfection: at the summit, the absolute perfection that is God's alone; then, the perfection of the love for God made possible only in the afterlife; and the lowest level of perfection which is 'the possibility of perfect love in this life' through charity, which is a necessity for salvation.[19] Very often, however, in the secular world, perfectionism is less lofty and is little more than a depressing preoccupation with (self-)improvement. Typically, such perfectionists strive compulsively and unceasingly to achieve unobtainable goals, sometimes to the point of neurosis.[20] This latter definition of the term seems to chime well with the character of Collopy and with his ceaseless campaign for the establishment of public conveniences for women in Dublin: at best, his purported concern for the plight of Dublin's women in the novel is a grotesque mockery of Thomistic perfection through earthly charity. Yet it is his determination to win this battle that eventually takes Collopy to Rome to take up the issue with no less a personage than Pope Pius X, whom he sees as a last court of appeal (Pius X was Pope from 1903 to 1914).

There is also, it might be argued, a carnivalesque mockery of perfectionism in Manus's endless (and spurious) self-help schemes, especially if we remember that psychologists speak of perfectionism in terms of obsessiveness. It is very much in this latter, fallen sense that perfectionism seems to be present in *The Hard Life* in its final form, and this feature connects the work quite directly with Laurence Sterne's variegated treatment of personal hobby-horses in *Tristram Shandy*, an undoubtedly important sourcebook for O'Nolan and his fellow (post-)modernists. O'Nolan seems to hint at this association when describing the 'episodically revealed' plot as 'sternly consecutive and conclusive'.[21] But if this is, in fact, a reference to Sterne, it is an ironic one as *The Hard Life* drives forward in a way that is very much at odds with Sterne's progressive-digressive method on which O'Nolan drew in his other novels and in the life and opinions expounded upon for decades in *Cruiskeen Lawn*. In the same letter, O'Nolan says of *The Hard Life*: 'Digression and expatiation would be easy but I feel would injure the book's spontaneity'.[22] However, the book's conversations between Collopy and Father Fahrt seem to owe something to those between Walter Shandy and Uncle Toby and do relatively little to push the plot forward even if they undoubtedly cement the friendship between the two.

As Myles announced in his 1953 column, for *The Hard Life* he had devised the 'very good pen-name' Felix Kulpa, a name which alludes to the Latin expression *'felix culpa'* deriving from the fifth-century Exultet of the Easter Vigil: '*O felix culpa quae talem et tantum meruit habere redemptorem*' [O happy fault that merited such and so great a Redeemer] and from Saint Augustine's *Enchiridion* in a passage regarding the Fall of Man, the source of original sin: '*Melius enim iudicavit de malis benefacere, quam mala nulla esse permittere*' [For God judged it better to bring good out of evil than not to permit any evil to exist]. Thus Adam's fall – following his defiance of the ultimate authority of God – can also be judged as not entirely unfortunate because it carries within it the subsequent possibility of redemption.

O'Nolan was far from the first writer or indeed the first Irish writer to draw attention to the phrase or indeed the theme in his fiction. It is a central Christian theme and a standard of Western thought. Joyce pre-empted O'Nolan by making the *felix culpa* a major motif in *Finnegans Wake* with, among others, plays on the words such as 'O foenix culprit!', 'phaymix cupplerts', 'felixed is who culpas does'.[23] O'Nolan would also have noticed Graham Greene's treatment of the same subject in *The Heart of the Matter* and may have seen Evelyn Waugh's review of this novel entitled 'Felix Culpa?' and published in *The Commonweal*.[24] This echo might even have contributed to O'Nolan's dedicating *The Hard Life* to Greene: 'I honourably present to Graham Greene whose own forms of gloom I admire, this misterpiece',[25] although this was also a way of thanking the English convert to Catholicism for his convinced early support for *At Swim-Two-Birds*. Whatever the contemporary literary connections suggested by Myles's citing of the *'felix culpa'* or 'kulpa', what is perhaps more important is that it draws attention to man's defiance of authority, his imperfection after the fall and to the possibility of his 'improving' his situation and eventually being saved – themes easily connected to the perfectionism of the title whether it is to be aspired to on earth or attained in Paradise.

All of which would be fine and useful if O'Nolan had stuck with his original title. Instead, as we know, he opted for *The Hard Life: An Exegesis of Squalor*, which puts the accent less on man having the possibility of redemption and more on the post-fall misery of the human condition as seen, in this case, in its Dublin variety with its distinctly seedy mix of alcohol and alcoholism, idleness, crime, illicit sex, sexual disease and vomit. As Taaffe summarises, it is 'a novel which fully exploits the comedy of disgust and squalor: from Annie's greasy mince balls to Fahrt's psoriasis, Mrs Crotty's rotted mattress and the sickly sexuality typified by Manus's fascinated discourse on venereal disease'.[26] Not for nothing, then, did O'Nolan, in a letter to his friend Niall Montgomery, refer to *The Hard Life* as 'my dirty book'[27] – as distinct from *Ulysses* which O'Nolan has Joyce describe in *The Dalkey Archive* as 'a dirty book, that collection of smut' (*CN*, 760). The word 'squalor' in English maintains the sense of the old Latin word, *squālor*, meaning dirtiness but it also suggests the condition of being squalid, of living in an almost Swiftian state of filth and misery. In his focus on this wretched condition, it is probable that O'Nolan had in mind Saint Augustine, a figure with whom he was entangled almost to the point of obsession: in the *Manchester Guardian* he wrote a late piece called 'The Saint and I' – published on 19 January 1966 – in which he described his ideas about Saint Augustine and 'how he suspected that the saint was the source of all he was suffering'. Augustine famously preached about the Sermon on the Mount, focusing on the line from 2 Corinthians iii, 18 which reads: 'From the squalor, therefore, by which the eye of God is offended, our face is to be washed'. As nineteenth-century Archbishop of Dublin Richard Chenevix Trench summarises, Augustine's target in this commentary is the pride that may also be attached to squalor by 'he who draws the eyes of men upon himself by an unusual squalor and self-neglect', with the church father warning that 'it is not merely in the pomp and splendour of worldly things that pride may display itself, but that also it may lurk under rags and in sackcloth, being then a pride the more perilous as being more veiled'.[28] In evoking this intertext, perhaps the subtitle implies a condemnation of Collopy's activism on behalf of the women of Dublin, or even a self-reflexive ironic dig at Brian O'Nolan himself, and his own intentions in writing this 'dirty book'.

And yet, O'Nolan's title does not seem so appropriate to the older generation in the novel, that is, to Collopy who manages to retain a degree of dignity and comfort until his sudden demise, or to the intellectual Father Fahrt who, despite his psoriasis, for the most part retains his clerical pomp and self-assurance. It more comfortably applies to Collopy's unfortunate daughter, Annie, and to the two young orphans who are brought under Collopy's roof and enjoy his rather eccentric protection: Finbarr, the docile narrator, and his older brother, Manus, the unstoppable, unscrupulous entrepreneur. Indeed, in Jonathan Bolton's view, the novel's main drive is the ways in which this younger generation of protagonists 'undergo paralyzing conflicts with adult authority' in moving through these squalid environments.[29] Perhaps the title is intended to extend to humanity itself – including Flann's or Myles's readers, whom he describes in *The Irish Times* as 'smug, self-righteous swine [...] ignorant self-opinionated sod-minded suet-brained ham-faced mealy-

mouthed streptococcus-ridden gang of natural gobdaws!' (*BM*, 81). In
choosing the word 'squalor' for his subtitle, then, O'Nolan was evoking a
tradition of condemnation and satire which had as its target human pride and
stretched from Augustine to Swift, and he was using his novel as a pessimistic
parable of the human condition, a condition which demanded one of two
responses, laughter or tears. He chose both, favouring the dark humour of a
comedy that ends in a farcical, almost slapstick tragedy.

Depictions of squalor are as old as literature itself and clearly O'Nolan was
revelling in having fun with the conventions while adding his contribution to
the many treatments of the subject in Irish literature. Squalor and degradation
were staple themes for Swift and Sterne, and the novel's clear connections
with the Swiftian grotesque in particular might go some way to accounting
not only for its Juvenalian emphasis on dirt and excremental humour, but also
its misogyny and disgust with the female body, a central feature of Swift's
scatological poems and in particular of his notorious 'The Lady's Dressing
Room'. In O'Nolan's own time the theme was perhaps nowhere more
memorably to be found than in Beckett's 1950s' trilogy *Molloy*, *Malone Dies*
and *The Unnameable*, but squalor of course abounds too in Joyce's *Ulysses*, and
Anne Clissmann has argued that *The Hard Life* parallels Joyce's 'overwhelming
evocation of squalor'.[30] In this key, George Bernard Shaw had found *Ulysses*
to be

> a revolting record of a disgusting phase of civilisation; but it is a truthful
> one [...]. It is [...] some consolation to find that at last somebody has
> felt deeply enough about it to face the horror of writing it all down and
> using his literary genius to force people to face it. In Ireland they try to
> make a cat cleanly by rubbing its nose in its own filth. Mr Joyce has tried
> the same treatment on the human subject.[31]

Indeed, 'squalor' had been a key trope in much of the novel's early reception,
with Rebecca West describing *Ulysses* in her 1928 *Bookman* piece 'The Strange
Case of James Joyce' as depicting 'the squalor of Dublin as seen by a man
with a cloacal obsession', thus implicitly linking Joyce back to Swift and by
association forward to *The Hard Life*.[32] The repetition of the concept of 'dirty
books', both in O'Nolan's private correspondence and in the text through
Collopy, align *The Hard Life* with both pornography and the Irish tradition
from Swift to Joyce, while evoking the 'cloacal' rhetoric that had condemned
that tradition and even his own place in it – as Taaffe summarises:

Back in 1946, Thomas Hogan had appropriated H.G. Wells's infamous judgement on *Ulysses* to declare that Myles, too, betrayed 'the cloacal obsession of the Irish'. Nearly two decades later *The Hard Life* obligingly fleshed out this critical caricature – perhaps as a comment on the reputation of Joyce, or Myles, or both. Indeed, Wells's literary judgement is closely echoed by Collopy, who on hearing that Manus has gone back into the book business, makes the kind of assumptions that would not embarrass the more excitable members of the Censorship Board: 'if those books are dirty books, lascivious peregrinations on the fringes of filthy indecency, cloacal spewings in the face of Providence, with pictures of prostitutes in their pelts, then out of this house they will go and their owner along with them'. [*CN*, 541][33]

I have previously considered Myles na gCopaleen as something of a reluctant 'Joyce scholar' in whose view Joyce's writing 'suffered at the hands of well-meaning but almost invariably misguided scholars'.[34] It is possible, in this vein, to read the subtitle 'An Exegesis of Squalor' as signalling the novel's implicit further engagement in that project, as a mock-scholarly exegesis of both Joyce's 'Holy text' (and perhaps the whole Irish comic tradition to which O'Nolan belonged) and its subsequent reception as 'cloacal spewings in the face of Providence'. However, just as it is a mistake to read the depiction of squalor as a predominant textual intention in *Ulysses*, so too is it of limited use to approach the complex and deceitful text that is *The Hard Life* in an analogous way. The covers of the welcome recent editions of *The Hard Life*, such as those from the Dalkey Archive Press (2006) and Souvenir Press (2011), are in some way indicative of what M. Keith Booker describes as 'the sterile squalor of everyday life in Dublin'.[35] At the same time, they rather unfortunately play into expectations of squalid realism of the sorts to be found in Joyce's *Dubliners* or in some of the narratives of the Blasket Islands which O'Nolan had already so brilliantly parodied and superseded in *An Béal Bocht*. They fail to signal the essential roguishness of O'Nolan's narrative (his lifelong distaste for the Cork school of realism is also well documented). In some not terribly successful way, it is as if O'Nolan is attempting here to both render homage to and at the same time challenge the realist strain in Irish fiction.

O'Nolan's novel (in common with his other works) openly plays with the conventions of realism and its presumed cultural authority even if it is set, rather precisely, in the late nineteenth and early twentieth centuries. It interrogates and pre-emptively deflates any claims for authentic portrayal.

Niall Sheridan, O'Nolan's close friend and trusted commentator, noted the 'very cunning simplicity' of O'Nolan's style but in so doing drew attention to the fact that it was not an end in itself but a mask.[36] As Thomas F. Shea contends: 'The "cunning simplicity" of style is definitely intended. It would be a mistake to read the novel for thematic plot development. "Narrative" is in fact faked, with *The Hard Life* exposing itself as a series of scenes loosely linked by cardboard character development'.[37] To suggest otherwise would be to imply that O'Nolan's work should be taken literally or at face value. If this were to be the case then O'Nolan had indeed become a very poor writer, one who had changed his entirely creative nature for the sake of hurrying a realistic novel out onto the market as quickly as possible. At the very least, as Shea has pointed out, 'Through its pose as realistic fiction, *The Hard Life* rebukes the reader looking for authenticity in the novel',[38] but O'Nolan is also questioning the conventions through which narrative portrays and poses as the 'real' and in so doing exerts its cultural status and power. As Brooker shrewdly intuits, this mock assumption and then refusal of the coordinates of the 'real' is intimately related to the book's engagements with authority, as signalled in its epigraph that constitutes an 'inversion of a norm' and of 'a legal precaution' at that: '*All the persons in this book are real and none is fictitious even in part*' (CN, 498).[39]

This inversion is as true of the Dublin sections (the bulk of the work) as it is of the Rome section. That said, the chapters that describe the visit undertaken by Manus, Collopy and Father Fahrt to Rome are those which definitively undermine any pretence of trustworthy realism. This is a visit which seems, in every sense of the word, to have been 'faked' either by the serial hoaxer Manus who writes home, or by Brian O'Nolan in the guise of Flann O'Brien, who inevitably fabricates the Rome descriptions, never having set foot in the city. These chapters in many ways exemplify and push to an extreme the novel's whole approach, that of fabrication, of playing with convention and of frustrating the reader's expectations. Although the reader is furnished with supposedly realistic descriptions of Rome, it quickly becomes clear that the city is little more than a simulacrum, a caricature or a 'cardboard' second-hand version of itself, much like the characters who briefly sojourn there. That the author does little or nothing to dress up the second-hand, depthless nature of the views and descriptions of Rome is not a sign of sloppiness, laziness or haste. Quite the opposite. This is all part of the game, a game which seems part of the late-modernist or postmodernist use of signs that parade their detachment from any reality beyond themselves. O'Nolan goes out of his way to cite monuments well-known even to those who have never laid eyes on the Eternal City and he enjoys parading these predictable scenes before his readers who will recognise them from having visited Rome, read through a guide book, or simply heard them mentioned.

The three characters arrive, we are told, after a three-week voyage aboard the '*Moravia*', a name which echoes that of the Roman novelist and journalist Alberto Moravia (1907–90), whose *Racconti romani* [*Roman Tales*] had documented Roman life and The Plain People of Rome (*Roma popolana*) in the pages of the leading Italian daily paper *Il Corriere della Sera* in the early 1950s, much as Myles's *Cruiskeen Lawn* had done for Dublin and The Plain People of Ireland in *The Irish Times*. Despite these seeming analogies, these two authors could not have been more different – Moravia, the popular and successful anti-fascist figure writing of 'the transforming and revealing power of sexual love'[40] in stark and controlled prose; O'Nolan, the Catholic satirist who wrote of sexuality in purely coded or Swiftian grotesque modes, if at all. And yet, the *Irish Times* review of *Roman Tales* emphasised its most Mylesian qualities, describing its stories as a 'technically expert' mix of the 'very funny' and a mood that is 'dry, ironic, or just plain pessimistic'.[41] Perhaps the significance of the Moravia allusion lies in O'Nolan's stated intention to have *The Hard Life* banned through its focus on bodily ailments and the bawdy naming of Fr Fahrt. Moravia's was a perennial name on the Irish banned books list issued by the Censorship of Publications Board, just as he was also a fixture on the Vatican's Holy Office Index of forbidden literature, a fact which undoubtedly did wonders for his book sales in Italy.[42] It might be argued that O'Nolan's allusion signals an implied alliance with the banned author on his trip to Rome to challenge the Catholic patriarchy and the Censorship Board which represents and enforces its strictest views on sexuality back in Ireland. However, it might also be the case that the reference supports the charge that in trying to have his own comeback novel censured, O'Nolan was endeavouring to claim for himself some of the cultural capital bestowed on banned authors such as Moravia, whom Kees Van Hoek described in an extended 1952 *Irish Times* piece on the author as 'the talk of the literary *salons* and a best-seller to boot'[43] – purportedly two of O'Nolan's most pressing objectives when setting about having *The Hard Life* published. Moravia's banned status was a topic of much discussion in the paper's pages, and thus in Irish literary and intellectual discourse. Seán O'Faoláin, claiming to '[speak] as a Puritan Catholic, i.e. as a normal Irishman', condemned the banning of *Agostino* in a 1948 letter to the paper's editor.[44] In a thickly sarcastic mock-literary 'review' of the Stationery Office's 'Register of Prohibited Publications', Donagh MacDonagh, listing Moravia among its most prestigious entries, contended that 'The work deserves a considerable circulation outside this country' as it offers 'a concise index to modern literature'.[45] MacDonagh continues, 'As in the case of the Irish writers there are few of the more outstanding writers – English, American, or those Europeans who have been translated into the Anglo-Saxon tongue – who have gone unnoted by the Censorship Board'. It seems then that, having his protagonists arrive in Rome aboard the *Moravia* before they go to take the piss out of the Pope was O'Nolan's none-too-cunning stratagem to have his own novel noted by the Censorship Board and to have himself thus numbered among the prestigious and successful literary company of Moravia and his banned European companions.

In any case, the *Moravia* arrives in Ostia which had once been a Roman port but had long ceased to function as such at the time of the novel and was never used as a port for large passenger ships, which would have docked instead at Civitavecchia. Perhaps the error is strategic, in line with the text's foregrounding of fakery and illusion, or perhaps O'Nolan simply liked the thematic resonances of the word 'Ostia', which also means 'host' as used in the Eucharist and carries with it the promise of salvation and Christian Perfection. Once they are settled in Rome, the travelling Irishmen take time to look around: 'In the afternoons we usually hire a wagonette and go for a slow tour of sights such as the Colosseum and the Forum; we have twice been to the piazza of St Peter's' (*CN*, 586–87). The whole trip can be read as a satirical version of the classic Irish pilgrimage to Rome where there is always a helpful Irish monsignor – usually the Rector of the Pontifical Irish College – to pull a few strings and even organise an audience with the Pope. (Perhaps, it even has in mind Seán O'Faoláin's travel books *A Summer in Italy* (1950) and *An Autumn in Italy* (1953).) In this case it is 'a Monsignor Cahill, a remarkable character and a Corkman. He is a sort of Vatican civil servant and attends on the Holy Father personally'. An interpreter and stenographer, he is, more importantly, in Manus's words 'a most friendly man, […] always genuinely delighted to see anybody from Ireland, and knows exactly what to do with a good glass of wine. He took a great fancy to Collopy who, to my own great surprise, has a detailed knowledge of Cork city' (*CN*, 587). And yet, in these scenes Manus's (and Flann O'Brien's) own supposedly 'detailed knowledge' of the Eternal City comes under constant stress.

The Hard Life's description of the main Franciscan monastery shows O'Nolan's mastery of the bland, clichéd, wilfully empty sentence, which flatters to initially deceive the reader into thinking he is being treated to a bird's eye view: 'The Monastery was a simple, austere place but apparently very big. The reception room was comfortable enough but full of holy pictures'

(*CN*, 588). This description is adamantly vague, drawing on predictable adjectives almost as if to direct the reader's attention to its contrived, hollow nature. Being a monastery, of course it is simple, austere, 'apparently very big' and full of non-descript holy pictures. Like all of Rome as it appears in the novel, the monastery remains as 'opaque and mysterious' as Collopy's 'crock'. The monastery is home to 'a certain Cardinal Baldini' with whom Father Fahrt establishes a connection in the hope of expediting the visit to the Pope.[46] According to Manus, Baldini was 'what they call a domestic prelate' which reads like another error as the title of domestic prelate is more usually given to a priest being promoted to monsignor rather than to cardinal. The question arises whether this is Manus's mistake or Brian O'Nolan's (one would expect the former), or another strategic gap in the chapter's threadbare realism. Similarly, the mention of a church of 'Santo Antonio di Padua' is an error, not because a church to Saint Anthony was not to be found in the vicinity but rather because the phrase is a mangling of what the Italian should be, that is 'Sant'Antonio di Padova'. In the text's version, the English 'Padua' usurps the Italian 'Padova'. The Padua reference is immediately followed by a telling admission in brackets: '(My Italian is improving fast.)'. The alert reader is immediately wondering just whose Italian exactly is improving. Is it Manus's? Finbarr's? The author's?

The trip to the Vatican is drawn in a similarly flimsy manner. Cardinal Baldini, the reader learns, gives each of the visitors 'a thick guide or catalogue', which is pretty much what the author himself appears to have had in front of him as he conjured up the Roman scenes of the novel. To kill the time before the papal audience, Baldini

> led us through this enormous and dazzling place talking all the time, showing us the loggia of Gregory XIII, a wonderful gallery; the Throne Room; the Sala Rotunda, a round hall full of statues; the Raphael salon, with many of the great man's paintings; part of the Vatican Museum; the Sistine Chapel. (*CN*, 590)

Only Manus's comment gives the slightest hint of them ever actually having been to the Vatican: 'The splendor of it all was stupendous. God forgive me, I thought it was a bit vulgar in places and that all the gilt and gold was sometimes a bit overdone' (*CN*, 590). But his description also seems intentionally hyperbolic and empty.

All this leaves the reader to wonder whether this trip to Rome is to be believed at all or if it is nothing more than a figment or the construction of one of the imaginations at work. Is the habitual narrator, Finbarr, making it up, or is Manus, the author of the Roman letters, simply pulling his reader brother's leg (again) in another instance of 'inside trickery' (*CN*, 587). Is Flann O'Brien just playing with the idea of a Roman holiday in an ironic retake of William Wyler's 1953 *Vacanze romane* with Gregory Peck and Audrey Hepburn? The second-hand nature of the narrative makes perfect sense. Without his brother Manus, Finbarr has no story to tell. This second-handedness also corresponds perfectly with Manus's other work – which involves pilfering other people's ideas and regurgitating them for a gullible and usually paying public. This is also, however, in a very real sense, behind the layers of obfuscation, O'Nolan's own late-Revival method. He draws on source texts, divests them of their original context and authority, and regurgitates them within his own always shifting frames.

Two other Roman locations are worthy of mention in so far as they appear to further the impression of Collopy's messianic mission to Rome as an untrustworthy (post-)modernist travesty of Christian salvation and perfection. The first is the hotel where they stay for the entire Roman sojourn. The fact that it is called the 'Hotel Élite et des Étrangers' and is located on via Basilicata is interesting because a hotel of that name did actually exist on via Basilicata. And it was not just any hotel, even if Manus dismisses it with a bland description as 'a big place near the station' (*CN*, 582). The Hôtel Élite et des Étrangers was home to a cabaret hall which had been established there by Italian poet Gino Gori in April 1922 and decorated by Italian artist Fortunato Depero. The cabaret, called 'La Bottega del Diavolo' (the Devil's workshop), was divided into three large Dantesque rooms: Paradiso, Purgatorio and, in the cellars, the Inferno. Many of Italy's leading experimental and Futurist artists performed and gave readings there, including Enrico Prampolini and Filippo Tommaso Marinetti. Great attention was given to the decor and even the armchairs were in the form of little devils. There were regular 'infernal' performances with Gori playing Minos, the judge of the dead in the Underworld, and other actors playing Cerberus, the three-headed hell-hound, Barbariccia and Lucifer himself. Locating his Irish contingent in this hotel – which aligns modernist innovation with a Dantean infernal topography – in light of their subsequent visit to the Vatican was indeed an ironic move for O'Nolan to make, especially in light of the themes of '*felix culpa*' and perfectionism developed in his earlier Myles column and travestied in Manus, Fahrt and Collopy's drunken pilgrimage to Rome.

All of these Italian connections can easily be dismissed as coincidence (also because the cabaret hall had not yet opened in the years in which the novel is set and was long closed by the time O'Nolan was writing) but it is not hard to imagine that O'Nolan had a compliant informant, possibly in the shape of a once Rome-based Irish Jesuit, later returned, perhaps to take up residence in the order's house in Leeson Street. From such a figure O'Nolan may have achieved not only the excellent Italian and Latin used in the farcical papal audience – which reads better than its English translation – but also the peculiar and tantalising Italian connections I have been discussing. His source may even have doubled as the prototype of Father Fahrt.

Alternatively, O'Nolan could have drawn on help from non-Jesuit Irish clerical friends who had trained or served in Rome, presumably at the Pontifical Irish College. In fact some of the Roman locations mentioned in the novel are situated close by the College. We read of the 'Franciscan monastery at the Via Merulana, where there is also the fine church of Santo Antonio di Padua' (*CN*, 587). O'Nolan presumably chose Via Merulana because it was a stone's throw from the Irish College although he may also have wanted to render homage to Carlo Emilio Gadda's *Quer pasticciaccio brutto de via Merulana* [*That Awful Mess on Via Merulana*].[47] (Gadda's novel also features the 'Sant'Antonio di Padova', correctly spelt.) Unfortunately no firm evidence exists of O'Nolan's being aware of Gadda but the two writers did have much in common, not least the fact that both only belatedly achieved a degree of popular success. (Gadda was over sixty when *Quer pasticciaccio brutto de via Merulana* came out and finally gave him the recognition he richly deserved.) Neither ever seemed to know how to complete a book and Gadda's *Quer pasticciaccio*, a work that masquerades as a crime novel initially involving a robbery and subsequently two murders, exists in several different versions, including a film adaptation. Just as O'Nolan was at odds with the realist school of Irish fiction as practised, principally, by Seán O'Faoláin and Frank O'Connor, the *avant-garde* Gadda had little in common with the dominant tradition of realist fiction of the second half of the twentieth century in Italy, to be found, among others, in the novels of Moravia, Cesare Pavese and Pier Paolo Pasolini.

Without wishing to stretch the connection too far, Collopy, as we know, eventually dies as a result of his huge weight. Gadda's grumpy, squat philosopher-detective Francesco Ingravallo is also overweight (like Gadda himself) and would fit well into the dialogue between Collopy and Fahrt as a lover of philosophy and obscure words. Furthermore, his theory of unforeseen catastrophes could serve as a remarkable description of Collopy's own dismal end:

He sustained, among other things, that unforeseen catastrophes are never the consequence or the effect, if you prefer, of a single motive, of *a* cause singular; but they are rather like a whirlpool, a cyclonic point of depression in the consciousness of the world, towards which a whole multitude of converging causes have contributed. He also used words like knot or tangle, or muddle, or *gnommero*, which in Roman dialect means skein. But the legal term, 'the motive, the motives', escaped his lips by preference, though as if against his will. The opinion that we must 'reform within ourselves the meaning of the category of cause', as handed down by the philosophers from Aristotle to Immanuel Kant, and replace cause with causes was for him a central, persistent opinion, almost a fixation.[48]

Collopy's catastrophic death is not brought about by a single motive but by an accumulation of causes: a prolonged and excessive intake of gravid water, failing timber, 'a fractured skull, a broken arm and leg and severe rupture of the whole stomach region. Even if none of those injuries was individually fatal, no man of Collopy's age could survive the shock of such an accident' (*CN*, 598). Even if the O'Nolan—Gadda link is entirely accidental, it points to the stakes of the Rome chapters, beyond their absurd logic, flimsy facades and clowning with the Pope, as a contemplation on contingency, ephemerality and catastrophic death.

The foregrounding of this theme through Collopy's deadly fall (which is anything but '*felix*') in a Roman setting links the narrative to another of O'Nolan's obsessions, the poet John Keats who lived his last months in Rome. Keats died of consumption and emaciation and was a victim of poor medical practice while Collopy's health deteriorates because of his taking excessive doses of Manus's 'Gravid Water' which causes rapid weight gain and eventually leads to his death. O'Nolan was well acquainted with Keats's final months and his terrible death which took place when he was just twenty-five, and twice wrote about this tragic event through comic means, firstly in *The Hard Life* and later in a 1965 *Cruiskeen Lawn* column entitled 'Keats in Rome'.[49] Here Myles recounts how a 'tall, well-dressed man' joins him in a pub and buys him a drink before asking him if he would 'help on a little business matter. You see our crowd are thinking of taking a stand at the Horse Show next August'. What the man really wants to know is whether Myles 'could induce' his friend Keats to take charge of the stand: 'The firm, of course, would be responsible for decking him out properly in striped trousers, a cutaway claw-hammer, canary waistcoat and cravat'. Myles reports that he 'demurred somewhat' on the grounds that 'Keats had died in Rome and was buried there. An exhumation order would be necessary and it might be that the Holy Father had an attitude on this matter'. He then goes on to 'reminisce' about Sir Walter Scott and Keats 'after the latter had had a quarrel with Chapman' describing how they had gone to a lido near Rome 'but Sir Walter, who was a coarse, belching type, having donned his tiniest of togs, lay face-down on the sand and went asleep'. Keats then 'got a sheet of brown paper, scrawled his name on it in enormous characters and, borrowing a scissors, in effect cut the signature out. He then laid the sheet on Sir Walter's naked back, knowing that the hot sun was his fellow-conspirator'. Later, on his deathbed, Keats gave instructions as to his own burial: 'Have the following cut on the stone: *Here lies one whose name is writ on Walter*'. This is of course a playful punning version of what Keats had actually requested, that is, the wish that on his gravestone in Rome no name or date should be written, only the inscription 'Here lies one whose name was writ in water'.

In *The Hard Life*, Manus quotes this epitaph to Finbarr, whom he describes as 'a bit of a literary man' (*CN*, 601), reminding him that 'Like Collopy, he [Keats] died in Rome and he is buried there. I saw his grave. [...] It is beautiful and very well kept' (*CN*, 602). All of which feeds into Collopy's own gravestone which, unlike Keats's, carries his own surname, place and year of birth. Neil Murphy points out 'Manus's adjustment of Keats's epitaph ("Here lies one whose name is writ in water") to read "Here lies one whose name is writ in water", that is, invisible'.[50] Murphy continues: 'He takes an already precarious scripted image and makes it vanish completely, and the world of the novel becomes less and less tangible, a quality that also extends to the narrator himself'. I am not so sure that there is much of a tangible difference between 'writ in water' and the original 'writ on water'. Both suggest the fluidity and fragility of existence, the intangibility of life, the impalpability of remembrance. Keats dies wrongly and tragically believing his life has been a failure; Collopy declines (or expands) towards death knowing that he has failed in his final mission; in 1965, just a year before his own death, the 'truly fear-shaken Irish Catholic' (*SP*, 207) O'Nolan, feeling (like Keats) that life has probably gotten the better of any perfectionist impulse he may once have had, tries to laugh and face off the spectre of death in the *Cruiskeen Lawn* with another, somewhat strained 'water/Walter' pun, as ever seeking to circumvent or at least approach the tragic through its comic flip side. *The Hard Life*'s chapters depicting Collopy's one-way, failed and fatal trip to Rome, *caput mundi*, reveal a similar intent to confront the levelling authority of death.

PART III

GROSS IMPIETIES
O'Nolan *vs.* the sacred texts

'a scholar manqué'?

further notes on Brian Ó Nualláin's engagement with Early Irish literature

LOUIS DE PAOR

The only source of inspiration he acknowledged without qualification – though he took care to define it in his own idiosyncratic way – was the native Irish tradition for which he had a genuine love, and typically on the grounds of its uselessness and total separation from modern concerns. His MA thesis on nature in Irish poetry was on a subject with clear and fundamental attraction for him, but, characteristically, from all reports it was impeccably academic.[1]

We in the Irish Times *thought he was a scholar manqué, and there is a rare note of sincerity in a generous appreciation which he wrote to mark the twenty-fifth anniversary of the death of Standish Hayes O'Grady, editor of Silva Gadelica:* 'He combined with profound learning other qualities of humour and imagination which enabled him to deal with early texts in a lively creative way that lifted his work far out of the repellent rut traversed by most philologists'. *Given another lifetime, this might have been his own obituary.*[2]

Despite the contributions of a growing number of Irish language scholars, and of Breandán Ó Conaire (1986) and Eva Wäppling (1984) in particular, the extent to which Brian Ó Nualláin's relationship with Irish and the Gaelic literary tradition is a defining influence on his writing is less evident than might be expected in the growing corpus of critical research on his work. Ó Conaire's detailed study of *An Béal Bocht* provides evidence of Ó Nualláin's extensive reading of native Irish autobiography, citing several other works by Ulster and Munster authors as supplementary sources for his response to Tomás Ó Criomhthain's *An tOileánach*, 'the superbest of all books I have ever read',[3] while Wäppling's thesis remains the most compelling study of the central role of medieval Irish narrative in the architecture of *At Swim-Two-Birds*.[4] The ambivalence of the author's own attitudes and the difficulty of ascribing any stable position to a writer determined to undermine all forms of verbal authority, and particularly the authority of authorship, might be cited amongst other mitigating factors in this regard. This essay does not propose to resolve the instability and ambiguity that are central to Ó Nualláin's achievement, but rather to provide further evidence of the central importance of the Irish language element in the early work which remains the pinnacle of his achievement despite legitimate claims made for more generous consideration of the later writing. It will argue that the aesthetic principles identified by Ó Nualláin in his MA thesis on nature poetry in Irish provide a basis for a poetics that is applicable not only to the material covered in his research but also to Ó Nualláin's own work.[5]

University College Dublin, 1929–35

Carol Taaffe has drawn attention to Ó Nualláin's academic training in University College Dublin (UCD) at a time when a precocious generation of students were contesting received ideas about Irish identity and literature, more sceptical of the native tradition than many of their predecessors in the revolutionary period, more inclined to look towards Paris than Tara for inspiration.[6] Confronted by the contest between nativists and Europhiles, Ó Nualláin 'continued to see the alternatives as falsely opposed and yet as inescapable'.[7] Given his own background in a bilingual family steeped in the cultural revival, his further education as a student-scholar of Irish language writing in Old and Middle, Early Modern, and Modern Irish, and the particular orientation of his own verbal imagination, Ó Nualláin was well placed to explore the dynamic tension between the Gaelic Irish tradition and contemporary European models as the basis for new writing that would integrate these disparate, but ultimately complementary, elements. The realignment of native Irish and European models had already been established as a key element of Irish language poetics during Pádraig Mac Piarais's tenure as editor of the Gaelic League journal *An Claidheamh Soluis* (1903–09). In 1906, Mac Piarais insisted that 'Irish literature if it [is] to live and grow, must get into contact on the one hand with its own past and on the other with the mind of contemporary Europe'.[8] Rejecting the nativism of the more myopic cultural nationalists and the provincialism of those who confused 'cosmopolitanism' with Anglicisation, he argued that the European connection was a feature of the pre-colonial Gaelic Irish tradition: 'Were we then completely aloof from European thought when we were Irish, and are we more in touch with it now that we are more than half English?'[9]

Among his UCD associates, Ó Nualláin was the most familiar with the pre-colonial Gaelic tradition.[10] In addition to Irish nationalist histories, nineteenth-century Anglo-Irish writing, 'the standard English authors and the Latin and Greek Classics', Brian and his brothers had access to Irish language material in their father's library before they were sent to school, belatedly, in Synge Street and Blackrock College.[11] Their admission to school in 1923 coincided with their father's transfer to Dublin following the establishment of the Free State and the introduction of a more national aspect to the secondary school curriculum, more in keeping with the atmosphere and values of the Ó Nualláin family home. That his father's cultural nationalist politics were not uncongenial to his son might be inferred from his choosing to study Irish at UCD where, despite his criticism of Douglas Hyde and Úna Ní Fhaircheallaigh (Agnes O'Farrelly), his teachers included some of the most distinguished scholars of early Irish literature. Given the idiosyncrasies noted by critics in his own use of Irish, the Irish proverb '*An té a bhíonn ag gáire, bíonn a leath faoi fhéin*' [When someone laughs, half the laughter is at himself] might be an appropriate response to Ó Nualláin's claim 'that Douggie Hyde spoke atrocious Irish, as also did Agnes O'Farrelly'.[12]

The inconsistency of Ó Nualláin's written Irish is hardly surprising, given that Irish was largely a private, familial language, supplemented by extensive reading and occasional visits to the Donegal Gaeltacht of Cloich Cheannfhaola. His recourse to archaism, for instance, in a note of condolence on the death of a child, quoted by Niall Montgomery in his note of appreciation the day after Ó Nualláin's own death, confirms his ability to imitate the patterns of the older language but also suggests an inability to use the contemporary idioms of the spoken language to communicate sympathy with the bereaved.[13] Ó Nualláin's opinion of Hyde and Ní Fhaircheallaigh was, however, shared by Liam S. Gógan (1891–1979), the most accomplished poet in Irish in the period from 1916 to the early 1940s. Gógan's work is characterised by erudition and artifice and he receives passing mention in *Cruiskeen Lawn*:

How many of us think back, I wonder, to that far day when a handful
of us, then young, ardent, met in a certain hotel to found the celebrated
Irish-American syndicate to write under the name of 'James Joyce'? We
had Aodh de Blacam, Niall Sheridan, myself, the Bird, Sam Beckett,
Kenneth Reddin, Father Prout, Liam Gogan, Tim O'Neill, Con Curran,
Beirt Fhear, Proust, Oliver Gogarty, Tom McGreevey, Joe Pike, Freud,
Jimmy Joyce, poor O'Leary Curtis *and* myself – I appear twice because
I was in the Chair, with a casting vote. Our motto was silence, exile and
cunningham if I remember aright.[14]

Brian Ó Nualláin, MA

As Cathal Ó hÁinle has demonstrated, the undergraduate curriculum in Irish
at UCD extended Ó Nualláin's knowledge of literature in Irish from early
Irish nature poetry and heroic prose narratives through to the court poetry of
the bardic period and the songpoems of the oral folk tradition. The Middle
Irish narrative *Buile Suibhne*, the poetry and prose of the *Fiannaíocht*, stories
from *Táin Bó Cuailgne*, *Oidhe Chloinne Lir*, and other material that would
feature in *At Swim-Two-Birds*, were among the set texts for study in the
BA programme. For all his much-vaunted non-attendance at lectures, there
is 'ample evidence to prove that either as an undergraduate or later while
writing his M.A. thesis he read quite assiduously those works prescribed
for the primary degree'.[15] Despite his younger brother Kevin's assertion that
he chose Úna Ní Fhaircheallaigh as his supervisor as she was likely to be
less rigorous than Osborn Bergin, Ní Fhaircheallaigh was one of the most
prominent women involved in the cultural revival of the early twentieth
century and principal of Coláiste Uladh, the Irish language summer school
for teachers in Cloich Chionnaola where the Ó Nualláin family had spent
summer holidays since 1927. She was also committed to improving the
status of Irish and opportunities for women in the education system, and
was appointed Professor of Modern Irish Poetry at UCD in 1932 following
Hyde's retirement.[16] If the mutual connection with the Donegal Gaeltacht
had any impact on his choice of supervisor, it did not diminish the rigour of
Ní Fhaircheallaigh's assessment of Ó Nualláin's postgraduate research when
he submitted his thesis in August 1934. The thesis failed and a revised version
was submitted and passed a year later. Copies of both versions are extant and
a comparison of the two is sufficient to disprove the rumour circulated by
the author that he had done very little with the thesis except to retype it on
pink paper with minor changes.[17] The copy of the later thesis, signed and

dated 1940 and 1941, which is among Ó Nualláin's papers in Boston College, is typed on pink paper but has been significantly revised from the 1934 version which is in the library of University College Dublin.

While acknowledging the extent of the revision, Anthony Cronin suggests the 1935 thesis was as 'pedestrian' as the 1934 version, and Kevin O'Nolan's assessment of his brother's work would seem to confirm that judgement. 'He really liked it, I think, and got a lot out of doing it, but the actual thesis was a very straightforward sort of thing, you know, cataloguing different poems and all that sort of thing, and talking about them in a critical way'.[18] Ciarán Ó Nualláin also dismissed the thesis as lacking originality, a way of passing the time before Brian entered the civil service.[19] In fact, the thesis might be cited as evidence of the fault lines that have run through Irish language scholarship from the nineteenth century to the present, the tension between a philological approach that privileges textual editing of manuscript material and a literary critical approach to the close reading of texts in their several contexts. The title of the revised thesis *Nádúir-fhilíocht na Gaedhilge: Tráchtas Maraon le Duanaire* [Nature-Poetry in Irish: A Thesis with an Accompanying Anthology] indicates clearly the scope of the project. The anthology includes material from Old and Middle Irish, Early Modern and Modern Irish, and the bibliography comprises a list of the best contemporary scholarship on the subject by Irish and European scholars. The essay runs to fifty pages in the earlier draft and sixty-four pages in the revised text; both versions attempt to provide the basis for a critical assessment of the generous selection of poems included in the anthology. The revised essay is more carefully structured and more precise in its articulation of the young scholar's insights into nature poetry in Irish, but the argument presented is consistent, for the most part, in the two versions of the thesis.

The essay makes clear the young scholar's interest in the literary dimension of the poems he has chosen rather than their textual history or linguistic attributes. He also makes clear the extent of the difficulty entailed in devising a reading method appropriate to the material he is presenting:

> *Is leamh an obair í triall a bhaint as sídheoig le scian dochtúra, agus ní mór an tairbhe nó an t-eolas a thiocfas aisti do fhear na sceana. An té a rachas ag iarraidh fhíor-fhilíochta a bhreithniú agus a mhion-scrúdú agus a mhíniú, tá scian-dochtúra ina láimh aige agus tá obair chigilteach chruaidh leagtha roimhe aige. Is cosamhail go sroichfidh sé ceann-scríbe agus é comh h-aineolach is abhí sé i dtosach mara ndéanann sé acht briathra an fhile a scaramhaint agus a tharraingt ó chéile agus a mhiondhealú ar bhealach an dhuine léigheannta atá dall ar gach nídh acht luathas*

agus clisteacht inntleachta. Ní bhuaidhfidh sé rún na filíochta agus ní bhainfidh sé
acht beag-mhíniú aisti, óir sí canamhaint an chroidhe í agus is iomdha rud, ceilte
ar an chionn, a thuigeann an croidhe go réidh.[20]

[It is dull work taking on a fairy with a doctor's knife, and the man with
the knife derives little benefit or knowledge from it. Anyone attempting
to examine, scrutinise and explain real poetry has a doctor's knife in his
hand and difficult tricky work ahead of him. It seems he will reach the
end as ignorant as he was when he started if all he does is separate and
isolate and parse words as a learned person might do who is blind to
everything except intellectual agility and acuity. He will not attain the
secret of poetry and he will draw little of its meaning, because poetry
is the dialect of the heart and there are many things, hidden from the
head, that the heart readily understands.]

Given the precedence of philological approaches in the academic study of
Irish language writing, and of the older literature in particular, Ó Nualláin's
attempt at developing a more literary critical response to the material
presented in the thesis was both innovative and ambitious for a postgraduate
student in the 1930s. The need to devise an appropriate terminology is evident
in his analysis, which, as John Wyse Jackson has pointed out, is 'often couched
in circumlocutions newly minted by O'Nolan to convey literary concepts
that the Irish language had not yet successfully tackled' (_MBM_, 253). The
instability of the terminology and the occasional awkwardness in some of his
formulations indicate something of the difficulty involved in a language not
yet fluent in literary criticism.

Standish Hayes O'Grady (1832–1915)

In October 1940, the same month as his first _Cruiskeen Lawn_ column,
Ó Nualláin published an essay in _The Irish Times_ which commemorated the
twenty-fifth anniversary of the death of Standish Hayes O'Grady, whose
1892 compendium _Silva Gadelica_ was a key influence on his understanding of
the older literature. Writing under the byline 'Flann O'Brien', Ó Nualláin
quotes O'Grady's rebuke to 'the omniscient impeccable leviathans of science
that headlong sound the linguistic ocean to its most horrid depths, and (in
the intervals of ramming each other) ply their flukes on such audacious
small fry as even on the mere surface will venture within their danger'.[21]
In the contest between literary criticism and those O'Grady characterised

as 'the lordly cetaceans of philology', Ó Nualláin sides with his brilliantly idiosyncratic predecessor. The young 'scholar manqué' notes O'Grady's careful manipulation of English in his translations from Irish

> to render to the student the last glint of colour in any Irish word. Dr Hyde has described it as 'half Latin, half early English phraseology, subtly inverted and highly Romanised; as: "he was a covetous and unconscionable man who, though it were but a solitary scruple whether of gold or of silver that he heard of as possessed by any in his country, would by force of arms make his own of it" (*fer sanntach díchuibsech ata comnaieside, ocus cin co cluined acht mad aenscrupal óir no airgit oc duine ina thír dobeired ar éicin chuice féin*)'.

While acknowledging that, on occasion, 'the queer English seems to acquire a peculiar luminance of its own, casting a ghostly charm over passages which read pedestrian enough in the Irish', Ó Nualláin insists that, generally, O'Grady 'gets not only the exact meaning of the Irish but the atmosphere and emotional content'.

O'Grady's foreignising approach to translation from Irish to English is clearly a source for the treatment of much of the early Irish material in *At Swim-Two-Birds*, but the extent to which Ó Nualláin's deployment of 'queer English' in his translation of the *Fiannaíocht* and *Buile Suibhne* is intended to ridicule O'Grady is a moot point.[22] In his preoccupation with accuracy and fidelity to the original text and his determination to distort conventional English if necessary to accommodate the alternative patterns of the source language, O'Grady is an enabling precedent for some of Ó Nualláin's own most impressive translations. O'Grady's influence can be detected also in Myles na gCopaleen's later rendering of Hugh O'Neill's 6 February 1600 letter to his adversary Mac Cochlain, where the undomesticated subterranean pressure of Irish is evident in Myles's unorthodox treatment of English syntax: 'For that reason, in each place in which ye do your own good, pray do also our ill to the fullest extent ye can and we will do your ill to the absolute utmost of our ability, with God's will'.[23] Myles describes the letter as an 'exceptional achievement in the sphere of written nastiness and the original exudes the charm attaching to all instances of complete precision in the use of words'. In the same column, he emphasises aspects of the Irish language and its literature which are central to his own aesthetic: 'its precision, elegance and capacity for the subtler literary nuances. [...] True Irish prose has a steely latinistic line that does not exist in the fragmented English patois'.

J.G. O'Keeffe and *Buile Suibhne*

There is some disagreement as to the extent of Ó Nualláin's debt to J.G. O'Keeffe's 1913 bilingual edition of *Buile Suibhne* in *At Swim-Two-Birds*. For Cathal Ó hÁinle, the similarities between the two translations of the medieval tale are such that Ó Nualláin's claim to have composed his version independently of O'Keeffe 'should not be taken too seriously'.[24] Wäppling focuses on the differences between the two versions, finding Ó Nualláin's translation 'For the most part [...] serious and accurate' and, in some instances, 'more intense and serious' than O'Keeffe's.[25] Where the *At Swim-Two-Birds* version deviates from O'Keeffe, it might be argued that Ó Nualláin is attempting a greater fidelity to the original and a higher degree of verbal precision, emphasising the strangeness of the Irish to the conventional patterns of orthodox English.[26] Where, for example, O'Keeffe translates '*sliocht bharr a throighedh a mbruach na glaisi*' as 'the track of his feet by the brink of the stream',[27] Ó Nualláin favours the more economical 'toe-tracks by the stream-mud' (*CN*, 65). O'Keeffe renders '*Marbh do mac atbeiredh a phop friot*' as 'Dead is your son who used to call you Daddy',[28] but Ó Nualláin's alliteration and his transliteration of the Irish 'pop' has a greater degree of poignancy: 'Ah, dumb dead is the little son that called you pop' (*CN*, 67). Alliteration and transliteration are foregrounded again in Ó Nualláin's version of '*guth cléirigh astoigh ag meiligh agus ag meigeallaigh*' which replaces O'Keefe's 'the voice of a cleric within/a-baaing and a-bleating'[29] with 'the voice of a cleric/melling and megling within' (*CN*, 88). In the earlier version of his MA thesis, Ó Nualláin characterised the language of the poems inset in the prose narrative at moments of heightened drama in *Buile Suibhne* as follows: '*bíonn cuma mearaithe, cuma briste sáruighthe neamh-choitchianta ar an fhilíocht, ag cur 'na luighe ar an léightheoir, eadar aisteacht meadarachta agus ciotacht ráidhte, an stád ina bhfuil inteann Shuibhne*' [the poetry has an agitated aspect to it, a strange, broken, capitulated quality which, in the strangeness of the metre and the awkwardness of expression, persuades the reader of the state of Sweeny's mind]. While some of the poetry has the quality and sweetness of *Fiannaíocht* poetry, he says, there are other verses, disjointed and fractured in meaning ('*sgártha agus briste i gcéill*') in which the disturbance of the madman is truthfully revealed ('*siabhrán an fhir mhire luaidhte go maith fírinneach*').[30] In a neglected essay cited by Caoimhghin Ó Brolcháin, Ciarán Ó Nualláin suggested that Suibhne, in the original text, practises a kind of '*caint crann*' [tree-talk], similar to the '*caint linbh*' [child-talk] a woman might speak to a child or the '*caint cat*' [cat-talk] one might address to a cat.[31] Clearly, there is an element of grotesque humour in all of this but there is also poignancy in Brian Ó Nualláin's more literal translation from *Buile Suibhne* that corresponds to the original, emotionally and linguistically, in giving voice to the trauma of the banished king.

Celtic realism

While Dinneen's dictionary provided Myles with ample evidence of the language's capacity for ambiguity and confusion, Ó Nualláin's insistence on the precision of Irish is crucial to understanding what Brendan Kennelly has identified as a defining element of his artistic practice and aesthetic:

> This love of verbal precision is the expression of an essentially moral imagination. Cliché is not only the truth worn dull by repetition; it can also be a form of immoral evasion, a refusal to exercise the mind at a moment when it should be exercised, even to one's own discomfort or distress. [...] It is also the work of that most driven kind of moralist – the writer for whom the precise use of language is evidence of the mind's capacity for intellectual passion, the heart's capacity for sincerity.[32]

As with many of the contradictions in Ó Nualláin's work, the tension between precision, profusion and confusion in his numerous references to the Irish language reflects competing tendencies in his own imagination. That tension may also indicate an anxiety that the facility for inflation and exaggeration was more pronounced in his own verbal imagination than the linguistic austerity and truth-telling he applauded in his MA thesis.

Ó Nualláin's thesis argues that early Irish literature is the primary source for a particular attitude to the natural world which is characteristic of the Celtic imagination at its height. He draws comparisons with Welsh and Scots-Gaelic poetry but points to the greater antiquity of the Irish material to support his argument that the Celtic attitude to the natural world originated in Ireland. Throughout the discussion, he distinguishes the Celtic Irish attitude from the English perception of the natural world, suggesting that where there is a similarity between the two it is due to the presence of Irish influence in the English material. In support of his argument, he draws on the work of some of the foremost Celtic scholars of the Revival period, occasionally including references to English and European literatures to provide a comparative dimension to his study. The 'Celtic realism' he identifies as characteristic of a distinctive response to nature flourished, he says, in the Old and Middle Irish period but began to decline in the twelfth century due to significant changes in Irish society and literature, including political turmoil and greater contact with the English world. The decline, he argues, is even more precipitous from the seventeenth century onwards although he detects the residual influence of the older attitude to nature in contemporary Irish and Anglo-Irish poetry. As Adrian Naughton has demonstrated, this approach to early Irish literature has been much revised by more recent scholarship but is in keeping with the work of some of the most distinguished Celticists of the early twentieth century.[33]

The key features of the literary sensibility Ó Nualláin sought to define are identified in both versions of the thesis: '*míphearsantacht*' [impersonality], '*géarfhéachain & cruinneas tuairisce*' [sharp observation and precise description], '*géarchomaoine leis an nádúr*' [intense communion with nature], '*fírinne-tuairisce*' [truth-telling] and '*gontacht-cainte*' [economy of expression].[34] The autonomy of the natural world is crucial to the aesthetic Ó Nualláin juxtaposes to the 'pathetic fallacy' he associates with later foreign influence. The Gaelic attitude, he says, did not regard the natural world as a mirror reflecting the poet's thoughts ('*scáthán ar a mbíonn aigne an fhile breacaighthe*') or as a manifest of God's presence in the world deflecting the poet from the beauty and wonder of the natural world to the divine power that created it ('*a thairngeas smaoineamh an fhile ó shaibhreas agus áilneacht an domhain chuig comhacht an dé a chruthaigh é*').[35] Rather, it acknowledged the stable truth ('*fírinne sheasmhach*') of the observed world independent of the mind of the observer.[36] Commenting on verses attributed to Saint Colmcille, Ó Nualláin notes the absence of a sense of the divine in the saint's wonder at the natural world ('*is beag an feith diadha le faghail ins na dántaí seo*').[37] The 1935 text extends the argument before retreating from the implication that the Gaelic Irish imagination considered the natural world to be sufficient to itself, intimately related to human existence, but independent of divine creation:

> *Ní raibh fonn ar an mheon cheilteach cumhacht Dé a fheiceáil 'sa Dúlraidh mórthimpeall air nó uathbhás do-eolais na síorraíochta a bhaint as an bhláth feochta. Ba leor leis an fhile an radharc a chonnaic sé agus an glór a chuala sé gan aon mheabhrú a dhéanamh ortha. Ní leanann sé ó seo go rabh an Ceilteach dall ar mhórtas agus ar uaisleacht na Dúlraidhe agus nár thuig sé go rabh dia nó cruthaitheoir taoibh thiar do'n iomlán. Níor dhúil leis a leithéid a admháil nuair abhí an Nádúir dá canadh agus dá moladh aige. Bhí dlúth-charadas eadar an fhile agus an Nádúir, bhí sé ar aon-chéim leithi. Níor mhian leis an dá rud, an domhan corportha agus anam-cheist na síorraíochta, a mheascadh ar a chéile, agus is feairrde a chuid filíochta nár mhian.*[38]

[The Celtic mind did not wish to see God's power in Nature all around it or infer the incomprehensible horror of eternity from the withered flower. What he saw and heard was sufficient to the poet without further contemplation. It does not follow from this that the Celt was oblivious to the pride and dignity of Nature or that he did not understand that there was a god or creator behind everything. He did not wish to acknowledge that when he was singing and praising Nature. There was a close relationship between the poet and Nature; he and she were equal. He did not wish to mix the two things, the corporeal world and the spiritual question of eternity, and his poetry is all the better for that.]

While it remains undeveloped, Ó Nualláin's perception that the Gaelic literary imagination perceived the natural world as permanent and autonomous, rather than as a cipher for God's presence in the world or an intimation of a Christian afterlife, is not inconsistent with Seán Ó Tuama's suggestion in a seminal essay on the sense of place in Irish writing: 'Can it be then that the half-concealed pre-Christian perception which lies deeply in the Irish subconscious is that the natural world is itself eternal; that there is no personal Creator, no transcendental afterlife?'[39]

Finn and Sweeny

Adrian Naughton has drawn attention to recent scholarship which suggests the poems that survive from Old and Middle Irish represent the nostalgia of monastic scribes for an earlier period in which their predecessors, whether Christian anchorites or pre-Christian warriors, had a more direct relationship with the natural world than was possible in the relatively affluent circumstances in which the poems were written down and recorded.[40] The nostalgia for a less alienated sensibility that would integrate the carnal and the spiritual aspects of human existence is crucial to the treatment of Finn and Sweeny in *At Swim-Two-Birds*. Despite their occasional exasperation with his prolixity, Finn's companions acknowledge the source of his superior storytelling ability: 'He has seen more of the world than you or me, of course, that's the secret of it' (*CN*, 59–60). While Finn attempts to restrict his stories to those directly drawn from his own experience, he is sometimes reluctant to tell even those stories whose truth he can vouch for: 'It is true, said Finn, that I will not' (*CN*, 12). His anxiety is related to the principle of *'fírinne-tuairisce'* [truth-telling] identified in Ó Nualláin's thesis as central to early Irish nature poetry. Finn is aware of the impossibility of upholding that principle once he commits himself to language. His first intervention in the novel begins in a manner reminiscent of the 'Celtic realism' analysed in the thesis but is gradually inflated to the point where the link between language, imagination and reality is shattered. His catalogue of the sweetest music opens with '*géarfhéachain & cruinneas tuairisce*' [sharp observation and precise description] drawn from empirical experience:

> When the seven companies of my warriors are gathered together on the one plain and the truant clean-cold loud-voiced wind goes through them, too sweet to me is that. Echo-blow of a goblet-base against the tables of the palace, sweet to me is that. I like gull-cries and the twittering together of fine cranes. I like the surf-roar at Tralee, the songs of the three sons of Meadhra and the whistle of Mac Lughaidh. (*CN*, 10)

Gradually, however, language becomes rampant, and the obsessive cataloguing of the natural world a travesty of the precision and economy noted with approval in the thesis:

> I am friend to the pilibeen, the red-necked chough, the parsnip land-rail, the pilibeen móna, the bottle-tailed tit, the common marsh-coot, the speckle-toed guillemot, the pilibeen sléibhe, the Mohar gannet, the peregrine plough-gull, the long-eared bush-owl, the Wicklow small-fowl, the bevil-beaked chough, the hooded tit, the pilibeen uisce, the common corby, the fish-tailed mud-piper, the crúiskeen lawn, the carrion sea-cock, the green-lidded parakeet, the brown bog-martin, the maritime wren, the dove-tailed wheatcrake, the beaded daw, the Galway hill-bantam and the pilibeen cathrach. (*CN*, 10)

Finn is tormented by the propensity of narrative to distort the truth of lived experience: 'it is true that there has been ill-usage to the men of Erin from the book-poets of the world and dishonor to Finn, with no knowing the nearness of disgrace or the sorrow of death, or the hour when they may swim for swans or trot for ponies or bell for stags or croak for frogs or fester for the wounds on a man's back' (*CN*, 16). The stories of Ceallach, Sweeny, the Children of Lir and others that 'dishonour the God-big Finn for the sake of a gap-worded story' (*CN*, 15) are cited as evidence of the treacherous slippage between rhetoric and reality. The counterfactual capacity of language to override empirical truth compromises his own ability to harness words and stories to give an accurate account of the world as he has known it: 'They go above me and around me and through me, said Finn. It is true that I cannot make them' (*CN*, 14).

Given his refusal to relate stories that misrepresent himself or cannot be vouched for by his own experience, Finn's willingness to tell the story of Sweeny, 'the turning point of the book',[41] requires further elucidation. Seamus Heaney notes the tension between the heroic pagan past and Christianity at the heart of *Buile Suibhne* before suggesting that this aspect of the story

> does not exhaust its significance. For example, insofar as Sweeney [*sic*] is also a figure of the artist, displaced, guilty, assuaging himself by his utterance, it is possible to read the work as an aspect of the quarrel between free creative imagination and the constraints of religious, political and domestic obligations.[42]

Sweeny's story in both the medieval Irish narrative and in *At Swim-Two-Birds* is a morality tale that reminds readers of the dangers of intellectual pride and unbounded imagination. The physical torment of Sweeny and Dermot Trellis is a reminder that reason and imagination must be anchored to the corporeal dimension of human existence. When Sweeny punctures Saint Ronan's bell (*CN*, 62), he is refusing the order of the Christian life it symbolises. In the world of the student narrator, the bell regulates the lives of the university professors who might otherwise remain 'distant in the web of their fine thought' (*CN*, 41). When he himself gradually abandons the world of imagination for the mundane routines of domestic life, his uncle's kindness 'induced in [him] an emotion of surprise and contrition extremely difficult of literary rendition or description' (*CN*, 214). His rediscovery of a shared humanity and humility beyond expression is marked by 'the Angelus pealing out from far away' (*CN*, 214). In the passage immediately following this, the destruction of the manuscript in which Orlick had turned the tyrannical power of language and narrative on his creator rescues Trellis from a world of his own design not subject to the laws of empirical reality or divine redemption. Orlick and his companions are consigned to fire, their remains 'taking flight as if to heaven through the chimney, a flight of light things red-flecked and wrinkled hurrying to the sky' (*CN*, 215). Sweeny too, although restored to equilibrium and reconciled to divine salvation through the intercession of Saint Moling, remains estranged from human society, betrayed by yet another 'crooked and dishonourable story' (*CN*, 15).

Kim McMullen has drawn attention to another aspect of Sweeny's story: the contest between oral and written tradition, between a landscape mapped and delimited by ecclesiastical authority and an undomesticated terrain beyond the control of a new Christian dispensation:

> By drowning the psalter, Sweeny challenges the emblem of the priest's Christian devotion and earthly authority. If the Word is God, language becomes monologic and absolute, its repository the unchanging, because scripted, holy text. In his attempted logocide, the Celtic Sweeny whose culture is oral, desires to submerge the authority upon which the Church's subsequent occupation of the Irish landscape is to be built – the Word. In turn, Ronan invokes the power of that Word to condemn Sweeny to madness and exile by uttering a 'melodious lay' that 'will banish thee to branches' and 'put thee on a par with fowls' [*CN*, 62]. Maddened through this clash of cultures, exiled by and within language, Sweeny flies across Ireland, singing intensely beautiful lyrics that rehearse the spirituality of the land itself as an alternative to Christian psalmody. It is a wild terrain, bountiful and harsh, not yet bounded by the Church. [...] And, in yet another twist to this complex and equivocal convergence of cultures, Sweeny's ephemeral (because oral) lyrics are preserved by a self-appointed scribe – the literate Christian Moling – and Sweeny's own words become textbound.[43]

Sweeny's predicament is similar to Finn's: in the contest between reality and representation, the ephemeral truth of lived experience becomes text, contained, elided, supplanted in the act and art of articulation. Myles na gCopaleen's preference for the perceived immediacy of orality, 'the illiterate's acute observation of the real world as distinct from the pale print-interpreted thing that means life for most of us' (*BM*, 238), is reminiscent of the nostalgia for a fully integrated relationship between language and reality that is central to the treatment of both Finn and Sweeny in *At Swim-Two-Birds* and of the tension between pagan past and Christian present in early Irish literature.

A dreamed-of language

It is a commonplace of twentieth-century literary criticism that the sense of being 'exiled by and within language' is a feature of the modern condition reflected in the narrative modes of modern fiction. As Roland Barthes has it, narrative 'burdens the unfolding of History with a parasitical unity, and gives the novel the ambiguity of a testimony which may well be false'.[44] Like all modern art, he says, 'literary writing carries at the same time the alienation of History and the dream of History [...] it hastens towards a dreamed-of language whose freshness, by a kind of ideal anticipation, might portray the perfection of some new Adamic world where language would no longer be alienated'.[45] The dream of an unalienated language is a defining element of Brian Ó Nualláin's writing, intensified by his knowledge of pre-colonial Gaelic Irish literature and his own ambiguous relationship with the Irish language. While modernism and post-modernism provide their own insights into his work, the extent to which Ó Nualláin's poetics derives from his reading of early Irish literature and a linguistic self-consciousness aware of the inadequacies of an incomplete bilingualism requires further sustained investigation.

12

In defence of 'gap-worded' stories

Brian O'Nolan on authority, reading and writing

ALANA GILLESPIE

For a writer whose work so attentively challenged the authority of institutions, ideas, authors, critics and politicians, Brian O'Nolan's author personae and characters frequently present themselves as unassailable authorities. In *Cruiskeen Lawn*, Myles styles himself 'Assistant Secretary of the World' (*FC*, 98), complains about not being consulted by world leaders about post-war planning and expresses haughty annoyance with 'the revolting manifestations and exercises which go by the name of "gaelicism" today' – none of which he authorised.[1] In this last complaint, Myles speaks in his capacity as co-founder of the Gaelic League in 1881, an example of a practice that can be considered the temporal equivalent of namedropping: time-dropping. The Myles persona time-drops into so many momentous events that it appears he would have us believe he worked closely with, or was even related to, the likes of Lloyd George, Georges Clemenceau and Marshal Tim O'Shenko.[2] These tactics ostensibly validate him as a speaker worth listening to and make it easier for him to hold court uninterrupted and unchallenged by thimbleriggers. Yet as we will see, O'Nolan's engagement with the concept of authority suggests that it is hardly unassailable; no cow is too sacred and no story is so solid it cannot be questioned. His writing demonstrates that all canonical narratives are constructed and edited and as a result, riddled with gaps, omissions and insertions – both authorised and unauthorised. Authority in O'Nolan's work is never stable or a given, but a flexible construct: if it is to be maintained within a given cultural moment and space of remembrance, those that perceive authority must affirm it and adjust it to suit their presentist needs. Ultimately, O'Nolan mocks claims to authority and suggests they are spurious by using techniques of time-dropping or impossible timelines. Neither old age nor the long-standing validity or greatness of a tradition are stable foundations on which authority can rest unchallenged.

This essay explores the complexity with which O'Nolan engages the concept of authority in relation to acts of reading and writing and the interrelated processes of editing, translating, remembering and forgetting. By making acts of construction and editing key themes, O'Nolan can exploit narrative gaps and demonstrate that true authority cannot be achieved through creation or intention alone – audience reception and approval are just as important, if not more so. By engaging with narratives in this way, O'Nolan achieves a radical reassessment of some aspects of authority and canonicity, in particular as they relate to the doctrines and myths of cultural nationalism and catholic tradition in an Irish context. I examine these points in *At Swim-Two-Birds* and *The Dalkey Archive*, two novels in which narratives function as tools or media of cultural memory,[3] of which the use-value can vary and be adjusted over time. Written texts can function as both containers and communicators of cultural memory which reproduce, repeat and shape shared cultural memories. Drawing on twentieth-century theories of cultural memory, reproduction and repetition, in particular Walter Benjamin's 'The Work of Art in the Age of Mechanical Reproduction' (1936) and Jacques Derrida's *Specters of Marx* (1993), I argue that O'Nolan's treatment of time and insistence on the mutability of (interpreting) narratives represent a radical critique not only of historical authority itself, but also of a non-critical attitude to history.

Focusing on the centrality of these processes and acts of reproduction, repetition and recycling to *At Swim-Two-Birds* and *The Dalkey Archive*, I consider how O'Nolan actively challenges and redesigns concepts of authority directly in relation to texts. Treating existing texts as raw materials with which to construct new ones, O'Nolan has his characters repurpose and recontextualise culturally authoritative narratives conveyed or produced by these texts.[4] By selecting fragments for inclusion or omission in a new narrative that they can put to use in their particular historical moment, the characters effectively choose which narratives they wish to call home. I will develop this concept of narrative as a form of habitation in relation to Benjamin and Derrida, arguing that readers as users of texts and inhabitants of narratives are instrumental in determining which texts are meaningful enough to exercise authority either over time or in a specific moment.

O'Nolan's temporal experiments or time-dropping are important in this regard, and I will discuss how time, whether immemorial or fleeting, can be called upon to influence the authority and (shifting) use-value of texts in different eras. Narratives are constantly deployed in service of crystallising or 'concretising' a shared cultural identity and memory (whether national, religious or both) during a given era.[5] Yet in so far as people use them to imagine the past and thus also the future, narratives are treated in *At Swim-Two-Birds* and *The Dalkey Archive* not as immovable and immortal monuments, but rather as squats we can all temporarily inhabit – and refurbish, destroy or restore to suit our present needs. If, as Denell Downum writes, O'Nolan 'illuminates the dilemma of the writer who cannot fully cede authority and yet who also understands the false premises on which [it] rests', then these two novels go furthest in revealing the gaps and holes in the authority of past texts, narratives and figures of memory that can be deconstructed and reinvented into something that is easier to live with and more appropriate for the present.[6]

The narrative as mosaic habitation: *At Swim-Two-Birds*

In *At Swim-Two-Birds*, Finn Mac Cool's epic proportions and authoritative standing in Irish letters and legend are set up early, but chipped away by degrees as the other characters in the Red Swan Hotel usurp authority and authorship from 'Finn that is a better man than God' (*CN*, 15), reducing him to a withered old man ranting beside the fireplace with the status of a valuable relic – one preserved in the knowledge that it is valuable, but which is covered in dust and seems unloved. By the hotel fireside, Finn begins to tell his version of *Buile Suibhne* [*The Frenzy of Sweeny*], engaging in his own act of time-dropping by relating a story 'set four centuries after Finn's own adventures'.[7] However, his audience tires of his traditional poetic form and he is soon displaced, first by Lamont's own retelling of the Sweeny myth as a convoluted nationalistic tale of a jumping contest between an Irish-speaking local and an English-speaking policeman, then by Shanahan's pulp-western version of *Táin Bó Cúailnge* [*Cattle Raid of Cooley*] in the style of William Tracy, 'the eminent writer of Western romances' (*CN*, 37). By flouting Finn's standing, new voices and claims to authority can emerge and be heard, possibly replacing, at least temporarily, the authority of the 'god-big' Finn. Downum argues that the novel's many retellings of *Buile Suibhne* have an effect similar to what Walter Benjamin describes in 'The Work of Art in the Age of Mechanical Reproduction' as 'detach[ing] the reproduced object from the domain of tradition' and eventually leading to the 'liquidation of the traditional value of the cultural heritage'.[8] But for O'Nolan, as for Benjamin, tradition-shattering was not the end: after their traditional values or 'auras' are diminished or liquidated, O'Nolan's manifold retellings of *Buile Suibhne*, *Táin Bó Cúailnge* and the Finn saga 'reactivate the object reproduced', giving them a new functionality that better harmonises with the audience's current desires and demands.[9]

The upside of mechanical reproduction in Benjamin's view is that even as it liquidates the work's aura, it democratically liberates the artwork from its original ritualistic context and brings it to more people than the original could ever reach. The new functionality achieved by the work of art in new, political contexts is highly valuable and can boost perceived authority and use-value. Carol Taaffe notes characteristics of mass production and reshuffled chronology in O'Nolan's text: '*At Swim* often reads not only as a novel produced by committee, but as an experiment in assembly line fiction – albeit with all the pieces inserted in the wrong order'.[10] Taaffe's insight and historicising approach has initiated a series of investigations of O'Nolan's engagements particularly with mass culture against Benjamin's (and the Frankfurt School's) coordinates.[11] What these arguments overlook, however, and what I will focus on in my own reading of O'Nolan against Benjamin here, is the fact that these strategies speak not only to O'Nolan's engagements with the modern drives of mass culture but also to his deconstruction of the aura of history's authoritative texts and their place in cultural memory (*vis-à-vis* Revivalist discourse and post-independence cultural nationalism).

The retellings in *At Swim-Two-Birds* are 'mechanically' reproduced along an imaginative conveyor belt in the factory of the novel, but this process also presents a modern twist on Benjamin's reading of Paul Klee's painting *Angelus Novus* (1920) in which the Angel of History sees the debris of the past and proceeds to reduce, reuse and recycle it in new political and cultural contexts and rituals. In the Red Swan Hotel, the traditional value of Sweeny is shattered but acquires new value when the shards are pieced together in a new constellation, like a mosaic, which reinvigorates the cultural heritage of the Sweeny story reproduced.

As writers, Shanahan and Lamont reject Finn's storytelling and the Old Irish literary tradition associated with it even though they respect it. As listeners or readers, they are uninspired by Finn's telling of the Sweeny story, particularly his droning and distant delivery, hence the passive-aggressive label of 'Mr Storybook'. They feel more affinity with Jem Casey's 'Workman's Friend', which they estimate to be a fine piece of writing that will 'live' (*CN*, 74). Unlike the poetry and tales Finn recites, Casey's doggerel can be read and reread without boredom. This critical praise for Casey indirectly diminishes the authority traditionally associated with Finn and ancient Irish poetry. It is not stimulating enough to the modern man. Shanahan, Lamont and Furriskey believe it is wrong to read and reread the stuff of the inherited tradition and 'read damn the bloody thing else', but they deem Casey's subjects eternally appealing because they identify with Casey as their own sort of man (*CN*, 73). Although they have great respect and pride for traditional Irish literature, they cannot relate to it and tire of listening to it. They seem to regard its main value as sentimental. It made their country great, but they would prefer to keep it as a monument, standing proudly in view but without dominating the landscape, leaving plenty of room for passers-by and the day-to-day business of the man on the street. Through O'Nolan's parody of both the source (Old Irish literature) and the critics who would claim it lacks value because it has no contemporary relevance, *At Swim-Two-Birds* raises several questions concerning readers' ideas about authority: how many transmutations can a text or narrative undergo and still retain enough of its original aura to create an authentic experience and have a contemporary use-value? What are the effects on authority of yoking a narrative to (different) political or cultural causes? As acts of memory, how do a narrative's repetition or transmediation augment or diminish (conceived) authenticity and authority?

Downum notes that Finn's listeners fail to 'grasp the democratizing potential of a narrative unmoored from nationalistic ritual and fetishist claims of originality' even though they 'exploit those possibilities unwittingly with their own stories and poems inspired by Sweeny's tale'.[12] O'Nolan's novel challenges us to explore further the democratising potential of a narrative freed from nationalistic ritual and to look at how users and consumers of narrative attribute or deny a given narrative's authority. Kimberley Bohman-Kalaja notes that Lamont's nationalist retelling of *Buile Suibhne* (about the jumping contest between Bagenal and the policeman) 'distorts the original story almost beyond recognition' as 'Lamont quickly sees the potential for stealing the spotlight from Finn by using the story to appeal to the nationalist bigotries of his audience'.[13] Lamont, Shanahan and Furriskey do not even realise they have appropriated Finn's narrative. How they appropriate it can be partly explained by drawing an analogy with Benjamin's discussion of the response of 'the distracted mass' to architecture in 'The Work of Art in the Age of Mechanical Reproduction'.[14] Benjamin emphasises the role of habit in the absorption of the work of art:

> Buildings are appropriated [...] by use and by perception – or rather, by touch and sight. [...] Tactile appropriation is accomplished not so much by attention as by habit. As regards architecture, habit determines to a large extent even optical reception [which occurs] by noticing the object in incidental fashion. *This mode of appropriation, developed with reference to architecture, in certain circumstances acquires canonical value. For the tasks which face the human apparatus of perception at the turning points of history cannot be solved by optical means, that is, by contemplation, alone. They are mastered gradually and by habit,* under the guidance of tactile appropriation. [my emphasis][15]

Benjamin's argument that buildings are appropriated as they become meaningful to the people who see, exploit and inhabit them can also be made of familiar narratives in general and, more particularly, of the Old Irish narratives and legends in the Revivalist discourse that O'Nolan satirises in *At Swim-Two-Birds*, *Cruiskeen Lawn* and *An Béal Bocht*. Repetition and recursivity are critical in realising a shared and meaningful cultural memory,[16] and this is exactly what the Revivalist movement was doing at the turn of the century: repeating and reproducing narratives that affirmed a shared cultural heritage. Throughout his work, O'Nolan also repeats and reproduces important narratives that affirm shared cultural heritage. But he digs with a critical spade, self-consciously foregrounding the transformation of these narratives through omission or addition by authors, translators, editors and other users of texts. Critical attention to editorial history and changes constitutes both affirmation and contestation of the authority of the canons and contexts to which these texts varyingly belong. Each new repetition of the Sweeny story in *At Swim-Two-Birds* introduces a new step or phase in the project of cultural memory. New value is given to the object of remembrance (narrative) by adapting it to reflect or criticise contemporary tastes and desires, giving it the potential to be linked to new contexts, rituals and commemorative acts.

Through habit and repeated commemorative acts and behaviours, narratives become institutionalised as part of official history and/or cultural memory.[17] Once a figure of memory becomes institutionalised, it begins to lead a life of its own and becomes detached from the historical context of its production. Ample textual evidence, not accuracy, is what is needed for a figure of memory to be selected and installed in working cultural memory, which, Aleida Assmann writes, 'is based on two separate functions':

> the presentation of a narrow selection of sacred texts, artistic master-pieces, or historic key events in a timeless framework; and the storing

of documents and artifacts of the past that do not at all meet these standards but are nevertheless deemed interesting or important enough to not let them vanish on the highway to total oblivion.[18]

Therefore, it is time, taste and posterity that determine which texts continue to be read and thus will survive.[19] Texts must remain useful and in circulation to continue to 'elicit [the] intense attention' that is needed to remain recursive enough to contribute to constructions of working cultural memory (as opposed to archival or reference memory – what could be, but is not necessarily actively drawn on).[20] Intense attention leads to a 'self-perpetuating vortex of symbolic investment' whereby an object or site of remembrance is repeated, reproduced, transformed, referred to, replicated and interpreted.[21]

In practice, through habit, repeated commemorative acts, and behaviours, a recurrent tragic paradigm of heroic suffering became common currency in the narratives circulating in nineteenth- and twentieth-century Ireland.[22] Narratives such as *Buile Suibhne* or *Táin Bo Cuailnge* had been reproduced and revived as translations, plays, songs, paintings and folk ballads for centuries and were transformed in the process.[23] They were used by various cultural and political authorities to inspire the Irish people with a sense of a rich past once characterised by suffering, which should somehow entitle them to a modern and sovereign state. Over years of exposure to these narratives, the Irish recipients of these stories formed a habitual relationship with them and began to use them as models for other stories of the Irish experience. However, Irish consumers of narratives were neither uncritical nor entirely autonomous in their acceptance of narratives of the past as used by the post-independence state. On some level, even those narratives imposed or endorsed by mid-century Irish governments or (sometimes oppressive) institutions were chosen and affirmed selectively because they supported hegemonic values and readings of the past. The narratives that stayed in circulation and gained enough authority to lead lives of their own succeeded precisely because they were useful to readers and listeners, who found in them, for example, inspiration, pride, justification, comfort or a thirst for revenge. As consumers of texts, the ('distracted') masses began to inhabit these narratives by appropriating them through habit. It is significant, then, that the theme of heroic suffering is the aspect of *Buile Suibhne* most emphasised in *At Swim-Two-Birds*.

O'Nolan vividly illustrates this principle in relation to Gaeltacht writing through the centrality of '*na dea-leabhair*' [the '*guid buiks*'] (*ABB*, 56; *CN*, 447) in the lives of the Gaels of *An Béal Bocht*. The novel satirically depicts how the 'good books' are thought to possess unwavering authority: the lessons of the 'good books' achieve this perceived timelessness through public and private repetition and celebration, and they are drawn on for direction and reassurance regarding the inevitability and implied rightness of tragic events. This powerful critique of (or even attack on) a certain Revivalist discourse and canon formation[24] also informs *At Swim-Two-Birds*, whose characters take matters into their own hands to fashion a narrative better suited to their particular cultural identity – which is not limited to the stuff of the native land but also draws on, among other 'non-native' genres, westerns, Victorian novels, textbooks and journalism.

Writers, canons and critics: reading us down the garden path

In order to explore more closely the importance of critics and editors in shaping worldviews, I would like to consider what it means to inhabit a narrative wilfully in *The Dalkey Archive*. In the novel, O'Nolan's Joyce elaborates the changes he foresees in Catholic doctrine should he manage to infiltrate the powers that be to rewrite church history and rectify what he regards as the mistranslation of *pneuma* and the subsequent groundless invention of the Holy Ghost. O'Nolan's Joyce compares the Hebrew *ruach* with the Latin *spiritus* and the Greek *pneuma*, stating that 'All these words mean life. Life, and breath of life. God's breath in man' and later, 'Life, death, eternity, recall of the past' (*CN*, 765–66, 768). Mick weakly voices his surprise at Joyce's account of the origins of the Holy Ghost by saying that he 'always understood that God was of three Divine Persons', to which Joyce remarks, 'Well you didn't get up early enough in the morning, my lad' (*CN*, 767). Joyce explains that the Holy Ghost was not 'officially invented' until AD 381 at the First Council of Constantinople and was hardly mentioned at the First Council of Nicaea (held in AD 325) from which the Nicene Creed takes its name (*CN*, 767).

Scholars distinguish between two creeds of this name, one that defends the orthodox faith against Arianism and another consisting of the original creed and appendages to it, known as the Niceno-Constantinopolitan Creed. What is commonly known as the Nicene Creed is the second version, complete with appendages. Mick confirms Joyce's assumption that he, despite his inexperience in Biblical studies, certainly knows the Nicene Creed because he is a Catholic: 'Sure everybody knows that', Mick replies, expressing the

casual confidence of one comfortable in what he knows he knows (*CN*, 767).
The canonical value of the Nicene Creed has wiped its dual origins from
popular memory. In lived experience or the day-to-day life of the text, it
is a statement of faith often (mindlessly) recited from beginning to end. In
an instance of time-dropping, by resurrecting Joyce from beyond the grave
to challenge the historicity of the Holy Ghost, O'Nolan calls attention to
Catholic Ireland's comfortable inhabitation of accepted and preordained
narratives. Few users of the Nicene Creed would think to speculate about
its origins or flinch at its anachronistic reference to the incarnation of Jesus
via the Holy Spirit. Furthermore, the creed's canonical position in the Irish
(Catholic) nationalist tradition as a text that everybody knows is shown to be
taken for granted. The non-Irish origins of the Nicene Creed and countless
other church texts have not prevented their integration into the Catholic
nationalist tradition, illustrating that religious texts could transcend the
nationally appropriate requirements of many other non-Irish texts. Where
At Swim-Two-Birds experiments with and rewrites existing narratives that
play an important role in Irish nationalism and historiography, *The Dalkey
Archive* liquidates or shatters the traditional value of comfortably inhabited,
canonical and ecclesiastical narratives that absolutely permeate Christian and
Western thought and worldviews in countless ways.

The Dalkey Archive also goes further than *At Swim-Two-Birds* in its
examination of readers' roles in evaluating and canonising texts. While
the trial of Trellis can be viewed as an opportunity for characters and/
or readers to enter into dialogue with authors and for authors to defend
themselves, it would be wrong to characterise the exchanges at the trial as
productive dialogue that leads to better understanding. The discussions
about particular texts between authors and readers in *The Dalkey Archive*
are also confrontational and inclined to create chaos, even as they generate
broader readings. While Mick tracks down Joyce to confront him with
questions about his work (most of which Joyce denies having authored[25]), De
Selby confronts Augustine with questions about the scriptures and his own
Confessions (which Augustine characterises as '*all shocking exaggeration*' [*CN*,
636]) and Hackett forms a plan to rehabilitate the apocryphal Gospel of Judas
Iscariot. Not only do denials of authorship or claims of spurious attribution
abound in *The Dalkey Archive* and *At Swim-Two-Birds*, but some characters
also try to distance themselves from their authorial personae or other authors'
representations of them. Finn complains of the 'ill-usage' writers have done
him and others by twisting words for the sake of a good story (*CN*, 16).
Although Augustine's view of storytelling recognises that the truth need not

get in the way of a good story, he still dislikes being associated with some of his work (and the '*obscene feats*' he '*invented*') and would rather be judged on his life's work than the *Confessions*'s youthful exaggeration (*CN*, 636). Despite having different motives and methods, Mick, Hackett, De Selby, Augustine and Joyce all question the authority of received interpretations or dominant narratives and seek to expose or destroy the foundations of established narratives or to erect new ones on top of ruins.

Through challenging the authority of authors and different texts and reintroducing apocryphal texts, both *At Swim-Two-Birds* and *The Dalkey Archive* indicate alternative traditions and historical trajectories. Tim Woods claims this is the only way to 'renew the course of history', namely, by 'releasing the suppressed otherness' of a 'conception of temporality [purified temporality] which generalizes the here-and-now as a once-and-for-all', a process which can only be accomplished by 'confront[ing] this temporality with its (invisible) ghosts'.[26] *The Dalkey Archive*'s playful reassessment of scriptural and literary canons unsettles an interpretation of history by forcing literary and historical spectres to intermingle, thus reinvigorating contemporary views of the course of history, and by extension – at least potentially – the future.

Serious reassessment of the Catholic canons was happening when O'Nolan wrote his final novel at the time of the Second Vatican Council (1962–65). Vatican II introduced more reforms than ever before in the Catholic Church, particularly on the level that concerned the average parishioner day-to-day. *The Dalkey Archive* questions why certain texts were taken by the church as foundational, canonical texts, while others were excluded. Hackett's interest in the apocryphal Gospel of Judas illustrates this questioning of scriptural canonicity directly, while Augustine's dismissal of Book II of his *Confessions* as 'bravado' enhances the novel's ironical re-evaluation of the church's authority. This reassessment of foundational texts and narratives allows O'Nolan to emphasise that truths now largely taken for granted used to be perceived otherwise. For example, Augustine was an embarrassment to the church before he became one of the church fathers, a fact that O'Nolan described with relish in a letter to Tim O'Keeffe about the novel-in-progress.[27] It follows that if things were not always this way, they may well change, and possibly sooner – and more unsettlingly – than one might like. The consequences that either Hackett's rehabilitation of Judas or Joyce's treatise on *pneuma* could have on Christian philosophy or faith if believers were convinced by their arguments would be as radically transformative, even destructive, as De Selby's DMP.

For example, the church and a great deal of Christian and even Western philosophy would be radically transformed if Joyce were right about the mistranslation of *pneuma* as it relates to the 'invention' of the Holy Spirit. Like writing and reading, translation is a creative and political act, one which also exemplifies problems and opportunities that can arise from gaps in meaning. Faced with a term in one language, translators select an equivalent in another language, which is an especially complicated choice when hundreds or thousands of years separate the original text and the moment of translation. Translators must often choose a near equivalent or just explain what is meant if no equivalent exists (what is ancient Greek for internet?). Furthermore, commissioners of translations can have very specific wishes about how a particular term should come across to the desired audience. Indeed, a single source text can result in several different target texts, as translators use different vocabulary, styles and registers to accommodate a variety of target audiences (e.g. experts and school children) as required by commissioning parties.[28] O'Nolan could have done much more with the potential of Joyce's etymological treatise, as could scholarly readings of *The Dalkey Archive*. What would it mean for church history and for contemporary believers if the Vatican issued an apology that the Holy Ghost and thus the Holy Trinity were actually based on a poor translation? What would it mean for philosophical conceptions of spirit? The mind boggles, but for O'Nolan (and his critics), when the metaphysical confounds, refuge can be sought in the bawdy. Rightly or wrongly, the maker of fart jokes is rarely valued as a font of philosophical insight and wisdom, even though a bit of joking and laughter has been known to make readers and audiences more receptive to unconventional beliefs and arguments.[29] Indeed, as Joyce points out when Mick suggests *pneuma* was involved in the conjuring up of Augustine: 'One must not be astonished at a thing merely because it looks impossible' (*CN*, 768). O'Nolan's teetering along the border between the impossible and the absurd enabled him to broach subjects that would have otherwise been out of the ambit of the acceptable in his time. His sense of playing with fire in his treatment of religious subjects is palpable in *The Dalkey Archive*.

Certainly, O'Nolan exceeded his original intentions of taking critics of the church, religion and God to task in *The Dalkey Archive*. He maintained that he had 'no intention to jeer at God or religion; the idea is to roast the people who seriously do so, and also to chide the Church in certain of its aspects. I seem to be wholly at one with Vatican Council II'.[30] The church was still seen as unchanged and unchanging in the early 1960s until finally challenged by Vatican II. The dialogues during the Council and the dialogic assessment of apocryphal texts in the novel reveal the processes by which the church selects and reproduces their defining texts, all of which are heavily edited to fit specific purposes. The parallels O'Nolan draws between the church and literature necessitate contemplation of why it is acceptable to question the authority of the church's critics but not of the church itself. Perhaps for O'Nolan, *The Dalkey Archive*'s most radical step was to present the church as a powerful editor who selects the narratives it deems most worthy of illustrating its principles and rejects – suppresses, even – those which could challenge its authoritative reading of history and its vision of the future.

We might see the novel as O'Nolan's private Council. His criticism of the church and its detractors indicates gaps in the received texts of the church and underscores the textuality of religious belief. The scientist De Selby's desire to correct details in the Bible and biographical details of the lives of the saints illustrates this textuality, as does Joyce's desire to set right hundreds of years of church history with an etymological treatise on the use of the word *pneuma*. By signposting such narrative holes, O'Nolan invites the reader to peer in and see what might be missing – and who can resist looking into a crevasse?

Readers and writers, pacts and conspiracies

Close examination of the gaps in received narratives demands that we accept and never forget that our reality is mediated. We must consider what has been omitted or changed; we must ask why this text and not that one, why this version and not that one. Readers have an ethical responsibility that corresponds to the author's ethical responsibility to select which narrative she or he relates, to question the narratives they receive from her or him. Writing and reading, seen in this way, form a pact – or a conspiracy – between at least two parties. Readers are implicated as conspirators who affirm the validity of certain privileged narratives; they are the final ratifying party in creating an official version in that they must invest in it, identify with it and reproduce it for posterity. To decide with what to identify, 'to reaffirm by choosing' whether consciously or unconsciously, is a question of sifting and criticising; Derrida even describes it as an obligation: 'one must filter, sift, criticize, one must sort out several different possibles'.[31]

O'Nolan destabilises narratives that have been taken for granted; what he uncovers may be unsettling – Finn, Sweeny, the Holy Ghost, Judas, Augustine and Joyce may not be who we thought they were. The discomfort this disclosure can occasion begs the question of what else we might be mistaken about, and in this way O'Nolan shows that we as readers must also sift and choose and that choosing is an ethical and political act. He also anticipates Derrida's rejection of the existence of a pure present and makes this rejection a thematic crux throughout his writing by both drawing attention to the 'non-contemporaneity with itself of the living present'[32] and celebrating the 'plurality of spirits', pasts and narratives that make up the layered and mixed temporality of the living present.[33] An aversion to what Fredric Jameson has aptly called the 'unmixed' is present in both O'Nolan and Derrida's visions of history, which reject the idea of a history without spectres and disturbances.[34]

Maebh Long has shown how Derrida's work resonates with O'Nolan's writing in her discussion of *The Third Policeman*, among others. Long argues that 'the act of remembering – writing, storing, archiving – an event is itself a creative and destructive event', noting how the philosopher underlines the absence of some 'unconscious truth to be rediscovered by virtue of having been written elsewhere [...]. The unconscious text is already a weave of pure traces, differences in which meaning and force are united – a text nowhere present, consisting of archives which are always already transcriptions'.[35] While Long applies this theory to the death drive in her discussion of *The Third Policeman*, I want to expand and develop this conversation by emphasising how the simultaneously creative and destructive act of remembrance informs the processing of certain versions of mythical, historical and religious narratives and events in *The Dalkey Archive* and *At Swim-Two-Birds*. Just as remembering always involves forgetting, so the acts of writing or identifying with a given narrative always involve editing, sifting and choosing.

Derrida's work, according to Woods, is focused on 'the tracking down and stigmatizing of just such nostalgias for some originary simplicity, of the unmixed in all its forms, in favour of mixed, miscegenated, hybridized and multivalenced forms'.[36] O'Nolan's treatment of the handling and (re-) shaping of narratives in these two novels reveals the absence of simple or pure histories and narratives by foregrounding how other narratives leave traces in, intrude upon or hide behind narratives presented or perceived as unchanging and immutable, whether it be a favoured nationalist narrative of heroic suffering epitomised in the selective retellings of *Buile Suibhne* or the accuracy and canonicity of Augustine's influential *Confessions*.[37] By resurrecting and inserting apocryphal and forgotten versions and narratives, part of O'Nolan's objective is the tracking down and stigmatising of pure forms that Woods identifies as the hallmark of Derrida's work. In these two novels, among others, O'Nolan creates and destroys threads of mid-century Irish and

Catholic cultural remembrance to remind readers that unadulterated versions do not exist – there is no pure, unconscious truth buried in originals. Even texts presented as unedited originals are usually edited hybrids with omissions and insertions. O'Nolan parodies claims to authority based solely on the significance of their origins in a specific and distant historical context and temporality to illustrate that history is a nebulous amalgamation of narratives and points of view, thus rejecting the false purity of the unmixed. And so O'Nolan mixes. Dissatisfied with singular readings, he confronts narratives with their omissions and insertions, while merging eras and conflating different readings from different times in order to create new meaning. *At Swim-Two-Birds* and *The Dalkey Archive* are concerned with revealing the gaps in the written weave of historical narratives and provoking us to ask what they conceal. The mixed temporality that unites multiple historical periods in both texts conforms to a conception of the (postmodern) novel as a 'temporal experimentation field' that is conducive to 'confronting history with its ghostly others'.[38]

The narrative strategy of the student author in *At Swim-Two-Birds* enables several characters from different periods and settings to coexist in a chaotically unified environment and to share in that present. According to the student, this strategy would ensure that the 'modern novel [...] be largely a work of reference' in which interchangeable characters are 'allowed a private life, self-determination and a decent standard of living' (*CN*, 21). While permitting them such frivolities may be as impossible as representing characters in all their fullness, O'Nolan seems to suggest that because of the power they wield, authors have an ethical obligation to try, if only to understand these characters better. In many cases, as the mixed temporality of these novels betrays, attempts to achieve the task of proper representation in full require experimenting with temporality itself by conflating several times and perspectives, which often results in highly comic constellations. These experiments with temporality bring characters together beyond the borders of their original or authentic historical contexts and lead to an openly, often impossibly, hybridised and multivalent representation of the subject – as in *At Swim-Two-Birds*, where the seventh-century story of Sweeny is retold from the disparate points of view of the multi-centuried Finn and the twentieth-century fictional characters; or in *The Dalkey Archive* where De Selby obliterates time altogether, enabling him to discuss Descartes with the dead Augustine.

The 'resuscitation of the past in the present', according to Benjamin, is 'a form of blasting away the nostalgic promises of a pure present and temporal transparency'.[39] O'Nolan collapses the linearity of narrative, making narratives that once seemed authoritative and static appear absurd and comic, while also opening up possibilities and alternative modes of interpretation. By these means, O'Nolan reveals how history could have been otherwise and in turn, how it might be possible to change the *status quo* in the future. By introducing, reproducing and transforming alternative narratives and ways of telling – and forcing them to engage in dialogue with each other so as to uncover and point to their gaps – O'Nolan calls attention to authors' and readers' shared responsibility to sift, choose and reaffirm, to inhabit a narrative wilfully. Finn Mac Cool's heart breaks and blood boils at the thought of reckless book-poets doing him dishonour with inaccurate, incomplete and unauthorised stories, but surely these 'book-web[s]' that O'Nolan spins show that 'a gap-worded story' is the only kind there is (*CN*, 15).

13

Reading Flann with Paul

modernism and the trope of conversion*

RUBEN BORG

In this essay I advance the idea that at the heart of Brian O'Nolan's writing is a sustained reflection on the trope of conversion. My argument rests on three subordinate claims:

a. First, that *conversion narratives* are thematically and formally connected to a representation of *life-in-death*, or to an uncanny experience of afterlife on earth;

b. Secondly, that this broader focus on the afterlife, or life-in-death, is pervasive in O'Nolan's fiction – but is also a recurrent theme in modernism, from Pirandello to Beckett, through Joyce and Woolf. In dealing with this trope, O'Nolan may thus be seen to participate in a conversation with contemporary writers;

c. And finally, that a creative engagement with the writings of the apostle Paul constitutes O'Nolan's main contribution to this conversation, his take on a pre-eminently modernist theme: the enquiry into the historical present (the now of modernism) in its contradictory relation to tradition.

As I will argue, the chief appeal of Paul's rhetoric is the invention of a paradoxical relation to the law (and to citizenship), a *neither/nor-but-both-at-once* logic of self-identification with a legal subject or a legal community. O'Nolan looks to Paul, and in particular, to a Pauline rhetoric of conversion, to characterise his own ambiguous status as an experimental modernist writer, and, simultaneously, a critic of modernist *avant-garde* pretensions.[1]

The paradoxical structure of the conversion trope thus comes to inform his attitude towards modernism. But it also provides the existential coordinates of a time out of joint, the very texture of the present in which his characters exist.

A key context for my reading is the critical conversation on O'Nolan's peculiar standing as an anti-modernist modernist writer. I use the word anti-modernist in a sense that is directly indebted to Keith Hopper's discussion of *The Third Policeman* as a post-modernist anti-novel (all hyphenated). However, I wish to mobilise a different definition of modernism to the one contemplated in Hopper's book.[2]

Drawing on ideas developed by Jean-Michel Rabaté in *The Ghosts of Modernity* I want to return to the notion of modernism as a moment characterised by an excess of historical self-consciousness – modernism as an over-extension, if you will, of the project of ideal history. Rabaté argues that a certain spectrality, a metaphorics of the ghost, characterises the modern writer's self-inscription in history. The idea harks back to an image from Chateaubriand: that of a memoirist 'who imagines himself posthumous' in an effort to contain or coordinate the unruly temporalities of his autobiography.[3] The autobiographical aspect is important, here, not because modernism is especially interested in the mysteries of personality, but because of the temporal relations set up by the image. The anachronism of a memoir written from beyond the grave captures the tensions inherent in a modernist theory of tradition when it gives us to think the madness of an impossible deixis – that is to say, when it puts self-presence in conflict with the now.

In this respect, the figure of the ghost expresses the anxieties at issue in the modern writer's fraught relation with the past and ultimately frames modernism itself as a ghost-like moment arising within the historical programme of modernity. The resulting picture is one of a 'haunted modernity [...] that is by definition never contemporaneous with itself',[4] a modernity that is seen always to inhabit a threshold space, looking to the authority of the past and the innovation of the future simultaneously. The idea of O'Nolan's anti-modernist modernism crystallises around a discourse of testament and tradition, and a peculiar conception of the event as a grotesque double of the present. If we understand the present as continuity, as the time of conscious *live* experience, we might think of the Mylesian event as a present shot through with the reality (the after-effects) of one's own death. It is not life that is lived in real time but death itself.

This narrative paradigm recurs throughout O'Nolan's body of work. It inspires a running gag in the *Irish Times* column on the testamentary troubles of Sir Myles (the da) and is a central conceit of the Gothic short story 'Two in One'. Most notably, it features in *The Third Policeman* (easily the most sustained treatment of living death in O'Nolan's canon)[5] and in *The Dalkey Archive*, where the apostle Paul makes a brief cameo appearance as one of Augustine's 'encorpified' companions and is openly acknowledged as Augustine's very first literary influence:

> *I sometimes roar after him 'You're not on the road to Damascus now!' Puts him in his place. All the same that* Tolle Lege *incident was no conjuring trick. It was a miracle. The first book I picked up was by Paul and the lines that struck my eyes were these: 'Not in rioting or drunkenness, nor in chambering or wantonness, nor in strife or envying: but put ye on the Lord Jesus Christ and make not provision for the flesh in the lust thereof'.* (CN, 639)

The 'Tolle Lege *incident*' refers to the conversion of Augustine, the moment when Augustine was inspired by a disembodied voice to 'take up and read', specifically, to take up and read Paul's epistle to the Romans. Indeed Paul's authority presides over the entire afterlife of the novel. It is also implicit in the later discussion of *Pneuma*, the breath of life, or the living spirit which gives life to the body.

Testament, figure and cliché

The same narrative formula – the model of a present shot through with the reality of one's own death – is developed further in the vignette on Sir Myles from the *Cruiskeen Lawn* column. The piece returns to the premise of *The Third Policeman*, in which a character appears to survive, or somehow surpass, the instant of his death. But there are a few notable differences: first, the experience of death-in-life is given a more overtly humorous treatment; secondly, the narrative makes no secret of the character's absurd existential condition: the narrator, the reader and Sir Myles himself are all perfectly aware of Sir Myles's mock-resurrection; and finally, the humour relies on a parody of legal jargon rather than a mock-scientific frame of reference.[6]

> 'I considered carefully', Sir Myles said, 'the advisability of dying intestate but rejected the idea as too dangerous [...] I would have placed upon me the onus of establishing quite novel juridical theses. For example, I would have to show that there is an alternative to testacy or intestacy, viz., extestacy, which would be the condition I would claim to be in. I

would have to show that death is not final and conclusive. This in itself would involve equally recondite definitions of life. My own "existence" would be called in question and I would have to prove — on oath, mind you! — that I was not dead, notwithstanding my recent decease and the hasty nuptials of my dear widow [...] Even my undoubted right to participate as next-of-kin in my own estate would be called in question. The income tax authorities would challenge the inclusion of funeral charges under allowable expenses and would probably insist on sticking me for death duties. It would all be far too troublesome. I would not like it at all. Gentlemen, I would rather be dead'. (*BM*, 158–59)

Here one cannot help being reminded of Beckett: of the puns on the quick and the dead in *More Pricks than Kicks* and of Victor's anxiety in *Eleutheria*, that if he died, he might not even realise he was dead ('I want to enjoy my death. That's where liberty lies: to see oneself dead'[7]); not to mention, of course, the countless narrators who appear to be speaking from beyond the grave, as in 'The Calmative', or 'First Love'.

In particular, the emphasis on legal jargon is reminiscent of *Echo's Bones* (an early short story written as a coda to *More Pricks than Kicks*, and then discarded, only to appear in print in 2014); but more concretely, it puts O'Nolan's work in dialogue with Pirandello's *The Late Mattia Pascal*. There too, the paradox of surpassing one's own death provides the narrative with its central premise. And once again afterlife is experienced as a kind of legal nuisance – or, more precisely, a bureaucratic impossibility. In the words of Don Egidio, Pascal's one remaining friend at the end of the novel, life is impossible 'outside of the law, and without those individual characteristics which, happy or sad as they may be, make us ourselves'.[8] For Pirandello this premise serves to explore a philosophical opposition between social reality and plain life. Life lived by the individual, within social bounds, is set against life in its pure state, freed of ties and social conventions; the latter promises to describe a more authentic existence, but ultimately proves impracticable. For Myles, by contrast, the stakes are moral and metaphysical. The joke of the 'Sir Myles' vignette has a lot to do with the suspicion that death, in modern representation, has become a trivial event – at best a legal technicality. What happens when the afterlife becomes the purview of lawyers and bureaucrats is a triumph of cliché. Being alive is scarcely distinguished from being dead.[9]

The lesson has a direct allegorical application for the craft of the modern writer. As several critics have pointed out, part of O'Nolan's genius was the recasting of English as a sort of mummified tongue. For Anthony Cronin,

'The basic prose style of the first person narrator of *At Swim-Two-Birds* had sometimes read like a translation from the Irish [...]. At others its very meticulousness, a sort of painstaking clarity and flatness, had given the impression that English was being written as a dead language'.[10] The effect is an upturned picture of the state of Anglo-Irish power relations. But the move also resonates beyond immediate language-politics to include matters of law, of testament and tradition.

In this respect, too, the afterlife of Sir Myles (the da) reads like a comic riff on Saint Paul. Paul famously stakes the authority of his word on two moments. The first is the moment of grace on the road to Damascus, an event by which the Apostle symbolically relives the passion and resurrection of Christ, and in doing so, rewrites the old covenant on Mt Sinai. The second is a systematic critique of legalism that seeks to redefine the relation of all free men to the law to which they are subject.[11] Ultimately, both strategies address the question of what it means to be under the law – under its protection, but also under its jurisdiction.

Ostensibly Paul's aim is to promote a doctrine of inclusiveness and universalism, but the polemical thrust of his writings is directed towards a supersession of both Jewish law and Roman citizenship. In this regard, the *Epistle to the Romans* wants to be two things at once: a reaffirmation of the past and a new beginning; conjunction *and* disjunction.[12] Paul's rhetoric relies throughout on a series of conceptual oppositions and chiastic reversals: the old is of course pitted against the new, the letter of the law against the spirit, loyalty to the dead against loyalty to the living. Thus, for example, in *Romans 7*:

> For when we were in the flesh, the motions of sins, which were by the law, did work in our members to bring forth fruit unto death. But now we are delivered from the law [having died to the law], that being dead wherein we were held; that we should serve in newness of spirit, and not *in* the oldness of the letter. [...] For I was alive without the law once: but when the commandment came, sin revived, and I died. And the commandment, which was ordained to life, I found to be unto death.[13]

In these reversals we observe a strange logic of simultaneous affirmation and disavowal, of having one's cake and eating it too. The Self is turned inside out. I am reborn to a present free from the burdens of the past. By the grace of God I am given a new start. But my new life is only justified to the extent that it repeats and redeems my old one; and the authority of my testimony depends on what I have suffered in the throes of death. The importance of this move in establishing Paul's literary authority cannot be overstated. Paul can speak against the Jews because he is one of them in the flesh. And he can speak for them because his covenant repeats and updates the marriage contract God signed with Moses.[14] But he also speaks for Christ because, like Christ, he died and came back among the living.

> Are they Hebrews? So am I. Are they Israelites? So am I. Are they the seed of Abraham? So *am* I. Are they ministers of Christ? (I speak as a fool) I *am* more; in labors more abundantly, in prisons more abundantly, in stripes above measure, in deaths oft. [...] Thrice was I beaten with rods, once was I stoned, thrice I suffered shipwreck, a night and a day I have been in the deep.[15]

The epic adventure of the Second Epistle to the Corinthians goes on to list numerous near-death (and actual death) experiences, followed by a vision of the third heaven. How can an apostle speak on behalf of Christ without going through the harrowing process of death and resurrection? Paul returns to this question time and time again – it is what justifies his entire mission. But we fail to understand that mission altogether if we treat the question as a mere figure of speech, or a thought experiment.

> I knew a man in Christ above fourteen years ago, (whether in the body, I cannot tell; or whether out of the body, I cannot tell: God knoweth), such an one caught up to the third heaven. And I knew such a man (whether in the body, or out of the body, I cannot tell: God knoweth), how that he was caught up into paradise, and heard unspeakable words, which it is not lawful for a man to utter. Of such an one will I glory: yet of myself I will not glory, but in mine infirmities.[16]

In the 'Sir Myles' vignette, Paul's militant rhetoric against the dead letter of the Old Testament is rewritten as a mock-legal problem: a reflection on the minutiae of testamentary law. The parody may well be an end in itself; but viewed in light of several other scenes of death-in-life featured in O'Nolan's work, it lends itself to a broader commentary on the author's poetics. Myles seems to be using Paul to engage an eminently modernist idea: that the task of the writer is to infuse life into a dead medium, to pour spirit into the dead letter of tradition.[17]

However, his fiction participates in this programme as it participates in the Gaelic Revival: by playing up the pretentiousness of its rhetoric. More precisely, it targets the century's bad-faith secularism and the falseness of its universalist politics. In place of the modern writer as a purveyor of the living word, as a Pentecostal figure or as a champion of Spirit, we come upon the allegory of writing as an insoluble testamentary problem. Once again, there is a sense of having only dead words to play with, of being able to speak with authority only from beyond the grave.

Two in one – or, the tell-tale foreskin

The parody of Pauline rhetoric is given a macabre twist in the short story 'Two in One'. Here, life and death are folded into each other, as are, quite literally, flesh and spirit, when the narrator, having killed his employer, provides an alibi for himself by wearing the skin of his victim. The plot follows a perfect symmetry. In the flesh, Murphy is mistaken for Kelly; but in spirit, Kelly is found guilty of Murphy's crime, and sentenced to death in his place.

Encoded in this pot-boiler premise is thus another anti-modernist, modernist metaphor: the figure of the storyteller as a homicidal taxidermist. It is important to take note of the overlap between taxidermy and Murphy's literary craft. The opening paragraph already hints at a connection. The very first words draw attention to the act of storytelling and to the field of literary activity:

> The story I have to tell is a strange one, perhaps unbelievable. I will try to set it down as simply as I can. I do not expect to be disturbed in my literary labours, for I am writing this in the condemned cell. (*SF*, 84)

Murphy then talks at length about the skill and patience required of the taxidermist, and later names low job-satisfaction as his major grievance against his employer.

> Kelly carried on a taxidermy business and I was his assistant. [...] He knew I had a real interest in the work, and a desire to broaden my experience. For that reason, he threw me all the common-place jobs that came in. If some old lady sent her favourite terrier to be done, that was me; foxes and cats and Shetland ponies and white rabbits – they were all strictly *my* department. I could do a perfect job on such animals in my sleep, and got to hate them. But if a crocodile came in, or a Great Borneo spider, or (as once happened) a giraffe – Kelly kept them all for

himself. In the meantime he would treat my own painstaking work with sourness and sneers and complaints. (*SF*, 84–85)

The frustrations of an under-appreciated artist thus provide the motive for Murphy's violent act. The murder doubles as the subject of a good story and as the pretext for the most challenging, most rewarding job a taxidermist can hope to take on. In short, it is an opportunity for the narrator to ply his trade and to take pride in his art.

Paul Fagan has unpacked the connection between taxidermy and writing by looking at the confessional strategies encoded in the story's narrative situation. From within his 'condemned cell' (*SF*, 84) Murphy appears to implicate the reader into a work of self-fashioning and self-justification. The confession is 'ostensibly directed towards the goal of formulating the text's "I" as a coherent, communicable [...] whole',[18] but, subsumed in the artist-murderer's craft, it is transformed into an act of dissimulation and self-effacement. In this sense, as Fagan observes, 'Two in One' reads as 'an autobiography of how Murphy's self comes not to be, or, perhaps, how it unbecomes'.[19]

Jennika Baines continues the exploration of the narrator's confessional stance by pointing to the central conceit of the story as a variation on those impossible, infinitely regressive structures to which O'Nolan resorts so often in the earlier novels: MacCruiskeen's chests of drawers, de Selby's series of mirrors reflecting all the way back into the past, the story within a story construction of *At Swim-Two-Birds*. In this case:

> The narrator of 'Two in One' sits quite literally within another character: 'that night I was able to look into a glass and see Kelly looking back at me, perfect in every detail except for the teeth and eyes, which had to be my own but which I knew other people would never notice' (*SF*, 86). From within this narrator, too, comes the voice of every other character as all dialogue is provided through the narrator's voice rather than within direct quotes. [...] In this way every character comes from within this murderous character, who sits within another character, who sits within a cell and waits for death.[20]

Fagan and Baines both frame the central conceit of 'Two in One' (Murphy's decision to wear the skin of his murder victim) as the literalisation of an idiom – and in both cases this ploy is shown to organise the game of doubles in the narrative. In Fagan's reading, the theme of getting under someone's skin points to an unsettling of the confessional scene, involving reader and narrator in a transformative power-exchange, a kind of reluctant complicity; for Baines, the sense of a character sitting 'literally within another character' establishes the murderer's position as the (dubious, unreliable) foundation of the entire narrative construction, a perspective that inhabits and controls all perspectives.

Joining this conversation, but adjusting the focus slightly, I want to claim that Paul's rhetoric on the letter and the spirit of the law informs not only the central conceit of 'Two in One' but also its figural strategies. Thus, while Murphy's confessional narrative positions itself precisely on the borderline between the literal and the figural, the writings of Paul provide a theoretical backdrop to the story's staging of its own use of literalised conceits for narrative composition.

Paul's intuition in *Romans* strikes a modern, almost Kafkaesque note. We are only subjects insofar as we submit to the authority of the law; indeed the law is the agency that *makes* us subjects, and in doing so it is able at once to condemn us *and* to save us. Without knowledge of the law we have no relation to sin; we are innocent by definition. At the same time, it is only by coming under its protection that we are capable of being redeemed. Paul resorts to the rhetoric of the living spirit and the dead letter precisely in order to resolve this contradiction. The move is accompanied by a distrust of literalism and a flat condemnation of all things of the flesh – and right at the centre of the argument are some well-rehearsed opinions on circumcision:

> For he is not a Jew, which is one outwardly; neither is that circumcision, which is outward in the flesh: But he is a Jew, which is one inwardly; and circumcision is that of the heart, in the spirit, and not in the letter; whose praise is not of men, but of God.[21]

Paul's hostility is directed at those who would see circumcision as a condition of salvation, or who would equate ritual with righteousness. By and large, the argument breaks down into three main objections: first, that they are far too literal in their interpretation of the law; secondly, that they ignore the primacy of spiritual reality over physical evidence; and finally, in a characteristically aggressive jibe, that in their eagerness to show off their piety, or to gauge the piety of their peers, they betray their exhibitionist and voyeuristic tendencies ('As many as desire to make a fair shew in the flesh, they constrain you to be circumcised; [or they] desire to have you circumcised, that they may glory in your flesh'[22]). On all three counts, the issue is with circumcision understood as a physical marking, as a *material* sign of belonging to a community. It is best to quote from different *Epistles* to highlight the recurrence of strategic phrases: 'For in Christ Jesus neither circumcision availeth anything, nor uncircumcision, but a new creature'.[23] And again:

> Lie not one to another, seeing that ye have put off the old man with his deeds; And have put on the new man, which is renewed in knowledge after the image of him that created him. Where there is neither Greek nor Jew, circumcision nor uncircumcision, Barbarian, Scythian, bond *nor* free: but Christ *is* all, and in all.[24]

Two figures, in particular, come into sharp relief here: Paul's insistence on a 'neither/nor' logic as the condition of the appearance of someone new; and the sartorial metaphor of *putting off* the old man and *putting on* a new one.

The pertinence of the latter to a reading of 'Two in One' is obvious enough. We may add *putting on the new man* to the string of literalised idioms that includes *inhabiting a character*, and, from the title of Fagan's essay, *getting under one's skin*. But the broader implications of the Pauline intertext also bear on O'Nolan's treatment of the *Doppelgänger* theme — specifically, the scene in which Murphy morphs into his victim, and the final twist which provides the ironic moral upshot of the story. After the applied skin becomes unstable it fuses with Murphy's own until the two, dead spirit ('dead spit') and live flesh, become inseparable: 'Kelly's skin got to live again, to breathe, to perspire. [...] My Kelliness, so to speak, was permanent' (*SF*, 87).

Baines has touched on the topic of the law in 'Two in One', noting that at the start of the narrative 'the murderer is already imprisoned by a swift and reasonably efficient judicial system. The police have the right man, they just have him for the wrong reasons'.[25] That last qualification is not negligible. The point of the story, of course, is that in a sense they have the right man *and* the wrong man at the same time. One way to read the ending, following Baines's lead, is as an affirmation of the infallibility of the law. By hook or by crook, a murderer will get his comeuppance and justice will be served. But then again, the same twist can also be interpreted as a demonstration of the arbitrary ways of justice. Truth is produced not by a process of unmasking, not by revealing the inner man, but by allowing a false appearance to *become* reality ('when the legend becomes fact print the legend').

In sum, 'Two in One' takes its place alongside other Mylesian texts, other allegories of writing in which life and death (or life and afterlife) are strangely folded into each other. But it ups the ante by reworking the premise into a modernist allegory of the act of figuration. I want to stress that the reversal of spiritual values entailed in these texts does not automatically signal a materialist turn in O'Nolan's thought. I believe, rather, that the main thrust of the allegory is diagnostic. O'Nolan's writing testifies to a strange moment in the history of Spirit, to a sense of living a time-out-of-joint. In well-worn modernist terms, what is demanded of the writer at such a time is an ambitious remapping of the relation of the present with tradition.

As I suggested earlier, the originality of O'Nolan's response to this diagnosis consists first in playing up the materialist rhetoric; then in subjecting it to a moral, satirical critique. At stake is the invention of a new way of being in the world and a new way of being in history, by which one at once belongs to and sets oneself apart from the authority of the past, from moral consensus, from the parochialisms that determine membership in one's community.

By this allegorical reading, O'Nolan's fiction opens up in two directions:

a. *existential*, calling for a complete reorganisation of the order of reality: to be sure, the blinding light on the road to Damascus is not commensurate with experience. It is a violent event, occurring outside any margin of expectation – hence the comparison with dying and being born again. It is reductive to think of such an event as a change in the circumstances of a person. What comes undone is a person's entire system of values; and

b. *political*, enacting a '*neither/nor-but-both-at-once*' gesture of resistance to the law: in Paul's case a refusal of both the Imperial order of Rome and the authority of the Mosaic covenant – but in that refusal is also an appropriation of the concepts of citizenship and election for the purpose of a new relation to history; in O'Nolan, a diagnosis of modernity as a time out of joint, a mad juncture in the history of Spirit, coupled with an anti-modernist critique of that same diagnosis.

14

The Dalkey Archive

a Menippean satire against authority

DIETER FUCHS

'Il faut cultiver notre jardin'.[1]

This essay analyses *The Dalkey Archive* as a text written in the tradition of Menippean satire. Although Mikhail Bakhtin,[2] Northrop Frye[3] and many others wrote about this tradition in great detail in the past century,[4] Menippean satire has remained a relatively little known literary phenomenon in the scholarly world. As Frye noted in 1975, before he wrote about Menippean satire in *The Anatomy of Criticism* (1957) 'there was not one in a thousand university English Teachers […] who knew what Menippean satire was: now there must be two or three'.[5]

As Menippean satire is widely unknown, I will take a closer look at this genre by way of introduction and situate my approach *vis-à-vis* the most important studies in the field of Brian O'Nolan as a Menippean satirist: M. Keith Booker's *Flann O'Brien, Bakhtin, and Menippean Satire* (1996) and José Lanters's *Unauthorized Versions* (2000).[6] Whereas Booker's main focus lies on the Bakhtinian concept of the dialogic imagination and the carnivalesque subversion of authority as essential aspects of the Menippean worldview, Lanters's Menippean reading of *At Swim-Two-Birds* and *The Third Policeman* applies the vantage point of modern Ireland from 1919–52. In contrast to Booker's archetypal and Lanters's more topical Menippean reading, my approach is informed by the history of literature and philosophy: it focuses on O'Nolan's intertextual dialogue with the Menippean corpus of the past and on the fact that the Menippean tradition is, epistemologically speaking, deeply imbued with the philosophy of Socrates.

Owing to this Socratic dimension, the Menippean mode may be character-ised as philosophical rather than literary satire. Rather than exposing human follies and vices in terms of topical allusion, the Menippean tradition is understandable in more radical terms as an anthropological satire on the species of humankind. In contrast to the Aristotelian notion of man as a rational being gifted with the blessings of intellect, Menippean satire emphasises the animal, or creature-like aspect of the human condition and posits that our claim to be a knowledgeable species is nothing more than a cultural myth. As knowledge is inevitably linked with power, the Menippean mode may be called not only a satire on man, but also a satire on man's intellectual authority – hence my intention here is to read *The Dalkey Archive* as a Menippean satire against authority.

My Menippean reading of *The Dalkey Archive* shows how Mick Shaughnessy meets, considers and resists various facets of patriarchal authority such as executive state power, patristic theology, philosophy and science. His attempts to reject patriarchal discourse, however, inevitably result in Mick's loss of phallogocentric self-control when he encounters and succumbs to matriarchal authority as a final ironic twist.

A very short sketch of the history and worldview of Menippean satire

The Menippean worldview is deeply rooted in the philosophy of Socrates, owing to its claim that the highest wisdom attainable for man is to acknowledge that all we can know is to know that we know nothing at all – hence the Socratic maxim which summarises the Menippean approach to human knowledge in a nutshell: 'I know that I know nothing'.[7] If we address the ultimate questions of our existence – the nature of the gods, the limits of the universe, the question of life after death, the meaning of life – we have to admit that there are no convincing final answers despite all our intellectual effort. Hence the Menippean emphasis on how little can be known. Acknowledging its Socratic roots, the Menippean tradition presents a philosophical quest for ultimate knowledge which inevitably results in epistemological disappointment.[8] Rather than encourage the search for absolute wisdom unattainable for man, the Menippean mode praises the qualities of a simple down-to-earth life. This is the case, for instance, at the end of Voltaire's Menippean satire *Candide, ou l'Optimisme* (1759), where rather than travel the world to search for the meaning of life, the best thing for humans to do, Candide's final statement suggests, is to refrain from asking unanswerable and thus silly questions, and to settle down and do simple work such as farm work to cater for our basic needs: '*Il faut cultiver notre jardin*', 'we have to cultivate our garden'.[9]

To contextualise Brian O'Nolan as a modern Irish Menippean satirist, it is important to look at the history of Menippean satire, which subdivides into a Hellenistic and a Roman tradition.[10] The Hellenistic tradition derives from the non-classical fringe of the Hellenistic world in the Levant region. It may be attributed to the highly fantastic if not to say eccentric works of Lucian which, *via* François Rabelais as a mediating figure, inspired what Vivian Mercier has called the Irish comic tradition[11]: the works of Jonathan Swift, Laurence Sterne, James Joyce and Flann O'Brien.[12]

The second Menippean tradition goes back to the Roman polymath Varro and is also known by the name of Varronian satire.[13] In contrast to the Lucianic tradition of eccentric fantasy, the Varronian counterpart presents a self-ironic compendium of schoolbook knowledge, which turns out to be unmanageable owing to its pedantic collation of a flood of non-contextualised circumstantial details: the more scattered raw data we collect, the less capable we are to wrest useful knowledge results from these analytically unconnected fragments. This parody of omniscience is not only elucidated in a modernist context by the questioning and answering catalogues from the 'Ithaca' episode of James Joyce's *Ulysses*, but also in earlier contexts by the self-ironic pedantry of Robert Burton's *The Anatomy of Melancholy* and Laurence Sterne's digressive telling *ab ovo* in *The Life and Opinions of Tristram Shandy, Gentleman*. In the dark ages of the decline and fall of the Roman Empire, the Varronian compendium was further elaborated into the satirical encyclopaedia known as the Menippean *summa*,[14] an ironic echo of the attempts of church fathers to summarise the Christian world picture by way of pedantically constructed encyclopaedic systems of scriptural thought – an aspect which culminates in the thirteenth-century *Summa Theologica* written by Thomas Aquinas.

In *The Aesthetics of Chaosmos: The Middle Ages of James Joyce*, Umberto Eco explains the medieval summarising approach satirised by the Menippean *Summa*:

> The medieval thinker cannot conceive, explain, or manage the world without inserting it into the framework of an Order [...] For the medieval thinker, the objects and events which the universe comprises are numerous. A key, therefore, must be found to help the scholar discover and catalogue them. The first approach to the reality of the

universe was of an encyclopedic type. [...] The encyclopedic approach uses the techniques of the Inventory, the List, the Catalogue or, in classical rhetorical terms, the *Enumeratio*. In order to describe a place or a fact, the early poets of the Latin Middle Ages first provide a list of detailed aspects.[15]

Taking this very brief historical and epistemological sketch as a starting point, I will now contextualise *The Dalkey Archive* within the Menippean pedigree. I begin with the Hellenistic tradition of Lucian's eccentric Menippean fantasy before moving on to the Roman tradition of Varro's self-ironic Menippean encyclopaedia continued by the medieval tradition of the 'mock-Aquinian' or anti-patristic *Summa*. My discussion of *The Dalkey Archive* is going to show that – although the allegedly superannuated tradition of Menippean satire and its philosophy have become all but forgotten in other parts of the world – the genre still holds a firm place in modern and postmodern Ireland. The circumstance that it has fused with the Irish comic tradition from the eighteenth century onward may be attributed not only to the proverbial eccentricity of Hibernian wit; it may be attributed first of all to the fact that, among other systems of authoritarian thought, Menippean satire debunks the authority of the Roman Catholic Church and the collective knowledge produced by its world picture. Whereas the church has lost its monopoly to produce and objectify public knowledge in the Age of Enlightenment in other places, it has kept Ireland as a priest- and past-ridden country under paralytic control until the end of the twentieth century – hence the enduring relevance of Menippean satire for Hibernian culture.

The Dalkey Archive and Lucianic satire

When De Selby invites Mick and Hackett to join the subterranean interview with the long-deceased Saint Augustine, O'Nolan's text evokes Lucian's *Nekyomantia: Menippus or the Descent into Hades* and *Dialogues of the Dead* – a series of thirty satirical encounters set in the Underworld. As in Lucian's Menippean dialogues, O'Nolan presents a character from the world of the living who sneaks into the world of the dead to observe and interview the great authorities of the past.[16] Although Menippus and De Selby are driven by curiosity and lust for new knowledge, each ultimately is forced to realise that the ancient authorities have nothing to say which might contribute to their own intellectual enlightenment.[17]

As their statements from beyond the grave turn out to be either vain, trite or merely commonsensical, Lucian diminishes the authorities of the pagan world, whether Homer, Socrates or the Homeric heroes including the Underworld traveller Odysseus. Whereas Lucian summons pagan authorities, De Selby conjures up an interview with Saint Augustine, one of the greatest authorities of the Roman Catholic Church. Subsequently we learn that De Selby has a sealed subterranean room in his house where he meets many other church fathers on a regular basis. However, rather than ask Saint Augustine for the divine enlightenment presented in the main part of the church father's spiritual autobiography *Confessiones*, De Selby delves into the scandalous excesses of the flesh committed during Augustine's sinful pre-Christianised youth. What really interests De Selby are titbits of sexual debauchery, pagan orgies and Babylonian lust (*CN*, 636, 638–39) and the question of whether the sexually potent North Africa-born pagan turned church potentate was a white man or '*a Nigger*' (*CN*, 642).

Unwittingly debunked as a mock-philosopher in quest of saucy gossip rather than spiritual enlightenment, De Selby strongly resembles Lucian's Menippus, who interviews the deceased Socrates in Hades. In this Underworld meeting, Menippus feigns to misunderstand the trope of Socratic irony at work in the dictum 'I know that I know nothing' in order to imply that the father of Western philosophy was a hypocritical would-be intellectual rather than a truly wise person.[18] Referring to the circumstance that he finds the Hades-bound philosopher in the Underworld company of men who died young, he also alludes to the well-known defamatory rumour that Socrates was a pederast:

> MENIPPUS: Bravo, Socrates! Still following your own special line here! Still an eye for beauty![19]

De Selby's enquiry into the sexual debaucheries enacted during the church father's youth may be thus considered an intertextual allusion to the Underworld encounter of Menippus with Socrates, who is satirised as a dirty old man in pursuit of young boys in Lucian's *Dialogues of the Dead*.[20] As Lucian's Menippean satire does with its pagan authorities, so O'Nolan's *The Dalkey Archive* reduces the authorities of the Christian world to all too human corporeal terms.

Like the Lucianic Menippus – who misrepresents Socrates as an intellectual impostor rather than a master ironist – De Selby challenges Saint Augustine's authority when he asks the heretic question 'Don't you know everything?'

However, the church father proves to be a man of Socratic wisdom and wit rather than an ignorant fake: '*I do not. I can, but the first wisdom is sometimes not to know*' (CN, 637). Albeit a Christian church father, Saint Augustine echoes the pagan Socrates-character from Lucian's *Dialogues of the Dead* in so far as he acknowledges that a truly wise man knows exactly what he does not know rather than *vice versa*. Like O'Nolan's Augustine as interviewed by De Selby, the Lucianic Socrates ironically admits to his Menippean interlocutor that he is truly wise, owing to the fact that he knows that he knows nothing:

> SOCRATES: And what do they [i.e. what does posterity] think of me?
> MENIPPUS: [...], you're a lucky fellow, Socrates. At any rate they all think you were a wonderful man, and knew everything, though – I think I am right saying so – you knew nothing.
> SOCRATES: That's what I myself kept telling them, but they thought it was all pretence on my part.[21]

Another rather Catholic, or Irish, reference to Lucian's Hellenistic Menippean fantasy occurs when De Selby and Mick discuss the case of the Old-Testamentarian prophet Jonas swallowed by a whale. When De Selby mentions that 'The Bible merely says that [Jonas] spent three days and nights in the *belly* of the creature' (CN, 670) that swallowed him, he echoes Lucian's *A True Story*, in which an entire galley and its crew disappears in the stomach of a giant sea mammal. This set of allusions is further specified when De Selby continues that a 'whale's stomach is like a house or a flat – it has several compartments. You could have a dining-room there, a bedroom, a kitchen, perhaps a library' (CN, 670). The idea of the inside of a whale as a world *en miniature* with fully furnished flats is quite obviously borrowed from Lucian's allegedly 'true' story:

> with a gulp [the whale] swallowed us down, ship and all. [...] When we were inside [...] we saw a great cavity, flat all over and high, and large enough for the housing of a great city. [...] In the middle there was land with hills on it, which to my thinking was formed of the mud that he had swallowed. Indeed, a forest of all kinds of trees had grown on it, garden stuff had come up, and everything appeared to be under cultivation. [...]
> I took seven of my comrades and went into the forest, wishing to have a look at everything. I had not yet gone quite five furlongs when I found a temple of Poseidon [...]. We also heard the barking of a dog,

smoke appeared in the distance, and we made out something like a
farmhouse, too.

Advancing eagerly, we came upon an old man [...]. He took us with
him to the house. It was a commodious structure, had bunks built in it
and was fully furnished in other ways.[22]

By evoking Lucian's *A True Story*, O'Nolan rewrites a literary motif which
recurs in the Hellenistic pedigree of Menippean satire and the Irish comic
tradition alike. As elucidated by Werner von Koppenfels,[23] the archetype
of a *world en miniature* such as the one within the whale may be traced back
to the Cyclops episode of Homer's *Odyssey*. Whereas the prison-like and
cannibalistic dimension of the Cyclops's cave inspired later dystopian spaces
such as Swift's Island of Balnibarbi – darkened and starved by the coloniser
Laputa – its less claustrophobic and more playful representation by Lucian
served as a prototype for eutopian or 'good' places, such as the Land of
Cokaygne-esque world in Pantagruel's mouth from Rabelais's *Gargantua et
Pantagruel*.[24] Like his Underworld dialogue with Saint Augustine, De Selby's
summoning of the ghost of the Biblical prophet Jonas in a Cyclopean or
whale-belly-like underwater cave, or the sealed underground room of his
house, turns out to be heuristically disappointing. Rather than instruct him
with new knowledge, Jonas just repeats well-known commonplaces:

– But you talked to Jonas. Did he make any remark himself about the
   inside of the monster that gobbled him?
– Not at all. He talked bull, like a cheap politician, or a first-year Jesuit
   novice.
– That was disappointing. (*CN*, 670)

Thus staging a dialogue with the Socratic background of Menippean satires
by Lucian, Rabelais, Swift and Joyce, O'Nolan's aesthetics of heuristic
disappointment may be identified as an important aspect of the Irish comic
tradition. Although the Socratic dimension of the Menippean worldview
has only recently been reconstructed in the field of theoretical debate,[25] this
archetypal dimension is still at work in the realm of modern and postmodern
Irish literary practice. Albeit no longer actively remembered, it still affects
the world of the present: in Jungian terms of the 'collective unconscious'
resurfacing in literary and other cultural production.[26]

Having discussed the Lucianic framework from the Hellenistic Menippean
pedigree relevant for *The Dalkey Archive*, I will now proceed to its Roman

counterpart: the tradition of Varro's self-ironic Menippean encyclopaedia, which inspired the medieval Menippean prototype known as the anti-patristic *Summa*.

The Dalkey Archive and Varronian satire

As highlighted in the title of O'Nolan's book, the archive plays a dominant role for the Menippean dimension of *The Dalkey Archive*. As far as the plot is concerned, the archive does not appear at all. The flood of pedantic circumstantial references to all sorts of schoolbook knowledge transformed into eccentric pseudo-philosophical speculation, however, may be duly labelled a Menippean mock-archive – an ironic *Summa* or mock-encyclopaedia that sums up all sorts of useless speculative knowledge which turns out to be deductively true but empirically absurd.

Although it refers to the patristic *Summa* proper rather than its Menippean parody, Maebh Long's *Assembling Flann O'Brien* (2014) draws an explicit link between the medieval genre of the *Summa* and the archive mentioned in the title of *The Dalkey Archive*. Long first of all elucidates that *The Dalkey Archive* was recognised as a playfully rewritten *Summa* from its very beginning:

> At the work's early stages, O'Nolan responded to a letter from Timothy O'Keeffe, stating 'It's amusing and even eerie that you should say "the new novel sounds like a Summa"'. [...] A Summa, meaning to 'sum up', is a compendium which summarizes and stores knowledge in a field, and as such, a summa is an archive, a repository for knowledge and information pertaining to a particular field, event or person. *The Dalkey Archive* is a summa or archive of accurate information of varying degrees of 'objective' truth, as the text's overriding engagement is with presenting, attributing and discrediting information and received wisdom; its scenes attempt to reveal fact, employ authentic etymology, present accurate details, ridicule error and short-sightedness, lament wasted ability, correct mistakes, mock an interest in minutiae, and use information to both witty and solemn ends.[27]

Long's reading of *The Dalkey Archive* thus functions as an important cornerstone for the Menippean approach of this essay. Yet it is not only the ironic quotation of all sorts of theological, philosophical and scientific authorities to support the absurd theories resulting from patristic reasoning which presents *The Dalkey Archive* as a mock-*Summa* in the truest sense of the word. It is also the presentation of Saint Augustine, De Selby, Sergeant Fottrell and even the character of James Joyce as mock-philosophers or scientists gone mad which fashions *The Dalkey Archive* as a Menippean rebellion against the authority of institutionalised knowledge and its representatives.

As already noted with regard to Lucianic fantasy and fancy, De Selby is presented as a pedantic genius gone mad. As far as the Roman tradition of Menippean satire and its medieval continuation is concerned, this disposition may be attributed to the stock figure of the pseudo-Varronian polymath. In his *Anatomy of Criticism*, Northrop Frye calls this stock figure of the blathering would-be philosopher *philosophus gloriosus*.[28] It is in line with this type of characterisation that O'Nolan's earlier work *The Third Policeman* presents de Selby as an *idiot savant* and features a pedantic flood of pseudo-scholarly footnotes inserted by the mad narrator.[29]

A Varronian collection of pedantic but heuristically useless bits of knowledge – which is continued by the medieval tradition of the anti-scholastic Menippean *Summa* – may also be observed in the discussion of Jonas and the whale in *The Dalkey Archive*. When De Selby and Mick debate the case of whether Jonas was swallowed by a whale or a giant fish, they do so in order to dispute whether a whale dish may be considered fish or flesh in terms of Catholic dietary regulations. Rather than ask for the spiritual meaning of the Biblical Jonas episode, they discuss the gluttonous, if not to say Rabelaisian, question of whether a whale dish might circumvent the Catholic prohibition of eating flesh on Fridays:

> the whale is not a fish. Scientists hold, with ample documentation in support, that the whale was formerly a land animal, its organs now modified for sea-living. It is a mammal, suckles its young, is warm-blooded and must come to the surface for breath, like man himself. [...] the creature has been the subject of much casuistry, no doubt stimulated by the Jesuits. Its flesh is quite edible, like the dolphin's. Roman Catholics are forbidden, as we know, to eat fleshmeat on Fridays. But on those days they have not hesitated to eat whale, on the specious ground that it is a fish. (*CN*, 669)

Furthermore, the Varronian tradition of Menippean satire is reflected by the atomic molecule, or 'Mollycule', theory featured in *The Third Policeman* and *The Dalkey Archive* alike. This weird and pedantic construct of pseudo-Varronian polymath thought is unfolded by the mock authority of the idle Sergeant Fottrell. Rather than follow his job description and enforce the law, the Sergeant engages in natural would-be philosophy as a hobby horse: a hobby horse gone mad comparable to the weird pseudo-scholarly pastime endeavours presented in *Tristram Shandy* or the mock-scientific experiments performed at the academy of Lagado in the third book of *Gulliver's Travels*.[30]

A final example of O'Nolan's rewriting of the Roman tradition of Varro's self-ironic Menippean compendium of knowledge and the medieval tradition of the anti-patristic *Summa* is the anti-Jesuit satire on the all too worldly Father Cobble via the fictitious *persona* of James Joyce. In contrast to the empirical figure traumatised by his Jesuit education, Joyce's fictitious counterpart is fashioned as a devout teetotaller Catholic. When O'Nolan's Joyce tells Mick that his greatest wish is to join the Jesuit order, Mick offers to arrange an interview with Father Cobble. Whereas Joyce is presented as a person 'steeled in the school of old Aquinas',[31] Mick characterises Father Cobble as 'an Englishman but quite intelligent' (*CN*, 765). When Joyce further inquires whether the Jesuit father is a 'severe sort of holy man', Mick specifies his opinion about the clergyman: 'I told you he is an Englishman, and the only danger is that he may be stupid' (*CN*, 773). Whereas Joyce resembles De Selby in so far as he is a truly knowledgeable authority in the field of the doctrines of the church fathers, Father Cobble turns out to be a very poor caricature of patristic authority indeed.

As he fails to understand Joyce's genius, Cobble makes him a queer offer: rather than being initiated into the field of Augustinian and Aquinian theology, Joyce is asked to sew and take care of the Jesuit Fathers' underwear. To stress the all too worldly rather than spiritual Jesuit approach to life, *The Dalkey Archive* employs the motif of underwear to foreground the digestive bodily region of the rump: instead of using their brains to think and to cater for the salvation of the human soul, the Jesuits engage in the bodily gluttony of excessive eating and drinking, as foregrounded in Rabelais's *Gargantua et Pantagruel*. Hence O'Nolan's Varronian Satire on Jesuit patristic authority is fused with the Rabelaisian concept of the grotesque.

Although he is presented as shocked or even enraged when he receives the offer to take care of the Jesuit Fathers' underwear, the reader does not know whether Joyce agrees to join the Jesuits or leaves the interview in an enraged shock of recognition. In other words, the reader does not know whether Joyce's 'medieval method' derived from the summarising approach of the church fathers[32] makes him realise Cobble's stupidity as a Menippean satirist, or if he subscribes to the authority of an all too worldly, if not to say Simoniac, Jesuit order that betrays its patristic heritage. All we know is that the enraged Mick leaves the room where Joyce's job interview takes place.

Conclusion

Thus the protagonist Mick finds himself alone at the end of *The Dalkey Archive*. As Saint Augustine, De Selby, Sergeant Fottrell, Father Cobble and James Joyce have left, Mick is finally in the position to rely on his own judgement rather than that of other authorities. He has succeeded in resisting all the facets of patriarchal authority these characters represent: patristic theology, philosophy, science, extremist fundamentalism, executive state power, religion and art.[33] It may be attributed to this newly gained intellectual independence that Mick does not leave his girlfriend Mary and that he suspends his plan to retire into the homo-social all-masculine monastic world of the Trappists as an extreme way of succumbing to the authority of others. Rather than embracing the authority of the Roman Catholic Church as a monk, he agrees to marry, settle down and father a baby. Mick thus subscribes to the Menippean ideal of a simple down-to-earth life unspoiled by embracing the wrong kind of knowledge, and this decision may be considered a variant of the final maxim of Voltaire's *Candide* presented as the motto of this essay: '*Il faut cultiver notre jardin*'.

That Mick's fate to marry and father a child is ironically contrasted with Father Cobble's statement that he has 'the embryo of an idea' (*CN*, 778) may be considered a final clue to O'Nolan's purpose in recalling Socrates as the archetypal Menippean satirist against the wrong kind of knowledge devoid of practical use. In comparison to the notably foolish Father Cobble, the future family father Mick seems to have emerged from his encounters with patriarchal authority a much wiser person, owing to the fact that he decides not to engage the pursuit of useless speculative thought any longer: like Socrates, Mick acknowledges that little or nothing can be known in the realms of theoretical, literary or religious philosophy. In this respect, the ignorant church father's claim of an embryonic idea echoes the fact that Socrates compared his own approach to practical rather than speculative philosophy with the art of *maieutics*, or midwifery: rather than indoctrinate his disciples with what has already been said by other authorities, Socrates considered himself an intellectual midwife who helps those 'pregnant with thought' to give birth to their own ideas.[34]

What looks like a perfect happy resolution at first glance, however, is not devoid of a final ambivalence which O'Nolan might have called 'queer': as we only get to know Mary's final thoughts, we do not know whether Mick really wishes to settle down for a family life devoid of speculation, or is rather coerced into this decision by his future wife. In addition, we do not know whether Mary's final statement 'I'm certain I'm going to have a baby' (*CN*, 787) expresses her wish to marry, have children and settle down in the near future, or hints at premarital pregnancy. In this case, we do not know whether the baby's father is Mick – who has neglected his girlfriend for the sake of his quest for the wrong kind of knowledge – or another man such as Hackett. In other words, we do not know whether the baby represents Mick's Socratic thoughts made flesh as an act of intellectual self-liberation or midwifery, or indicates that Mick is being tricked into marriage as a 'Joseph the Joiner'-like husband of the unfaithful mock-virgin Mary. As 'Paternity may be a legal fiction'[35] backed by the patristic authority of the Roman Catholic Church, Mick's alleged fatherhood might be a changeling trick wrought by his unfaithful spouse. Thus Mary's pregnancy may turn out to be a blackmailing scheme to get married in order to secure her own authority over her husband as a mock Socrates: like Socrates – whom popular culture characterises as a henpecked husband ruled by his shrewish spouse Xanthippe – Mick's fate seems to point towards a laboursome family life under the harsh rule of his future wife.[36]

It may be due to these final textual silences that we cannot decide whether Mick resembles Socrates as a truly wise man – who gets to know that all we can know is to know that we know nothing – or as a henpecked husband who has become subjected to the authority of a shrewish Xanthippean wife. Hence we do not know whether Mick has succeeded in overcoming his problems with authority or if these problems are just about to begin as a never-ending domestic nightmare with his unfaithful quarrelsome spouse: i.e. whether he has to pay the price for succumbing to matriarchal authority in order to emancipate himself from the patristic rule of the church. Thus there remains the unanswerable question of whether Mick is punished as the cuckold husband of a Marian mock-virgin figure, owing to the fact that he has abandoned 'mother church' ruled by patristic discourse in favour of a shrewish woman of the world. Should he have followed the example of the church father Origines in order to cope with the matriarchal challenge of patristic authority by way of self-castration, as discussed in one of De Selby and Saint Augustine's subterranean meetings (*CN*, 636–37)?

Thus the end of Brian O'Nolan's Menippean satire *The Dalkey Archive* casts the reader into the position of Socrates: if the reader is truly wise, a reading of O'Nolan's book results in the Socratic insight that all that one knows is that one knows that one knows nothing.

15

'walking forever on falling ground'

closure, hypertext and the textures of possibility in *The Third Policeman*

Tamara Radak

Having rejected the idea of 'One beginning and one ending for a book', the student narrator of *At Swim-Two-Birds* famously argues that 'A good book may have three openings entirely dissimilar and inter-related only in the prescience of the author, or for that matter one hundred times as many endings' (*CN*, 5) and proceeds to sketch three such possible openings. The narrator's comments, seemingly nothing more than inconsequential aphoristic quips, play a vital role in establishing his work in progress as a branching text, a set of parallel storylines that run alongside each other without being subject to hierarchical structuring. Such a narrative design is directly opposed to linear narrative and anticipates Barthes's concept of the 'ideal text' to which 'we gain access [...] by several entrances, none of which can be authoritatively declared to be the main one'.[1] At the same time, the notion of not one but 'many endings' posits an understanding of closure as a tentative construct. Indeed, we find, the plot's resolution is not only delayed by means of '*antepenultimate*' and '*penultimate*' conclusions (*CN*, 207, 214), but is in fact infinitely deferred. In line with the text's many metafictional devices that work to foreground literary discourse's inherent artificiality, even the self-labelling of the last section as an '*ultimate*' conclusion (*CN*, 215) cannot be taken at face value.[2] As Maebh Long notes, 'These false monuments to traditional progression are derided' from the very outset of the novel, which 'begins with Chapter 1, but never proffers Chapter 2'.[3] As such, *At Swim-Two-Birds* offers 'a non-progressive series of beginnings that never present a secure foundation' and 'a non-linear series of endings that never offer closure'.[4] Introducing a new set of characters and events that are narratologically unrelated to those already developed, the novel's *'ultimate'* conclusion contradicts the very idea of *dénouement* as a neat, final resolution of individual narrative strands. Given the novel's portrayal of authorial creation in terms of an abuse of power, this refusal of traditional closure implies that claims to the ability to definitively delimit textual boundaries are a ruse maintained not only for the sake of convention, but also for the leveraging of authority. O'Nolan thus challenges any text 'whose authority derives from the force of closure, from the capacity to say: here is where it began, here is what it became'.[5] By revealing that 'closure [...] also uncloses', the branching text of *At Swim-Two-Birds* bears out Peter Brooks's contention that novels 'may in essence be interminable'.[6]

Albeit in more covert and subtle ways, *The Third Policeman* also advances the notion that narrative 'closure or termination' is always 'merely provisional'.[7] In this essay, I will draw on hypertext and possible worlds theories to demonstrate three ways in which O'Nolan's posthumous text problematises, tests and challenges the authority of narrative closure. First, the radically unstable nature of the text's temporality and spatiality makes it impossible to pinpoint its narrative in terms of a normative, linear understanding of time or space and suggests that any sense of closure must necessarily remain relative to the observer. Secondly, the Kermodean 'sense of an ending'[8] typically found in traditional narratives is endlessly deferred on the level of content with the novel's Möbius strip-like narrative structure: its closing question, 'Is it about a bicycle?' (*CN*, 404) takes the reader, along with the narrator, back to The Parish (*CN*, 267) to experience the Sisyphean cycle of the 'beginning of the unfinished, [...] the re-experience of the already suffered, the fresh-forgetting of the unremembered' anew (*CN*, 406). Thirdly, the text's employment of fictional footnotes establishes O'Nolan's novel as a branching text, which introduces multiple narrative strands that defy hierarchical textual organisation and thereby challenge the authority of the linear, teleological and monolithic narrative composition popularised in the well-made novel. Arguing that hypertext is a particularly apt concept for theorising the unstable, oscillatory status of footnotes in *The Third Policeman*, I will show how the nonlinear structure of this branching text is further related to its refusal of closure in terms of the reading process(es) it necessitates. Throughout the essay, I will examine the ontological stakes of these arguments, employing Tzvetan Todorov's theory of the fantastic and Gilles Deleuze's concept of incompossibility to explore the idea of the narrative world of *The Third Policeman* with regard to the 'radical incompleteness of fictional worlds' at large.[9]

In search of lost timepieces

The refusal of closure in *The Third Policeman* is indexed in its employment of non-linear theories on time. These engagements take the form of O'Nolan's oft-noted dual debts to J.W. Dunne's concept of serialism, which is connected to the concepts of infinity and infinite regress by definition,[10] and to central concepts of quantum mechanics, such as the dual nature of light or Sergeant Pluck's Atomic theory (*CN*, 293ff), which mirror the text's dialogic, non-linear narrative structure.[11] The abolition of a Newtonian view of time and absolute physical values becomes explicit through the introduction of the idea that time passes differently in the fantastic world of The Parish as opposed to the realist rules of temporal progression witnessed in Divney's world. De Selby's view of human existence as 'a succession of static experiences each infinitely brief', which Keith Hopper characterises as a comic appropriation of Zeno's paradox,[12] is particularly noteworthy in this context as it 'denies that time can pass as such in the accepted sense and attributes to hallucinations the commonly experienced sensation of progression' (*CN*, 263). Such a successive concept of time refutes the idea of teleological progression and denies the notion of a measurable starting and ending point in the narrative.

In a world where 'it was always five o'clock in the afternoon' (*CN*, 291) in some parts and '*eternity was up the lane*' (*CN*, 334), the narrator's search for a non-existent American gold watch becomes a powerful metaphor for the text's elusive temporality. The absence of a watch is directly equated with the narrator's inability to discern the time of day: 'It was still early morning, perhaps. If I had not lost my American gold watch it would be possible for me to tell the time. *You have no American gold watch*' (*CN*, 265). The absent/non-existent watch further acts as a reminder of an abstract underlying problem: the narrator's inability to impose any kind of order onto the chaotic (and therefore frightening) world of The Parish. The narrator's Sisyphean suffering is directly related to his failure to 'understand all the terrible things which had happened to [him]' (*CN*, 242), as conventional rules of cause and effect do not apply in the strange netherworld of the policemen, which makes it impossible for the narrator to predict what will happen next. *The Third*

Policeman thus introduces its own uncertainty principle in the sense that the narrator neither knows the spatial direction in which he is going nor the speed at which events happen. This circumstance considerably intensifies his exasperation ('the horror of my situation descended upon me like a heavy blanket flung upon my head, enveloping and smothering me and making me afraid of death'; *CN*, 242) and leaves him at the mercy of the policemen and their seemingly arbitrary displays of justice.

While the search for the narrator's gold watch replicates the unsettled (and unsettling) temporal order of the narrative, the fictional footnotes found in the text can be read as an index of its spatial displacement. They contribute to the 'dislocation of time and space'[13] in the narrative in the sense that all such 'digressions "stop time", stop the *orderly progress of events* to tell another story' [my emphasis], as Shari Benstock suggests in the context of marginalia in *Finnegans Wake*.[14] Furthermore, although the footnotes in *The Third Policeman* do cause power relations and hierarchies to 'slide and crumble',[15] they never supplant the main narrative altogether. The footnotes come asymptotically close to assuming absolute power, but never quite succeed,[16] reinforcing a sense of unstable and oscillating power structures. The dialogic and dynamic nature of power relations in the topographical arrangement of *The Third Policeman* correlates with the narrator's insecurity with regard to his identity, as he is endlessly suspended between two incompossible ontological realities, belonging neither to the real world nor the fantastic world of The Parish. In this way, The Parish takes on qualities of Gilles Deleuze's 'ever expanding zone of indiscernibility or indetermination'[17]: by blurring the boundaries between the real and the fantastic, O'Nolan's text not only renders them essentially indistinguishable, it also dismantles the concept of such distinctions by demonstrating their futility in a world where basic rules of common sense or logic do not apply.

Both the lost watch as the epitome of socially constructed clock time and the footnotes as an academically constructed convention serve as ways of ordering discourse and structuring the narrative, but are essentially exposed as mere scaffoldings or, like the police barracks itself, as 'false and unconvincing' ruses (*CN*, 265, 402). It is particularly noteworthy that the 'unconvincing' nature of that 'very poorly painted [...] "building"' is invoked twice (at the beginning and the end of the text) *verbatim* (*CN*, 265, 402), while other aspects of the narrator's Sisyphean *ricorso* are minimally or considerably changed. Not only does the text explicitly comment on its own textuality at this point (for a certain sense of deception is, of course, inherent in any fictional text or artefact), the narrator's realisation also exposes the police barracks, conventionally coded as a zone of legal authority, as a sham that 'would not deceive a child' (*CN*, 265, 402–03). Nevertheless, he abides by the rules set up by the policemen and participates in their daily routine, as the policemen exert authority over the narrator through their ability to superimpose an illusion of causality (which presupposes a linear view of time) onto the unpredictable world of The Parish. Not only do the policemen (as opposed to the narrator) have names, and thus stable identities, they also claim to have the ability (which the narrator lacks) to structure temporal experience by establishing daily routines, performing weekly lever readings and distinguishing one day from the preceding one ('This is not today, this is yesterday'; *CN*, 273). In the fantastic world of The Parish, far removed from conventional temporal or spatial coordinates, claims to authority are thus inextricably connected to establishing a sense of order and structuring experience. Even though the nameless narrator exposes the policemen's barracks – and as a result, their authority – as a poorly veiled fiction and acknowledges the constructed nature of their claim to power, he succumbs to their macabre games and questionings for lack of an alternative set of coordinates by which he could measure or structure his experience in The Parish. Unlike the reader, who can actualise the dialogic potential inherent in the text's nonlinear form, the narrator is bound to endlessly perpetuate the hierarchical structures established by the policemen as the only figures of (self-proclaimed) authority present in the distressingly unstable world of The Parish.

Return to no-man's land

After the chaotic array of unconventional and unforeseeable events taking place in The Parish, the last chapter of *The Third Policeman* starts out, quite inconspicuously, with the narrator returning to the land of his birth feeling 'comfortable in mind and body, happy in the growing lightness of [his] heart' (*CN*, 399). His calmness, however, is soon unsettled when he experiences 'another of those chilling shocks which [he] thought [he] had left behind [him] forever' (*CN*, 400). The narrator's observation that Pegeen Meers and John Divney have 'grown old, very fat and very grey' (*CN*, 400), seemingly a throwaway remark, has important repercussions for the multi-layered temporal organisation of O'Nolan's text, implying that time obeys realist and thus linear rules of progression in Divney's world as opposed to the non-locatable temporal and spatial coordinates of The Parish. The narrator's epiphanic moment of self-realisation similarly offers a rational explanation for 'all the terrible things which had happened to [him]' (*CN*, 242):

> He told me to keep away. He said I was not there. He said I was dead.
> He said that what he had put under the boards in the big house was not
> the black box but a mine, a bomb. It had gone up when I touched it. He
> had watched the bursting of it from where I had left him. The house
> was blown to bits. I was dead. He screamed to me to keep away. I was
> dead for sixteen years. (*CN*, 401–02)

At this point, the narrative takes a turn away from the fantastic, which in
Tzvetan Todorov's view occupies the moment of hesitation 'experienced
by a person who knows only the laws of nature, confronting an apparently
supernatural event'.[18] Todorov considers the fantastic as an ephemeral state
that only lasts for the duration of this hesitation shared by readers and
characters of fantastic texts before the narrative is resolved as either 'uncanny'
or 'marvellous'.[19] The world of The Parish could be said to belong to the
category of the marvellous, since 'new laws of nature must be entertained to
account for the phenomena' taking place in it.[20] However, once the narrator
returns to his place of birth, the narrative leaves the liminal realm of the
fantastic, providing a rational explanation of events, with Divney revealing
the mysterious black box to be a bomb and explaining to the narrator that he
has been 'dead for sixteen years'. In this time zone, events are thus subject to
linear temporal progression and 'the laws of reality remain intact and permit
an explanation of the phenomena described'.[21] However, beyond giving a
rational explanation of events, Divney's revelation draws attention to the
paradox inherent in the narrator's ability to recount his story beyond the
natural threshold of death, thus producing an irresolvable aporia. By the time
the narrator sets out on his Sisyphean quest anew and re-enters the world
of The Parish, the boundaries between the real and the unreal have been
considerably blurred once again and the sense of ontological hesitation about
reality, or indeed, about two (or more) incompatible realities, resurfaces.[22]

The merging of the uncanny world of the narrator's birthplace with the
marvellous world of The Parish is initiated by the narrator's and Divney's
journey to the police barracks, which transports the reader, along with
the two characters, back to the scene already encountered in Chapter 4.
While the last section of *The Third Policeman* is characterised by repetition
and citation with a difference, the very last question asked in the text, 'Is
it about a bicycle?' (*CN*, 404) is an exact replication of its first occurrence
(*CN*, 267). In the context of closure and its discontents, it is both noteworthy
and symptomatic that the text should end with a question mark rather than
a full stop. The question not only acts as a link between two possible, yet

incompatible worlds, but also as a porous threshold between these worlds, highlighting their interconnectedness and creating an infinite loop in the narrative. This link, or in the terminology of hypertext theory, this 'node', makes it impossible for the reader to truly leave the realm of the fantastic, as that would require unambiguously resolving the narrative to either extreme of the uncanny/marvellous divide. The link is thus a key factor in the moment of hesitation about reality, which is prolonged *ad infinitum*.[23]

Despite remaining embedded within the structuralist tradition, Todorov gestures towards a more fluid definition of the fantastic when he acknowledges the 'dialectical vocation' of fantastic literature and comments on its ability to 'question [...] the existence of an irreducible opposition between real and unreal [...] by the hesitation it engenders'.[24] Rather than resolving this opposition, *The Third Policeman* indeed dwells on the moment of tension, amplifying rather than reducing the ontological hesitation envisaged by Todorov. In *The Third Policeman*, the relationship between the real and the unreal is not presented as one between mutually exclusive categories (or time zones) but rather as a fluid, permeable border that can be framed in terms of Deleuze's concept of 'incompossibility'.[25] Modifying Leibniz's notion of possible worlds, Deleuze dwells on the 'infinity of possible worlds'[26] which Leibniz eschews in favour of the actual(ised) world as the best of all worlds chosen by God.[27] Evoking Jorge Luis Borges's 'Garden of Forking Paths' and its 'baroque labyrinth whose infinite series converge or diverge, forming a webbing of time embracing all possibilities',[28] Deleuze establishes incompossibility as 'a relation other than one of contradiction [...] a vice-diction', 'an original relation, distinct from impossibility or contradiction'.[29] The acknowledgement of *all* possibilities, whether they are actualised or remain virtual, counteracts the implicit argument in Leibniz's theologically founded view that 'because divinely conceived worlds are defined by the convergence of series of events, the relation between incompossible worlds is ultimately one of exclusion'.[30] Apart from his explicit linking of incompossibility with discontinuity,[31] the most pertinent of Deleuze's arguments regarding the present context of closure in literary texts is his suggestion that 'if incompossible worlds are affirmed as incompossible, then persons, unable finally to resolve divergences, remain forever "open" to further (re-)determinations'.[32] In contrast to Leibniz, Deleuze thus calls for an affirmation, rather than suppression, of divergence and incompossibility. The concept of incompossibility seems particularly apt to *The Third Policeman* in its ability to describe and account for the deliberately unresolvable tension between two seemingly contradictory worlds that nevertheless converge in the sense that they belong to one and the same fictional world, presenting two possibilities that both exclude each other and at the same time cannot be separated. Furthermore, the notion of entities[33] that are never closed but 'remain forever open to' revision proves a particularly appropriate image for O'Nolan's chimeric text, the flaunted 'divergences' of which necessitate a never-ending reading process of (attempted) (re-)determinations which can still never exploit the text's full range of possibilities and potentialities.[34]

By assuming a position outside the text, however, a reader who adopts nonlinear reading strategies such as 'reading with hypertext'[35] acquires an awareness for the 'roads not taken', i.e. all possible reading paths beyond the choices that have been made. In the words of Louis Armand, 'the solicitation of [the] hypertextual apparatus [...] is located in the structure of possibility itself'.[36] The relatively large number of nodes present in hypertext narratives generally, and in O'Nolan's foot-noted branching text more specifically, poses ambivalent implications. On the one hand, the reader is free to choose which path to follow; on the other hand, due to the considerably obscure nature of O'Nolan's text and the footnotes in particular, the reader is faced with the same uncertainty as the narrator: as the fantastic world of The Parish lacks a logical sense of cause and effect, so the first-time reader cannot be sure where the divergent path presented by a particular footnote will lead or which further ramifications a particular choice will entail. The paths which the reader encounters on the way uncannily resemble the road to The Parish described in *The Third Policeman*: 'The road was narrow, white, old, hard and scarred with shadow. It ran away westwards in the mist of the early morning, running cunningly through the little hills and going to some trouble to visit tiny towns which were not, strictly speaking, on its way' (*CN*, 251). Indeed, the many paths of *The Third Policeman* occasionally appear to 'run away', or at least go 'to some trouble' to take detours which do not, strictly speaking, lie on the text's way. Such detours form part of a general penchant for prolepsis, digression and 'deliberate confusion'[37] exhibited throughout *The Third Policeman*, which has a paradoxical effect: it enhances the reader's feeling of alienation while at the same time forging a bond between reader and narrator by way of their shared experiences of bewilderment.

Stuart Moulthrop (1991) and George P. Landow (1995, 1997) argue that the role of the reader in 'reading with hypertext' is not limited to a mere actualisation of virtualities in the text; the reader is also perceived as a de-constructor of pre-defined hierarchies in the sense that the 'ability to pursue links should encourage' the reader 'to subject those [power] arrangements to inquiry'.[38] Still, as Moulthrop argues, while hypertexts seem to propagate infinite openness with regard to form and structure, a pre-defined set of options created by an author-like figure or function – the 'undead presence in the literary machine, the inevitable Hand that turns the time'[39] – is necessary lest the text disintegrate into randomly generated nonsense. However, in a world such as The Parish, in which conventional logic does not hold true, the existence and authority of an 'undead presence' itself eventually becomes a fiction, as the linear hierarchies begin to 'crumble and slide' in the hands of a reader who sees through the matrix of possible paths and thus comes to explore and question the very structure of possibility. Such a reader is both literally and figuratively on the same page as the author, able to expose any kind of order superimposed by a figure of authority as an artificially constructed illusion.

The roads (not) taken

O'Nolan's introduction of fictional footnotes is another way in which *The Third Policeman* engages with the issue of possibility and, as a consequence, with the question of closure. As an additional textual block that obeys its own rules and logic and adheres to a temporality of its own, the fictional paratext contributes to *The Third Policeman*'s rejection of linear time progression. On the one hand, simple cross-references made in the footnotes, such as those to '*Country Album*, p. 1,034', '*Golden Hours*, vi, 156', etc. (*CN*, 236, 251), presuppose a body of criticism that predates the completion of the narrator's story or to the material text that the reader is holding. By thus pointing to a manuscript which is non-existent even within the fictional world of *The Third Policeman*, the text once again draws attention to its own materiality by way of metalepsis. On the other hand, the 'adventure stor[ies]'[40] taking place within the counternarrative of the footnotes create a semblance of simultaneity when paired with the primary narrative: even though it is impossible for the reader to read both blocks of discourse simultaneously, as in a newspaper, s/he is aware that both events happen in parallel, rather than sequentially. This awareness in turn introduces a bifurcation typical of hypertext narratives: the reader has to choose among different possible paths which cannot be actualised simultaneously. As Hopper reminds us, 'the spatial displacement of this split-text format frustrates our attempts at linear, monological absorption'.[41] Regarding 'fictional notes' as a particular type of paratext, Gérard Genette highlights their unstable and oscillatory status as 'an often indefinite fringe between text and off-text'.[42] The endorsement of 'indefiniteness' and 'slipperiness' which Genette identifies as key features of footnotes[43] rings particularly true for *The Third Policeman*, where these paratextual elements further reinforce the text's rejection of univocality.[44] By virtue of the metaleptic processes that Hopper emphasises,[45] the footnotes in *The Third Policeman* foreground the status of the text as artifice and draw attention to its constructedness,[46] but also complicate the generic classification of the narrative for, by common consensus, 'Novels are not supposed to have footnotes'.[47] These fictional footnotes thus unsettle unequivocal generic ascriptions. They give us pause, inviting us to consider a range of possibilities and to use alternative paths, implicitly questioning the legitimacy of linear narration and its rigid structure of exposition, peripeteia and *dénouement*. The split-text format necessitates nonlinear reading practices which foreground unactualised possibilities, Iserian gaps and alternative paths. Reading *The Third Policeman* thus becomes an unfinishable, never-ending work in progress, questioning the very possibility of closure in nonlinear, branching texts.

In recent decades, the significance of possible worlds theory to modernism has been explored by critics such as Margot Norris, who reads Joyce's *Ulysses* as a textual world that constantly blurs and transgresses the lines between the actual Dublin of 16 June 1904 and an alternative, virtual Dublin populated by Dedalus, Bloom, *et al.*[48] The same period has seen the concept of hypertextual modernism gain increased purchase, as Louis Armand, Darren Tofts and Annalisa Volpone, among others, have posited that the intertextual and metaleptic poetics of modernists such as Joyce anticipate digital hypertext technologies.[49] Given their common concern with transgressions of narrative and ontological boundaries, it is surprising that these rubrics have seldom been placed into conversation with each other.[50] While many essays that deal with hypertextual literature *avant la lettre* (or that trace a prehistory of hypertext in the textual inventions of modernism) typically limit their conclusions to matters of interactivity and use, the ties between hypertextual theory and possible worlds theory remain under-analysed.

Considering its experimental employment of fictional footnotes and its necessitation of nonlinear reading practices, *The Third Policeman* can be seen as a text that concurs with Ted Nelson's definition of hypertext as 'non-sequential writing – text that branches and allows choices to the reader'.[51] Furthermore, the novel's oscillating power structures in terms of the struggle for textual space between primary and secondary text suggest a non-hierarchical mode of thought, which is a central element of hypertext narratives.[52] In *Hypertext 2.0* (1997), Landow explicitly states that 'The standard scholarly article' (a genre which *The Third Policeman* obviously pastiches) 'perfectly embodies the underlying notions of hypertext as multisequentially read text'.[53] Other contemporary and even earlier experimental print texts – such as Laurence Sterne's *Tristram Shandy* or Borges's 'Garden of Forking Paths' – are frequently invoked as typical examples of hypertexts *avant la lettre*.[54] In that respect, hypertext can indeed be seen 'as much [as] a concept as [...] a form of technology'.[55]

Arguing that hypertextuality can be seen as 'a way of characterising textual behaviour [...] as a form of poetics', Darren Tofts focuses on *Ulysses* as a representative instance of a range of texts which 'actively foreground disjunctive structure, thematic multi-layering and a machinic tendency to generate prodigious systems of meaning that are in excess of the sum of its parts'.[56] Most importantly for the present context, Tofts draws attention to the fact that 'Reading such texts is an indeterminate and highly differential process that frustrates any sense of an ending or closure'.[57] Tofts's mention of 'indeterminate' processes re-introduces Deleuze's idea of entities (or, in the present context, texts) which remain open to 're-determination'; however, it also brings the 'infinity of possible worlds' – or the potentially endless bifurcations that branching texts entail – into direct relation with the lack of closure in a text, placing the act of reading at the heart of this transaction. In the same article, Tofts proposes the useful idea of 'an intransitive sense of unending, the building up of a rich mosaic of understanding that develops over time through many re-readings'.[58] Tofts furthermore explicitly ties what he calls 'vectoral events'[59] to a rejection of a linear understanding of time:

> It is therefore inappropriate to speak of events occurring one after the other in these episodes [of *Ulysses*], in the linear, concatenated Forsterian manner of 'and then, and then'. It is more appropriate to describe the vectoral cross-links in terms of syncopation, of 'elsewhere and elsewhere'. What we experience as synchronicities are non-linear instances of convergence and juxtaposition, links within a discontinuous narrative space.[60]

When he speaks of 'elsewhere and elsewhere', Tofts implicitly acknowledges the virtual co-existence of several possible worlds alongside each other. The arrangement that he envisages is clearly a parallel one rather than one of sequence or hierarchy. Even more so than Joyce's text, which, though certainly daring in its content and style, displays a mostly linear layout (a few notable exceptions aside), *The Third Policeman*, with its two blocks of discourse that compete for the reader's attention, can be considered a 'discontinuous narrative space' that rejects 'Forsterian notions' of teleological plot development.

An issue that Tofts does not elaborate, but implicitly touches upon through the notion of indeterminacy, is the 'radical incompleteness of fictional words' highlighted in some strands of possible worlds theory. Lubomír Doležel's seminal work *Heterocosmica: Fiction and Possible Worlds*, for instance, makes the case that 'because it is impossible for the human mind to imagine an object (much less a world) in all of its properties, every fictional world presents areas of radical indeterminacy', which in turn, foreground the 'ontological gap inherent to fictional worlds'.[61] Ruth Ronen expands on this issue in her cogent study of *Possible Worlds in Literary Theory*, claiming that 'Fictional entities are inherently incomplete'.[62] Ronen summarises the 'three basic facets revealed in the mode of existence of fictional entities', the last of which being the idea that 'while reading a literary work we are seldom aware of any gaps or spots of indeterminacy'.[63] In the same context, Ronen posits that 'Literary theorists address the incompleteness of fictional entities by claiming that although the constituents of fictional worlds are inherently incomplete, they are not necessarily grasped as such; incompleteness is hence rhetorically neutralized'.[64] While it may hold true that incompleteness can be 'explained away'[65] in texts which do not actively foreground their inconsistencies and incompossible realities (such as realist novels, particular types of genre fiction and any other genres intent on upholding the suspension of disbelief in its readers from start to finish), it is certainly not the case in *The Third Policeman*. Rather than limiting elements which would jolt the reader out of their complacent pact with the author, *The Third Policeman* thrives on metafiction and metalepsis, using its gaps, lacunae and ambiguities as ways of testing ontological boundaries and making radical incompleteness the very principle of its composition.

Conclusion: a wrinkle in the fold of time

The infinite loop of events created in *The Third Policeman* by way of the hypertextual node 'Is it about a bicycle?' brings together two incompossible worlds. By offering both a natural and a supernatural explanation for events taking place in its storyworld at the same time, this visual link becomes, in Tofts's words, a 'vectoral event' that prolongs endlessly the moment of hesitation between two incompossible realities, or two possible worlds. The moment of hesitation experienced by the narrator and the reader with regard to questions of reality is mirrored in the text's 'split-text format' and the co-existence of realist and non-realist notions of temporal progression. Both the form and the content of *The Third Policeman* thus sustain a degree of tension throughout the novel and endlessly defer the moment of resolution. In this context, it is noteworthy that the very last passages in the text are, with some minor alterations, almost *verbatim* quotations of the narrator's earlier account of his journey. Both the similar phrasing of these experiences and O'Nolan's 14 February 1940 letter to William Saroyan (published as a coda to most editions of *The Third Policeman*) make it unmistakably 'clear that this sort of thing goes on for ever', indicating that in 'the world of the dead – and the damned' (*CN*, 405) the rules of teleology do not apply and that the narrator's Sisyphean suffering extends beyond the margins of his narration. In *The Third Policeman*, closure is infinitely deferred, as is the resolution of the many 'lacuna[e] in the palimpsest' (*CN*, 184). Rather than reiterating a linear, monological discourse, the text openly acknowledges and indeed celebrates its 'unfinalizability'[66] by creating multiple pathways that lead to different possible worlds as well as a surplus of possible meanings that can never be completely exhausted. The textual layout of *The Third Policeman* as such already necessitates nonlinear reading strategies; readers who adopt a hypertextual approach are able, not only to acknowledge the plethora of unexplored possibilities encoded in the novel's form, but indeed to interrogate the 'structure of possibility itself'. Within this interpretive paradigm, a sustained investigation of the value of possibility and incompossibility constitutes an overt challenge to discourses of power, such as those exerted by the policemen in the chaotic and frightening world of The Parish. Whether reading *The Third Policeman* is a matter of 'running cunningly' through the shadows, or of 'walking forever on falling ground' (*CN*, 252), the paths encountered in O'Nolan's chimeric text, with their occasional detours to eternity, only ever lead us to a (re-)'beginning of the unfinished' (*CN*, 406), never to an unequivocal sense of closure.

Endnotes

EDITORS' INTRODUCTION

1 *Blather*, vol. 1, no. 1, August 1934, repr. in *MBM*, 96–98.

2 An undifferentiated, deathly non-place in which 'the infant Peter [...] playing among the ashes' looks out at his native land with the declaration: 'God help us [...] the world is brown' (*SF*, 42).

3 It is particularly suggestive that these bland commodities are all rendered in English in the original text: '*tá siopaí ar an phortach anois, agus tá bus-ticket agus cigarette agus daily mail le faghāil ann*'. Brian Ó Nualláin, 'Aistear Pheadair Dhuibh', *Inisfail* vol. 1. no. 1, March 1933, p. 64. See Carol Taaffe, *Ireland Through the Looking-Glass: Flann O'Brien, Myles na gCopaleen and Irish Cultural Debate* (Cork: Cork University Press, 2008), p. 94.

4 'Caruthers McDaid is a man I created one night when I had swallowed nine stouts and felt vaguely blasphemous. I gave him a good but worn-out mother and an industrious father, and coolly negativing fifty years of eugenics, made him a worthless scoundrel, a betrayer of women and a secret drinker' (*SF*, 50).

5 Keith Hopper, *Flann O'Brien: A Portrait of the Artist as a Young Post-Modernist* (Cork: Cork University Press, 1995), p. 37.

6 Kimberly Bohman-Kalaja, *Reading Games: An Aesthetics of Play in Flann O'Brien, Samuel Beckett and Georges Perec* (Champaign, IL: Dalkey Archive Press, 2007), p. 94.

7 See Paul Fagan, '"I've got you under my skin": "John Duffy's Brother", "Two in One" and the Confessions of Narcissus', in Ruben Borg, Paul Fagan and Werner Huber (eds), *Flann O'Brien: Contesting Legacies* (Cork: Cork University Press, 2014), p. 70.

8 See Paul Fagan, '"Expert diagnosis has averted still another tragedy": Misreading and the Paranoia of Expertise in *The Third Policeman*', *The Parish Review*, vol. 3, no. 1, Fall 2014, pp. 8–28.

9 *CL*, 12 February 1943, p. 3.

10 John James Doe, 'A Weekly Look Around', *Southern Star*, Skibbereen, 15 January 1955–3 November 1956; George Knowall, *Bones of Contention* a.k.a. *George Knowall's Peepshow*, *The Nationalist and Leinster Times*, Carlow, 1960–66.

11 *CL*, 4 October 1944, p. 3; *CL*, 6 October 1945, p. 4.

12 *CL*, 13 May 1946, p. 4.

13 Joseph Brooker, *Flann O'Brien* (Tavistock: Northcote House, 2005), p. 26.

14 Aristotle, *The Poetics*, trans. S.H. Butcher (London: Macmillan, 1902), pp. iii–iv.

15 M. Keith Booker, *Flann O'Brien, Bakhtin, and Menippean Satire* (Syracuse, NY: Syracuse University Press, 1995); Keith Hopper, *Flann O'Brien: A Portrait of the Artist as a Young Post-Modernist*, 2nd edn, J. Hillis Miller (foreword) (Cork: Cork University Press, 2009).

16 Brooker, *Flann O'Brien*; Taaffe, *Ireland Through the Looking-Glass*.

17 Julian Murphet, Rónán McDonald and Sascha Morrell (eds), *Flann O'Brien & Modernism* (London: Bloomsbury, 2014).

18 Maebh Long, *Assembling Flann O'Brien* (London: Bloomsbury, 2014).

19 Ruben Borg, Paul Fagan and Werner Huber, 'Editors' Introduction', in Borg, Fagan and Huber (eds), p. 4.

20 David J. Gunkel, 'What Does it Matter Who is Speaking? Authorship, Authority, and the Mashup', *Popular Music and Society*, vol. 35, no. 1, 2012, p. 82.

21 Flann O'Brien, *The Short Fiction of Flann O'Brien*, Neil Murphy and Keith Hopper (eds), Jack Fennell (trans.) (Champaign, IL: Dalkey Archive Press, 2013); Flann O'Brien, *Plays and Teleplays*, Daniel Keith Jernigan (ed.) (Champaign, IL: Dalkey Archive Press, 2013).

22 *Flann O'Brien: The Lives of Brian* (dir. Maurice Sweeney; Ireland: Mint Productions, 2006), 53 mins.

23 Ute Anna Mittermaier, 'In Search of Mr Love; or, The Internationalist Credentials of "Myles before Myles"', in Borg, Fagan and Huber (eds), p. 109.

24 Hopper, p. 206.

25 Joseph Brooker, 'Ploughmen without Land: Flann O'Brien and Patrick Kavanagh', in Murphet, McDonald and Morrell (eds), p. 93.

26 David Herman, 'Re-Minding Modernism', in David Herman (ed.), *The Emergence of Mind: Representations of Consciousness in Narrative Discourse in English* (Lincoln, NE: University of Nebraska Press, 2011), p. 266.

27 Shelly Brivic, '*The Third Policeman* as Lacanian Deity: O'Brien's Critique of Language and Subjectivity', *New Hibernia Review*, vol. 16, no. 2, Summer 2012, p. 114.

28 Carlos Villar Flor, 'Flann O'Brien: A Postmodernist Who Happens to Be a Thomist', in Neil Murphy and Keith Hopper (eds), *Flann O'Brien: Centenary Essays*, *The Review of Contemporary Fiction*, vol. 31, no. 3, Fall 2011 (Champaign, IL: Dalkey Archive Press, 2011), p. 62.

29 See Booker; José Lanters, *Unauthorized Versions: Irish Menippean Satire, 1919–1952* (Washington: Catholic University of America Press, 2000).

30 Hopper, p. 133.

I. TAAFFE

1 See Jorge Luis Borges, 'When Fiction Lives in Fiction', in *The Total Library: Non-Fiction 1922–1986*, Eliot Weinberger (ed.), Esther Allen, Suzanne Jill Levine and Eliot Weinberger (trans.) (London: Allen Lane, 2000), pp. 160–62.

2 Brian O'Nolan, 'A Sheaf of Letters', Robert Hogan and Gordon Henderson (eds), *The Journal of Irish Literature*, vol. 3, no. 1, *A Flann O'Brien–Myles na Gopaleen Number*, January 1974, pp. 68–69. See also Anthony Cronin, *No Laughing Matter: The Life and Times of Flann O'Brien* (New York, NY: Fromm, 1989), p. 94.

3 See Gerard Windsor, 'The Shrinkage of the Book' and 'Handling the Effects: Pedalling Flann O'Brien in Australia', in *The Mansions of Bedlam: Stories and Essays* (St Lucia: University of Queensland Press, 2000), pp. 78–91, 220–30.

4 Letter to 'Thomas' (16 January 1939), Donagh MacDonagh File, Lot 5, Montgomery Papers, National Library of Ireland.

5 Anon. ['Our Correspondent'], 'University College Notes: The Reincarnation of "Brother Barnabus"', *The Irish Times*, 8 May 1939, p. 9.

6 Anon., 'Irish Author's Experiment: Erudite Humour in Novel Form', *The Irish Times*, 25 March 1939, p. 7.

7 Colm Tóibín, 'Flann O'Brien's Lies', *The London Review of Books*, vol. 34, no. 1, 5 January 2012, p. 32.

8 Ibid.

9 *Dáil Éireann Debates*, vol. 25, no. 5, 18 October 1928, p. 626.

10 James Devane, 'Is an Irish Culture Possible?', *Ireland Today*, vol. 1, no. 5, October 1936, p. 23.

11 For a fuller discussion of these issues see Joseph Brooker, *Flann O'Brien* (London: Northcote, 2005), pp. 102–08.

12 Jon Day, 'Cuttings from *Cruiskeen Lawn*', in Jennika Baines (ed.), *'Is it about a bicycle?': Flann O'Brien in the Twenty-First Century* (Dublin: Four Courts Press, 2011), p. 34. In making a case for a critical re-assessment of *Cruiskeen Lawn* see Flore Coulouma, 'Tall Tales and Short Stories: *Cruiskeen Lawn* and the Dialogic Imagination', in Neil Murphy and Keith Hopper (eds), *Flann O'Brien: Centenary Essays, The Review of Contemporary Fiction*, vol. 31, no. 3, Fall 2011 (Champaign, IL: Dalkey Archive Press, 2011), pp. 162–77.

13 Kevin O'Nolan's *The Best of Myles* (1968), *Further Cuttings from Cruiskeen Lawn* (1976) and *The Hair of the Dogma: A Further Selection from 'Cruiskeen Lawn'* (1977), Benedict Kiely's *The Various Lives of Keats and Chapman and The Brother* (1976) and John Wyse Jackson's *Flann O'Brien at War: Myles na gCopaleen, 1940–1945* (1999).

14 Stephen Young, 'Fact/Fiction: *Cruiskeen Lawn*, 1945–66', in Anne Clune [Clissmann] and Tess Hurson (eds), *Conjuring Complexities: Essays on Flann O'Brien* (Belfast: Institute of Irish Studies, 1997), p. 117.

15 Andrew Gibson, *Joyce's Revenge: History, Politics and Aesthetics in Ulysses* (Oxford: Oxford University Press, 2002), p. 20.

16 See Cronin, p. 52.

17 See Samuel Beckett, 'Recent Irish Poetry', in *Disjecta* (London: John Calder, 1983), pp. 70–76.

18 W.B. Yeats, 'Ireland After the Revolution', in *Explorations* (London: Macmillan, 1962), pp. 438–43.

19 For a sustained discussion of the magazine see Joseph Brooker, 'A Balloon Filled With Verbal Gas: *Blather* and the Irish Ready-Made School', *Precursors and Aftermaths*, vol. 2, no. 1, 2003, 74–98.

20 See L. Perry Curtis Jr, *Apes and Angels: The Irishman in Victorian Caricature* (Washington, DC: Smithsonian Institution Press, 1971), pp. 68–88.

21 *Blather*, vol. 1, no. 1, August 1934, repr. in *MBM*, 97.

22 Ibid.

23 Ibid.

24 'The Abbey Theatre Subsidy', *Blather*, vol. 1, no. 5, January 1935, repr. in *MBM*, 143.

25 Ciarán Ó Nualláin, 'The West's Awake! A Heart-Pounding Melodrama', *Comhthrom Féinne*, vol. 5, no. 4, May 1933, pp. 66–67.

26 'An Impudent Scoundrel Unmasked!', repr. in *MBM*, 120–23, and 'The Mystery of the Yellow Limousine', *Blather*, vol. 1, no. 3, November 1934, pp. 44–46.

27 '*Eachtraí Shearluic*', *Blather*, vol. 1, no. 4, Christmas 1934, p. 77.

28 Frank O'Connor, *The Mirror in the Roadway* (London: Hamish Hamilton, 1957), p. 3. While popular Victorian writers were parodied in *Blather*, Niall Sheridan recorded more contemporary influences on O'Nolan's circle: T.S. Eliot, Ezra Pound, 'the French writers *The Waste Land* had brought back into vogue […] Hergesheimer, Cabell, Dos Passos, Hemingway, and Scott Fitzgerald', as well as Proust, Kafka and Kierkegaard. Niall Sheridan, 'Brian, Flann and Myles', in Timothy O'Keeffe (ed.), *Myles: Portraits of Brian O'Nolan* (London: Martin Brian & O'Keeffe, 1973), p. 39.

29 Philip O'Leary, *Gaelic Prose in the Irish Free State 1922–1939* (Dublin: UCD Press, 2004), p. 377.

30 Ibid., p. 387.

31 Ibid., p. 389.

32 Elizabeth Russell, 'Themes in Popular Reading Material in the 1930s', in Joost Augusteijn (ed.), *Ireland in the 1930s* (Dublin: Four Courts Press, 1999), p. 23. In recounting his experiences as a librarian in the 1930s, Hubert Butler deplored the censorship climate in which he had worked, but also the unending popular appetite for romantic novels about

English duchesses. Hubert Butler, 'The County Libraries: Sex, Religion, and Censorship', in *Grandmother and Wolfe Tone* (Dublin: Lilliput Press, 1990), pp. 58–59.

33 'Has Hitler Gone Too Far?', *Blather*, vol 1, no. 2, October 1934, repr. in *MBM*, 137.

34 See Matthew Potter, 'Keeping an Eye on the Tsar: Frederick Potter and the *Skibbereen Eagle*', in Kevin Rafter (ed.), *Irish Journalism Before Independence: More a Disease than a Profession* (Manchester: Manchester University Press, 2011), pp. 49–61.

35 *The Daily Express*, 24 March 1933.

36 See Cronin, p. 105.

37 Seamus Deane, *Strange Country: Modernity and Nationhood in Irish Writing Since 1790* (Oxford: Clarendon Press, 1997), p. 157.

38 Young, p. 118. For a reading of the multivocal nature of *Cruiskeen Lawn* in terms of dialogism see Coulouma.

39 Tóibín, p. 33.

40 Flann O'Brien, 'Going to the Dogs!', *The Bell*, vol. 1, no. 1, October 1940, pp. 19–24; 'The Trade in Dublin', *The Bell*, vol. 1, no. 2, November 1940, pp. 6–15; 'The Dance Halls', *The Bell*, vol. 1, no. 5, February 1941, pp. 44–52.

41 Seán O'Faoláin, 'Why Don't We See It?', *The Bell*, vol. 5, no. 3, December 1942, p. 163. The popular impact of *The Bell* in Ireland was hardly as broad as O'Faoláin might have liked, though he invited submissions from people in all walks of life. It had a print run of only 3,000 copies, 1,000 of which usually went overseas. Terence Brown, *Ireland: A Social and Cultural History* (London: Harper Perennial, 2004), p. 191.

42 It is possibly the multi-authored nature of *Cruiskeen Lawn* to which O'Nolan was referring in the 5 September 1960 letter to the poet Leslie Daiken: 'I am taxably answerable for certain materials which I "promote" but which are not mine at all' (MS 33,566, NLI). For further details on O'Nolan's forays into advertising and his attempts to monetise the Myles brand see Amy Nejezchleb, 'The Myles Brand Franchise', *The Parish Review*, vol. 1, no. 2, Winter 2013, pp. 51–57.

43 For a discussion of this topic see Brooker, pp. 107–08.

2. LONG

1 *CL*, 1 November 1945, p. 2.

2 The typescripts of the television series, housed in the Brian O'Nolan Papers at the Southern Illinois University, Carbondale, name it *The Ideas of O'Dea* but the series was broadcast as *O'Dea's Your Man*.

3 William Shakespeare [falsely attributed], *The True and Honorable History of the Life of Sir John Oldcastle, the Good Lord Cobham* (London: R. Walker, 1734), 5.vi.

4 G.B. Shaw, *John Bull's Other Island and Major Barbara* (New York, NY: Brentano's, 1911), p. 6.

5 Ibid., p. 15.

6 J.O. Bartely and D.L. Sims 'Pre-Nineteenth Century Stage Irish and Welsh Pronunciation', *Proceedings of the American Philosophical Society*, vol. 93, no. 5, 1949, p. 439.

7 Ben Jonson, 'Irish Masque at Court', *The Works of Ben Jonson vol. 7*, W. Gifford (ed.) (London: Nicol *et al.*, 1816), p. 238.

8 Shakespeare [falsely attributed], *Sir John Oldcastle*, 5.x.

9 Ibid., 5.ii.

10 David Hayton, 'From Barbarian to Burlesque: The Changing Stereotype of the Irish', in *The Anglo-Irish Experience, 1680–1730: Religion, Identity and Patriotism* (Woodbridge: The Boydell Press, 2012), p. 2. See also J.O. Bartley, 'The Development of a Stock Character I. The Stage Irishman to 1800', *The Modern Language Review*, vol. 37, no. 4. 1942, pp. 438–47; Florence R. Scott, 'Teg: The Stage Irishman', *The Modern Language Review*, vol. 42, no. 3,

1947, pp. 314–20; Richard Allen Cave, 'Staging the Irishman', in Jacqueline S. Bratton *et al.* (eds), *Acts of Supremacy: The British Empire and the Stage, 1790–1930* (Manchester: Manchester University Press, 1991), pp. 62–128; Nicholas Grene, *The Politics of Irish Drama: Plays in Context from Boucicault to Friel* (Cambridge: Cambridge University Press, 2004).

11 Hayton, p. 22.

12 Henry J. Byron, *Miss Eily O'Connor: A New and Original Burlesque, Founded on the Great Sensational Drama of The Colleen Bawn* (London: Thomas Hailes Lacy, n.d.), p. 2.

13 Ibid., pp. 13–14.

14 *CL*, 24 March 1953, p. 6.

15 Announcement bill for *The Colleen Bawn*, as quoted by Townsend Walsh, *The Career of Dion Boucicault* (New York, NY: Benjamin Blom, 1967), p. 74.

16 Ibid.

17 Augusta Gregory, *Our Irish Theatre* (New York, NY: G.P. Putnam's Sons, 1911), p. 9.

18 See Deirdre McFeely, *Dion Boucicault: Irish Identity on Stage* (Cambridge: Cambridge University Press, 2012).

19 Gregory, p. 9.

20 Frank Hugh O'Donnell, 'The Stage Irishman of Pseudo-Celtic Drama' (London: John Long, 1904), p. 13.

21 Ibid., p. 9.

22 Ibid., p. 10.

23 Ibid., pp. 29–30.

24 Declan Kiberd, 'The Fall of the Stage Irishman', in *The Irish Writer and the World* (Cambridge: Cambridge University Press, 2005), p. 29.

25 Aristotle, *Politics*, as quoted by Walter Lippmann, *Public Opinion* (Minneapolis, MN: Filiquarian Publishing, 2007), p. 94.

26 Ibid., pp. 95–96.

27 Homi K. Bhabha, 'The Other Question: Stereotype, Discrimination and the Discourse of Colonialism', in *The Location of Culture* (London: Routledge, 2000), p. 75.

28 Ibid., p. 77.

29 Christopher Salvsen, 'Irish Myles', *New Society* (London), 5 September 1968, pp. 346–47.

30 Gregory Castle, *Modernism and the Celtic Revival* (Cambridge: Cambridge University Press, 2001), p. 250.

31 Ibid.

32 *CL*, 28 August 1942, p. 3.

33 Dion Boucicault, *The Colleen Bawn* (New York, NY: S. French, n.d.), 1.ii.

34 L. Perry Curtis Jr's *Apes and Angels: The Irishman in Victorian Caricature* (Washington, DC: Smithsonian Institution Press, 1971) offers a useful overview of these Irish comic weeklies.

35 *CL*, 28 August 1956, p. 6.

36 Joseph Holloway, Manuscript Diaries, National Library of Ireland, as quoted by Robert Tracy, 'Introduction', in Flann O'Brien, *Rhapsody in Stephen's Green*, Robert Tracy (ed.) (Dublin: Lilliput Press, 2001), pp. 11–12.

37 Anon., 'Faustus Kelly', *The Irish Times*, 26 January 1943, p. 3.

38 Anthony Cronin, *No Laughing Matter: The Life and Times of Flann O'Brien* (New York, NY: Fromm International, 1998), p. 134. Daniel Keith Jernigan traces out the tendencies for these theatrical performances to permeate O'Nolan's life in '"Simulato Ergo Est": Brian O'Nolan's Metaperformative Simulations', *New Hibernia Review*, vol. 21, no. 1, Spring 2016, pp. 87–104. See also Stefan Solomon, '"The outward accidents of illusion": O'Brien and the Theatrical', in Julian Murphet, Rónán McDonald and Sascha Morrell (eds), *Flann O'Brien & Modernism* (London: Bloomsbury, 2014), pp. 41–54.

39 A three-act version of *The Boy from Ballytearim* was written in 1955 for the BBC in Northern Ireland. The major differences between the two are that the later version no longer includes a grandfather, Annie and Peter's reaction to Hugh's sweetheart is less aggressive and Hugh is far less likeable.

40 *CL*, 3 September 1941, p. 4. My thanks to Paul Fagan for alerting me to this column.

41 Joseph Brooker, 'Ploughmen without Land: Flann O'Brien and Patrick Kavanagh', in Murphet, McDonald, Morrell (eds), *Flann O'Brien & Modernism* (London: Bloomsbury, 2014), pp. 104–05.

42 W.B. Yeats, *Fairy and Folk Tales of the Irish Peasantry* (New York; NY: The Modern Library, n.d.), p. xiv.

43 Shaw, p. 15.

44 William Shakespeare, *Henry V*, 3.ii.

45 *CL*, 28 August 1942, p. 3.

46 Section 17, Broadcasting Authority Act, 1960, <http://www.irishstatutebook.ie/eli/1960/act/10/section/17/enacted/en/html>.

47 Lance Pettitt, *Screening Ireland: Film and Television Representation* (Manchester: Manchester University Press, 2000), p. 144. See also Robert J. Savage, *Irish Television: The Political and Social Origins* (Westport, CT: Greenwood, 1996).

48 Farrel Corcoran, *RTÉ and the Globalisation of Irish Television* (Bristol: Intellect, 2004), p. 16.

49 Brian O'Nolan, 'The Meaning of Malt', *The Ideas of O'Dea*, Brian O'Nolan papers, 1914–66, ID: 1/4/MSS 051, Special Collections, Southern Illinois University, Carbondale, US. Hereafter SIUC.

50 Ibid.

51 Ibid.

52 Ibid.

53 O'Nolan, 'The New Arrival', *The Ideas of O'Dea*, SIUC.

54 O'Nolan, 'The Horse Show', *The Ideas of O'Dea*, SIUC.

55 See, for example, 'Liverpool Grand National: The Story of Tipperary Tim', *The Adelaide Chronicle*, 19 May 1928. This contamination strongly figures in O'Nolan's atomic/mollycule theory, and, as Thierry Robin establishes, in Brian Nolan's 'The Martyr's Crown' (1950), in which 'the elegant young man "*born* for Ireland" is every bit as British as he is Irish' given that his father is an English soldier. Thierry Robin, 'Tall Tales or "Petites Histoires": History and the Void in "The Martyr's Crown" and *Thirst*', in Ruben Borg, Paul Fagan and Werner Huber (eds), *Flann O'Brien: Contesting Legacies* (Cork: Cork University Press, 2014), p. 85.

56 O'Nolan, 'The New Arrival', *The Ideas of O'Dea*, SIUC. This reference to *Fanny Hill* is unexpected, but topical. Mayflower Books published an uncensored version of *Fanny Hill* in 1963, which was involved in an obscenity trial in 1964.

57 Brian O'Nolan, 'Trouble About Names', *Th'oul Lad of Kilsalaher*, Brian O'Nolan papers, 1914–66, ID: 1/4/MSS 051, Special Collections, Southern Illinois University, Carbondale, US.

58 O'Nolan, 'Animals of Erin', *Th'oul Lad of Kilsalaher*, SIUC.

59 O'Nolan, 'The New Abbey Theatre', *Th'oul Lad of Kilsalaher*, SIUC.

60 O'Nolan, 'The Language Question, *The Ideas of O'Dea*, SIUC.

61 Ibid.

62 Ibid.

63 O'Nolan, 'The Ballad Wave', *Th'oul Lad of Kilsalaher*, SIUC.

64 O'Nolan, 'Beirt Eile', *Th'oul Lad of Kilsalaher*, SIUC.

65 Ibid.

66 O'Nolan, 'Apples and Nuts', *Th'oul Lad of Kilsalaher*, SIUC.
67 O'Nolan, 'Hughie for Pres!', *Th'oul Lad of Kilsalaher*, SIUC.
68 O'Nolan, 'The Language Question', *The Ideas of O'Dea*, SIUC.
69 Ibid.
70 Ibid.

3. KAGER

1 See Elizabeth Klosty Beaujour, *Alien Tongues: Bilingual Russian Writers of the 'First' Emigration* (Ithaca, NY: Cornell University Press, 1989).

2 Beaujour explains that bilingualism is 'very difficult to deal with because the elements that determine the relationships of the languages commanded by any bi- or multilingual person are idiosyncratic. Each bilingual is a special case; the manner of acquisition and the associative complexes of the languages in individuals are almost impossible to measure or to compare statistically'. Elizabeth Klosty Beaujour, 'Prolegomena to a Study of Russian Bilingual Writers', *The Slavic and East European Journal*, vol. 28, no. 1, Spring 1984, p. 59.

3 Although this switch is rarely absolute: both Beckett and Nabokov continued to be creatively engaged with their previous writing language.

4 Carol Taaffe, *Ireland Through the Looking-Glass: Flann O'Brien, Myles na gCopaleen and Irish Cultural Debate* (Cork: Cork University Press, 2008), p. 91.

5 Ciaran Carson, *The Midnight Court* (Oldcastle: Gallery, 2005), p. 14.

6 My account of O'Nolan's linguistic background is based mainly on Anthony Cronin, *No Laughing Matter: The Life and Times of Flann O'Brien* (Dublin: New Island, 2003).

7 O'Nolan's example shows perhaps not only the complexities of being an Irish speaker in a predominantly Anglophone Ireland, but also the problematic nature of the concept of a 'mother tongue'. For more on this topic, see Yasemin Yildiz, *Beyond the Mother Tongue: The Postmonolingual Condition* (New York, NY: Fordham University Press, 2011); and Juliane Prade (ed.), *(M)Other Tongues: Literary Reflexions on a Difficult Distinction* (Newcastle upon Tyne: Cambridge Scholars Publishing, 2013).

8 Taaffe, p. 93.

9 Cronin, p. 13.

10 Ibid.

11 Ibid., p. 33.

12 See Jack Fennell, 'Irelands Enough and Time: Brian O'Nolan's Science Fiction', in Ruben Borg, Paul Fagan and Werner Huber (eds), *Flann O'Brien: Contesting Legacies* (Cork: Cork University Press, 2014), pp. 33–36; and Joseph LaBine, '"the words I taught to him": Interfusional Language Play and Brian O'Nolan's "Revenge on the English"', *The Parish Review*, vol. 3, no. 2, Spring 2016, pp. 26–38.

13 Qtd. in Taaffe, p. 175.

14 Annette de Groot, *Language and Cognition in Bilinguals and Multilinguals: An Introduction* (New York, NY: Psychology Press, 2011), p. 340.

15 Ton Dijkstra, 'Bilingual Visual Word Recognition and Lexical Access', in Judith F. Kroll and Annette de Groot (eds), *Handbook of Bilingualism: Psycholinguistic Approaches* (Oxford: Oxford University Press, 2005), p. 179.

16 De Groot, p. 279.

17 Vivian Cook, 'Consequences of Multi-Competence for Second Language Acquisition', *article forthcoming*. Cook is quoting a study of interlexical homographs by Beauvillain and Grainger (1987). Cook also cites research by Hermans *et al.* (2011) that shows that both phonological systems are activated when bilingual speakers produce cognates.

C. Beauvillain and J. Grainger, 'Accessing Interlexical Homographs: Some Limitations of a Language Selective Access', *Journal of Memory and Language*, no. 26, 1987, pp. 658–72; D. Hermans, *et al.*, 'Lexical Activation in Bilinguals' Speech Production is Dynamic: How Language Ambiguous Words Can Affect Cross-Language Activation', *Language and Cognitive Processes*, vol. 26, no. 10, 2011, pp. 1687–1709.

18 Judith Kroll and D. Hermans, 'Psycholinguistic Perspectives on Language Processing in Bilinguals', in Monika Schmid and Wander Lowie (eds), *Modeling Bilingualism: From Structure to Chaos* (Amsterdam: John Benjamins Publishing, 2011), p. 15. In fact, something similar happens in monolingual word recognition. When a monolingual reads, 'many possible words initially become active on the presentation of a letter string, and the reader is usually not aware of them; only the word that is eventually recognized becomes available to awareness'. In the case of bilingual (or multilingual) word recognition, this process is more complex because there are not just one but two (or more) languages involved (Dijkstra, p. 179).

19 Ellen Bialystok, I. Fergus, M. Craik and G. Luk, 'Bilingualism: Consequences for Mind and Brain', *Trends in Cognitive Sciences*, vol. 16, no. 4, 2012, p. 242.

20 De Groot, p. 393.

21 E. Bialystok and R. Barac, 'Cognitive Effects', in François Grosjean and Ping Li (eds), *The Psycholinguistics of Bilingualism* (Oxford: Blackwell Publishing, 2013), p. 193.

22 Bialystok *et al.*, 'Bilingualism', pp. 241–42.

23 C.A. Dreifus, Conversation with Ellen Bialystok, *New York Times*, 2011, May 31, p. D2.

24 A number of recent neuroimaging studies have reported that bilinguals have more grey matter than monolinguals in several areas of the brain that are involved in language. Volker Ressel, *et al.* write, for instance, that neuroimaging studies have shown larger grey matter in Heschl's gyrus in bilinguals, resulting in larger Heschl's gyri overall. Heschl's gyrus is the structure that houses the auditory cortex, and in fact, earlier studies had already shown that a larger volume of Heschl's gyrus resulted in an increased ability to perceive speech: 'participants with larger left Heschl's gyri learned consonantal or tonal contrasts faster than those with smaller HG'. Volker Ressel, *et al.*, 'An Effect of Bilingualism on the Auditory Cortex', *The Journal of Neuroscience*, vol. 32, no. 47, 2012, p. 16597. Consequently, bilinguals, who have larger Heschl's gyri than monolinguals and thus a larger auditory cortex, have an anatomically more complex brain that allows them to perceive and produce speech in a distinct way.

25 De Groot, p. 320.

26 Ibid., p. 342.

27 See de Groot, p. 390; Penelope Gardner Chloros, *Code-Switching* (Cambridge: Cambridge University Press, 2009), p. 169.

28 De Groot, p. 390. De Groot bases her argument here on two earlier studies: Sandra Ben-Zeev, 'The Influence of Bilingualism on Cognitive Strategy and Cognitive Development', *Child Development*, vol. 48, no. 3, September 1977, pp. 1009–18; and Anita D. Ianco-Worrall, 'Bilingualism and Cognitive Development', *Child Development*, vol. 43, no. 4, December 1972, pp. 1390–1400.

29 De Groot, p. 390. The idea that bilingualism can promote recognition of the separation of sound and meaning is not a new one. In the 1930s and 1940s, Werner Leopold kept a diary of the linguistic development of his bilingual daughter Hildegard and concluded that bilingualism encouraged an early separation of the word and its referent. Leopold detected 'a noticeable looseness of the link between the phonetic word and its meaning'. Werner Leopold, 'Patterning in Children's Language Learning', in S. Saporta (ed.), *Psycholinguistics* (New York, NY: Holt, Rinehart, & Winston, 1961), p. 358. Leopold also suggested a relation between the cognitive and semantic development of bilingual children,

in the sense that the separation of meaning from sound leads to an early awareness of the 'conventionality of words and the arbitrariness of language. This awareness could promote, in turn, more abstract levels of thinking'. Kenji Hakuta and Rafael Diaz, 'The Relationship Between Degree of Bilingualism and Cognitive Ability: A Critical Discussion and Some New Longitudinal Data', in K.E. Nelson (ed.), *Children's Language: Vol. 5* (Hillsdale, NJ: L. Erlbaum, 1985), p. 324.

30 Bialystok and Barac, p. 195.

31 Anatoliy Kharkurin, *Multilingualism and Creativity* (Bristol: Multilingual Matters 2012), p. 89.

32 Ellen Bialystok, 'Consequences of Bilingualism for Cognitive Development', in Kroll and de Groot (eds), p. 428.

33 Li Wei, *The Bilingualism Reader* (London: Routledge, 2000), p. 21.

34 'Shawn Beg' is a phonetic rendering of the Irish *'Sean Beag'*, or 'little Sean'. It is interesting that, in an item on the (im)possibility of translating contemporary English into Irish, the name of one of the protagonists has been transliterated, but not translated, from Irish into English.

35 *CL*, 4 October 1940, p. 4.

36 Anon., 'Irish in the Home', *The Irish Times*, 28 September 1940, p. 6.

37 Ibid.

38 *CL*, 4 October 1940, p. 4.

39 This transliteration is done in a manner similar to that employed by the English in 'translating' Irish names, by which process Brian Ua Nualláin becomes Brian O'Nolan.

40 Anne Clissmann, *Flann O'Brien: A Critical Introduction to His Writings* (Dublin: Gill & Macmillan, 1975), p. 235.

41 *CL*, 8 February 1944, p. 3.

42 *CL*, 11 January 1941, p. 8.

43 David Wheatley, rev. of *Comhar: Brian Ó Nualláin: Eagrán Comórtha Speisialta, The Parish Review*, vol. 1, no. 1, Summer 2012, p. 33.

44 *CL*, 10 March 1942, p. 3.

45 *CL*, 23 May 1942, p. 2.

46 Joseph Brooker, 'Myles' Tones', in Jennika Baines (ed.), *'Is it about a bicycle?': Flann O'Brien in the Twenty-First Century* (Dublin: Four Courts Press, 2011), p. 18.

47 Ibid.

48 Cronin, pp. 247, 213.

49 *CL*, 12 August 1946, p. 4.

50 The manner in which Myles records these conversations, often 'in the snug of a public house', is reminiscent of the way in which the young James Joyce recorded his epiphanies, which were often snippets of Dublin speech similar to those noted down by O'Nolan in *Cruiskeen Lawn* and recorded with a similar meticulous attention to the peculiarities of people's speech. Oliver St John Gogarty has described the following instance, which also occurred in a Dublin public house: 'James Augustine Joyce slipped politely from the snug with an "Excuse me!" "Whist! He's gone to put it all down!" "Put what down?" "Put *us* down. A chiel's among us takin' notes. And, faith, he'll print it"'. 'Which of us', Gogarty wonders, 'had endowed him with an "Epiphany" and sent him to the lavatory to take it down?' Qtd. in Robert Scholes and Richard M. Kain, *The Workshop of Daedalus: James Joyce and the Raw Materials for 'A Portrait of the Artist as a Young Man'* (Evanston, IL: Northwestern University Press, 1975), p. 7.

51 Discussing *At Swim-Two-Birds*, Declan Kiberd has remarked: 'The plots, for all their fantastic complications, are secondary to that language, which is the real hero of the book'. Declan Kiberd, 'Gaelic Absurdism in *At Swim-Two-Birds*', in *Irish Classics* (London: Granta, 2000), p. 503. The same could be said about much of *Cruiskeen Lawn*.

4. FLYNN

1   Anon., 'Common Cause', *The Irish Times*, 11 October 1940, p. 4.

2   Reprinted in full in David J. Lu (ed.), *Japan, A Documentary History, Volume 2: The Late Tokugawa Period to the Present* (New York, NY: East Gate, 1997), p. 424.

3   Anon., 'Common Cause', p. 4.

4   Anthony Cronin writes that Smyllie 'wanted to show that [*The Irish Times*] was not against the Irish language but only against the chauvinism and hypocrisy that went with it. He must have seen immediately that this potential new contributor was ideally fitted to serve his purposes'. Anthony Cronin, *No Laughing Matter: The Life and Times of Flann O'Brien* (London: Grafton, 1989), p. 112.

5   Carol Taaffe quotes Smyllie's comment, upon the ending of censorship of the press in 1945, that it had been 'in some respects as Draconian and irrational as anything that ever was devised in the fertile brain of the late Josef Goebbels'. Carol Taaffe, *Ireland Through the Looking-Glass: Flann O'Brien, Myles na gCopaleen and Irish Cultural Debate* (Cork: Cork University Press, 2008), p. 154.

6   Hugh Kenner, *A Colder Eye: The Irish Modern Writers* (Middlesex: Penguin, 1983), p. 326.

7   Anon., 'Common Cause', p. 4.

8   *CL*, 28 October 1940, p. 4.

9   See Anon. [Reuters Correspondent], 'Japan to Implement Three-Power Pact: "New Order in Greater East-Asia"', *The Irish Times*, 21 January 1941, p. 6.

10 For a discussion of the term and its historical context see Delmer M. Brown, *Nationalism in Japan: An Introductory Historical Analysis* (Berkeley, CA: University of California Press, 1955); John Dower, *Japan in War & Peace: Selected Essays* (New York, NY: New Press, 1993); Walter Edwards, 'Forging Tradition for a Holy War: The *Hakkō Ichiu* Tower in Miyazaki and Japanese Wartime Ideology', *Journal of Japanese Studies*, no. 29, 2003, pp. 289–324; and Andrew Gordon, *A Modern History of Japan* (Oxford: Oxford University Press, 2003).

11 *CL*, 28 October 1940, p. 4.

12 Fr Dineen translates '*connlán*' as 'a family, *esp* a large and helpless family', and a 'group, party, [...] a band of companions'. Patrick S. Dinneen, *Foclóir Gaedhilge agus Béarla: An Irish-English Dictionary; Being a Thesaurus of the Words, Phrases and Idioms of the Modern Irish Language, with Explanations in English* (Dublin: M.H. Gill & Son, 1904), p. 245.

13 I am grateful to Daniel Cuong O'Neill of the Department of East Asian Languages and Cultures at UC Berkeley for this translation.

14 *CL*, 16 November 1940, p. 6.

15 Frank O'Connor, *Kings, Lords and Commons: An Anthology from the Irish* (New York, NY: Knopf, 1959), p. 132.

16 While this essay focuses upon *Cruiskeen Lawn*'s discussion of Japan in the early war years, the column also undoes Irish regional identifiers. The 'Sun/Son of Heaven' takes up a *Cruiskeen Lawn* meme of '*mac-eolas*', which might be called 'filology' or 'sonology', in which compound nouns are invented by adding words to 'son'. Relatively simple in Irish, these neologisms become the pretext for a display of English lexical inventiveness, as '*Mac-cathrach*', literally 'son of the city', is translated by O'Nolan as 'a towny, a jazzer, a mickey-dazzler'. Comic in its unbridled vituperation, the meme exemplifies a rural animus towards urban dwellers, ridiculing a more local kind of territorial animosity.

17 Anon., 'Invasion of Indo-China: Reported Attack by Thailand, Japan to Present Demands?', *The Irish Times*, 15 November 1940, p. 5.

18 Ibid.

19 Dermot Keogh, *Ireland in World War Two: Diplomacy and Survival* (Cork: Mercier Press, 2004), p. 120.

20 Meyer's comparison between the Celts and the Japanese dates from 1911 and is confined entirely to these lines. Kuno Meyer, *Selections from Ancient Irish Poetry* (London: Constable, 1913), p. xiii. Andreas Huether writes that, in 1914, Meyer 'published a number of articles by Roger Casement in German, a sign that some within the imperial administration were aware of the Irish case and its potential value for German military plans'; Meyer, who died in 1919, 'continued to lobby for an inclusion of Ireland in German military plans'. Andreas Heuther, '"*In Politik verschieden, in Freundschaft wie immer*": The German Celtic Scholar Kuno Meyer and the First World War', in Fred Bridgham (ed.), *The First World War as a Clash of Cultures* (Woodbridge: Boydell & Brewer, 2006), pp. 232, 240.

21 Anon. [Reuters Correspondent], 'Japan to Implement Three-Power Pact: "New Order in Greater East-Asia"', *The Irish Times*, 21 January 1941, p. 6.

22 *CL*, 21 January 1941, p. 6.

23 *CL*, 18 February 1942, p. 6.

24 *CL*, 20 August 1945, p. 3.

5. EBURY

1 Bertrand Russell, *The ABC of Relativity* (London: Unwin, 1925), pp. 4–5.

2 Arthur Stanley Eddington, *The Nature of the Physical World* (London: Dent, 1929), p. 342.

3 Charles Kemnitz, 'Beyond the Zone of Middle Dimensions: A Relativistic Reading of *The Third Policeman*', *Irish University Review*, vol. 15, no. 1, Spring 1985, pp. 56–72; M. Keith Booker, 'Science, Philosophy, and *The Third Policeman*: Flann O'Brien and the Epistemology of Futility', *South Atlantic Review*, vol. 56, no. 4, November 1991, pp. 37–56; Andrew Spenser, 'Many Worlds: The New Physics in Flann O'Brien's *The Third Policeman*', *Éire-Ireland*, vol. 30, no. 1, Spring 1995, pp. 145–58; Samuel Whybrow, 'Flann O'Brien's Science Fiction: An "Illusion of Progression" in *The Third Policeman*', in Jennika Baines (ed.), '*Is it about a bicycle?*': *Flann O'Brien in the Twenty-First Century* (Dublin: Four Courts Press, 2011), pp. 127–41; Jack Fennell, 'Irelands Enough and Time: Brian O'Nolan's Science Fiction', in Ruben Borg, Paul Fagan and Werner Huber (eds), *Flann O'Brien: Contesting Legacies* (Cork: Cork University Press, 2014), pp. 33–45.

4 Brian O'Nolan, letter to Timothy O'Keeffe, 21 September 1962, in 'A Sheaf of Letters', Robert Hogan and Gordon Henderson (eds), *The Journal of Irish Literature*, vol. 3, no. 1, *A Flann O'Brien–Myles na Gopaleen Number*, January 1974, p. 80.

5 Keith Hopper, *Flann O'Brien: A Portrait of the Artist as a Young Post-Modernist* (Cork: Cork University Press, 1995), p. 206.

6 Mary A. O'Toole, 'The Theory of Serialism in *The Third Policeman*', *Irish University Review*, vol. 18, no. 2, Autumn 1988, pp. 215–25; Mark O'Connell, '"How to handle eternity": Infinity and the Theories of J.W. Dunne in the Fiction of Jorge Luis Borges and Flann O'Brien's *The Third Policeman*', *Irish Studies Review*, vol. 17, no. 2, Summer 2009, pp. 223–37; Alana Gillespie, '"Banjaxed and Bewildered": *Cruiskeen Lawn* and the Role of Science in Independent Ireland', in Borg, Fagan and Huber (eds), pp. 169–80.

7 O'Connell, p. 224.

8 Ibid., p. 231.

9 Gillian Beer, 'Eddington and the Idiom of Modernism', in Henry Krips, J.E. McGuire and Trevor Melia (eds), *Science, Reason and Rhetoric* (Pittsburgh, PA: University of Pittsburgh Press, 1995), p. 312.

10 *CL*, 18 June 1943, p. 3.

11 For example: 'Some years ago [1943] a stamp was issued in memory of Rowan Hamilton, discoverer of quaternions. Not a half dozen people in the country knew what quaternions were, or what they were good for. Some thought quaternions should in no circumstances

be taken with whiskey, as they dried up in the stomach like oysters. [...] A knowledgeable man will take out the pipe and say that the word means "the quotient of two vectors, or operator that changes one vector into another". That does not get us very far. [...] Would my own Excellency get my face on a stamp [...] if I were to devise and scratch on a canal bridge a formula so recondite that nobody but myself could comprehend it?' (*CL*, 9 November 1954, p. 6).

12 As the story goes that Hamilton discovered the fundamental formula for quaternion multiplication ($i^2 = j^2 = k^2 = ijk = -1$) while out walking and cut the formula in a stone of the Broom Bridge crossing the Royal Canal, so Myles reports that 'Sir Myles (the da), out for a walk' one day came up with the concept '$a+b+c-j=a$' and 'reached the nearest canal bridge at a run' (*CL*, 6 December 1943, p. 3). In another column listing the history of the na gCopaleen family's achievements, Myles writes, 'We were materially implicated in the discovery of quaternions' (*CL*, 31 March 1948, p. 4).

13 *CL*, 18 June 1943, p. 3.

14 *CL*, 5 July 1944, p. 3.

15 The article is written by 'A Correspondent'; it seems likely that this was J.G. Crowther who was then a scientific correspondent at both *The Observer* and *The Guardian*.

16 *CL*, 10 March 1947, p. 4.

17 Eddington, *Nature of the Physical World*, p. 139.

18 Arthur Stanley Eddington, *Space, Time and Gravitation* (Cambridge: Cambridge University Press, 1920), p. 201.

19 Eddington, *Nature of the Physical World*, p. 229.

20 Michael Whitworth, *Einstein's Wake: Relativity, Metaphor and Modernist Literature* (Oxford: Oxford University Press, 2001), p. 135.

21 Gillespie, p. 177.

22 Qtd. in *CL*, 3 August 1942, p. 3; Gillespie, p. 172.

23 Ibid., pp. 172–73.

24 Whybrow, p. 128.

25 Gillespie, pp. 171–72.

26 See *CL*, 10 April 1942, p. 3; 2 February 1946, p. 4; 25 January 1950, p. 5; 6 March 1950, p. 4.

27 For a detailed study of O'Nolan's involvement with debates about the DIAS and science in the Free State, see Gillespie, pp. 156–69. On the O'Nolan/Schrödinger connection, see Walter Moore, *Schrödinger: Life and Thought* (Cambridge: Cambridge University Press, 1989), pp. 377–79; Ondřej Pilný, 'My Kingdom for a Pun: Myles na gCopaleen, Erwin Schrödinger and *The Third Policeman* in Improbable Frequency', *Irish Theatre International*, vol. 1, no. 1, 2008, pp. 47–48; and Paddy Leahy, 'How Myles na gCopaleen Belled Schrödinger's Cat', *The Irish Times*, 22 February 2001, p. 15.

28 Peter J. Bowler, *Science for All: The Popularization of Science in Early Twentieth-Century Britain* (Chicago, IL: University of Chicago Press, 2009), p. 17.

29 Val Nolan, 'Flann, Fantasy, and Science Fiction: O'Brien's Surprising Synthesis', in Neil Murphy and Keith Hopper (eds), *Flann O'Brien: Centenary Essays*, *The Review of Contemporary Fiction*, vol. 31, no. 3, Fall 2011 (Champaign, IL: Dalkey Archive Press, 2011), pp. 172, 186.

30 Fennell, p. 37.

31 Famously, even the agnostic Einstein allows the language of religion to enter his rhetoric, finding 'God does not play dice with the universe' a fitting rebuke to what he saw as the excesses of quantum mechanics: 'The theory certainly says a lot, but it does not really bring us any closer to the secrets of the "Old One". I, at any rate, am convinced that He does not play dice'. Walter Isaacson, *Einstein: His Life and Universe* (New York, NY: Simon & Schuster, 2007), p. 335.

32 Fennell, p. 67.

33 See, for example, Wim Tigges, *An Anatomy of Literary Nonsense* (Amsterdam: Rodopi, 1988), p. 208; Wim Tigges, 'Ireland in Wonderland: Flann O'Brien's *The Third Policeman* as a Nonsense Novel', in C.C. Barfoot and Theo d'Haen (eds), *The Clash of Ireland: Literary Contrasts and Connections* (Amsterdam: Rodopi, 1989), pp. 204–06; Carol Taaffe, *Ireland Through the Looking-Glass: Flann O'Brien, Myles na gCopaleen and Irish Cultural Debate* (Cork: Cork University Press, 2008), pp. 69–76 (and title); and Gillespie, p. 180.

34 Bernard O'Donoghue, 'Irish Humour and Verbal Logic', *Critical Quarterly*, no. 24, 1982, pp. 33–40. See also Ondřej Pilný, '"Did you put charcoal adroitly in the vent?": Brian O'Nolan and Pataphysics', in Borg, Fagan and Huber (eds), pp. 163–64.

35 Eddington, *Nature of the Physical World*, p. 359.

36 Katy Price, *Loving Faster than Light: Romance and Readers in Einstein's Universe* (Chicago, IL: University of Chicago Press, 2012), p. 26.

37 George Gamow's *Mr Tompkins in Wonderland* (1940) seems to build directly on Eddington's intertextual references to Alice, which he had been using since *Space, Time and Gravitation* (1920). Interestingly, Booker reads *The Third Policeman* against the example of Gamow. Apparently, 'Gamow was a physicist whose stories […] were written exclusively to demonstrate scientific principles. O'Brien, by contrast, is a novelist whose fiction happens to resonate with certain concepts from science'. Following this somewhat clumsy distinction between literature and science writing, Booker notes that, 'for those interested in zeitgeist arguments', Gamow's stories were written at the same time as *The Third Policeman*. The missing explanation for this 'zeitgeist' congruity is the influence of Eddington, which both Gamow and O'Nolan shared. George Gamow, *Mr Tompkins in Wonderland* (Cambridge: The University Press, 1940); M. Keith Booker, *Flann O'Brien, Bakhtin, and Menippean Satire* (Syracuse, NY: Syracuse University Press, 1995), p. 55, n. 13.

38 Eddington, *Space, Time and Gravitation*, p. 32.

39 Booker briefly but convincingly connects these changes in scale to the tradition of Menippean satire (*Menippean Satire*, pp. 146–47). However, it is important to acknowledge Eddington's more contemporary example, since changes of scale also occur at moments in O'Nolan's fiction that are not obviously satirical: for example, the dreamlike moment, to be discussed at the close of this essay, when the narrator of *The Third Policeman* is alone in bed and loses 'definition, position and magnitude' (*CN*, 327), which seems perhaps more poignant than anything else in the novel.

40 Eddington, *Space, Time and Gravitation*, pp. 23–24.

41 Arthur Stanley Eddington, *The Expanding Universe* (Cambridge: Cambridge University Press, 1933), p. 97.

42 Whybrow, p. 130.

43 *CL*, 1 September 1945, p. 3; Nolan, p. 185.

44 Whybrow, p. 140.

45 James Jeans, *The New Background of Science* (Cambridge: Cambridge University Press, 1933), p. 5.

46 Eddington, *Space, Time and Gravitation*, p. 31.

47 Eddington, *Nature of the Physical World*, p. 13.

48 Ibid., p. 39.

49 Many versions of this thought experiment existed in popularisations: the most common name for it was 'the twin paradox'.

50 Eddington, *Space, Time and Gravitation*, p. 51.

51 Ibid., p. 69.

6. VAN HULLE

1   Susan Stanford Friedman, 'Definitional Excursions: The Meanings of Modern/Modernity/
    Modernism', *Modernism/modernity*, vol. 8, no. 3, September 2001, p. 494.
2   Keith Hopper, *Flann O'Brien: A Portrait of the Artist as a Young Post-Modernist* (Cork: Cork
    University Press, 1995). Carol Taaffe notes that Hopper's study 'provocatively argued
    in 1995 that the critical reception of [O'Nolan's] work had been largely split between
    an indigenous school of criticism, "invariably folksy and anecdotal, and often lacking
    in critical acumen" and that of international post-structuralists'. Framing the debate in
    O'Nolan studies, Taaffe comments that 'As with Hopper's "tribal retrieval" of O'Nolan as
    a post-modernist in 1995, the most recent tendency in criticism (originating in Ireland or
    otherwise) has been to consciously merge formalist and cultural approaches to his fiction'.
    Carol Taaffe, *Ireland Through the Looking-Glass: Flann O'Brien, Myles na gCopaleen and Irish
    Cultural Debate* (Cork: Cork University Press, 2008), pp. 5–6.
3   Brian McHale, *Constructing Postmodernism* (London: Routledge, 1992), pp. 28, 155, 157.
4   Ibid., p. 34.
5   Ibid.
6   Wang Ning, 'Introduction: Historicizing Postmodernist Fiction', *Narrative*, vol. 21, no. 3,
    October 2013, p. 265. In his 'Afterword: Reconstructing Postmodernism' in the same issue
    of *Narrative*, McHale observes that 'even as postmodernist fiction has waned in its North
    American and European homelands […], it seems to have flourished elsewhere'. Brian
    McHale, 'Afterword: Reconstructing Postmodernism', *Narrative*, vol. 21, no. 3, October
    2013, p. 362. At the same time, 'the term "modernism" has overshadowed cognate terms
    like "postmodernism", which now often seems a contrapuntal extension of "modernism"
    rather than a rejection or inversion of it', as Rónán McDonald and Julian Murphet argue in
    their 'Introduction' to Julian Murphet, Rónán McDonald and Sascha Morrell (eds), *Flann
    O'Brien & Modernism* (London: Bloomsbury, 2014), p. 3.
7   Ibid.
8   Tyrus Miller situates late modernism in the 1920s and especially the 1930s. Tyrus Miller,
    Late Modernism: Politics, Fiction, and the Arts Between the World Wars (Berkeley, CA: University
    of California Press, 1999), pp. 63–64. In Beckett studies, however, most critics seem to agree
    with Fredric Jameson's *A Singular Modernity* (London: Verso, 2002) that late modernism
    reached its peak after the Second World War; see, for instance, Conor Carville, 'Autonomy
    and the Everyday: Beckett, Late Modernism and Post-War Visual Art', *Samuel Beckett Today/
    Aujourd'hui*, no. 23, 2011, pp. 63–78. According to Peter Fifield, Beckett's post-war work is
    late modernist 'because it responds to the disaster of the war' and shows the experience of
    an 'historical collapse', resulting in writings that question 'the capacity of literature and
    philosophy to produce a systematic, rigorous, and comprehensive account of the world'.
    Peter Fifield, *Late Modernist Style in Samuel Beckett and Emmanuel Levinas* (Basingstoke:
    Palgrave Macmillan, 2013), p. 12.
9   McDonald and Murphet, 'Introduction', p. 4.
10 David Herman refers to Evan Thompson to define this postcognitivist paradigm:
    'enactivists and others developing postcognitivist models maintain that intelligent agents
    "do not operate on the basis of internal representations in the subjectivist/objectivist sense.
    Instead of internally representing an external world in some Cartesian sense, they enact an
    environment inseparable from their own structure and actions"'. Evan Thompson, *Mind in
    Life: Biology, Phenomenology, and the Sciences of Mind* (Cambridge, MA: Harvard University
    Press, 2007), p. 59; qtd. in David Herman, 'Re-Minding Modernism', in David Herman
    (ed.), *The Emergence of Mind: Representations of Consciousness in Narrative Discourse in English*
    (Lincoln, NE: University of Nebraska Press, 2011), p. 257.

11 Ibid., p. 249.

12 Ibid., p. 266.

13 For instance, von Uexküll tried to find out what the *Umwelt* of a sea urchin (1909) or of a tick (1956) looked like. Jakob von Uexküll, *Umwelt und Innenwelt der Tiere* (Berlin: Julius Springer, 1909), p. 5; Jakob von Uexküll, *Streifzüge durch die Umwelten von Tieren und Menschen: Ein Bilderbuch Unsichtbarer Welten* (Hamburg: Rowohlt, 1956), p. 3.

14 See Dirk Van Hulle, 'Flann O'Brien's *Ulysses*: Marginalia and the Modernist Mind', in Murphet, McDonald and Morrell (eds), p. 118.

15 Lambros Malafouris, *How Things Shape the Mind: A Theory of Material Engagement* (Cambridge, MA: MIT Press, 2013), pp. 177, 118.

16 Virginia Woolf, *Collected Essays, vol. 2* (London: Hogarth Press, 1972), p. 106.

17 James Joyce, *Dubliners* (London: Penguin, 2000), p. 103.

18 Ibid., pp. 103–04.

19 As a young man, Joyce had himself translated Hauptmann's *Vor Sonnenaufgang* and *Michael Kramer*. Richard Ellmann, *James Joyce*, rev. edn (New York, NY: Oxford University Press, 1982), p. 87.

20 Joyce, *Dubliners*, p. 104.

21 Ibid.

22 Ibid., p. 106.

23 Ibid., p. 107.

24 Ibid.

25 Ibid., pp. 107–08.

26 Ibid., p. 108

27 For example, the following passage from *At Swim-Two-Birds* plays on the ambiguity between the sexual meaning of 'intercourse' and 'joking' as a form of 'intercourse of a social character': '*Relevant excerpt from the Press*: An examination of the galley and servants' sleeping-quarters revealed no trace of the negro maids. [...] Detective-Officer Snodgrass found a pearl-handled shooting-iron under the pillow in the bed of Liza Roberts, the youngest of the maids. No great importance is attached by the police to this discovery, however, as ownership has been traced to Peter (Shorty) Andrews, a cowboy, who states that though at a loss to explain the presence of his property in the maid's bed, it is possible that she appropriated the article in order to clean it in her spare time in bed (she was an industrious girl) or in order to play a joke. It is stated that the former explanation is the more likely of the two as there is *no intercourse of a social character* between the men and the scullery-maids. A number of minor clues have been found and an arrest is expected in the near future. Conclusion of excerpt' [my emphasis] (*CN*, 51). Also, there is a recurrence of this play with intercourse in the *At Swim-Two-Birds* court case, when William Tracy accuses Trellis of having impregnated one of his female characters and states that as a result he 'discontinued all social intercourse with the accused' (*CN*, 198).

28 Samuel Beckett, *Murphy*, J.C.C. Mays (ed.) (London: Faber & Faber, 2009), p. 70.

29 Joyce, *Dubliners*, p. 108.

30 Ibid., pp. 109, 112, 113.

31 Ibid., p. 113.

32 Ibid., p. 114.

33 John Keats, *The Complete Works of John Keats, Volume 1*, Harry Buxton Forman (ed.) (New York, NY: Thomas Y. Crowell & Company, 1817), p. 47.

34 James Joyce, *Ulysses*, Oxford World's Classics, Jeri Johnson (introd. and ed.) (Oxford: Oxford University Press, 1998), p. 53.

35 Herman, 'Re-Minding Modernism', p. 266.

36 Qtd. in Dirk Van Hulle, *Modern Manuscripts: The Extended Mind and Creative Undoing from Darwin to Beckett and Beyond* (London: Bloomsbury, 2014), p. 105.

37 Sue Asbee, *Flann O'Brien* (Boston, MA: Twayne, 1991), p. 220.

38 Samuel Beckett, *The Unnamable*, Steven Connor (ed.) (London: Faber & Faber, 2010), p. 11.

39 Paul Fagan, '"I've got you under my skin": "John Duffy's Brother", "Two in One", and the Confessions of Narcissus', in Ruben Borg, Paul Fagan and Werner Huber (eds), *Flann O'Brien: Contesting Legacies* (Cork: Cork University Press, 2014), p. 64.

40 Ibid., pp. 65, 67.

41 J.W. Dunne, *An Experiment with Time* (London: Faber & Faber, 1934), p. 160.

42 Samuel Beckett, *The Letters of Samuel Beckett, vol. II: 1941–1956*, George Craig, Martha Dow Fehsenfeld, Dan Gunn and Lois More Overbeck (eds) (Cambridge: Cambridge University Press, 2011), p. 129.

43 Dirk Van Hulle and Shane Weller, *The Making of Samuel Beckett's 'L'Innommable / The Unnamable'* (Brussels/London: University Press Antwerp/Bloomsbury, 2014), p. 160.

44 Beckett, *Letters*, p. 140.

45 Beckett, *The Unnamable*, p. 100.

46 'Every joint became loose and foolish and devoid of true utility. Every inch of my person gained weight with every second until the total burden on the bed was approximately five hundred thousand tons. This was evenly distributed on the four wooden legs of the bed, which had by now become an integral part of the universe. [...] United with the bed I became momentous and planetary. Far away from the bed I could see the outside night framed neatly in the window as if it were a picture on the wall. There was a bright star in one corner with other smaller stars elsewhere littered about in sublime profusion. [...] Robbing me of the reassurance of my eyesight, it [the night] was *disintegrating my bodily personality into a flux of colour, smell, recollection, desire* – all the strange uncounted essences of terrestrial and spiritual existence. I was deprived of definition, position and magnitude and my significance was considerably diminished' [my emphasis] (*CN*, 324–27).

47 Samuel Beckett, *Company, Ill Seen Ill Said, Worstward Ho, Stirrings Still*, Dirk Van Hulle (ed.) (London: Faber & Faber, 2009), p. 109.

48 Ibid., p. 111.

49 Ibid.

50 Ibid., pp. 112, 113.

51 Ibid., p. 114.

52 Ibid.

53 The notion of failing visual and aural perception is also thematised in *The Third Policeman*. When MacCruiskeen mangles the light, the narrator simultaneously hears a shout, and when he asks MacCruiskeen, 'What was that shouting', the latter replies, 'I will tell you that in a tick [...] if you will inform me what you think the words of the shout were. What would you say was said in the shout now?':

> 'I could not make it out', I said, vaguely and feebly, 'but I think it was railway-station talk'.
>
> 'I have been listening to shouts and screams for years', he said, 'but I can never surely catch the words. Would you say that he said "Don't press so hard"?'
>
> 'No'.
>
> 'Second favourites always win?'
>
> 'Not that'.
>
> 'It is a difficult pancake', MacCruiskeen said. (*CN*, 316–17)

54 For a more detailed discussion of this section's genesis, see Beckett, *The Beckett Digital Manuscript Project, Module 1: Stirrings Still / Soubresauts and 'Comment dire' / 'what is the*

word': An Electronic Genetic Edition, Dirk Van Hulle and Vincent Neyt (eds) (Brussels: ASP/ University Press Antwerp, 2010), <http://www.beckettarchive.org>

55 Beckett, *Company, Ill Seen Ill Said, Worstward Ho, Stirrings Still*, p. 115.

56 Ibid., p. 114.

57 John Keats, *The Complete Works of John Keats, Volume 2*, Harry Buxton Forman (ed.) (New York, NY, Thomas Y., Crowell & Company, 1818), p. 104.

58 Beckett, *Company, Ill Seen Ill Said, Worstward Ho, Stirrings Still*, p. 114.

59 Joyce, *Dubliners*, p. 227.

60 Fagan, p. 65.

61 Keith Hopper, 'Coming Off the Rails: The Strange Case of "John Duffy's Brother"', in Borg, Fagan and Huber (eds), p. 25.

62 Ibid.

63 Ibid.

7. CROWLEY

* This essay was completed during the author's term as Humboldt research fellow at the University of Passau.

1 D.J. O'Donoghue, 'Post Bag: Irish Pseudonyms', *The Irish Book Lover*, vol. 1, no. 9, April 1910, p. 121.

2 Keith Hopper, *Flann O'Brien: A Portrait of the Artist as a Young Post-Modernist*. 2nd edn (Cork: Cork University Press, 2009), p. 16.

3 Most book-length studies of O'Nolan still open with this familiar motif. See, for example, the 'profusion of names' enumerated at the beginning of Maebh Long's excellent *Assembling Flann O'Brien* (London: Bloomsbury Publishing, 2014), p. 1, or the 'pseudonymous creations' dutifully listed in Rónán McDonald and Julian Murphet's 'Introduction', in Julian Murphet, Rónán McDonald and Sascha Morrell (eds), *Flann O'Brien & Modernism* (London: Bloomsbury Publishing, 2014), p. 1.

4 Pierre Bourdieu, 'The Field of Cultural Production, or: The Economic World Reversed', in *The Field of Cultural Production: Essays on Art and Literature*, Randal Johnson (trans.) (New York, NY: Columbia University Press, 1993), p. 29.

5 Ibid.

6 Timothy Dalrymple, 'Abraham: Framing *Fear and Trembling*', in Lee C. Barrett and Jon Stewart (eds), *Kierkegaard and the Bible: Vol. 1, The Old Testament* (Farnham: Ashgate, 2010), p. 52.

7 M. Keith Booker provides a useful run-through of critics who link O'Nolan to the experimental and metafictional writers who came after him. Many of these writers (Donald Barthelme, Alasdair Gray and B.S. Johnson among them) themselves adopted pseudonyms. See M. Keith Booker, *Flann O'Brien, Bakhtin, and Menippean Satire* (Syracuse, NY: Syracuse University Press, 1995), p. 122.

8 Susan Stanford Friedman, 'Definitional Excursions: The Meanings of Modern/Modernity/ Modernism', *Modernism/modernity*, vol. 8, no. 3, September 2001, p. 494.

9 For the now-standard account of modernism's changed critical fortunes, see Douglas Mao and Rebecca L. Walkowitz, 'The New Modernist Studies', *PMLA*, vol. 123, no. 3, May 2008, pp. 737–48.

10 Stephen Abblitt, 'The Ghost of "Poor Jimmy Joyce": A Portrait of the Artist as a Reluctant Modernist', in Murphet, McDonald and Morrell (eds), p. 55 and *passim*. The 'Introduction' to Murphet, McDonald and Morrell (eds) usefully charts the implications for O'Nolan studies of a revitalised and reconfigured modernist field (pp. 1–10).

11 Joseph Conrad, letter to Charles Chassé, 31 January 1924, *The Collected Letters of Joseph Conrad: Vol. 8, 1923–1924*, Laurence Davies and Gene M. Moore (eds) (Cambridge:

Cambridge University Press, 2008), p. 290; Lorelei Guidry, *'The Mask': Introduction and Index* (New York, NY: Blom, 1968), p. 8.

12 Paul Valéry, 'Stendhal' [1927], in *Variety: Second Series*, William A. Bradley (trans.) (New York, NY: Harcourt, Brace & Company, 1938), p. 133.

13 Ralph Schoolcraft, 'For Whom the Beyle Toils: Stendhal and Pseudonymous Authorship', *PMLA*, vol. 119, no. 2, March 2004, p. 247.

14 Adrian Oțoiu, '"Compartmentation of personality for the purpose of literary utterance": Pseudonymity and Heteronymity in the Various Lives of Flann O'Brien', *Word and Text: A Journal of Literary Studies and Linguistics*, vol. 1, no. 1, 2011, pp. 128–38; Fernando Pessoa, *The Book of Disquiet*, Richard Zenith (trans.) (New York, NY: Penguin Books, 2002), p. 299. The text is presented as the work of Bernardo Soares, an assistant bookkeeper, whom Zenith describes as 'a mutilated Pessoa, with missing parts' (p. xi).

15 Adrian Oțoiu, 'Hibernian Choices: The Politics of Naming in Flann O'Brien's *At Swim-Two-Birds*', in Oliviu Felecan (ed.), *Name and Naming: Synchronic and Diachronic Perspectives* (Newcastle upon Tyne: Cambridge Scholars Publishing, 2012), p. 297.

16 *CL*, 16 May 1951, p. 4.

17 *CL*, 11 May 1944, p. 3; *CL*, 9 May 1947, p. 4.

18 *CL*, 30 April 1946, p. 4; *CL*, 19 March 1951, p. 6; *CL*, 9 October 1945, p. 2.

19 Qtd in Anthony Cronin, *No Laughing Matter: The Life and Times of Flann O'Brien* (London: Grafton, 1989), p. 197.

20 Albert J. DeGiacomo, *T.C. Murray, Dramatist: Voice of the Irish Peasant* (Syracuse, NY: Syracuse University Press, 2002), p. 76.

21 Qtd in ibid., pp. 75, 81.

22 The obituary of O'Donoghue in *The Irish Book Lover* promised that his 'long projected work' on Irish pseudonyms was 'almost ready for publication, and only awaits the return to normal conditions'. 'David James O'Donoghue', *The Irish Book Lover*, vol. 9, nos. 1–2, August and September 1917, p. 6. The D.J. O'Donoghue Archive at Belfast Central Library now houses the manuscript of 'Pseudonyms' as well as some four archival boxes of material relating to the project.

23 Declan Kiely, 'The Go-Between: Ernest Boyd, John Quinn and Ireland's Literary Renaissance', in Janis Londraville and Richard Londraville (eds), *John Quinn: Selected Irish Writers from his Library* (West Cornwall, CT: Locust Hill Press, 2001), p. 32. The pamphlet was published under the pen-name 'Gnathaí gan Iarraidh' and, in his Dublin letter, Boyd protests that 'this little book has been ascribed to various hands, including my own!'. Boyd, 'Dublin, November 16', *The Dial*, vol. 65, 14 December 1918, p. 559.

24 B.M. [Brinsley MacNamara], 'Satire in Disguise: A Disciple of Swift', *Irish Independent*, 15 November 1920, p. 7. *The Irishman* was the London edition of *In Clay and in Bronze*, published by Brentano's in New York under the 'Brinsley MacNamara' pseudonym.

25 *CL*, 12 December 1941, p. 4; *CL*, 13 December 1965, p. 10.

26 Cronin, p. 190.

27 Though more widely known for his political career, in the 1910s and into the early 1920s, Desmond FitzGerald was a poet, playwright and short-storyist. An intimate of Ezra Pound, he published so-so verse in *The New Age* and, in 1919, authored a one-acter, 'The Saint', that was staged at the Abbey Theatre. See Helen Carr, *The Verse Revolutionaries: Ezra Pound, H.D. and The Imagists* (London: Jonathan Cape, 2009), pp. 180–85 and *passim*.

28 W.B. Yeats, 'A General Introduction for my Work' [1937], in *Essays and Introductions* (New York, NY: Macmillan, 1961), p. 509.

29 For metrocolonial Ireland, see Joseph Valente, *The Myth of Manliness in Irish National Culture, 1880–1922* (Urbana, IL: University of Illinois Press, 2011), pp. 11, 13 and *passim*.

30 Susan Howe, *Kidnapped* (Tipperary: Coracle, 2002), p. 19.

31 See, for example, the series of articles collected and reprinted as D.P. Moran, *The Philosophy of Irish Ireland* (Dublin: James Duffy & Co., 1905), rpt. as Patrick Maume (ed.) (Dublin: UCD Press, 2006).

32 Terence Brown, 'The Church of Ireland and the Climax of the Ages', in *Ireland's Literature: Selected Essays* (Mullingar: Lilliput Press, 1988), p. 57. The essay is a revision of Brown's earlier 'The Church of Ireland: Some Literary Perspectives', *Search: A Church of Ireland Journal*, vol. 3, no. 2, Winter 1980, pp. 5–19.

33 Brown, 'The Church of Ireland and the Climax of the Ages', p. 57.

34 Edna Longley, 'Not Guilty?', *Dublin Review*, no. 16, Autumn 2004, p. 17.

35 Ibid.

36 Margaret Kelleher, 'Introduction', *Irish University Review*, vol. 33, no. 1, Spring–Summer 2003, p. viii.

37 Vivian Mercier, 'Literature in English, 1891–1921', in W.E. Vaughan (ed.), *A New History of Ireland: Vol. 6, Ireland under the Union, 1870–1921* (New York, NY: Oxford University Press, 1996), p. 369.

38 Clare Hutton, 'Joyce and the Institutions of Revivalism', *Irish University Review*, vol. 33, no. 1, Spring–Summer 2003, pp. 126–28.

39 See Sonja Tiernan, *Eva Gore-Booth: An Image of Such Politics* (Manchester: Manchester University Press, 2012); Lauren Arrington, *Revolutionary Lives: Constance and Casimir Markievicz* (Princeton, NJ: Princeton University Press, 2016).

40 James M. Cahalan, 'Forging a Tradition: Emily Lawless and the Irish Literary Canon', *Colby Quarterly*, vol. 27, no. 1, March 1991, p. 27.

41 Kevin Birmingham, *The Most Dangerous Book: The Battle for James Joyce's 'Ulysses'* (New York, NY: The Penguin Press, 2014), p. 44.

42 Flore Coulouma, '"Finn Mc Cool in his mind was wrestling with his people": Polyphonic Dialogues in Flann O'Brien's Comic Writing', in Clara-Ubaldina Lorda and Patrick Zabalbeascoa (eds), *Spaces of Polyphony* (Amsterdam: John Benjamins, 2012), p. 234.

43 Paul K. Saint-Amour, 'An Interlude: We Have Never Been Modernists', *English Literature in Transition, 1880–1920*, vol. 56, no. 2, 2013, pp. 201–04.

44 Kristin Bluemel, *Intermodernism: Literary Culture in Mid-Twentieth-Century Britain* (Edinburgh: Edinburgh University Press, 2009), p. 5.

45 Hopper, p. 23.

46 David Holdeman, *Much Labouring: The Texts and Authors of Yeats's First Modernist Books* (Ann Arbor, MI: University of Michigan Press, 1997), especially Chapter 1.

47 The phrase is Bruce Stewart's, though he resists its application to Joyce. Bruce Stewart, 'Lumberjacks and Surgeons' [rev. of *James Joyce: The Artist and the Labyrinth* by Augustine Martin; *James Joyce and the Politics of Desire* by Suzette A. Henke; *The Irish Beckett* by John P. Harrington; *Clongowes Wood: A History of Clongowes Wood College 1814–1989* by Peter Costello], *Books Ireland*, no. 154, November 1991, p. 215.

48 James Joyce, *Ulysses*, Hans Walter Gabler (ed.) (London: Vintage Classic, 2008), p. 274.

49 Richard Ellmann, *James Joyce*, rev. edn (New York, NY: Oxford University Press, 1982), p. 172.

50 R.F. Foster, *Vivid Faces: The Revolutionary Generation in Ireland, 1890–1923* (New York, NY: W.W. Norton & Company, 2015), p. 120.

51 McDonald and Murphet, 'Introduction', p. 1.

52 Richard Pine, 'Review Article: mac Liammóir in Wonderland', *Irish University Review*, vol. 28, no. 2, Autumn–Winter 1998, p. 373.

53 Joyce, *Ulysses*, p. 256. Janet Egleson Dunleavy and Gareth W. Dunleavy, *Douglas Hyde: A Maker of Modern Ireland* (Berkeley, CA: University of California Press, 1991), p. 95.

54 Dunleavy and Dunleavy, p. 95.

55 Clare Hutton, 'Reading *The Love Songs of Connacht*: Douglas Hyde and the Exigencies of Publication', *The Library*, vol. 2, no. 4, December 2001, p. 368.

56 Eamonn Hughes, 'Flann O'Brien's *At Swim-Two-Birds* in the Age of Mechanical Reproduction', in Edwina Keown and Carol Taaffe (eds), *Irish Modernism: Origins, Contexts, Publics* (Bern: Peter Lang, 2010), p. 113.

57 James Joyce, 'A Little Cloud', in *Dubliners* (London: Vintage Classic, 2012), p. 63.

58 Declan Kiberd notes in James Joyce, *Ulysses: Annotated Students' Edition* (London: Penguin, 2000), p. 956. See Ellmann, p. 164.

59 James Joyce, *Letters of James Joyce*, Stuart Gilbert (ed.) (New York, NY: Viking Press, 1957), p. 54.

60 The inscription, 'To | Harriet Weaver | Stephen Dedalus | London | Michaelmas: 1924', is quoted in Luca Crispi and Stacey Herbert with Lori N. Curtis, *In Good Company: James Joyce & Publishers, Readers, Friends* (Tulsa, OK: University of Tulsa, 2003), p. 55. The association copy is now part of the Harriet Shaw Weaver library in the McFarlin Library, University of Tulsa.

61 Austin Clarke, '"Stephen Dedalus": The Author of *Ulysses*', *The New Statesman*, vol. 22, no. 566, 23 February 1924, pp. 571–72.

62 Oliver St John Gogarty, *As I Was Going Down Sackville Street: A Phantasy in Fact* (London: Rich & Cowan, 1937), p. 310.

63 Brinsley MacNamara, 'Dr Oswald Brannigan', *The Irish Statesman*, vol. 1, no. 6, 2 August 1919, p. 144.

64 Ibid., p. 145.

65 Richard J. Finneran, 'Appendix A: The Date of James Stephens's Birth', in James Stephens, *Letters of James Stephens: With an Appendix Listing Stephens's Published Writings*, Richard J. Finneran (ed.) (London: Macmillan, 1974), p. 418.

66 See James Esse, 'An Interview with Mr James Stephens', *The Irish Statesman*, no. 1, 22 September 1923, pp. 48 and 50.

67 Russell to Gertrude Kurath, 9 September 1931, qtd in Frank Shovlin, 'The Pseudonyms of George W. Russell', *Notes and Queries*, vol. 49, no. 1, March 2002, p. 80.

68 J.H. Orwell [Seumas O'Sullivan], *Impressions: A Selection from the Notebooks of the Late J.H. Orwell, with a foreword by Seumas O'Sullivan* (Dublin: The New Nation Press, 1910); J.H. Orwell [Seumas O'Sullivan], *Facetiae et Curiosa, being a selection from the note-books of the late J.H. Orwell, made by his friend Seumas O'Sullivan* (Dublin: privately printed, 1937).

69 Padraic Colum, *The Road Round Ireland* (New York, NY: Macmillan Co., 1926), p. 299.

70 Patricia McCracken, quoting the Lennon Papers at the National Library of Ireland, writes '"Cuguan" is not really a word but we think it represents the sound made by a turtle dove'. See Patricia McCracken, 'Arthur Griffith's South African Sabbatical', *Southern African-Irish Studies*, vol. 3, 1996, p. 254.

71 Conn [Arthur Griffith], 'In a Real Wicklow Glen', *The United Irishman*, 24 October 1903, p. 3.

72 Virginia E. Glandon, *Arthur Griffith and the Advanced-Nationalist Press, Ireland, 1900–1922* (New York, NY: Peter Lang, 1985), p. 67 n. 30. Glandon avails of the comprehensive list of Griffith's pseudonyms that Seán Milroy supplied to Seán Ó Lúing, the statesman's first biographer.

73 P.J. Matthews, 'A Battle of Two Civilizations? D.P. Moran and William Rooney', *The Irish Review*, no. 29, Autumn 2002, pp. 28, 36 n. 35.

74 The poetry Casement published in *The Irish Review* appeared under his birth-name.

75 Ernest Boyd, 'The Literary Comrade: A Portrait', *The American Mercury*, vol. 40, no. 157, January 1937, p. 78. The portrait is something of a companion piece to Boyd's more widely known satire of the Greenwich Village literary coterie, 'Aesthete: Model 1924', *The American Mercury*, vol. 1, no. 1, January 1924, pp. 51–56.

76 See C.P. Curran, *James Joyce Remembered* (London: Oxford University Press, 1968), p. 68.

77 Norah Hoult, *Coming from the Fair* (New York, NY: Covici, Friede, 1937), p. 63 and *passim*.

78 *CL*, 17 April 1943, p. 3. Myles supplies an anagrammatic reworking of 'Myles na gCopaleen'.

79 Niall Montgomery, 'An Aristophanic Sorcerer', *The Irish Times*, 2 April 1966, p. 7.

80 Oțoiu, 'Compartmentation of personality', p. 128.

81 Seán O'Faoláin, 'Time's Pocket', letter, *The Irish Times*, 13 January 1939, p. 5. O'Nolan's provoking sally is Flann O'Brien, 'Time's Pocket', letter, *The Irish Times*, 11 January 1939, p. 5. He had twice tried to bait O'Faoláin in letters to the newspaper the previous year, but the latter left the jibes unanswered; see Flann O'Brien, 'Ideals for an Irish Theatre', letter, *The Irish Times*, 15 October 1938, p. 7 and 'At it Again!', letter, *The Irish Times*, 8 November 1938, p. 5. O'Faoláin's review of *At Swim-Two-Birds* is 'Irish Gasconade', *John O'London's Weekly*, 24 March 1939, p. 970.

82 Anon. '"A.E." Memorial Award: Trustees' Report', *The Irish Times*, 5 January 1940, p. 9.

83 Anon. [Stanford Lee Cooper], 'Eire's Columnist', *TIME*, vol. 42, no. 8, 23 August 1943, p. 88; Anon. 'Myles on the Front Page', *The Irish Times*, 3 July 1943, p. 3.

84 Quidnunc, 'An Irishman's Diary', *The Irish Times*, 30 April 1947, p. 5.

85 Brian Nolan, 'The Martyr's Crown', *Envoy*, vol. 1, no. 3, February 1950, p. 57.

86 Quidnunc, 'An Irishman's Diary', *The Irish Times*, 9 June 1955, p. 6.

87 Brendan Behan, 'Secret Scripture' [rev. of *At Swim-Two-Birds*], *The Irish Times*, 30 July 1960, p. 6.

88 J.J., 'Laughter Rings Out as Saints Cycle In', *The Irish Times*, 28 September 1965, p. 6.

89 Rüdiger Imhof (ed.), *Alive-Alive O! Flann O'Brien's 'At Swim-Two-Birds'* (Dublin: Wolfhound Press, 1985), p. 8.

90 See Nichevo, 'Problems of Finance', *The Irish Times*, 1 October 1921, p. 6; 'In Search of a Scapegoat for University Failure', *The Irish Times Pictorial*, 14 August 1954, p. 4.

91 See 'Windsor Card: Birdcatcher's Selections', *The Irish Times*, 10 April 1943, p. 4; Birdcatcher, 'Sporting Link Best at Liverpool', *The Irish Times*, 2 December 1953, p. 2. For Montgomery's bookending contributions, see Rosemary Lane, 'The Liberties', *The Irish Times*, 16 January 1964, p. 8 and Rosemary Lane, 'The Liberties', *The Irish Times*, 14 December 1964, p. 8. A late letter to the editor signed 'Rosemary Lane' appears in the *Times* for 12 October 1968 (p. 16). See also Christine O'Neill, 'An Irishwoman's Diary on Architect, Poet, Artist and Literary Critic Niall Montgomery', *The Irish Times*, 8 June 2015, p. 15.

92 Carol Taaffe, *Ireland Through the Looking-Glass: Flann O'Brien, Myles na gCopaleen and Irish Cultural Debate* (Cork: Cork University Press, 2008), pp. 15, 163–66; Tony Gray, '"Old Days" of the Diary', letter, *The Irish Times*, 3 June 1999, p. 17.

93 The first Quidnunc column is 'An Irishman's Diary', *The Irish Times*, 16 December 1927, p. 4. To judge from the columns reproduced in Patrick Campbell's *An Irishman's Diary*, Ronald Searle (illustrations) (London: Cassell, 1950), his tenure as Quidnunc ran, after a brief Nichevo interlude, from 30 May 1944 to 5 August 1946. But even after Inglis started writing 'An Irishman's Diary' as Pro-Quidnunc in August 1946, occasional contributions signed 'Quidnunc' still appeared, attesting to Campbell's continued presence as late as 1947.

94 *CL*, 13 December 1950, p. 4.

95 Joseph Brooker, 'A Balloon Filled with Verbal Gas: *Blather* and the Irish Ready-Made School', *Precursors and Aftermaths*, vol. 2, no. 1, 2003, p. 75.

96 Cronin, p. 225.

97 Myles Na Gopaleen, 'De Me', *New Ireland: Magazine of the New Ireland Society of the Queen's University of Belfast*, no. 2, March 1964, pp. 41–42.

98 Ibid. The paragraph is reproduced, however, in Eva Wäppling, *Four Irish Legendary Figures in 'At Swim-Two-Birds': A Study of Flann O'Brien's use of Finn, Suibhne, the Pooka and the Good Fairy* (Stockholm: Almqvist och Wiksell, 1984), pp. 22–23.

8. MASLEN

1   Anon., 'Tall Talk', *The Times Literary Supplement*, 7 September 1967, p. 793. On Stephens's relationship with Joyce see Hilary Pyle, *James Stephens: His Work and an Account of His Life* (London: Routledge & Kegan Paul, 1965), pp. 114–15; the detailed account in James Stephens, *James, Seumas and Jacques: Unpublished Writings of James Stephens*, Lloyd Frankenberg (ed.) (London: Macmillan & Co., 1964), pp. xxiii–xxx; and Stephens's own broadcasts on Joyce in the same book, pp. 147–62.

2   Keith Hopper, *Flann O'Brien: A Portrait of the Artist as a Young Post-Modernist* (Cork: Cork University Press, 1995), p. 126.

3   Carol Taaffe, *Ireland Through the Looking-Glass: Flann O'Brien, Myles na gCopaleen and Irish Cultural Debate* (Cork: Cork University Press, 2008), p. 80.

4   Ibid., p. 65. For O'Nolan's attitude to de Valera see also John Coyle, 'Flann O'Brien in the Devil Era', in Paddy Lyons and Alison O'Malley-Younger (eds), *No Country for Old Men: Fresh Perspectives on Irish Literature* (London: Peter Lang, 2009), pp. 69–85.

5   Shelly Brivic, '*The Third Policeman* as Lacanian Deity: O'Brien's Critique of Language and Subjectivity', *New Hibernia Review*, vol. 16, no. 2, Summer 2012, p. 114.

6   The best picture of Stephens's politics is painted in the political essays reprinted in James Stephens, *Uncollected Prose of James Stephens*, 2 vols, Patricia McFate (ed.) (New York, NY: St Martin's, 1983).

7   Pyle, p. 3.

8   Ibid., p. 5.

9   See Anthony Cronin, *No Laughing Matter: The Life and Times of Flann O'Brien* (London: Grafton, 1989).

10 James Stephens, *The Crock of Gold* (London: Macmillan & Co., 1928), pp. 172–73.

11 Ibid., p. 186.

12 Ibid., pp. 187–89.

13 See Pyle, 'Part One: Dublin – 1880–1925', pp. 3–107. See also A. Norman Jeffares, 'Introduction', in James Stephens, *The Poems of James Stephens*, Shirley Stevens Mulligan (ed.) (Buckinghamshire: Colin Smythe, 2006), pp. xi–xxxiv.

14 Taaffe, p. 80.

15 Ibid.

16 Stephens, 'There is a Tavern in the Town', in *Here Are Ladies* (London: Macmillan, 1914), pp. 277–349.

17 Stephens, *The Charwoman's Daughter* (London: Macmillan & Co., 1912), p. 62.

18 Stephens, *Crock of Gold*, p. 76.

19 Ibid., p. 209.

20 Ibid., p. 206.

21 Ibid., p. 218.

22 Ibid., pp. 219–20.

23 Ibid., pp. 226–27.

24 Ibid., p. 246.

25 Ibid., p. 262.

26 Ibid., p. 308.

27 One writer who took advantage of the detachable quality of 'The Happy March' was C.S. Lewis, who adapted it in the final section of his second Narnia book, *Prince Caspian*. C.S. Lewis, *Prince Caspian: The Return to Narnia*, Pauline Baynes (illustrations) (London: G. Bles, 1951).

28 It is worth noting that one of de Selby's commentators, Le Fournier, seems to assign the philosopher a portion of blame for the outbreak of the First World War (*CN*, 246, n. 4). For a fuller account of violence in *The Third Policeman* see my 'Flann O'Brien's Bombshells:

At Swim-Two-Birds and *The Third Policeman*', *New Hibernia Review*, vol. 10, no. 4, Winter 2006, pp. 84–104.

29 See Keith Hopper, 'Coming Off the Rails: The Strange Case of "John Duffy's Brother"', in Ruben Borg, Paul Fagan and Werner Huber (eds), *Flann O'Brien: Contesting Legacies* (Cork: Cork University Press, 2014), p. 30.

30 Stephens, *Crock of Gold*, p. 140.

31 For Ciceronian amity see Cicero, 'Laelius de amicitia', in *Cicero in Twenty-Eight Volumes*, vol. 20, *De senectute, de amicitia, de divinatione*, The Loeb Classical Library, W.A. Falconer (trans.) (Cambridge, MA: Harvard University Press, 1971), xxi. 80: '*est enim is qui est tamquam alter idem*'; 'for he is, as it were, another self'.

32 Stephens, *Crock of Gold*, p. 244.

33 'My mind was completely void. I did not recall who I was, where I was or what my business was upon earth' (*CN*, 402).

34 Stephens, *Crock of Gold*, p. 100.

35 Ibid., p. 106.

36 See ibid., p. 91: 'Every person who is hungry is a good person, and every person who is not hungry is a bad person. It is better to be hungry than rich'.

37 See: '[Divney] had a quiet civil face with eyes like cow's eyes, brooding, brown, and patient' (*CN*, 228).

38 Stephens, *Crock of Gold*, p. 311.

39 Ibid., p. 312.

40 See Pyle, Chapters 3 and 4, pp. 31–76.

9. Ó CAOIMH

1   I am grateful to Peadar Ó Riada and the University College Cork Library Archives Service for permission to quote from this material.

2   Máiréad Ní Chinnéide, *An Damer: Stair Amharclainne* (Baile Átha Cliath: Gael-Linn, 2008), p. 59. I am grateful to the late Mairéad Ní Chinnéide for clarifying the possible link between the 1967 production and the undated typescript. Email correspondence with the current author, 09 November 2011.

3   Seán Ó Riada, item BL/PP/OR/528, Bailiúchán Sheáin Uí Riada, UCC Library Archives Service, UCC Library, University College Cork.

4   Máirín Nic Eoin, *An Litríocht Réigiúnach* (Baile Átha Cliath: An Clóchomhar, 1982), pp. 130, 211.

5   All translations from Irish are my own unless otherwise stated.

6   Alan Titley, *An tÚrscéal Gaeilge* (Baile Átha Cliath: An Clóchomhar, 1991), pp. 124, 45.

7   Robert Welch (ed.), *The Oxford Companion to Irish Literature* (Oxford: Oxford University Press, 1996), p. 451.

8   Diarmuid Breathnach and Máire Ní Mhurchú (eds), *1882–1982: Beathaisnéis a Dó* (Baile Átha Cliath: An Clóchomhar, 1990), p. 131.

9   A sketch with the same title, without the exclamation mark, but different content appeared in the first edition of *Blather* in August 1934.

10 Ciarán Ó Nualláin, 'Cúrsaí Báis!', *The New Irish Magazine/An Sgeulaidhe Nuadh*, August 1934, p. 43.

11 Joseph Brooker, 'A Balloon Filled With Verbal Gas: *Blather* and the Irish Ready-Made School', *Precursors and Aftermaths*, vol. 2, no. 1, 2003, pp. 74–98.

12 See R.M. Douglas, *Architects of the Resurrection: Ailtirí na hAiséirighe and the Fascist 'New Order' in Ireland* (Manchester: Manchester University Press, 2009), and Clair Wills, *That Neutral Island: A Cultural History of Ireland During the Second World War* (London: Faber & Faber, 2007).

13 I am grateful to Dr de Paor for raising this point in response to a version of this chapter presented at the National University of Ireland, Galway's *Comhdháil ar Litríocht agus ar Chultúr na Gaeilge* conference in 2014. De Paor has elsewhere described Brian's attitude to the Irish language as 'deeply conflicted', 'an unresolved domestic dispute, an uncivil war with himself, his family and his background', in particular with his uncle Gearóid Ó Nualláin. I would suggest that the familial tensions de Paor refers to be extended to include Ciarán, and if de Paor's reading is correct, *Óige an Dearthár* might be taken as a mature reconsideration of its author's youthful worldview. Louis de Paor, 'Twisting the Knife', *The Irish Times*, 29 March 2002, p. 12.

14 Ciarán Ó Nualláin, *Amaidí* (Baile Átha Cliath: Foilseacháin Náisiúnta Teoranta, 1983), p. 134.

15 See Ian Ó Caoimh, 'An Tríú Leathchúpla: Caoimhín Ó Nualláin, Colúnaí' / 'The Third Twin: Caoimhín Ó Nualláin as Columnist', *The American Journal of Irish Studies* (New York, NY: New York University, *forthcoming*).

16 Kevin O'Nolan, 'The Functioning of Long Formulae in Irish Heroic Folktales', in Bo Almqvist, Séamas Ó Catháin and Pádraig Ó Héalaí (eds), *The Heroic Process: Form, Function and Fantasy in Folk Epic* (Dublin: The Glendale Press, 1987), p. 474.

17 Regarding this attitude to linguistic impenetrability in *Cruiskeen Lawn*, see Breandán Ó Conaire, *Myles na Gaeilge: Lámhleabhar ar Shaothar Gaeilge Bhrian Ó Nualláin* (Baile Átha Cliath: An Clóchomhar, 1986), p. 302, n. 59, where Ó Conaire also isolates this statement on the theme in the autobiography of the siblings' uncle Gearóid Ó Nualláin: '*Is ionann na deacrachtaí agus na háillneachtaí*' [The difficulties are the same as the beauties]. Gearóid Ó Nualláin, *Beatha Dhuine a Thoil* (Baile Átha Cliath: Oifig an tSoláthair, 1950), p. 67.

18 Caitríona Ó Torna, *Cruthú na Gaeltachta 1893–1922* (Baile Átha Cliath: Cois Life, 2005), p. 22.

19 The *Cat Mara* is referred to as the 'Sea-cat' in Power's direct translation, although the phrase itself means both 'angel-fish' and 'calamity, mischance'; the latter meaning is perhaps more in keeping with the fateful atmosphere of Corca Dhorcha itself, especially as the awfulness of the *Cat Mara* and the wretched fate of Ireland are equated in a footnote accompanying the illustration.

20 It is important to note that 'Corca Dhorcha' is the form used in the novel, not 'Corca Dorcha' as it is frequently amended by commentators. This latter form, in removing the lenition, gives the sense of *dorcha*, 'dark', as a qualifying adjective only. The lenited form conveys a more tangible idea of a proper noun, an actual placename 'Darkness'.

21 There is an abstract noun *gealtacht*, meaning 'lunacy, insanity, wildness, panic'; Niall Ó Dónaill (ed.), *Foclóir Gaeilge-Béarla* (Baile Átha Cliath: An Gúm, 2005), p. 620, sv *gealtacht*. One of the usages given in the dictionary is that to be in this state, '*ar gealtacht*', is 'to run away in terror': as echoed in the figure of the mad Sweeny in *At Swim-Two-Birds*.

22 Qtd. in Maebh Long, *Assembling Flann O'Brien* (London: Bloomsbury, 2014), p. 134. Writing to an Australian correspondent in 1978, Gearóid Ó Nualláin said of *An Béal Bocht*: 'there exists no translation even remotely adequate. Indeed it is a question whether the English Language can capture of the flavour of the original book'. Qtd. in Ó Conaire, p. 423, n. 21.

23 Anthony Cronin, *No Laughing Matter: The Life and Times of Flann O'Brien* (London: Grafton, 1989).

24 John Cronin has also composed an unpublished English translation of *Óige an Dearthár*, as noted in John Cronin, 'Brother of the More Famous Flann: Ciarán Ó Nualláin', *New Hibernia Review / Iris Éireannach Nua*, vol. 3, no. 4, Winter 1999, p. 9.

25 Max Saunders, *Self Impression: Life-Writing, Autobiografiction, and the Forms of Modern Literature* (Oxford: Oxford University Press, 2010), p. 2.

26 Ibid., pp. 5, 22. For a discussion of these themes in Irish-language autobiography see Máirín Nic Eoin, 'Ó *An tOileánach* go *Kinderszenen*: An toise dírbheathaisnéiseach i bprós-scríbhneoireacht na Gaeilge', *The Irish Review*, no. 13, Winter 1992/1993, pp. 14–21.

27 Pádraig Ó Héalaí, 'Fear an Leabhair', in Eoin Mac Cárthaigh and Jürgen Uhlich (eds), *Féilscríbhinn do Chathal Ó Háinle* (Indreabhán: Cló Iar-Chonnacht, 2012), pp. xx–xxi.

28 Cronin, *No Laughing Matter*, p. 102.

29 Brendan Duffin [rev. of *The Early Years of Brian O'Nolan/Flann O'Brien/Myles na Gopaleen* by Ciaran O'Nuallain [*sic*]], *Fortnight*, no. 378, May 1999, p. 31.

30 Ciarán Ó Nualláin, *Óige an Dearthár .i. Myles na gCopaleen* (Baile Átha Cliath: Foilseacháin Náisiúnta Teoranta, 1973), p. 107.

31 Cronin, 'Brother of the More Famous Flann', p. 14. In the chapter in question Ciarán writes: '*Léigh mé arís agus arís eile gur aoir é An Béal Bocht. Ní rud ar bith den tsórt é* ' [I read again and again that *An Béal Bocht* is a satire. It is nothing of the kind]. From here, Ciarán's stance appears to take a literalist turn, as though the novel should be read as reportage: '*Cad chuige, ar chaoi ar bith, an mbeadh aoir ar a intinn ag duine nár bhain as a chuairteanna ar an Ghaeltacht ach pléisiúr agus sult agus nach bhfaca riamh na rudaí ann atá curtha i leith Gaeltachta sa leabhar?*' [For what reason, in any case, would a person have a satirical intent who only ever took pleasure and enjoyment in his visits to the Gaeltacht and never saw there those things ascribed to a Gaeltacht in the book?]. Next he deploys pastoral simile: '*Ach murar aoir é caidé atá ann? Rud chomh nádúrtha le aoibheall uain nó leis an rith mhire a ligeann an coileán madaidh – an greann a dhéantar ar a shon féin*' [But if it is not a satire what is it? Something as natural as the gambolling of a lamb or the crazy run the young dog makes – humour done for its own sake]. Ó Nualláin, *Óige an Dearthár*, p. 107.

32 Ciarán Ó Nualláin, *The Early Years of Brian O'Nolan/Flann O'Brien/Myles na gCopaleen*, Niall O'Nolan (ed.), Róisín Ní Nualláin (trans.) (Dublin: Lilliput Press, 1998), p. 107.

33 Ó Nualláin, *Óige an Dearthár*, p. 85.

34 Ibid., p. 73.

35 Cronin, *No Laughing Matter*, p. 39.

36 Ó Nualláin, *Óige an Dearthár*, p. 78.

37 Ibid.

38 Ibid.

39 Cronin, *No Laughing Matter*, p. 26.

40 Qtd. in J.J. Lee, *Ireland 1912–1985: Politics and Society* (Cambridge: Cambridge University Press, 1989), p. 334.

41 Joseph Lee and Gearóid Ó Tuathaigh, *The Age of de Valera* (Dublin: Ward River Press in association with Radio Telefís Éireann, 1982), p. 165.

42 Ó Nualláin, *Óige an Dearthár*, p. 78.

43 Ibid., p. 87.

44 Qtd. in Breandán Ó Conaire, '*An Béal Bocht*: an lámhscríbhinn agus an leabhar', in Seán Ó Coileáin, Liam P. Ó Murchú and Pádraigín Riggs (eds), *Séimhfhear Suairc: Aistí in Ómós don Ollamh Breandán Ó Conchúir* (Má Nuad: An Sagart, 2013), p. 443.

45 Ó Nualláin, *Óige an Dearthár*, p. 88.

46 Ibid., pp. 90, 88.

47 Another aspect of Máire Ní Ghallchóir's reputation may have increased her appeal for Ciarán. Known in Gortahork as Máire Cholm, she was said to be a good storyteller, to both children and adult audiences, and a gifted composer of curses, with people sometimes goading her deliberately for the purpose of hearing her retorts. Her stories concerned evil stepmothers, and she even blamed one for the loss of her leg. One incident, collected by the Irish Folklore Commission illustrates the finely calibrated navigation through interpersonal sensitivities informed by perceptions of relative want/plenty in a close community which Ciarán details in *Óige an Dearthár*. A neighbour, Eibhlín Ní Dhubhthaigh, bought Máire a load of turf and had her husband deliver it to her house. Máire came to thank Eibhlín shortly afterwards, and said '*Go dtuga an tAthair Síoraí a luach duit, agus go raibh an mhóin sin*

insa tsíoraíocht romhat le teas agus téadh a choinneáil leat ar feadh shaol na saol' [May the Eternal Father recompense you for it, and may that turf be in the afterlife before you to provide you with heat and warmth for ever and ever]. This ambiguous entreaty demonstrates a facility for withering sarcasm, and while there is no evidence to suggest Ciarán was aware of these details, they lend our image of the person behind the portrait a little more agency. National Folklore Collection, University College Dublin 818: 186–188; Niall Ó Dubhthaigh (c. 66), An Bhealtaine, Gortahork, Co. Donegal. Collector: Seán Ó hEochaidh, April 1942. I am grateful to the Director of the NFC for permission to quote from this material. Liam Lillis Ó Laoire, 'Gort an Choirce agus Toraigh', in Gearóid Ó Tuathaigh, Liam Lillis Ó Laoire and Seán Ua Súilleabháin (eds), *Pobal na Gaeltachta: A Scéal agus a Dhán* (Indreabhán: Raidió na Gaeltachta i gcomhar le Cló Iar-Chonnachta, 2000), p. 90. I am grateful to Dr Ó Laoire for drawing my attention to this material.

48 Louis de Paor, 'Myles na gCopaleen agus Drochshampla na nDealeabhar', *The Irish Review*, no. 23, Winter 1998, p. 28.

49 Ibid., p. 29.

50 Alf Mac Lochlainn, 'An Chéad Phearsa Uaigneach: Idir an Réaltacht agus an tSamhailt' [rev. of *Óige an Dearthár .i. Myles na gCopaleen* by Ciarán Ó Nualláin], *Comhar*, vol. 33, no. 1, January 1974, p. 17. Another potential point of connection here is the pseudonymous *feis* attendee *Ochtar Fear* [Eight Men] in *An Béal Bocht* who considers himself sufficient by dint of his *alter ego* to undertake alone a dance usually requiring eight participants.

51 Cronin, *No Laughing Matter*, pp. 37–38. For the sake of completeness, Cronin's choice of the term 'Cow-jumps' in this context (*No Laughing Matter*, p. 38) as a translation of Ó Nualláin's '*ag bocléimnigh*' (*Óige an Dearthár*, p. 89) would be more accurately rendered 'buck-leaps' or 'buck-jumps'.

52 For a detailed discussion of these connections, see Angela Partridge [Bourke], 'Wild Men and Wailing Women', *Éigse: A Journal of Irish Studies*, vol. 18, no. 1, 1980, pp. 25–37. Liam Mac Mathúna cites evidence from *An tOileánach* of the term *geilt* being used in the sense of 'a naked person'. Liam Mac Mathúna, '"Geilt" sa chiall "duine lomnocht"', *Éigse: A Journal of Irish Studies*, vol. 18, no. 1, 1980, pp. 39–42.

53 Ó Nualláin, *Óige an Dearthár*, p. 89.

54 Ibid.

55 See Deasún Breathnach, *Chugat an Púca* (Baile Átha Cliath: An Clóchomhar, 1993).

56 In this phrase, the use of *cangarú* is similar to that of the word *crúiskeen* in *At Swim-Two-Birds* (with the source- and target-language pairing inverted), in that instance supposedly as the name of a bird, and more than likely mocking indirectly the prolixity of Dineen's dictionary (*CN*, 10). What links the two terms is that *crúiskeen*, a word Anglicised from the Irish, is also a hybrid, as the retention in the target language of the length-mark over the letter u marks it as an incomplete transition, rather than one which might be expected to convey its pronunciation by orthography alone. The incongruous lexical element used to emphasise a thematic concern with 'foreignness' is a device with which Brian would have been familiar as a student of early Irish poetry. Here we may also recall the Gaeltacht visitor to Corca Dhorcha who smashes Sitric Ó Sánasa's bottle of water '[mar gur] *spile sé an effect*' (*ABB*, 77).

57 Ó Nualláin, *Óige an Dearthár*, p. 88.

58 Long, p. 123.

59 Ó Nualláin, *Óige an Dearthár*, p. 90.

60 Vivian Mercier, *The Irish Comic Tradition* (Oxford: Oxford University Press, 1969), p. 164.

61 Allan Rodway, 'Terms for Comedy', *Renaissance and Modern Studies*, vol. 6, no. 1, 1962, p. 113.

62 Anthony Cronin, *Dead as Doornails* (Dublin: The Lilliput Press, 1999), p. 117.

63 The late Eoghan Ó hAnluain, Senior Lecturer in the Department of Modern Irish, UCD, interview with current author in 2005 for documentary broadcast on RTÉ Raidió na Gaeltachta.

64 Ó Nualláin, *Óige an Dearthár*, p. 104.

65 John Cronin, *Irish Fiction 1900–1940* (Belfast: Appletree, 1992), p. 170.

10. MCCOURT

1 Keith Hopper, *Flann O'Brien: A Portrait of the Artist as a Young Post-Modernist*, 2nd edn, J. Hillis Miller (foreword) (Cork: Cork University Press, 2009), p. 44.

2 Joseph Brooker, *Flann O'Brien* (Tavistock: Northcote House, 2005), p. 78.

3 Hopper, p. 44.

4 Ibid.

5 Carol Taaffe, *Ireland Through the Looking-Glass: Flann O'Brien, Myles na gCopaleen and Irish Cultural Debate* (Cork: Cork University Press, 2008), pp. 183–84.

6 Ibid., p. 183.

7 Jennika Baines, 'A Portrait of the Artist as a Dubliner: Eroding the Künstlerroman in *The Hard Life*', in Jennika Baines (ed.), *'Is it about a bicycle?': Flann O'Brien in the Twenty-First Century* (Dublin: Four Courts Press, 2011), pp. 143–44.

8 Qtd. in Peter Costello and Peter Van de Kamp, *Flann O'Brien: An Illustrated Biography* (London: Bloomsbury, 1987), p. 122.

9 Letter of 16 December 1962 to Timothy O'Keeffe, qtd. in Taaffe, p. 186.

10 Undated letter to Mark Hamilton, qtd. in Taaffe, p.186. Taaffe speculates that the letter was written in December 1960.

11 Letter of 15 October 1964 to Miss Hester Green. The original of the letter is kept as part of the Milberg collection of Irish prose writers at Princeton University.

12 Hopper, p. 55.

13 Taaffe, p. 192.

14 Maebh Long, *Assembling Flann O'Brien* (London: Bloomsbury, 2014), p. 152.

15 Keith Donohue, 'Introduction', in *CN*, xvi.

16 *CL*, February 10 1953, p. 4.

17 See Carlos Villar Flor, 'Flann O'Brien: A Postmodernist Who Happens to Be a Thomist', in Neil Murphy and Keith Hopper (eds), *Flann O'Brien: Centenary Essays, The Review of Contemporary Fiction*, vol. 31, no. 3, Fall 2011 (Champaign, IL: Dalkey Archive Press, 2011), p. 62.

18 Thomas Aquinas, *Summa Theologiae*, Fathers of the English Dominican Province (trans.) (Westminster: Christian Classics, 1981), Ia 6.1.

19 See T.A. Noble, *Holy Trinity: Holy People: The Theology of Christian Perfecting* (Eugene, OR: Cascade, 2013), p. 66.

20 See D.E. Hamachek, 'Psychodynamics of Normal and Neurotic Perfectionism', *Psychology*, no. 15, 1978, pp. 27–33.

21 Letter to Mark Hamilton, 20 February 1961, qtd. in Taaffe, p. 186.

22 Ibid.

23 James Joyce, *Finnegans Wake* (New York, NY: Viking Press, 1939), pp. 23, 331, 246.

24 Evelyn Waugh, 'Felix Culpa?', *The Commonweal*, no. 48, 16 July 1948, p. 323.

25 Graham Greene, *Conversations with Graham Greene*, Edward J. Donaghy (ed.) (Mississippi, MS: University Press of Mississippi, 1992), p. 164.

26 Taaffe, p. 186.

27 Costello and van de Kamp, p. 122.

28 Augustine, *Exposition of the Sermon on the Mount, Drawn from the Writings of St Augustine*, Richard Chenevix Trench (introd.) (London: John W. Parker, West Strand, 1851), pp. 278–79.

29 Jonathan Bolton, 'Comedies of Failure: O'Brien's *The Hard Life* and Moore's *The Emperor of Ice Cream*', *New Hibernia Review*, vol. 12, no. 3, Autumn 2008, p. 120.

30 Anne Clissmann, *Flann O'Brien: A Critical Introduction to His Writings* (Dublin: Gill & Macmillan, 1975), p. 273.

31 George Bernard Shaw, letter to Sylvia Beach, 10 October 1921. A copy of this letter is kept in Box 14 of the James Joyce Collection at Cornell University.

32 West notes that Bloom 'guides Stephen through the filthy squalor of nocturnal Dublin' and summarises, 'Except when the book is at its greatest, I resent being rapt into the squalor of Dublin'. Rebecca West, 'The Strange Case of James Joyce', *Bookman*, no. 68, September 1928, pp. 9–23.

33 Taaffe, p. 189.

34 John McCourt, 'Myles na gCopaleen: A Portrait of the Artist as a Joyce Scholar', in Ruben Borg, Paul Fagan and Werner Huber (eds), *Flann O'Brien: Contesting Legacies* (Cork: Cork University Press, 2014), p. 111.

35 M. Keith Booker, *Flann O'Brien, Bakhtin, and Menippean Satire* (Syracuse, NY: Syracuse University Press, 1995), p. 134.

36 Letter from Niall Sheridan to Brian O'Nolan, no date, labelled 'Saturday', probably fall 1960, O'Nolan Collection, Southern Illinois University, Carbondale, qtd. in Thomas F. Shea, 'The Craft of Seeming Pedestrian: Flann O'Brien's *The Hard Life*', *Colby Quarterly*, vol. 25, no. 4, December 1989, p. 258.

37 Ibid., p. 259.

38 Ibid., p. 266.

39 Brooker, p. 72.

40 B.W., 'Recent Novels', *The Irish Times*, 29 August 1953, p. 6.

41 E.A.O., 'Recent Fiction: Casualty Ward', *The Irish Times*, 27 October 1956, p. 6.

42 *The Irish Times* duly reported the orders which had banned Moravia's *Le ambizioni sbagliate* [*Wheel of Fortune*]; *La romana* [*The Woman of Rome*]; *La disobbidienza* [*Disobedience*] (ironically, in the very same issue in which the paper's reviewer B.W. praised the novel and declared that Moravia's 'talent is considerable, and his purpose is serious'); *L'amore coniugale* [*Conjugal Love*] (the *Irish Times* review declared the novel proof that 'Signor Moravia is an important novelist'); *Il Conformista* [*The Conformist*], *Gli indifferenti* [*The Time of Indifference*], *Agostino* [*Two Adolescents*] and *Luna di miele, sole di fiele* [*Bitter Honeymoon and Other Stories*]: 'Banned Publications', *The Irish Times*, 12 March 1938, p. 6; 'Additions to Banned Publications', *The Irish Times*, 24 September 1949, p. 10; '19 Books Banned', *The Irish Times*, 18 June 1958, p. 5; 'Big List of Banned Books', *The Irish Times*, 14 October 1950, p. 3; B.W., 'Recent Fiction', *The Irish Times*, 14 October 1950, p. 6; 'Many Books and Publications Banned', *The Irish Times*, 22 March 1951, p. 4; B.W., 'Recent Fiction', 22 March 1951, p. 6; B.W. 'Recent Novels', 15 March 1952, p. 6; 'Books Banned', *The Irish Times*, 14 April 1952, p. 5; B.W., 'Recent Novels', 29 August 1953, p. 6; '150 Books and Periodicals Banned by Censor', *The Irish Times*, 29 September 1953, p. 5; 'Books on Banned List', *The Irish Times*, 19 April 1954, p. 5; 'Censors Ban 116 Books and Six Periodicals', *The Irish Times*, 25 May 1954, p. 5.

43 Kees van Hoek, 'The Way of the World', *The Irish Times*, 22 January 1952, p. 4. Van Hoek followed this up a year later with another long piece praising the Roman author ('Moravia: Italy's Leading Novelist', *The Irish Times*, 5 January 1953, p. 4). In an editorial from November 1959, as O'Nolan was quickly composing *The Hard Life*, Moravia was also mentioned as having been slighted in the awarding of the Nobel Prize to Italian poet Salvatore Quasimodo ('The Nobel Prize Furore', *The Irish Times*, 25 November 1959, p. 8).

Given the recurrence of Moravia's name in *The Irish Times*, it is almost certain that O'Nolan would have had at the very least a casual acquaintance with his work through the paper's reporting.

44 Seán O'Faoláin, 'Banned and Unbanned', letter, *The Irish Times*, 3 January 1948, p. 4.

45 Donagh MacDonagh, 'Names and Numbers', *The Irish Times*, 1 November 1952, p. 6.

46 Baldini appears to be a randomly chosen character name, although an Italian called Baldini served as Bishop of Massa Marittima, Tuscany from 1933 to 1966. Readers of *The Third Policeman* may be amused to note that the Italian Ercole Baldini was one the world's foremost cyclists at the time that O'Nolan was composing *The Hard Life*, winning an Olympic medal in 1956, the World Road Cycling Championships in 1958 and the *Grand Prix des Nations* in 1960.

47 Carlo Emilio Gadda, *That Awful Mess on Via Merulana*, William Weaver (trans.) (New York, NY: George Braziller, 1965). *Quer pasticciaccio brutto de via Merulana* was published in instalments in 1946 and 1947 and later in book form in 1957 by Garzanti, and in 1965 in English as *That Awful Mess on Via Merulana*.

48 Gadda, p. 5.

49 *CL*, 'Keats in Rome', 25 January 1965, p. 11.

50 Neil Murphy, 'Flann O'Brien's *The Hard Life* & the Gaze of the Medusa', Neil Murphy and Keith Hopper (eds), *Flann O'Brien: Centenary Essays, The Review of Contemporary Fiction*, vol. 31, no. 3, Fall 2011 (Champaign, IL: Dalkey Archive Press, 2011), p. 153.

II. DE PAOR

1 J.C.C. Mays, 'Brian O'Nolan: Literalist of the Imagination', in Timothy O'Keeffe (ed.), *Myles: Portraits of Brian O'Nolan* (London: Martin Brian & O'Keeffe, 1973), p. 84.

2 Jack White, 'Myles, Flann and Brian', in O'Keeffe (ed.), pp. 75–76.

3 Breandán Ó Conaire, *Myles na Gaeilge: Lámhleabhar ar Shaothar Gaeilge Bhrian Ó Nualláin* (Baile Átha Cliath: An Clóchomhar, 1986); *CL*, 3 January 1957, p. 6.

4 Eva Wäppling, *Four Irish Legendary Figures in 'At Swim-Two-Birds': A Study of Flann O'Brien's Use of Finn, Suibhne, the Pooka and the Good Fairy* (Stockholm: Almqvist och Wiksell, 1984). See also Jane Farnon, 'Motifs of Gaelic Lore and Literature in *An Béal Bocht*', in Anne Clune [Clissmann] and Tess Hurson (eds), *Conjuring Complexities: Essays on Flann O'Brien* (Belfast: Queen's University of Belfast, 1997), pp. 89–109; Neil Murphy, 'Myles na gCopaleen, Flann O'Brien and *An Béal Bocht*: Intertextuality and Aesthetic Play', in Ruben Borg, Paul Fagan and Werner Huber (eds), *Flann O'Brien: Contesting Legacies* (Cork: Cork University Press, 2014), pp. 143–55.

5 Louis de Paor, 'An tSídheoig is an Scian Dochtúra: Flann O'Brien agus Seanlitríocht na Gaeilge', in John Carey, Máire Herbert and Kevin Murray (eds), *Cín Chille Cúile: Texts, Saints and Places: Essays in Honour of Pádraig Ó Riain* (Aberystwyth: Celtic Studies Publications, 2004), pp. 64–76.

6 Carol Taaffe, *Ireland Through the Looking-Glass: Flann O'Brien, Myles na gCopaleen and Irish Cultural Debate* (Cork: Cork University Press, 2008).

7 Mays, p. 77.

8 Frank O'Brien, *Filíocht Ghaeilge na Linne Seo* (Baile Átha Cliath: An Clóchomhar, 1968), p. 31.

9 Philip O'Leary, *The Prose Literature of the Gaelic Revival, 1881–1921: Ideology and Innovation* (Philadelphia, PA: The Pennsylvania State University Press, 1994), p. 56.

10 For discussion of Ó Nualláin's treatment of Irish language material in work published while he was still a student at UCD, see Ó Conaire, *Myles na Gaeilge*; Thomas F. Shea, *Flann O'Brien's Exorbitant Novels* (Lewisburg, PA: Bucknell University Press, 1992), pp. 18–24; Caoimhghín Ó Brolcháin, 'Comparatively Untapped Sources', in Clune and Hurson (eds),

pp. 9–16; and Jack Fennell, 'Irelands Enough and Time: Brian O'Nolan's Science Fiction', in Borg, Fagan and Huber (eds), pp. 33–36.

11 Cathal G. Ó hÁinle, 'Fionn and Suibhne in *At Swim-Two-Birds*', *Hermathena*, no. 142, Summer 1987, p. 17.

12 Ríona Nic Congáil, *Úna Ní Fhaircheallaigh agus an Fhís Útóipeach Ghaelach* (Dublin: Arlen House, 2010), p. 187.

13 Niall Montgomery, 'An Aristophanic Sorcerer', *The Irish Times*, 2 April 1966, p. 7.

14 *CL*, 7 July 1950, p. 4.

15 Ó hÁinle, 'Fionn and Suibhne [1987]', pp. 17–19.

16 Nic Congáil, p. 187.

17 Anthony Cronin, *No Laughing Matter: The Life and Times of Flann O'Brien* (London: Grafton, 1989), p. 73.

18 Qtd. in ibid.

19 Ciarán Ó Nualláin, *Óige an Dearthár .i. Myles na gCopaleen* (Baile Átha Cliath: Foilseacháin Náisiúnta Teoranta, 1973), p. 103.

20 Brian Ó Nualláin, 'Nádúir-fhilíocht na Gaedhilge: Tráchtas Maraon le Duanaire', unpublished MA thesis, University College Dublin, 1935 [Burns Library, Boston College], p. 5.

21 Flann O'Brien, 'Standish Hayes O'Grady', *The Irish Times*, 16 October 1940, p. 3.

22 Cathal Ó hÁinle, 'Fionn and Suibhne in *At Swim-Two-Birds*', in Clune and Hurson (eds), pp. 24–25.

23 *CL*, 11 October 1943, p. 3.

24 Ó hÁinle, 'Fionn and Suibhne [1987]', p. 41.

25 Wäppling, p. 61.

26 De Paor, 'Flann O'Brien agus Seanlitríocht na Gaeilge', p. 76.

27 J.G. O'Keeffe (ed. and trans.), *Buile Suibhne: The Frenzy of Suibhne* (London: Irish Texts Society, 1910), pp. 36–37.

28 Ibid., pp. 52–53.

29 Ibid., pp. 152–53.

30 Brian Ó Nualláin, 'Tráchtas ar Nádúir-fhilíocht na Gaedhilge', unpublished MA thesis, University College Dublin, 1934, p. 36.

31 Caoimhghin Ó Brolcháin, 'Flann, Ó Caoimh agus Suibhne Geilt', *Irish Studies Review*, no. 9, 1994–95, pp. 31–34; see also Caoimhghin Ó Brolcháin, 'Comparatively Untapped Sources', in Clune and Hurson (eds), pp. 15–16; Ciarán Ó Nualláin, 'Amaidí: *Buile Shuibhne* mar Chothú Tionscail', *Inniu*, no. 5, Meán Fómhair, 1980, p. 5.

32 Brendan Kennelly, '*An Béal Bocht*, Myles na gCopaleen (1911–1966)', in John Jordan (ed.), *The Pleasures of Gaelic Literature* (Cork: Mercier Press, 1977), pp. 90, 96.

33 Adrian Naughton, '*Nádúir-fhilíocht na Gaedhilge* and Flann O'Brien's Fiction', in Jennika Baines (ed.), *'Is it about a bicycle?': Flann O'Brien in the Twenty-First Century* (Dublin: Four Courts Press, 2011), pp. 94–95.

34 Ó Nualláin, 1934 thesis, pp. 3, 10, 11, 13, 27; 1935 thesis, pp. 14, 15, 42–44.

35 Ó Nualláin, 1934 thesis, p. 2; 1935 thesis, pp. 8, 42.

36 Ó Nualláin, 1934 thesis, p. 11; 1935 thesis, p. 34.

37 Ó Nualláin, 1934 thesis, p. 25.

38 Ó Nualláin, 1935 thesis, pp. 8, 9.

39 Seán Ó Tuama, 'Celebration of Place in Irish Writing', in *Repossessions: Selected Essays on the Irish Literary Heritage* (Cork: Cork University Press, 1995), p. 264.

40 Naughton, p. 95.

41 Mays, p. 88.

42 Seamus Heaney, *Sweeney Astray* (London: Faber & Faber, 1990), p. ii.

43 Kim McMullen, 'Culture as Colloquy: Flann O'Brien's Postmodern Dialogue with Irish Tradition', *Novel: A Forum on Fiction*, vol. 27, no. 1, pp. 80–81.

44 Roland Barthes, 'The Utopia of Language', in *Writing Degree Zero*, Susan Sontag (foreword), Annette Lavers and Colin Smythe (trans.) (New York, NY: Hill & Wang, 1968), p. 85.

45 Ibid., pp. 87–88.

12. GILLESPIE

1 *CL*, 30 October 1946, p. 2.

2 For example: 'Were Clemenceau alive to-day, he would be the first to admit that he and I went rather too far in respect of "democracy" and "self-determination" some years back when in a Swiss city [...] we sought far into the night to . . to . . unmess the peoples of this hemisphere' (*CL*, 25 April 1944, p. 3).

3 Astrid Erll defines 'media of cultural memory' as 'a host of different media, operating within various symbolic systems' – such as 'religious texts, historical painting, historiography, TV documentaries, monuments, and commemorative rituals' – which 'create and mold collective images of the past'. Astrid Erll, 'Literature, Film, and the Mediality of Cultural Memory', in Astrid Erll and Ansgar Nünning (eds), *Cultural Memory Studies: An Interdisciplinary Handbook; Media and Cultural Memory* (Berlin: Walter de Gruyter, 2008), pp. 380–00

4 I distinguish between narrative and text in the sense that narratives can be transmitted by non-textual media and as such, are not text-bound. Narratives, such as the story of Irish nationalism, live beyond texts even as texts represent them and convey them, anchoring them to the material world. Texts can be disparate and edited; they are objects which can be reused to reinforce a living narrative – which is perceived by those who tell it and reaffirm it, and for whom it has use-value – as stable and the same regardless of textual iterations. But equally, the same texts can be employed to support a different narrative, so texts and narratives don't always 'say' the same thing.

5 Jan Assmann, 'Collective Memory and Cultural Identity', *New German Critique*, no. 65, 1995, pp. 125–33.

6 Denell Downum, 'Citation and Spectrality in Flann O'Brien's *At Swim-Two-Birds*', *Irish University Review*, vol. 36, no. 2, 2006, p. 310.

7 Kimberly Bohman-Kalaja, *Reading Games: An Aesthetics of Play in Flann O'Brien, Samuel Beckett, and Georges Perec* (Champaign, IL: Dalkey Archive Press, 2007), p. 79.

8 Walter Benjamin, 'The Work of Art in the Age of Mechanical Reproduction', in Vassiliki Kolocotroni, Jane Goldman and Olga Taxidou (eds), *Modernism: An Anthology of Sources and Documents* (Chicago, IL: University of Chicago Press, 1998), pp. 571–72; Downum, p. 308.

9 Benjamin, p. 572.

10 Carol Taaffe, *Ireland Through the Looking-Glass: Flann O'Brien, Myles na gCopaleen and Irish Cultural Debate* (Cork: Cork University Press, 2008), p. 35.

11 For example, *Flann O'Brien & Modernism* (2014) includes Sascha Morrell's consideration of drink manufacture as a launching point for O'Nolan 'to explore whether human life itself might be considered a mass product like Guinness or Coca-Cola' in the modern era. Elsewhere, Andrew V. McFeaters reads O'Nolan's sustained engagement with the ideology of Fordism against Benjamin's 'One-Way Street' (1928) to conclude that O'Nolan's writing 'reveals a deep distrust for capitalism as the sole justification for human pursuits'. Eamonn Hughes examines links between authority, authoritarianism and democracy in 'Flann O'Brien's *At Swim-Two-Birds* in the Age of Mechanical Reproduction', reading O'Nolan's debut as 'an anti-Fascist novel' that 'denies in Benjamin's terms its own authenticity (it is after all a "self-evident sham") and its own authority (it will not be despotic and attempt to fool its readers)'. And in a special number of *The Parish Review*, Jack Fennell has edited

a symposium on 'Flann and the Culture Industry' dedicated to teasing out the strategies by which O'Nolan 'means to disrupt the reading habits cultivated by soothing, easily-digested culture industry texts'. Sascha Morrell, 'Soft Drink, Hard Drink, and Literary (Re) Production in Flann O'Brien and Frank Moorhouse', in Julian Murphet, Rónán McDonald and Sascha Morrell (eds), *Flann O'Brien & Modernism* (London: Bloomsbury, 2014), p. 175; Andrew V. McFeaters, 'Reassembling Ford: Time is Money in Brian O'Nolan's Brave New Ireland', *The Parish Review*, vol. 3, no. 1, Fall 2014, p. 40; Eamonn Hughes, 'Flann O'Brien's *At Swim-Two-Birds* in the Age of Mechanical Reproduction', in Edwina Keown and Carol Taaffe (eds), *Irish Modernism: Origins, Contexts, Publics* (Bern: Peter Lang, 2010), p. 128; Jack Fennell, 'The Flannkfurt School: Brian O'Nolan and the Culture Industry', *The Parish Review*, vol. 3, no. 2, Spring 2014, pp. 4–5.

12 Downum, p. 309.

13 Bohman-Kalaja, p. 80

14 Benjamin, p. 575.

15 Ibid.

16 Ann Rigney, 'Plenitude, Scarcity and the Circulation of Cultural Memory', *Journal of European Studies*, vol. 35, no. 1, 2005, p. 20.

17 Rigney writes that 'it is through recursivity – visiting the same places, repeating the same stories – that a cultural memory is constructed as such' (ibid.).

18 Aleida Assmann, 'Canon and Archive', in Erll and Nünning (eds), p. 101.

19 Aleida Assmann, 'Texts, Traces, Trash: The Changing Media of Cultural Memory', *Representations*, no. 56, special issue, *The New Erudition*, Autumn 1996, p. 128.

20 Rigney, p. 18.

21 Ibid.

22 The rhetoric of heroic suffering in Irish national narratives is only one of many. It is not my intention to suggest that it dominated Irish cultural remembrance or national narratives, but I single it out here because of its predominance in *At Swim-Two-Birds*. David Fitzpatrick argues that the contentiousness of the paradigm of heroic suffering (shared or not) in Ireland stems from its link with death through conflicts related to the establishment of the independent state. David Fitzpatrick, 'Commemoration in the Irish Free State: A Chronicle of Embarrassment', in Ian McBride (ed.), *History and Memory in Modern Ireland* (Cambridge: Cambridge University Press, 2001), pp. 184–204. For a detailed account of which narratives were contested, see Joep Leerssen, *Remembrance and Imagination: Patterns in the Historical and Literary Representation of Ireland in the Nineteenth Century* (Cork: Cork University Press in association with Field Day, 1996).

23 Lady Gregory and Æ, for example, took up Cúchulainn's heroic suffering from Standish James O'Grady's own retellings of Irish myths in *History of Ireland: Heroic Period* (Dublin: Ponsonby, 1878, 1880). Leerssen notes that by the time Lady Gregory was retelling the *Táin*, it 'had come to be venerated as Ireland's oldest and most authentic native epic' (p. 198). Heroic suffering is also influential in the political rhetoric that positions Patrick Pearse as the archetype of the modern revolutionary male, and ultimately, in de Valera's choice of *The Death of Cúchulainn* by Oliver Sheppard for the GPO memorial to 1916.

24 Recognising that there is not one totalising Revivalist discourse, the strand critiqued here is perhaps best called what O'Nolan vilified as 'dawnburst brigade' Revivalism and which he criticises in *An Béal Bocht* and *Cruiskeen Lawn*. This Revivalist discourse was not Irish-language Revivalism *per se*, but widely circulated translations of Irish-language books (including autobiographies like *An tOileánach* or *Peig*) into English which came to represent cult-of-the-west Irish literature in English.

25 O'Nolan's personal views about *At Swim-Two-Birds* are hard to overlook in this regard. Even after its re-issue in 1960, he continued to denigrate it, insisting we must remember

it was 'written by a schoolboy'; qtd. in Anthony Cronin, *No Laughing Matter: The Life and Times of Flann O'Brien* (London: Grafton, 1989), pp. 211–12. As to why it was critically acclaimed, O'Nolan thought that '"there must be some diabolical code, some anagram buried in it" that he had not intended' (Cronin, p. 212). Readers and authors do not always see eye to eye.

26 Tim Woods, 'Spectres of History: Ethics and Postmodern Fictions of Temporality', in Dominic Rainsford and Tim Woods (eds), *Critical Ethics: Text, Theory and Responsibility* (London: Macmillan, 1999), pp. 118–19.

27 Letter to Timothy O'Keefe, 21 September 1962, SIUC.

28 The theory of translation skopos or functionality as defined by Christiane Nord holds that 'translation is always realized for a target situation with its determining factors (receiver, time and place of reception, etc.), in which the target text is supposed to fulfil a certain function which can and, indeed, must be specified in advance'. The determining factors enable the translator to decide 'which elements of the [source text-in-situation] can be "preserved" and which may, or must, be "adapted" to the target situation'. Christiane Nord, *Text Analysis in Translation: Theory, Methodology, and Didactic Application of a Model for Translation-Oriented Text Analysis*, 2nd edn (Amsterdam: Rodopi, 2005), p. 32. The example of English translations of the Nicene Creed illustrates this theory in that one version exists and is used to express faith and a sense of belonging with a community of Catholics, while an arguably more literal and therefore 'authentic' version that is truer to the original text also exists, which is of interest to scholars.

29 See, for example, Susan Purdie, *Comedy: The Mastery of Discourse* (Hemel Hempstead: Harvester Wheatsheaf, 1993).

30 Letter to Timothy O'Keeffe, 15 November 1963, SIUC.

31 Jacques Derrida, *Specters of Marx: The State of the Debt, the Work of Mourning and the New International*, Peggy Kamuf (trans.), Stephen Cullenberg and Bernd Magnus (eds) (New York, NY: Routledge, 1994), p. 16.

32 Ibid., p. xix.

33 Walter Montag, 'Spirits Armed and Unarmed: Derrida's Specters of Marx', in Michael Sprinker (ed.), *Ghostly Demarcations: A Symposium on Jacques Derrida's Specters of Marx* (London: Verso, 2008), p. 71.

34 Ibid., pp. 43–49; Fredric Jameson, *Late Marxism: Adorno, Or, the Persistence of the Dialectic* (London: Verso, 1996), p. 30.

35 Maebh Long, *Assembling Flann O'Brien* (London: Bloomsbury, 2014), p. 195; Derrida 'Freud and the Scene of Writing', in *Writing and Difference*, Alan Bass (trans.) (London: Routledge, 2001), pp. 253–54.

36 Woods, pp. 108–09.

37 Artistic artefacts are marked by traces of previous contexts, utterances, editors, curators and makers, which, according to Aleida Assmann, are usually decontextualised, unintentional or unaddressed, in contrast to the 'cultural messages that are addressed to posterity and intended for continuous repetition and reuse' ('Canon and Archive', p. 99). Aleida Assmann draws here on cultural historian Jakob Burckhardt's distinction between two categories of 'remains of former historical periods': 'messages' (texts and monuments addressed to posterity) and 'traces' (which are not addressed to posterity). These traces or 'cultural relics' which have 'lost their immediate addressees' can be taken from the archive and reactivated or reauthorised to become 'open to new contexts and lend themselves to new interpretations'. Assmann, 'Canon and Archive', pp. 98–99.

38 Woods, p. 119.

39 Ibid., p. 117.

13. BORG

* A version of this paper was presented at *Problems with Authority: The II International Flann O'Brien Conference* (Rome, June 2013). I would like to thank Adam Winstanley and Maebh Long for their comments during and after the session.

1 Stephen Abblitt has thematised this ambivalent attitude towards the modernist *avant-garde* by focusing on O'Nolan's parodic treatment of Joyce in *The Dalkey Archive*. His argument identifies O'Nolan as a reluctant or ironic modernist, divided between 'his repeated disavowals of Joyce's modernism, and his obvious dependency on the advances made by this literary movement'. Stephen Abblitt, 'The Ghost of "Poor Jimmy Joyce": A Portrait of the Artist as a Reluctant Modernist', in Julian Murphet, Rónán McDonald and Sascha Morrell (eds), *Flann O'Brien & Modernism* (London: Bloomsbury, 2014), p. 65.

2 Hopper describes O'Nolan as an early post-modernist whose 'repudiation of the author as the central signifying presence of the text rejects certain modernist (as well as realist) premises'. Keith Hopper, *Flann O'Brien: A Portrait of the Artist as a Young Post-Modernist*, 2nd edn, J. Hillis Miller (foreword) (Cork: Cork University Press, 2009), p. 14. The argument presupposes a post-modernist paradigm that conceives of the values of authorship in terms of displacement, pastiche and fragmentation, in contrast to the self-possessed, promethean author-figures affirmed in modernism.

3 Jean-Michel Rabaté, *The Ghosts of Modernity* (Gainesville, FL: University Press of Florida, 1996), p. 3.

4 Ibid.

5 Since my purpose is to show the recurrence of the theme in a number of works, and considering that a discussion of *The Third Policeman* would tend to overshadow the rest of my analysis, I have decided not to give the novel its due in this essay and to look instead at lesser known titles, or at marginal rhetorical figures deployed within other narratives.

6 To be sure, legal problems also inform the narrative of *The Third Policeman*. But in that novel they function as a prop for moral judgement – that is to say, they dramatise an absurd moral situation. In Sir Myles's case the *law* is a matter of bureaucratic competence, of being able to deal with abstruse details and fine print.

7 Samuel Beckett, *Eleutheria*, Barbara Wright (trans.) (London: Faber, 1996), p. 150.

8 Luigi Pirandello, *The Late Mattia Pascal*, William Weaver (trans.) (New York, NY: Marsilio, 1995), p. 250.

9 Pirandello and Beckett – but also, notably, Woolf and Joyce – return to the motif of death-in-life time and again throughout their fiction. Woolf's characters often speak of the sensation of being already dead: Bernard in *The Waves*; Septimus in *Mrs Dalloway*. Especially relevant is the following scene from *Orlando*:

> But now Orlando was to learn how little the most tempestuous flutter of excitement avails against the iron countenance of the law […] No sooner had she returned to her home in Blackfriars than she was made aware by a succession of Bow Street runners and other grave emissaries from the Law Courts that she was a party to three major suits which had been preferred against her during her absence, as well as innumerable minor litigations, some arising out of, others depending on them. The chief charges against her were (1) that she was dead, and therefore could not hold any property whatsoever; (2) that she was a woman, which amounts to much the same thing; (3) that she was an English Duke who had married one Rosina Pepita, a dancer; and had had by her three sons, which sons now declaring that their father was deceased, claimed that all his property descended to them.

Note the role played by the Law Courts in this excerpt (a detail that invites comparisons with the Sir Myles fragment, but also with Pirandello and Beckett). Virgina Woolf,

Orlando: A Biography (Harmondsworth: Penguin, 1963), p. 118. I develop these ideas in my essay 'Putting the Impossible to Work: Beckettian Afterlife and the Posthuman Future of Humanity', *Journal of Modern Literature*, vol. 35, no. 4, 2012, pp. 163–80; and again, in greater detail, in my forthcoming book, *Fantasies of Self-Mourning: Modernism, the Posthuman and the Problem of Genre*.

10 Anthony Cronin, *No Laughing Matter: The Life and Times of Flann O'Brien* (London: Grafton, 1989), p. 106.

11 'For the promise, that he should be the heir of the world, was not to Abraham, or to his seed, through the law, but through the righteousness of faith. For if they which are of the law be heirs, faith is made void, and the promise made of none effect: Because the law worketh wrath: for where no law is, there is no transgression'. *Romans* 4:13–15. All references to Biblical verse herein are to *Holy Bible: Containing the Old and New Testaments*, Revised Standard Version (Philadelphia, PA: National Publishing Company, 1995).

12 The clearest formulation of this double-focus is in Romans 9–13, to which Jacob Taubes provides an illuminating commentary: 'My thesis is that Paul understands himself as outbidding Moses. [...] Some hold, of course, that he is measuring himself against Christ, that he is now Christ and bears Christ's suffering on his own body. I regard that as a total exaggeration, because he is always *doulos*, he is always serving. No not that, but he does measure himself against Moses, that certainly. And his business is the same: the establishment of a people. That's what's accomplished by chapters 9–13'. Jacob Taubes, *The Political Theology of Paul*, Dana Hollander (trans.) (Stanford, CA: Stanford University Press, 2004), pp. 39–40.

13 *Romans* 7.

14 A self-styled Apostle to the Gentiles (or, as Taubes insists, an Apostle 'from the Jews to the Gentiles' [p. 38]), Paul challenges the privileged relationship between God and the people of Israel; and tests the possibility of universalising that privilege. Can the past survive such a revolutionary act? Does the *Epistle to the Romans* repeat the covenant at Sinai, extending its tenure both temporally and juridically, or does it simply close off one history to inaugurate another? The question is complicated by the fact that the covenant with Israel was never a wholly original event in the first place. Sinai repeats Abraham, who takes up from Noah, who redirects the promise to Adam. In what sense, then, is Paul's covenant an absolute break from the covenants that precede it? Might we not think of it as the continuation of a long tradition?

15 *2 Corinthians* 11.

16 *2 Corinthians* 12. In this connection consider also *The Apocalypse of Paul*, an Apocryphal text from the sixth century which tells of Paul's journey beyond the third heaven (all the way to tenth).

17 The other side of the coin – a life so stark, so far removed from social norms that it becomes indistinguishable from death – is suggested in the motif of decomposition that inspires the domestic scenes at the beginning of *The Poor Mouth*. The cliché of the 'child among the ashes' (*CN*, 416) introduces us to a world putrefied at its core, and the sense of pervasive rot is reinforced through the symbolic identification between Bonaparte O'Coonassa and the family pig Ambrose. Maternity is an issue in both cases: the pig is suckled on cow's milk, while Bonaparte is brought up among whispers that he 'was not born of [his] mother at all but of another woman' (*CN*, 414). Raised 'among the ashes', as cliché would have it, his first memory is of almost getting burnt while sitting too close to the fire. Like Ambrose, he is adopted by the Old Grey Fellow, and left to play in a bed of mud, muck, and chicken droppings – a youngster's natural habitat 'according to the old Gaelic tradition' (*CN*, 416). 'Later at midnight I was taken and put into bed but the foul stench of the fireplace stayed with me for a week; it was a stale, putrid smell and I do not think that the like will ever be there again' (*CN*, 416). The scene is echoed (and ideally completed) by the episode of

Ambrose's death: first, the pig stench drives Bonaparte's mother to set fire to the house; then, the steam from the sick, rotting pig is itself mistaken for smoke, and finally, the pig is found dead of its own stench on the hearthstone. 'Ambrose was an odd pig and I do not think that his like will be there again. Good luck to him if he be alive in another world today' (*CN*, 423). In its insistence on the grotesque, on the grotesquely pathetic, *The Poor Mouth* substitutes teeming cliché for the spirit that breathes life into the word.

18 Paul Fagan, '"I've got you under my skin": "John Duffy's Brother", "Two in One", and the Confessions of Narcissus', in Ruben Borg, Paul Fagan and Werner Huber (eds), *Flann O'Brien: Contesting Legacies* (Cork: Cork University Press, 2014), p. 72.

19 Ibid.

20 Jennika Baines, 'The Murders of Flann O'Brien: Death and Creation in *At Swim-Two-Birds*, *The Third Policeman*, *An Béal Bocht*, and "Two in One"', in Borg, Fagan and Huber (eds), p. 207.

21 *Romans* 2.

22 *Galatians* 6.

23 Ibid.

24 *Colossians* 3.

25 Baines, p. 208.

14. FUCHS

1 Voltaire, *Candide ou l'Optimisme*, Thomas Baldischwieler (ed.) (Stuttgart: Reclam, 2007), pp. 149–50.

2 Mikhail Bakhtin, *Problems of Dostoevsky's Poetics*, Caryl Emerson (ed. and trans.) (Manchester: Manchester University Press, 1984), pp. 109–21.

3 Northrop Frye, *Anatomy of Criticism* (Princeton, NJ: Princeton University Press, 1957), pp. 308–11.

4 See, among many others, Rudolf Helm, *Lucian und Menipp* (Hildesheim: Georg Olms Verlagsbuchhandlung, 1967); Eugene Paul Korkowski, 'Menippus and His Imitators: A Conspectus, up to Sterne, for a Misunderstood Genre', unpublished dissertation (University of California: San Diego, 1973); Eugene Kirk [*alias* 'Korkowski'], *Menippean Satire: An Annotated Catalogue of Texts and Criticism* (New York, NY: Garland, 1980); Hannu K. Rijkonen, 'Menippean Satire as a Literary Genre with Special Reference to Seneca's Apocolocyntosis', *Commentationes Humanorum Literarum*, no. 83, 1987; Joel C. Relihan, *Ancient Menippean Satire* (Baltimore, MD: Johns Hopkins University Press, 1993); Howard D. Weinbrot, *Menippean Satire Reconsidered: From Antiquity to the Eighteenth Century* (Baltimore, MD: Johns Hopkins University Press, 2005); Dieter Fuchs, *Joyce und Menippos: A Portrait of the Artist as an Old Dog*, ZAA Monograph Series 2 (Würzburg: Königshausen & Neumann, 2006); Werner von Koppenfels, *Der Andere Blick, oder Das Vermächtnis des Menippos in der Europäischen Literatur* (München: Beck, 2007).

5 Qtd. in Weinbrot, p. 11.

6 M. Keith Booker, *Flann O'Brien, Bakhtin, and Menippean Satire* (Syracuse, NY: Syracuse University Press, 1996); José Lanters, *Unauthorized Versions: Irish Menippean Satire, 1919–1952* (Washington, DC: Catholic University of America Press, 2000); see also José Lanters, 'Irish Satire', in Ruben Quintero (ed.), *Satire Ancient and Modern* (Oxford: Blackwell, 2007), pp. 476–91. Other Menippean-related contributions to O'Nolan studies inspired by Booker include Flore Coulouma, 'Tall Tales and Short Stories: *Cruiskeen Lawn* and the Dialogic Imagination', in Neil Murphy and Keith Hopper (eds), *Flann O'Brien: Centenary Essays*, *The Review of Contemporary Fiction*, vol. 31, no. 3, Fall 2011 (Champaign, IL: Dalkey Archive Press, 2011), pp. 162–78; Flore Coulouma, 'Transgressive and Subversive: Flann O'Brien's Tales of the In-Between', in Ciaran Ross (ed.), *Sub-Versions: Trans-National Readings of*

Modern Irish Literature (Amsterdam: Rodopi, 2010), pp. 65–85; Anthony Adams, 'Butter-Spades, Footnotes, and Omnium: *The Third Policeman* as "Pataphysical" Fiction', in Murphy and Hopper (eds), pp. 106–20; Jennika Baines, '"Un-Understandable Mystery": Catholic Faith and Revelation in *The Third Policeman*', in Murphy and Hopper (eds), pp. 78–91; Neil Murphy, 'Flann O'Brien's *The Hard Life* and the Gaze of the Medusa', in Murphy and Hopper (eds), pp. 148–62; and Maciej Ruczaj, 'Infernal Poetics/Infernal Ethics: *The Third Policeman* Between Medieval and (Post)Modern Netherworlds', in Murphy and Hopper (eds), pp. 91–107.

7   See Bakhtin, pp. 109–14. A more detailed archaeology of Menippean discourse and its Socratic heritage disseminated via the Cynic movement is presented by Fuchs, *Joyce und Menippos*, pp. 7–26.

8   Bakhtin, p. 115.

9   Voltaire, pp. 149–50. For a more recent example in a more contemporary medium, Monty Python's equally disappointed search for *The Meaning of Life* (1983) in the movie of the same title must be considered another sample of Menippean satire on human knowledge.

10   For a more detailed outline of these traditions, see Fuchs, *Joyce und Menippos*, pp. 7–11.

11   Vivian Mercier, *The Irish Comic Tradition* (Oxford: Oxford University Press, 1969).

12   See Lanters, 'Irish Satire', pp. 480–81.

13   See Relihan, Chapter 4.

14   See Fuchs, *Joyce und Menippos*, pp. 10–11; Rijkonen, p. 39; and Umberto Eco, *The Aesthetics of Chaosmos: The Middle Ages of James Joyce*, Ellen Esrock (trans.) (Tulsa, OK: Tulsa University Press, 1982), p. 33.

15   Eco, pp. 7–8.

16   It may be the case that O'Nolan's rewriting of Lucian was indirectly inspired by James Joyce's *Ulysses*. As far as the Joycean rewriting of the Lucianic Menippus in *Ulysses* is concerned, see Dieter Fuchs, 'Joyce, Lucian, and Menippus: An Undiscovered Rewriting of the Ulysses-Archetype', *James Joyce Quarterly*, vol. 47, no. 1, 2009, pp. 140–46.

17   See Relihan, pp. 46–47, 110–13; and Ulrich Rütten, *Phantasie und Lachkultur: Lukians 'Wahre Geschichten'* (Tübingen: Narr, 1997), p. 124.

18   See Lucian, 'Dialogues of the Dead', in *Lucian Vol. VII*, M.D. Macleod (trans.) (London: William Heinemann, 1961), p. 35.

19   Ibid.

20   It seems possible that James Joyce's 'The Sisters' served as a source of inspiration for O'Nolan's Irish rewriting of Lucian; see my reading of Father Flynn as an Irish mock Socrates in Dieter Fuchs, 'Rereading James Joyce's "The Sisters": A Bakhtinian Approach', *Anglia*, vol. 124, no. 3, 2006, pp. 474–83.

21   Lucian, 'Dialogues of the Dead', p. 35.

22   Lucian, 'A True Story' Book I & II, in *Lucian Vol. I*, A.M. Harmon (trans.) (London: William Heinemann, 1913), pp. 287–91.

23   See von Koppenfels, p. 130.

24   Concerning the eutopian world in Pantagruel's mouth, see Erich Auerbach, 'The World in Pantagruel's Mouth', in *Mimesis: The Representation of Reality in Western Literature, Fifteenth-Anniversary Edition*, Edward Said (introd.) (Princeton, NJ: Princeton University Press, 2003), pp. 262–84. With regard to the dystopian dimension of the Cyclopean cave archetype, it is important to note that the Irish comic tradition emphasises the motif of cannibalism as a way of representing the Irish people starved by its English colonisers: like the one-eyed Homeric Cyclops – who eats rather than caters for Odysseus's hungry peers – the xenophobic and blinkered pro-English landowning elite starves the indigenous Irish people to death as a means of imperial power politics. For a detailed analysis of Ireland cannibalised by England including texts such as Swift's 'A Modest Proposal', see

Dieter Fuchs, 'The Earl of Surrey's Geraldine-Sonnet Contextualized: Cultural (Mis-) Representations of Ireland in the Early Modern, the Enlightened and the Contemporary Period', in Sonja Fielitz and Uwe Meyer (eds), *Shakespeare, Satire, Academia: Essays in Honour of Wolfgang Weiss* (Heidelberg: Winter, 2012), pp. 167–85.

25 See Fuchs, *Joyce und Menippos*, and Fuchs, 'Joyce, Lucian, and Menippus'.

26 Carl Jung, 'The Personal and the Collective (or Transpersonal) Unconscious', in *Two Essays on Analytical Psychology*, Herbert Read, Michael Fordham and Gerhard Adler (eds), Richard Francis Carrington Hull (trans.) (London: Routledge, 1990), pp. 64–79.

27 Maebh Long, *Assembling Flann O'Brien* (London: Bloomsbury, 2014), p. 200. See O'Nolan's epistolary response to Timothy O'Keefe on 21 September 1962: Brian O'Nolan papers, 1914–1966, ID: 1/4/MSS 051, Special Collections, Southern Illinois University, Carbondale, US.

28 See Frye, pp. 308, 310.

29 To elucidate how *The Third Policeman* fuses the Lucianic tradition of the Underworld journey with the Varronian self-ironic compendium of knowledge, von Koppenfels calls this work (as well as Samuel Beckett's *Watt*) '*Eine irische Höllenfahrt mit Fußnoten*' [An Irish Descent into Hell with Footnotes]; Von Koppenfels, pp. 263–67.

30 Although this satire on pedantic theoretical knowledge without practical use dates back to ancient Rome and the Christian Middle Ages, the present analysis of *The Dalkey Archive* stresses the enduring popularity of the Varronian tradition for modern and postmodern Ireland owing to the still widely unbroken authority of the Roman Catholic Church in the country.

31 James Joyce, 'The Holy Office', in Harry Levin (ed.), *The Portable James Joyce*, rev. edn (London: Penguin, 1976), p. 82.

32 See Eco, *passim*.

33 In this allegedly successful, '*non serviam*'-like pose of self-authorisation, Mick resembles Stephen Dedalus from *A Portrait of the Artist as a Young Man*. Although a comparative reading goes beyond the scope of this essay, the Menippean tradition at work in *Portrait* has to be mentioned as a common feature of both texts; see Fuchs, *Joyce und Menippos*, pp. 72–96.

34 This figure of thought echoes the birth of Pallas Athena – the goddess of wisdom who was born from the head of Zeus as a 'brainchild'.

35 Joyce, *Ulysses*, p. 844.

36 As well as a source of inspiration for O'Nolan, this mock-Socratic dimension is also at work in *Ulysses*: Stephen's tongue-in-cheek Shakespeare theory fashions Shakespeare not only as a mock Odysseus, but also as a mock Socrates: a midwife philosopher ruled by a shrewish Xanthippean wife. For a detailed Menippean analysis see Dieter Fuchs, '"Poor Penelope. Penelope Rich": Sir Philip Sidney's *Astrophil and Stella* as a Source for the Rewriting of the Odysseus-Archetype in James Joyce's *Ulysses*', *James Joyce Quarterly*, vol. 48, no. 2, 2011, pp. 350–56.

15. RADAK

1 Roland Barthes, *S/Z*, Richard Miller (trans.) (New York, NY: Hill & Wang, 1974), pp. 5–6.

2 In this regard, I take a different view to that of David Cohen, who argues that *At Swim-Two-Birds* is ultimately a 'conventional novel', in which 'The three endings defy their labels and become the climax, denouement, and conclusion'. David Cohen, 'An Atomy of the Novel: Flann O'Brien's *At Swim-Two-Birds*', *Twentieth Century Literature*, vol. 39, no. 2, 1993, p. 208.

3 Maebh Long, *Assembling Flann O'Brien* (London: Bloomsbury, 2014), p. 23.

4 Ibid., p. 10.

5   Peter Brooks, *Reading for the Plot: Design and Intention in Narrative* (Cambridge, MA: Harvard University Press, 1992), p. 277.

6   Ibid., pp. 211–12.

7   Ibid., p. 260.

8   See Frank Kermode, *The Sense of an Ending: Studies in the Theory of Fiction* (Oxford: Oxford University Press, 2000).

9   Marie-Laure Ryan, 'Possible Worlds', in Peter Hühn, Jan Christoph Meister, John Pier and Wolf Schmid (eds), *Handbook of Narratology, Volume 1*, 2nd edn (Berlin: De Gruyter, 2014), p. 739.

10 For detailed investigations of O'Nolan's employment of theories of time and space, see J.M. Silverthorne, 'Time, Literature, and Failure: Flann O'Brien's *At Swim-Two-Birds* and *The Third Policeman*', *Éire-Ireland*, vol. 11, no. 4, Winter 1976, pp. 66–83; Richard F. Petersen, 'Flann O'Brien's Timefoolery', *Irish Renaissance Annual*, no. 3, 1982, pp. 30–46; Charles Kemnitz, 'Beyond the Zone of Middle Dimensions: A Relativistic Reading of *The Third Policeman*', *Irish University Review*, vol. 15, no. 1, Spring 1985, pp. 56–72; Mary A. O'Toole, 'The Theory of Serialism in *The Third Policeman*', *Irish University Review*, vol. 18, no. 2, Autumn 1988, pp. 215–25; M. Keith Booker, 'Science, Philosophy, and *The Third Policeman*: Flann O'Brien and the Epistemology of Futility', *South Atlantic Review*, vol. 56, no. 4, November 1991, pp. 37–56; Andrew Spenser, 'Many Worlds: The New Physics in Flann O'Brien's *The Third Policeman*', *Éire-Ireland*, vol. 30, no. 1, Spring 1995, pp. 145–58; Marguerite Quintelli-Neary, 'Flann O'Brien: *At Swim-Two-Birds*, *The Third Policeman* – Temporal and Spatial Incongruities', in *Folklore and the Fantastic in Twelve Modern Irish Novels* (Westport, CT: Greenwood, 1997), pp. 83–97; Ondřej Pilný, 'My Kingdom for a Pun: Myles na gCopaleen, Erwin Schrödinger and *The Third Policeman* in *Improbable Frequency*', *Irish Theatre International*, vol. 1, no. 1, 2008, pp. 38–52; Keith Hopper, *Flann O'Brien: A Portrait of the Artist as a Young Post-Modernist*, 2nd edn, J. Hillis Miller (foreword) (Cork: Cork University Press, 2009), pp. 185–91, 218–21; Mark O'Connell, '"How to handle eternity": Infinity and the Theories of J.W. Dunne in the Fiction of Jorge Luis Borges and Flann O'Brien's *The Third Policeman*', *Irish Studies Review*, vol. 17, no. 2, Summer 2009, pp. 223–37; Samuel Whybrow, 'Flann O'Brien's Science Fiction: An "Illusion of Progression" in *The Third Policeman*', in Jennika Baines (ed.), *'Is it about a bicycle?': Flann O'Brien in the Twenty-First Century* (Dublin: Four Courts Press, 2011), pp. 127–41; Jack Fennell, 'Irelands Enough and Time: Brian O'Nolan's Science Fiction', in Ruben Borg, Paul Fagan and Werner Huber (eds), *Flann O'Brien: Contesting Legacies* (Cork: Cork University Press, 2014), pp. 33–45.

11 Kemnitz (somewhat questionably) takes this idea even further by suggesting a direct parallel between the structure of the text and electromagnetic radiation: 'Nuclear physics in the nineteen-thirties was based upon the paradoxical situations connected with the dual nature of light, or, more generally, with electromagnetic radiation. [...] In a similar manner, *The Third Policeman* is based upon paradoxical information sources (remember that in science an experiment is merely an information source). The most obvious source is the narrative itself which interacts with the de Selby footnotes. The footnotes in turn act as an electromagnetic source upon the metal of the narrative: at times the footnotes interfere with the information in the text, at other times they augment the narrative, and at still other times they "kick-out" insights that aid in experiencing the text' (p. 57).

12 Hopper, p. 219.

13 Anne Clissmann, *Flann O'Brien: A Critical Introduction to His Writings* (Dublin: Gill & Macmillan, 1975), p. 157.

14 Shari Benstock, 'At the Margin of Discourse: Footnotes in the Fictional Text', *PMLA*, vol. 98, no. 2, 1983, p. 210.

15 Ibid., p. 212.

16 See Hopper, p. 155: 'In *The Third Policeman*, O'Brien gradually dismantles the textual apparatus to a point where the footnotes and the text compete for space and signifying supremacy. [...] a sub-narrative demanding a completely separate reading from the main body of work – in fact, for a while, [...] *is* the main body of work'.

17 Gilles Deleuze, 'Bartleby; Or, The Formula', in *Essays Critical and Clinical*, Daniel W. Smith and Michael A. Greco (trans.) (Minneapolis: University of Minnesota Press, 1997), p. 71. Although Deleuze uses this image in a different context (Herman Melville's 'Bartleby, the Scrivener'), the underlying concept of a narrative act that continually positions itself in a threshold space *between* mutually exclusive possibilities, rather than on either side of a binary opposition, is relevant here.

18 Tzvetan Todorov, *The Fantastic: A Structural Approach to a Literary Genre* (Ithaca, NY: Cornell University Press, 1975), p. 25.

19 'The fantastic occupies the duration of [the reader's or character's] uncertainty. Once we choose one answer or the other [i.e. decide whether what happens is real or not], we leave the fantastic for a neighbouring genre, the uncanny or the marvellous' (Todorov, p. 25).

20 Ibid., p. 41. Apart from the different 'time zones' that distinguish The Parish from the world of the narrator's birth, there are a number of other indications that the boundaries between the real and the unreal, or between the natural and the supernatural, have been blurred; for instance: the lack of commentary or confusion by other characters relating to the narrator's state of being suspended between two contradictory ontological realities; the absence of a framing device, which often marks the transition into a world adhering to supernatural logic in fantastic tales; the absence of anthropomorphic animals or other common indicators of supernatural genres (such as fairy tales); the metafictional commentary on the 'unconvincing' police barracks, etc.

21 Ibid., p. 41.

22 Hopper implicitly addresses the issue of incompossibility and draws it together with questions of temporality when he suggests that 'The simultaneity of two co-existent events in mutual contradiction is the antithesis of the seamless linearity demanded by realist narrative' (p. 147).

23 Hopper reads this question in the context of 'infinite regress', as a '"strange loop" which turns the novel into an endlessly repeating cycle' (p. 115).

24 Todorov, pp. 157, 158. See also Tobin Siebers's claim that 'Todorov's contribution to structuralist criticism has been overestimated'. Tobin Siebers, 'Hesitation, History, and Reading: Henry James's *The Turn of the Screw*', *Texas Studies in Literature and Language*, vol. 25, no. 4, 1983, p. 558.

25 Gilles Deleuze, *The Fold*, Tom Conley (trans.) (London: Athlone Press, 1993), p. 59.

26 Ibid., p. 60.

27 See also Sean Bowden's contention that 'Deleuze's constant criticism is that Leibniz ultimately subordinates the ideal play of events to a principle of converging differences under the hypothesis of a God who calculates and chooses for existence the "best" or maximally convergent series of possible events'. Sean Bowden, 'Deleuze's Neo-Leibnizianism, Events and the Logic of Sense's "Static Ontological Genesis"', *Deleuze Studies*, vol. 4, no. 3, November 2010, p. 302.

28 Deleuze, *The Fold*, p. 62.

29 Ibid., pp. 59, 62.

30 Gilles Deleuze, *The Logic of Sense*, Constantin Boundas (ed.), Mark Lester and Charles Stivale (trans.) (New York, NY: Columbia University Press, 1990), p. 172.

31 'You go on like that constructing, from one singularity to the next, what you will be able to call a continuity. The simplest case of a continuity is a straight line, but there is also

precisely a continuity of non-straight lines. [...] When there is a coincidence of values of two ordinary series encompassed in the two circles, you have a continuity. Thus you can construct a continuity made from continuity. [...] If the series of ordinaries that derive from singularities diverge, then you have a discontinuity. You will say that a world is constituted by a continuity of continuity. It's the composition of the continuous. A discontinuity is defined when the series of ordinaries or regulars that derive from two points diverge'. Gilles Deleuze, 'Cours Vincennes – 29/04/1980', <http://www.webdeleuze.com/textes/55>.

32 Bowden, p. 319.

33 'Persons' can, in both Leibniz's and Deleuze's view, be subsumed under 'monads'.

34 Bowden, p. 319. Similarly employing mathematical metaphors, Hopper implicitly acknowledges the branching nature of *The Third Policeman* and its essentially unfinisable nature when he calls it (after Jeremy Hawthorn) 'a parabolic text [...] an open plane curve formed by *a series of intersections*, i.e. an *open* narrative' [my emphasis] (p. 193).

35 George P. Landow, *Hypertext 2.0*, 2nd edn (Baltimore, MD: Johns Hopkins University Press, 1997), p. 2.

36 Louis Armand, *Technē: James Joyce, Hypertext & Technology*, 2nd edn (Prague: Charles University Press, 2007), p. 59.

37 Wayne C. Booth, *The Rhetoric of Fiction* (Chicago, IL: University of Chicago Press, 1961), p. 300.

38 Stuart Moulthrop, 'You Say You Want a Revolution? Hypertext and the Laws of Media', *Postmodern Culture: An Electronic Journal of Interdisciplinary Criticism*, vol. 1, no. 3, May 1991, par. 22. Landow is careful to highlight that 'not all current hypertext systems include the crucial democratizing features that permit readers to contribute to the text' and that it is vital 'not [to] confuse [...] the effects of read-only and read-and-write systems'. George P. Landow (ed.), *Hyper/Text/Theory*, 2nd edn (Baltimore, MD: Johns Hopkins University Press, 1995), p. 14. However, Landow later acknowledges that, to a certain extent, the very concept of 'hypertext blurs the boundaries between reader and writer' (*Hypertext 2.0*, p. 4).

39 Moulthrop, par. 21.

40 Brooker, p. 126.

41 Hopper, p. 147. See also P.G. Wodehouse's tongue-in-cheek charge that 'it is only a man of iron will who, coming on a[6] or a[7], can keep from dropping everything and bounding off after it like a basset hound after a basset[17]/[17]What is a *basset*? I've often wondered'. P.G. Wodehouse, *Over Seventy* (London: Herbert Jenkins, 1957), p. ii.

42 Gérard Genette, *Paratexts: Thresholds of Interpretation* (Cambridge: Cambridge University Press, 1997), p. 343.

43 Ibid.

44 As Hopper suggests, 'The very texture of language becomes the arena of conflict where Bakhtin's dialogic potential is actualised – a field of play where all utterances resist absolute resolution' (p. 171).

45 See Hopper, ch. 4.

46 See Malcah Effron's contention that 'footnotes call attention to the textuality of the narrative [...] the emphasied textuality calls attention to the fictionality because it calls attention to the narrative as text'. Malcah Effron, 'On the Borders of the Page, on the Borders of Genre: Artificial Paratexts in Golden Age Detective Fiction', *Narrative*, vol. 18, no. 2, May 2010, p. 202. Regarding the incompossible coexistence between fiction and reality in *The Third Policeman*, see Debra Malina's suggestion that metalepsis has a 'fundamentally disruptive effect on the fabric of narrative, on the possibilities for achieving coherent readings, *and on the very distinction between fiction and reality*' [my emphasis]. Debra Malina, *Breaking The Frame: Metalepsis and the Construction of the Subject* (Ohio, OH: Ohio State University Press, 2002), p. 1.

47 J. Hillis Miller, 'Foreword: A Portrait of the Critic as a Young Post-Modernist', in Hopper, p. iv.

48 Margot Norris, 'Possible-Worlds Theory and Joyce's "Wandering Rocks": The Case of Father Conmee', *Joyce Studies Annual*, vol. 2007, pp. 21–43. For more on possible worlds theory and its applications to literature see Thomas G. Pavel, *Fictional Worlds* (Cambridge, MA: Harvard University Press, 1986); Marie-Laure Ryan, *Possible Worlds, Artificial Intelligence, and Narrative Theory* (Bloomington, IN: Indiana University Press, 1991); Ruth Ronen, *Possible Worlds in Literary Theory* (Cambridge: Cambridge University Press, 1994); Lubomir Doležel, *Heterocosmica: Fiction and Possible Worlds* (Baltimore, MD: Johns Hopkins University Press, 1998); Margot Norris, 'Possible Worlds Theory and the Fantasy Universe of *Finnegans Wake*', *James Joyce Quarterly*, vol. 44, no. 3, Spring 2007, pp. 455–74.

49 See Armand, *Technē, passim*; Darren Tofts, 'A Retrospective Sort of Arrangement: *Ulysses* and the Poetics of Hypertextuality', *Hypermedia Joyce Studies*, vol. 3, no. 1, 2002, <http://hjs.ff.cuni.cz/archives/v3/tofts2.html>; Annalisa Volpone, *Joyce, Give and Take* (Rome: Aracne, 2012).

50 Alice Bell's work is a notable exception; for instance, she makes the case that possible worlds theory is able to model metalepses more accurately than other theories of narrative that do not have an ontological focus. Alice Bell, '"I felt like I'd stepped out of a different reality": Possible Worlds Theory, Metalepsis and Digital Fiction', in Joanna Gavins and Ernestine Lahey (eds), *World Building: Discourse in the Mind* (London: Bloomsbury, 2016). Similarly, in her contribution to Ruth Page and Bronwen Thomas (eds), *New Narratives: Stories and Storytelling in the Digital Age* (Lincoln, NE: University of Nebraska Press, 2011), Bell focuses on 'Ontological Boundaries and Methodological Leaps', highlighting the 'Importance of Possible Worlds Theory for Hypertext Fiction (and Beyond)'. With this method, Bell raises awareness for the ways in which 'the study of hypertext fiction [could] move away from the chronological focus of traditional narrative theory to address the ontological mechanics of hypertext narratives' (p. 63).

51 Ted Nelson, *Literary Machines: The Report on, and of, Project Xanadu*, 5th edn (Swarthmore PA: Ted Nelson, 1983), p. 2. Not only the text's visual layout, but also its many *non sequiturs* in terms of (non-)causal links between events reinforce the idea of 'non-sequential' writing on different levels.

52 See also J.Y. Douglas's comment that 'as a concept, hypertext has been rolling around for decades. The idea was *born in the thirties*, the child of a science adviser to Franklin Delano Roosevelt, Vannevar Bush, who envisioned a system that could support and improve human memory more efficiently than the printed word' [my emphasis]. J.Y. Douglas, *The End of Books – or Books Without End? Reading Interactive Narratives* (Ann Arbor, MI: University of Michigan Press, 2000), p. 25.

53 Landow, *Hypertext 2.0*, p. 4.

54 Landow introduces the concept of 'quasi hypertextuality in print text', referring to J.D. Bolter's *Writing Space: The Computer, Hypertext, and the History of Writing* (Hillsdale, NJ: Lawrence Erlbaum, 1991). Landow specifically mentions '*Tristram Shandy, In Memoriam, Ulysses*, and *Finnegan's* [*sic*] *Wake* and recent French, American, and Latin American fiction, particularly that by Michel Butor, Marc Saporta, Robert Coover, and Jorge Luis Borges' in this context (*Hypertext 2.0*, p. 182). *Ulysses* in particular is foregrounded in Landow's discussion of '*implicit* hypertext in nonelectronic form' (*Hypertext 2.0*, p. 35).

55 Douglas, p. 24.

56 Tofts, 'Poetics of Hypertextuality', n.p.

57 Ibid.

58 Ibid. In a similar vein, the concept of 'anagnostic reading' was coined by Fritz Senn in *Inductive Scrutinies: Focus on Joyce*, Christine O'Neill (ed.) (Baltimore, MD: Johns

Hopkins University Press, 1995), p. 91. Senn views the reading process of complex texts with multiple layers of signifiers as a constant work in progress and argues that only re-readers of a text (his example being *Finnegans Wake*) can fully appreciate certain allusions and prefigurations. This idea becomes especially important in the present context when we consider that the second- or third-time reader of *The Third Policeman* is endowed with much more knowledge than its first-time reader.

59 See Tofts, 'Poetics of Hypertextuality': 'the thematic cross-reference is a vectoral event, an exchange or link between the local and remote, immediate and mediated objects of narration' (n.p.). In the case of *The Third Policeman*, the question 'Is it about a bicycle?', which functions as a vectoral cross-link, is not only thematic in nature but also implies a call to action on the part of the reader.

60 Tofts, 'Poetics of Hypertextuality', n.p.

61 Ryan, 'Possible Worlds', p. 730.

62 Ronen, p. 114.

63 Ibid., p. 108.

64 Ibid., p. 116.

65 Ibid.

66 Although Bakhtin mainly applies this concept to the impossibility of accurately representing the human psyche in a linear, monologic fashion in novels, he eventually extends 'the rigorous unfinalizability and dialogic openness' of discourse to the whole of 'Dostoevsky's artistic world'. Michail M. Bakhtin, *Problems of Dostoevsky's Poetics*, Caryl Emerson (ed. and trans.) (Manchester: Manchester University Press, 1984), p. 272.

Bibliography

Primary

Na gCopaleen, Myles, *An Béal Bocht* (Cork: Mercier, 1999)

Na Gopaleen, Myles, 'De Me', *New Ireland*, March 1964, 41–42

Nolan, Brian, 'The Martyr's Crown', *Envoy*, vol. 1, no. 3, February 1950, 57–62

O'Brien, Flann, 'Going to the Dogs!', *The Bell*, vol. 1, no. 1, October 1940, 19–24

— 'The Trade in Dublin', *The Bell*, vol. 1, no. 2, November 1940, 6–15

— 'The Dance Halls', *The Bell*, vol. 1, no. 5, February 1941, 44–52

— *Stories and Plays*, Claud Cockburn (introd. and ed.) (London: Hart-Davis, MacGibbon, 1973)

— *The Hair of the Dogma* (London: Hart-Davis, MacGibbon, 1977)

— *Flann O'Brien at War: Myles na gCopaleen 1940–1945*, John Wyse Jackson (ed.) (London: Duckworth, 1999)

— *Further Cuttings from Cruiskeen Lawn* (Normal, IL: Dalkey Archive, 2000)

— *Rhapsody in Stephen's Green*, Robert Tracy (ed.) (Dublin: Lilliput Press, 2001)

— *The Complete Novels: At Swim-Two-Birds, The Third Policeman, The Poor Mouth, The Hard Life, The Dalkey Archive*, Keith Donohue (introd.) (New York, NY: Everyman's Library, 2007)

— *The Best of Myles*, Kevin O'Nolan (ed.) (London: Harper Perennial, 2007)

— *Myles Before Myles*, John Wyse Jackson (ed.) (Dublin: Lilliput Press, 2012)

— *The Short Fiction of Flann O'Brien*, Neil Murphy and Keith Hopper (eds), Jack Fennell (trans.) (Champaign, IL: Dalkey Archive Press, 2013)

— *Plays and Teleplays*, Daniel Keith Jernigan (ed.) (Champaign, IL: Dalkey Archive Press, 2013)

O'Nolan, Brian, 'A Sheaf of Letters', Robert Hogan and Gordon Henderson (eds), *The Journal of Irish Literature*, vol. 3, no. 1, *A Flann O'Brien–Myles na Gopaleen Number*, January 1974

Ó Nualláin, Brian, 'Aistear Pheadair Dhuibh', *Inisfail*, vol. 1. no. 1, March 1933, 63–64

Secondary

Almqvist, Bo, Séamas Ó Catháin and Pádraig Ó Héalaí (eds), *The Heroic Process: Form, Function and Fantasy in Folk Epic* (Dublin: The Glendale Press, 1987)

Aquinas, Thomas, *Summa Theologiae*, Fathers of the English Dominican Province (trans.) (Westminster: Christian Classics, 1981)

Aristotle, *The Poetics*, S.H. Butcher (trans.) (London: Macmillan, 1902)

Armand, Louis, *Technē: James Joyce, Hypertext & Technology*, 2nd edn (Prague: Charles University Press, 2007)

Arrington, Lauren, *Revolutionary Lives: Constance and Casimir Markievicz* (Princeton, NJ: Princeton University Press, 2016)

Asbee, Sue, *Flann O'Brien* (Boston, MA: Twayne, 1991)

Assmann, Aleida, 'Texts, Traces, Trash: The Changing Media of Cultural Memory', *Representations*, no. 56, special issue, *The New Erudition*, Autumn 1996, 123–34

Assmann, Jan, 'Collective Memory and Cultural Identity', *New German Critique*, no. 65, 1995, 125–33

Auerbach, Erich, *Mimesis: The Representation of Reality in Western Literature, Fifteenth-Anniversary Edition*, Edward Said (introd.) (Princeton, NJ: Princeton University Press, 2003)

Augusteijn, Joost (ed.), *Ireland in the 1930s* (Dublin: Four Courts Press, 1999)

Augustine, *Exposition of the Sermon on the Mount, Drawn from the Writings of St Augustine*, Richard Chenevix Trench (introd.) (London: John W. Parker, West Strand, 1851)

Bakhtin, Michail M., *Problems of Dostoevsky's Poetics*, Caryl Emerson (ed. and trans.) (Manchester: Manchester University Press, 1984)

Baines, Jennika (ed.), *'Is it about a bicycle?': Flann O'Brien in the Twenty-First Century* (Dublin: Four Courts Press, 2011)

Barfoot, C.C. and Theo d'Haen (eds), *The Clash of Ireland: Literary Contrasts and Connections* (Amsterdam: Rodopi, 1989)

Barrett, Lee C. and Jon Stewart (eds), *Kierkegaard and the Bible: Vol. 1, The Old Testament* (Farnham: Ashgate, 2010)

Bartely, J.O. and D.L. Sims, 'Pre-Nineteenth Century Stage Irish and Welsh Pronunciation', *Proceedings of the American Philosophical Society*, vol. 93, no. 5, 1949, 439–47

Barthes, Roland, *Writing Degree Zero*, Susan Sontag (foreword), Annette Lavers and Colin Smythe (trans.) (New York, NY: Hill & Wang, 1968)

— *S/Z*, Richard Miller (trans.) (New York, NY: Hill & Wang, 1974)

Beaujour, Elizabeth Klosty, 'Prolegomena to a Study of Russian Bilingual Writers', *The Slavic and East European Journal*, vol. 28, no. 1, Spring 1984, 58–75

— *Alien Tongues: Bilingual Russian Writers of the 'First' Emigration* (Ithaca, NY: Cornell University Press, 1989)

Beauvillain, C. and J. Grainger, 'Accessing Interlexical Homographs: Some Limitations of a Language Selective Access', *Journal of Memory and Language*, no. 26, 1987, 658–72

Beckett, Samuel, *Disjecta* (London: John Calder, 1983)

— *Eleutheria*, Barbara Wright (trans.) (London: Faber 1996)

— *Murphy*, J.C.C. Mays (ed.) (London: Faber & Faber, 2009)

— *Company, Ill Seen Ill Said, Worstward Ho, Stirrings Still*, Dirk Van Hulle (ed.) (London: Faber & Faber, 2009)

— *The Unnamable*, Steven Connor (ed.) (London: Faber & Faber, 2010)

— *The Beckett Digital Manuscript Project, Module 1: Stirrings Still / Soubresauts and 'Comment dire' / 'what is the word': An Electronic Genetic Edition*, Dirk Van Hulle and Vincent Neyt (eds) (Brussels: ASP / University Press Antwerp, 2010), <http://www.beckettarchive.org>

— *The Letters of Samuel Beckett, vol. II: 1941–1956*, George Craig, Martha Dow Fehsenfeld, Dan Gunn and Lois More Overbeck (eds) (Cambridge: Cambridge University Press, 2011)

Behan, Brendan, 'Secret Scripture' [rev. of *At Swim-Two-Birds*], *The Irish Times*, 30 July 1960, p. 6.

Benstock, Shari, 'At the Margin of Discourse: Footnotes in the Fictional Text', *PMLA*, vol. 98, no. 2, 1983, 204–25

Ben-Zeev, Sandra, 'The Influence of Bilingualism on Cognitive Strategy and Cognitive Development', *Child Development*, vol. 48, no. 3, September 1977, 1009–18

Bhabha, Homi K., *The Location of Culture* (London: Routledge, 2000)

Bialystok, Ellen, I. Fergus, M. Craik and G. Luk, 'Bilingualism: Consequences for Mind and Brain', *Trends in Cognitive Sciences*, vol. 16, no. 4, 2012, 240–50

Birmingham, Kevin, *The Most Dangerous Book: The Battle for James Joyce's 'Ulysses'* (New York, NY: The Penguin Press, 2014)

Bluemel, Kristin, *Intermodernism: Literary Culture in Mid-Twentieth-Century Britain* (Edinburgh: Edinburgh University Press, 2009)

Bolter, J.D., *Writing Space: The Computer, Hypertext, and the History of Writing* (Hillsdale, NJ: Lawrence Erlbaum, 1991)

Bolton, Jonathan, 'Comedies of Failure: O'Brien's *The Hard Life* and Moore's *The Emperor of Ice Cream*', *New Hibernia Review*, vol. 12, no. 3, Autumn 2008, 118–33

Bohman-Kalaja, Kimberly, *Reading Games: An Aesthetics of Play in Flann O'Brien, Samuel Beckett and Georges Perec* (Champaign, IL: Dalkey Archive Press, 2007)

Booker, M. Keith, 'Science, Philosophy, and *The Third Policeman*: Flann O'Brien and the Epistemology of Futility', *South Atlantic Review*, vol. 56, no. 4, November 1991, 37–56

— *Flann O'Brien, Bakhtin, and Menippean Satire* (Syracuse, NY: Syracuse University Press, 1995)

Booth, Wayne C., *The Rhetoric of Fiction* (Chicago, IL: University of Chicago Press, 1961)

Borg, Ruben, 'Putting the Impossible to Work: Beckettian Afterlife and the Posthuman Future of Humanity', *Journal of Modern Literature*, vol. 35, no. 4, 2012, 163–80

Borg, Ruben, Paul Fagan and Werner Huber (eds), *Flann O'Brien: Contesting Legacies* (Cork: Cork University Press, 2014)

Borges, Jorge Luis, *The Total Library: Non-Fiction 1922–1986*, Eliot Weinberger (ed.), Esther Allen, Suzanne Jill Levine and Eliot Weinberger (trans.) (London: Allen Lane, 2000)

Boucicault, Dion, *The Colleen Bawn* (New York, NY: S. French, n.d.)

Bourdieu, Pierre, *The Field of Cultural Production: Essays on Art and Literature*, Randal Johnson (trans.) (New York, NY: Columbia University Press, 1993)

Bowden, Sean, 'Deleuze's Neo-Leibnizianism, Events and the Logic of Sense's "Static Ontological Genesis"', *Deleuze Studies*, vol. 4, no. 3, November 2010, 301–28

Bowler, Peter J., *Science for All: The Popularization of Science in Early Twentieth-Century Britain* (Chicago, IL: University of Chicago Press, 2009)

Boyd, Ernest, 'Aesthete: Model 1924', *The American Mercury*, vol. 1, no. 1, January 1924, 51–56

— 'The Literary Comrade: A Portrait', *The American Mercury*, vol. 40, no. 157, January 1937

Bratton, Jacqueline S. *et al.* (eds), *Acts of Supremacy: The British Empire and the Stage, 1790–1930*, (Manchester: Manchester University Press, 1991)

Breathnach, Deasún, *Chugat an Púca* (Baile Átha Cliath: An Clóchomhar, 1993)

Breathnach, Diarmuid and Máire Ní Mhurchú (eds), *1882–1982: Beathaisnéis a Dó* (Baile Átha Cliath: An Clóchomhar, 1990)

Bridgham, Fred (ed.), *The First World War as a Clash of Cultures* (Woodbridge: Boydell & Brewer, 2006)

Brivic, Shelly, '*The Third Policeman* as Lacanian Deity: O'Brien's Critique of Language and Subjectivity', *New Hibernia Review*, vol. 16, no. 2, Summer 2012, 112–32

Brooker, Joseph, 'A Balloon Filled With Verbal Gas: *Blather* and the Irish Ready-Made School', *Precursors and Aftermaths, vol. 2, no. 1, 2003, 74–98

— *Flann O'Brien* (Tavistock: Northcote House, 2005)

Brooks, Peter, *Reading for the Plot: Design and Intention in Narrative* (Cambridge, MA: Harvard University Press, 1992)

Brown, Delmer M., *Nationalism in Japan: An Introductory Historical Analysis* (Berkeley, CA: University of California Press, 1955)

Brown, Terence, 'The Church of Ireland: Some Literary Perspectives', *Search: A Church of Ireland Journal*, vol. 3, no. 2, Winter 1980, 5–19

— *Ireland's Literature: Selected Essays* (Mullingar: Lilliput Press, 1988)

— *Ireland: A Social and Cultural History* (London: Harper Perennial, 2004)

Butler, Hubert, *Grandmother and Wolfe Tone* (Dublin: Lilliput Press, 1990)

Byron, Henry J., *Miss Eily O'Connor: A New and Original Burlesque, Founded on the Great Sensational Drama of The Colleen Bawn* (London: Thomas Hailes Lacy, n.d.)

Cahalan, James M., 'Forging a Tradition: Emily Lawless and the Irish Literary Canon', *Colby Quarterly*, vol. 27, no. 1, March 1991, 27–39

Campbell, Patrick, *An Irishman's Diary*, Ronald Searle (illustrations) (London: Cassell, 1950)

Carey, John, Máire Herbert and Kevin Murray (eds), *Cín Chille Cúile: Texts, Saints and Places: Essays in Honour of Pádraig Ó Riain* (Aberystwyth: Celtic Studies Publications, 2004)

Carr, Helen, *The Verse Revolutionaries: Ezra Pound, H.D. and The Imagists* (London: Jonathan Cape, 2009)

Carson, Ciaran, *The Midnight Court* (Oldcastle: Gallery, 2005)

Carville, Conor, 'Autonomy and the Everyday: Beckett, Late Modernism and Post-War Visual Art', *Samuel Beckett Today/Aujourd'hui*, no. 23, 2011, 63–78

Castle, Gregory, *Modernism and the Celtic Revival* (Cambridge: Cambridge University Press, 2001)

Chloros, Penelope Gardner, *Code-Switching* (Cambridge: Cambridge University Press, 2009)

Cicero, *Cicero in Twenty-Eight Volumes*, vol. 20, *De senectute, de amicitia, de divinatione*, The Loeb Classical Library, W.A. Falconer (trans.) (Cambridge, MA: Harvard University Press, 1971)

Clarke, Austin, '"Stephen Dedalus": The Author of *Ulysses*', *The New Statesman*, vol. 22, no. 566, 23 February 1924, 571–72

Clissmann, Anne, *Flann O'Brien: A Critical Introduction to His Writings* (Dublin: Gill & Macmillan, 1975)

Clune [Clissmann], Anne and Tess Hurson (eds), *Conjuring Complexities: Essays on Flann O'Brien* (Belfast: Institute of Irish Studies, 1997)

Cohen, David, 'An Atomy of the Novel: Flann O'Brien's *At Swim-Two-Birds*', *Twentieth Century Literature*, vol. 39, no. 2, 1993, 208–29

Colum, Padraic, *The Road Round Ireland* (New York, NY: Macmillan Co., 1926)

Conrad, Joseph, *The Collected Letters of Joseph Conrad: Vol. 8. 1923–1924*, Laurence Davies and Gene M. Moore (eds) (Cambridge: Cambridge University Press, 2008)

Corcoran, Farrel, *RTÉ and the Globalisation of Irish Television* (Bristol: Intellect, 2004)

Costello, Peter and Peter Van de Kamp, *Flann O'Brien: An Illustrated Biography* (London: Bloomsbury, 1987)

Crispi, Luca and Stacey Herbert with Lori N. Curtis, *In Good Company: James Joyce & Publishers, Readers, Friends* (Tulsa, OK: University of Tulsa, 2003)

Cronin, Anthony, *No Laughing Matter: The Life and Times of Flann O'Brien* (London: Grafton, 1989; New York, NY: Fromm, 1989; Dublin: New Island, 2003)

— *Dead as Doornails* (Dublin: Lilliput Press, 1999)

Cronin, John, *Irish Fiction 1900–1940* (Belfast: Appletree, 1992)

— 'Brother of the More Famous Flann: Ciarán Ó Nualláin', *New Hibernia Review/Iris Éireannach Nua*, vol. 3, no. 4, Winter 1999, 9–17

Curran, C.P., *James Joyce Remembered* (London: Oxford University Press, 1968)

Curtis Jr, L. Perry, *Apes and Angels: The Irishman in Victorian Caricature* (Washington, DC: Smithsonian Institution Press, 1971)

Deane, Seamus, *Strange Country: Modernity and Nationhood in Irish Writing Since 1790* (Oxford: Clarendon Press, 1997)

DeGiacomo, Albert J., *T.C. Murray, Dramatist: Voice of the Irish Peasant* (Syracuse, NY: Syracuse University Press, 2002)

De Groot, Annette, *Language and Cognition in Bilinguals and Multilinguals: An Introduction* (New York, NY: Psychology Press, 2011)

Deleuze, Gilles, *The Logic of Sense*, Constantin Boundas (ed.), Mark Lester and Charles Stivale (trans.) (New York, NY: Columbia University Press, 1990)

— *The Fold*, Tom Conley (trans.) (London: Athlone Press, 1993)

— *Essays Critical and Clinical*, Daniel W. Smith and Michael A. Greco (trans.) (Minneapolis, MN: University of Minnesota Press, 1997)

— 'Cours Vincennes – 29/04/1980', <http://www.webdeleuze.com/textes/55>

de Paor, Louis, 'Myles na gCopaleen agus Drochshampla na nDealeabhar', *The Irish Review*, no. 23, Winter 1998, 24–32

Derrida, Jacques, *Specters of Marx: The State of the Debt, the Work of Mourning and the New International*, Peggy Kamuf (trans.), Stephen Cullenberg and Bernd Magnus (eds) (New York, NY: Routledge, 1994)

— *Writing and Difference*, Alan Bass (trans.) (London: Routledge, 2001)

Devane, James, 'Is an Irish Culture Possible?', *Ireland Today*, vol. 1, no. 5, October 1936, 21–31

Dinneen, Patrick S., *Foclóir Gaedhilge agus Béarla: An Irish-English Dictionary; Being a Thesaurus of the Words, Phrases and Idioms of the Modern Irish Language, with Explanations in English* (Dublin: M.H. Gill & Son, 1904)

Doležel, Lubomir, *Heterocosmica: Fiction and Possible Worlds* (Baltimore, MD: Johns Hopkins University Press, 1998)

Douglas, J.Y., *The End of Books – or Books Without End? Reading Interactive Narratives* (Ann Arbor, MI: University of Michigan Press, 2000)

Douglas, R.M., *Architects of the Resurrection: Ailtirí na hAiséirighe and the Fascist 'New Order' in Ireland* (Manchester: Manchester University Press, 2009)

Dower, John, *Japan in War & Peace: Selected Essays* (New York, NY: New Press, 1993)

Downum, Denell, 'Citation and Spectrality in Flann O'Brien's *At Swim-Two-Birds*', *Irish University Review*, vol. 36, no. 2, 2006, 304–20

Duffin, Brendan, [rev. of *The Early Years of Brian O'Nolan/Flann O'Brien/Myles na Gopaleen* by Ciaran O'Nuallain [*sic*]], *Fortnight*, no. 378, May 1999, 31

Dunleavy, Janet Egleson and Gareth W. Dunleavy, *Douglas Hyde: A Maker of Modern Ireland* (Berkeley, CA: University of California Press, 1991)

Dunne, J.W., *An Experiment with Time* (London: Faber & Faber, 1934)

Eco, Umberto, *The Aesthetics of Chaosmos: The Middle Ages of James Joyce*, Ellen Esrock (trans.) (Tulsa, OK: Tulsa University Press, 1982)

Eddington, Arthur Stanley, *Space, Time and Gravitation* (Cambridge: Cambridge University Press, 1920)

— *The Nature of the Physical World* (London: Dent, 1929)

— *The Expanding Universe* (Cambridge: Cambridge University Press, 1933)

Edwards, Walter, 'Forging Tradition for a Holy War: The *Hakkō Ichiu* Tower in Miyazaki and Japanese Wartime Ideology', *Journal of Japanese Studies*, no. 29, 2003, 289–324

Effron, Malcah, 'On the Borders of the Page, on the Borders of Genre: Artificial Paratexts in Golden Age Detective Fiction', *Narrative*, vol. 18, no. 2, May 2010, 199–219

Ellmann, Richard, *James Joyce*, rev. edn (New York, NY: Oxford University Press, 1982)

Erll, Astrid and Ansgar Nünning (eds), *Cultural Memory Studies: An Interdisciplinary Handbook; Media and Cultural Memory* (Berlin: Walter de Gruyter, 2008)

Esse, James, 'An Interview with Mr James Stephens', *The Irish Statesman*, no. 1, 22 September 1923, 48, 50

Fagan, Paul, '"Expert diagnosis has averted still another tragedy": Misreading and the Paranoia of Expertise in *The Third Policeman*', *The Parish Review*, vol. 3, no. 1, Fall 2014, 8–28

Felecan, Oliviu (ed.), *Name and Naming: Synchronic and Diachronic Perspectives* (Newcastle upon Tyne: Cambridge Scholars Publishing, 2012)

Fennell, Jack, 'The Flannkfurt School: Brian O'Nolan and the Culture Industry', *The Parish Review* vol. 3, no. 2, Spring 2014, 1–5

Fielitz, Sonja and Uwe Meyer (eds), *Shakespeare, Satire, Academia: Essays in Honour of Wolfgang Weiss* (Heidelberg: Winter, 2012)

Fifield, Peter, *Late Modernist Style in Samuel Beckett and Emmanuel Levinas* (Basingstoke: Palgrave Macmillan, 2013)

Foster, R.F., *Vivid Faces: The Revolutionary Generation in Ireland, 1890–1923* (New York, NY: W.W. Norton & Company, 2015)

Frye, Northrop, *Anatomy of Criticism* (Princeton, NJ: Princeton University Press, 1957)

Fuchs, Dieter, *Joyce und Menippos: A Portrait of the Artist as an Old Dog*, ZAA Monograph Series 2 (Würzburg: Königshausen & Neumann, 2006)

— 'Rereading James Joyce's "The Sisters": A Bakhtinian Approach', *Anglia*, vol. 124, no. 3, 2006, 474–83

— 'Joyce, Lucian, and Menippus: An Undiscovered Rewriting of the Ulysses-Archetype', *James Joyce Quarterly*, vol. 47, no. 1, 2009, 140–46

— '"Poor Penelope. Penelope Rich": Sir Philip Sidney's *Astrophil and Stella* as a Source for the Rewriting of the Odysseus-Archetype in James Joyce's *Ulysses*', *James Joyce Quarterly*, vol. 48, no. 2, 2011, 350–56

Gadda, Carlo Emilio, *That Awful Mess on Via Merulana*, William Weaver (trans.) (New York, NY: George Braziller, 1965)

Gamow, George, *Mr Tompkins in Wonderland* (Cambridge: The University Press, 1940)

Gavins, Joanna and Ernestine Lahey (eds), *World Building: Discourse in the Mind* (London: Bloomsbury, 2016)

Genette, Gérard, *Paratexts: Thresholds of Interpretation* (Cambridge: Cambridge University Press, 1997)

Gibson, Andrew, *Joyce's Revenge: History, Politics and Aesthetics in Ulysses* (Oxford: Oxford University Press, 2002)

Glandon, Virginia E., *Arthur Griffith and the Advanced-Nationalist Press, Ireland, 1900–1922* (New York, NY: Peter Lang, 1985)

Gogarty, Oliver St John, *As I Was Going Down Sackville Street: A Phantasy in Fact* (London: Rich & Cowan, 1937)

Gordon, Andrew, *A Modern History of Japan* (Oxford: Oxford University Press, 2003)

Greene, Graham, *Conversations with Graham Greene*, Edward J. Donaghy (ed.) (Mississippi, MS: University Press of Mississippi, 1992)

Gregory, Augusta, *Our Irish Theatre* (New York, NY: G.P. Putnam's Sons, 1911)

Grene, Nicholas, *The Politics of Irish Drama: Plays in Context from Boucicault to Friel* (Cambridge: Cambridge University Press, 2004)

Grosjean, François and Ping Li (eds), *The Psycholinguistics of Bilingualism* (Oxford: Blackwell Publishing, 2013)

Guidry, Lorelei, *'The Mask': Introduction and Index* (New York, NY: Blom, 1968)

Gunkel, David J., 'What Does it Matter Who is Speaking? Authorship, Authority, and the Mashup', *Popular Music and Society*, vol. 35, no. 1, 2012, 71–91

Hamachek, D.E., 'Psychodynamics of Normal and Neurotic Perfectionism', *Psychology*, no. 15, 1978, 27–33

Hayton, David, *The Anglo-Irish Experience, 1680–1730: Religion, Identity and Patriotism* (Woodbridge: The Boydell Press, 2012)

Heaney, Seamus, *Sweeney Astray* (London: Faber & Faber, 1990)

Helm, Rudolf, *Lucian und Menipp* (Hildesheim: Georg Olms Verlagsbuchhandlung, 1967)

Herman, David (ed.), *The Emergence of Mind: Representations of Consciousness in Narrative Discourse in English* (Lincoln, NE: University of Nebraska Press, 2011)

Hermans, D. *et al.*, 'Lexical Activation in Bilinguals' Speech Production is Dynamic: How Language Ambiguous Words Can Affect Cross-Language Activation', *Language and Cognitive Processes*, vol. 26, no. 10, 2011, 1687–1709

Holdeman, David, *Much Labouring: The Texts and Authors of Yeats's First Modernist Books* (Ann Arbor, MI: University of Michigan Press, 1997)

Holy Bible: Containing the Old and New Testaments, Revised Standard Version (Philadelphia, PA: National Publishing Company, 1995)

Hopper, Keith, *Flann O'Brien: A Portrait of the Artist as a Young Post-Modernist* (Cork: Cork University Press, 1995)

— *Flann O'Brien: A Portrait of the Artist as a Young Post-Modernist*, 2nd edn, J. Hillis Miller (foreword) (Cork: Cork University Press, 2009)

Hoult, Norah, *Coming from the Fair* (New York, NY: Covici, Friede, 1937)

Howe, Susan, *Kidnapped* (Tipperary: Coracle, 2002)

Hühn, Peter, Jan Christoph Meister, John Pier and Wolf Schmid (eds), *Handbook of Narratology, Volume 1*, 2nd edn (Berlin: De Gruyter, 2014)

Hutton, Clare, 'Reading *The Love Songs of Connacht*: Douglas Hyde and the Exigencies of Publication', *The Library*, vol. 2, no. 4, December 2001, 364–93

— 'Joyce and the Institutions of Revivalism', *Irish University Review*, vol. 33, no. 1, Spring-Summer 2003, 117–32

Ianco-Worrall, Anita D., 'Bilingualism and Cognitive Development', *Child Development*, vol. 43, no. 4, December 1972, 1390–1400

Imhof, Rüdiger (ed.), *Alive Alive O! Flann O'Brien's 'At Swim-Two-Birds'* (Dublin: Wolfhound Press, 1985)

Isaacson, Walter, *Einstein: His Life and Universe* (New York, NY: Simon & Schuster, 2007)

Jameson, Fredric, *Late Marxism: Adorno, Or, the Persistence of the Dialectic* (London: Verso, 1996)

— *A Singular Modernity* (London: Verso, 2002)

Jeans, James, *The New Background of Science* (Cambridge: Cambridge University Press, 1933)

Jernigan, Daniel Keith, '"Simulato Ergo Est": Brian O'Nolan's Metaperformative Simulations', *New Hibernia Review*, vol. 21, no. 1, Spring 2016, 87–104

Jonson, Ben, *The Works of Ben Jonson vol. 7*, W. Gifford (ed.) (London: Nicol *et al.*, 1816)

Jordan, John (ed.), *The Pleasures of Gaelic Literature* (Cork: Mercier Press, 1977)

Joyce, James, *Finnegans Wake* (New York, NY: Viking Press, 1939)

— *Letters of James Joyce*, Stuart Gilbert (ed.) (New York, NY: Viking Press, 1957)

— *Ulysses*, Oxford World's Classics, Jeri Johnson (introd. and ed.) (Oxford: Oxford University Press, 1998)

— *Ulysses: Annotated Students' Edition*, Declan Kiberd (ed.) (London: Penguin, 2000)

— *Ulysses*, Hans Walter Gabler (ed.) (London: Vintage Classic, 2008)

— *Dubliners* (London: Penguin, 2000; London: Vintage Classic, 2012)

Jung, Carl, *Two Essays on Analytical Psychology*, Herbert Read, Michael Fordham and Gerhard Adler (eds), Richard Francis Carrington Hull (trans.) (London: Routledge, 1990)

Keats, John, *The Complete Works of John Keats, Volume 1*, Harry Buxton Forman (ed.) (New York, NY: Thomas Y. Crowell & Company, 1817)

— *The Complete Works of John Keats, Volume 2*, Harry Buxton Forman (ed.) (New York, NY: Thomas Y. Crowell & Company, 1818)

Kelleher, Margaret, 'Introduction', *Irish University Review*, vol. 33, no. 1, Spring–Summer 2003, viii–ix

Kemnitz, Charles, 'Beyond the Zone of Middle Dimensions: A Relativistic Reading of *The Third Policeman*', *Irish University Review*, vol. 15, no. 1, Spring 1985, 56–72

Kenner, Hugh, *A Colder Eye: The Irish Modern Writers* (Middlesex: Penguin, 1983)

Keogh, Dermot, *Ireland in World War Two: Diplomacy and Survival* (Cork: Mercier Press, 2004)

Keown, Edwina and Carol Taaffe (eds), *Irish Modernism: Origins, Contexts, Publics* (Bern: Peter Lang, 2010)

Kermode, Frank, *The Sense of an Ending: Studies in the Theory of Fiction* (Oxford: Oxford University Press, 2000)

Kharkhurin, Anatoliy, *Multilingualism and Creativity* (Bristol: Multilingual Matters, 2012)

Kiberd, Declan, *Irish Classics* (London: Granta, 2000)

— *The Irish Writer and the World* (Cambridge: Cambridge University Press, 2005)

Kirk, Eugene [alias 'Korkowski'], *Menippean Satire: An Annotated Catalogue of Texts and Criticism* (New York, NY: Garland, 1980)

Kolocotroni, Vassiliki, Jane Goldman and Olga Taxidou (eds), *Modernism: An Anthology of Sources and Documents* (Chicago, IL: University of Chicago Press, 1998)

Korkowski, Eugene Paul, 'Menippus and his Imitators: A Conspectus, up to Sterne, for a Misunderstood Genre', unpublished dissertation (University of California: San Diego, 1973)

Krips, Henry, J.E. McGuire and Trevor Melia (eds), *Science, Reason and Rhetoric* (Pittsburgh, PA: University of Pittsburgh Press, 1995)

Kroll, Judith F. and Annette de Groot (eds), *Handbook of Bilingualism: Psycholinguistic Approaches* (Oxford: Oxford University Press, 2005)

LaBine, Joseph. '"the words I taught to him": Interfusional Language Play and Brian O'Nolan's "Revenge on the English"', *The Parish Review*, vol. 3, no. 2, Spring 2016, 26–38

Landow, George P. (ed.), *Hyper/Text/Theory*, 2nd edn (Baltimore, MD: Johns Hopkins University Press, 1995)

— *Hypertext 2.0*, 2nd edn (Baltimore, MD: Johns Hopkins University Press, 1997)

Lanters, José, *Unauthorized Versions: Irish Menippean Satire, 1919–1952* (Washington, DC: Catholic University of America Press, 2000)

Lee, J.J., *Ireland 1912–1985: Politics and Society* (Cambridge: Cambridge University Press, 1989)

Lee, Joseph and Gearóid Ó Tuathaigh, *The Age of de Valera* (Dublin: Ward River Press in association with Radio Telefís Éireann, 1982)

Leerssen, Joep, *Remembrance and Imagination: Patterns in the Historical and Literary Representation of Ireland in the Nineteenth Century* (Cork: Cork University Press in association with Field Day, 1996)

Levin, Harry (ed.), *The Portable James Joyce*, rev. edn (London: Penguin, 1976)

Lewis, C.S., *Prince Caspian: The Return to Narnia*, Pauline Baynes (illustrations) (London: G. Bles, 1951)

Lewis, Pericles (ed.), *The Cambridge Companion to European Modernism* (Cambridge: Cambridge University Press, 2007)

Lippmann, Walter, *Public Opinion* (Minneapolis, MN: Filiquarian Publishing, 2007)

Londraville, Janis and Richard Londraville (eds), *John Quinn: Selected Irish Writers from his Library* (West Cornwall, CT: Locust Hill Press, 2001)

Long, Maebh, *Assembling Flann O'Brien* (London: Bloomsbury, 2014)

Longley, Edna, 'Not Guilty?', *Dublin Review*, no. 16, Autumn 2004, 17–31

Lorda, Clara-Ubaldina and Patrick Zabalbeascoa (eds), *Spaces of Polyphony* (Amsterdam: John Benjamins, 2012)

Lu, David J. (ed.), *Japan, A Documentary History, Volume 2: The Late Tokugawa Period to the Present* (New York, NY: East Gate, 1997)

Lucian, *Lucian Vol. I*, A.M. Harmon (trans.) (London: William Heinemann, 1913)

— *Lucian Vol. VII*, M.D. Macleod (trans.) (London: William Heinemann, 1961)

Lyons, Paddy and Alison O'Malley-Younger (eds), *No Country for Old Men: Fresh Perspectives on Irish Literature* (London: Peter Lang, 2009)

Mac Cárthaigh, Eoin and Jürgen Uhlich (eds), *Féilscríbhinn do Chathal Ó Háinle* (Indreabhán: Cló Iar-Chonnacht, 2012)

Mac Lochlainn, Alf, 'An Chéad Phearsa Uaigneach: Idir an Réaltacht agus an tSamhailt' [rev. of *Óige an Dearthár .i. Myles na gCopaleen* by Ciarán Ó Nualláin], *Comhar*, vol. 33, no. 1, January 1974, 16–17

Mac Mathúna, Liam, '"Geilt" sa chiall "duine lomnocht"', *Éigse: A Journal of Irish Studies*, vol. 18, no. 1, 1980, 39–42

MacNamara, Brinsley, 'Dr Oswald Brannigan', *The Irish Statesman*, vol. 1, no. 6, 2 August 1919, 144

Malafouris, Lambros, *How Things Shape the Mind: A Theory of Material Engagement* (Cambridge, MA: MIT Press, 2013)

Malina, Debra, *Breaking The Frame: Metalepsis and the Construction of the Subject* (Ohio, OH: Ohio State University Press, 2002)

Mao, Douglas and Rebecca L. Walkowitz, 'The New Modernist Studies', *PMLA*, vol. 123, no. 3, May 2008, 737–48

Maslen, R.W., 'Flann O'Brien's Bombshells: *At Swim-Two-Birds* and *The Third Policeman*', *New Hibernia Review*, vol. 10, no. 4, Winter 2006, 84–104

Matthews, P.J., 'A Battle of Two Civilizations? D.P. Moran and William Rooney', *The Irish Review*, no. 29, Autumn 2002, 22–37

McBride, Ian (ed.), *History and Memory in Modern Ireland* (Cambridge: Cambridge University Press, 2001)

McCracken, Patricia, 'Arthur Griffith's South African Sabbatical', *Southern African-Irish Studies*, vol. 3, 1996, 227–62

McFeaters, Andrew V., 'Reassembling Ford: Time is Money in Brian O'Nolan's Brave New Ireland', *The Parish Review*, vol. 3, no. 1, Fall 2014, 33–42

McFeely, Deirdre, *Dion Boucicault: Irish Identity on Stage* (Cambridge: Cambridge University Press, 2012)

McHale, Brian, *Constructing Postmodernism* (London: Routledge, 1992)

— 'Afterword: Reconstructing Postmodernism', *Narrative*, vol. 21, no. 3, October 2013, 357–64

McMullen, Kim, 'Culture as Colloquy: Flann O'Brien's Postmodern Dialogue with Irish Tradition', *Novel: A Forum on Fiction*, vol. 27, no. 1, 62–84

Mercier, Vivian, *The Irish Comic Tradition* (Oxford: Oxford University Press, 1969)

Meyer, Kuno, *Selections from Ancient Irish Poetry* (London: Constable, 1913)

Miller, Tyrus, *Late Modernism: Politics, Fiction, and the Arts Between the World Wars* (Berkeley, CA: University of California Press, 1999)

Moore, Walter, *Schrödinger: Life and Thought* (Cambridge: Cambridge University Press, 1989)

Moran, D.P., *The Philosophy of Irish Ireland* (Dublin: James Duffy & Co., 1905)

— *The Philosophy of Irish Ireland*, Patrick Maume (ed.) (Dublin: UCD Press, 2006)

Moulthrop, Stuart, 'You Say You Want a Revolution? Hypertext and the Laws of Media', *Postmodern Culture: An Electronic Journal of Interdisciplinary Criticism*, vol. 1, no. 3, May 1991, 53 pars

Murphet, Julian, Rónán McDonald and Sascha Morrell (eds), *Flann O'Brien & Modernism* (London: Bloomsbury, 2014)

Murphy, Neil and Keith Hopper (eds), *Flann O'Brien: Centenary Essays*, *The Review of Contemporary Fiction*, vol. 31, no. 3, Fall 2011 (Champaign, IL: Dalkey Archive Press, 2011)

Nejezchleb, Amy, 'The Myles Brand Franchise', *The Parish Review*, vol. 1, no. 2, Winter 2013, 51–57

Nelson, K.E. (ed.), *Children's Language: Vol. 5* (Hillsdale, NJ: L. Erlbaum, 1985)

Nelson, Ted, *Literary Machines: The Report on, and of, Project Xanadu*, 5th edn (Swarthmore PA: Ted Nelson, 1983)

Nic Congáil, Ríona, *Úna Ní Fhaircheallaigh agus an Fhís Útóipeach Ghaelach* (Dublin: Arlen House, 2010)

Nic Eoin, Máirín, *An Litríocht Réigiúnach* (Baile Átha Cliath: An Clóchomhar, 1982)

— 'Ó *An tOileánach* go *Kinderszenen*: An Toise Dírbheathaisnéiseach i bPrós-scríbhneoireacht na Gaeilge', *The Irish Review*, no. 13, Winter 1992/93, 14–21

Ní Chinnéide, Máiréad, *An Damer: Stair Amharclainne* (Baile Átha Cliath: Gael-Linn, 2008)

Ning, Wang, 'Introduction: Historicizing Postmodernist Fiction', *Narrative*, vol. 21, no. 3, October 2013, 263–70

Noble, T.A., *Holy Trinity: Holy People: The Theology of Christian Perfecting* (Eugene, OR: Cascade, 2013)

Nord, Christiane, *Text Analysis in Translation: Theory, Methodology, and Didactic Application of a Model for Translation-Oriented Text Analysis*, 2nd edn (Amsterdam: Rodopi, 2005)

Norris, Margot, 'Possible-Worlds Theory and Joyce's "Wandering Rocks": The Case of Father Conmee', *Joyce Studies Annual*, vol. 2007, 21–43

— 'Possible Worlds Theory and the Fantasy Universe of *Finnegans Wake*', *James Joyce Quarterly*, vol. 44, no. 3, Spring 2007, 455–74

O'Brien, Frank, *Filíocht Ghaeilge na Linne Seo* (Baile Átha Cliath: An Clóchomhar, 1968)

Ó Brolcháin, Caoimhghin, 'Flann, Ó Caoimh agus Suibhne Geilt', *Irish Studies Review*, no. 9, 1994–95, 31–34

Ó Coileáin, Seán, Liam P. Ó Murchú and Pádraigín Riggs (eds), *Séimhfhear Suairc: Aistí in Ómós don Ollamh Breandán Ó Conchúir* (Má Nuad: An Sagart, 2013)

Ó Conaire, Breandán, *Myles na Gaeilge: Lámhleabhar ar Shaothar Gaeilge Bhrian Ó Nualláin* (Baile Átha Cliath: An Clóchomhar, 1986)

O'Connell, Mark, '"How to handle eternity": Infinity and the Theories of J.W. Dunne in the Fiction of Jorge Luis Borges and Flann O'Brien's *The Third Policeman*', *Irish Studies Review*, vol. 17, no. 2, 2009, 223–37

O'Connor, Frank, *The Mirror in the Roadway* (London: Hamish Hamilton, 1957)

— *Kings, Lords and Commons: An Anthology from the Irish* (New York, NY: Knopf, 1959)

Ó Dónaill, Niall (ed.), *Foclóir Gaeilge-Béarla* (Baile Átha Cliath: An Gúm, 2005)

O'Donnell, Frank Hugh, 'The Stage Irishman of Pseudo-Celtic Drama' (London: John Long, 1904)

O'Donoghue, Bernard, 'Irish Humour and Verbal Logic', *Critical Quarterly*, no. 24, 1982, 33–40

O'Donoghue, D.J., 'Post Bag: Irish Pseudonyms', *The Irish Book Lover*, vol. 1, no. 9, April 1910, 121

O'Faoláin, Seán, 'Irish Gasconade', *John O'London's Weekly*, 24 March 1939, 970

— 'Why Don't We See It?', *The Bell*, vol. 5, no. 3, December 1942, 161–64

O'Grady, Standish James, *History of Ireland: Heroic Period* (Dublin: Ponsonby, 1878, 1880)

Ó hÁinle, Cathal G., 'Fionn and Suibhne in *At Swim-Two-Birds*', *Hermathena*, no. 142, Summer 1987, 11–49

O'Keeffe J.G. (ed. and trans.), *Buile Suibhne: The Frenzy of Suibhne* (London: Irish Texts Society, 1910)

O'Keeffe, Timothy (ed.), *Myles: Portraits of Brian O'Nolan* (London: Martin Brian & O'Keeffe, 1973)

O'Leary, Philip, *The Prose Literature of the Gaelic Revival, 1881–1921: Ideology and Innovation* (Philadelphia, PA: The Pennsylvania State University Press, 1994)

— *Gaelic Prose in the Irish Free State 1922–1939* (Dublin: UCD Press, 2004)

Ó Nualláin, Ciarán, 'The West's Awake! A Heart-Pounding Melodrama', *Comhthrom Féinne*, vol. 5, no. 4, May 1933, 66–67

— 'Cúrsaí Báis!', *The New Irish Magazine/An Sgeulaidhe Nuadh*, August 1934, 43

— *Óige an Dearthár .i. Myles na gCopaleen* (Baile Átha Cliath: Foilseacháin Náisiúnta Teoranta, 1973)

— *Amaidí* (Baile Átha Cliath: Foilseacháin Náisiúnta Teoranta, 1983)

— *The Early Years of Brian O'Nolan/Flann O'Brien/Myles na gCopaleen*, Niall O'Nolan (ed.), Róisín Ní Nualláin (trans.) (Dublin: Lilliput Press, 1998)

Ó Nualláin, Gearóid, *Beatha Dhuine a Thoil* (Baile Átha Cliath: Oifig an tSoláthair, 1950)

Orwell, J.H. [Seumas O'Sullivan], *Impressions: A Selection from the Notebooks of the Late J.H. Orwell, with a foreword by Seumas O'Sullivan* (Dublin: The New Nation Press, 1910)

— *Facetiae et Curiosa, being a selection from the note-books of the late J.H. Orwell, made by his friend Seumas O'Sullivan* (Dublin: privately printed, 1937)

Oţoiu, Adrian, '"Compartmentation of personality for the purpose of literary utterance": Pseudonymity and Heteronymity in the Various Lives of Flann O'Brien', *Word and Text: A Journal of Literary Studies and Linguistics*, vol. 1, no. 1, 2011, 128–38

O'Toole, Mary A., 'The Theory of Serialism in *The Third Policeman*', *Irish University Review*, vol. 18, no. 2, Autumn 1988, 215–25

Ó Torna, Caitríona, *Cruthú na Gaeltachta 1893–1922* (Baile Átha Cliath: Cois Life, 2005)

Ó Tuama, Seán, *Repossessions: Selected Essays on the Irish Literary Heritage* (Cork: Cork University Press, 1995)

Ó Tuathaigh, Gearóid, Liam Lillis Ó Laoire and Seán Ua Súilleabháin (eds), *Pobal na Gaeltachta: A Scéal agus a Dhán* (Indreabhán: Raidió na Gaeltachta i gcomhar le Cló Iar-Chonnachta, 2000)

Page, Ruth and Bronwen Thomas (eds), *New Narratives: Stories and Storytelling in the Digital Age* (Lincoln, NE: University of Nebraska Press, 2011)

Partridge [Bourke], Angela, 'Wild Men and Wailing Women', *Éigse: A Journal of Irish Studies*, vol. 18, no. 1, 1980, 25–37

Pavel, Thomas G., *Fictional Worlds* (Cambridge, MA: Harvard University Press, 1986)

Pessoa, Fernando, *The Book of Disquiet*, Richard Zenith (trans.) (New York, NY: Penguin Books, 2002)

Petersen, Richard F., 'Flann O'Brien's Timefoolery', *Irish Renaissance Annual*, no. 3, 1982, 30–46

Pettitt, Lance, *Screening Ireland: Film and Television Representation* (Manchester: Manchester University Press, 2000)

Pilný, Ondřej, 'My Kingdom for a Pun: Myles na gCopaleen, Erwin Schrödinger and *The Third Policeman* in *Improbable Frequency*', *Irish Theatre International*, vol. 1, no. 1, 2008, 38–52

Pine, Richard, 'Review Article: mac Liammóir, in Wonderland, *Irish University Review*, vol. 28, no. 2, Autumn-Winter 1998, 373–76

Pirandello, Luigi, *The Late Mattia Pascal*, William Weaver (trans.) (New York, NY: Marsilio, 1995)

Prade, Juliane (ed.), *(M)Other Tongues: Literary Reflexions on a Difficult Distinction* (Newcastle upon Tyne: Cambridge Scholars Publishing, 2013)

Price, Katy, *Loving Faster than Light: Romance and Readers in Einstein's Universe* (Chicago, IL: University of Chicago Press, 2012)

Purdie, Susan, *Comedy: The Mastery of Discourse* (Hemel Hempstead: Harvester Wheatsheaf, 1993)

Pyle, Hilary, *James Stephens: His Work and an Account of His Life* (London: Routledge & Kegan Paul, 1965)

Quintelli-Neary, Marguerite, *Folklore and the Fantastic in Twelve Modern Irish Novels* (Westport, CT: Greenwood, 1997)

Quintero, Ruben (ed.), *Satire Ancient and Modern* (Oxford: Blackwell, 2007)

Rabaté, Jean-Michel, *The Ghosts of Modernity* (Gainesville, FL: University Press of Florida, 1996)

Rafter, Kevin (ed.), *Irish Journalism Before Independence: More a Disease than a Profession* (Manchester: Manchester University Press, 2011)

Rainsford, Dominic and Tim Woods (eds), *Critical Ethics: Text, Theory and Responsibility* (London: Macmillan, 1999)

Relihan, Joel C., *Ancient Menippean Satire* (Baltimore, MD: Johns Hopkins University Press, 1993)

Ressel, Volker *et al.*, 'An Effect of Bilingualism on the Auditory Cortex', *The Journal of Neuroscience*, vol. 32, no. 47, 2012, 16597–601

Rigney, Ann, 'Plenitude, Scarcity and the Circulation of Cultural Memory', *Journal of European Studies*, vol. 35, no. 1, 2005, 11–28

Rijkonen, Hannu K., 'Menippean Satire as a Literary Genre with Special Reference to Seneca's Apocolocyntosis', *Commentationes Humanorum Literarum*, no. 83, 1987

Rodway, Allan, 'Terms for Comedy', *Renaissance and Modern Studies*, vol. 6, no. 1, 1962, 102–24

Ronen, Ruth, *Possible Worlds in Literary Theory* (Cambridge: Cambridge University Press, 1994)

Ross, Ciaran (ed.), *Sub-Versions: Trans-National Readings of Modern Irish Literature* (Amsterdam: Rodopi, 2010)

Russell, Bertrand, *The ABC of Relativity* (London: Unwin, 1925)

Rütten, Ulrich, *Phantasie und Lachkultur: Lukians 'Wahre Geschichten'* (Tübingen: Narr, 1997)

Ryan, Marie-Laure, *Possible Worlds, Artificial Intelligence, and Narrative Theory* (Bloomington, IN: Indiana University Press, 1991)

Saint-Amour, Paul K., 'An Interlude: We Have Never Been Modernists', *English Literature in Transition, 1880–1920*, vol. 56, no. 2, 2013, 201–04

Salvsen, Christopher, 'Irish Myles', *New Society* (London), 5 September 1968, 346–47

Saporta, S. (ed.), *Psycholinguistics* (New York, NY: Holt, Rinehart & Winston, 1961)

Saunders, Max, *Self Impression: Life-Writing, Autobiografiction, and the Forms of Modern Literature* (Oxford: Oxford University Press, 2010)

Savage, Robert J., *Irish Television: The Political and Social Origins* (Westport, CT: Greenwood, 1996)

Schmid, Monika and Wander Lowie (eds), *Modeling Bilingualism: From Structure to Chaos* (Amsterdam: John Benjamins Publishing, 2011)

Scholes, Robert and Richard M. Kain, *The Workshop of Daedalus: James Joyce and the Raw Materials for 'A Portrait of the Artist as a Young Man'* (Evanston, IL: Northwestern University Press, 1975)

Schoolcraft, Ralph, 'For Whom the Beyle Toils: Stendhal and Pseudonymous Authorship', *PMLA*, vol. 119, no. 2, March 2004, 247–64

Scott, Florence R., 'Teg: The Stage Irishman', *The Modern Language Review*, vol. 42, no. 3, 1947, 314–20

Senn, Fritz, *Inductive Scrutinies: Focus on Joyce*, Christine O'Neill (ed.) (Baltimore, MD: Johns Hopkins University Press, 1995)

Shakespeare, William [falsely attributed], *The True and Honorable History of the Life of Sir John Oldcastle, the Good Lord Cobham* (London: R. Walker, 1734)

Shaw, G.B., *John Bull's Other Island and Major Barbara* (New York, NY: Brentano's, 1911)

Shea, Thomas F., 'The Craft of Seeming Pedestrian: Flann O'Brien's *The Hard Life*', *Colby Quarterly*, vol. 25, no. 4, December 1989, 258–67

— *Flann O'Brien's Exorbitant Novels* (Lewisburg, PA: Bucknell University Press, 1992)

Shovlin, Frank, 'The Pseudonyms of George W. Russell', *Notes and Queries*, vol. 49, no. 1, March 2002, 79–80

Siebers, Tobin, 'Hesitation, History, and Reading: Henry James's *The Turn of the Screw*', *Texas Studies in Literature and Language*, vol. 25, no. 4, 1983, 558–73

Silverthorne, J.M., 'Time, Literature, and Failure: Flann O'Brien's *At Swim-Two-Birds* and *The Third Policeman*', *Éire-Ireland*, vol. 11, no. 4, Winter 1976, 66–83

Spenser, Andrew, 'Many Worlds: The New Physics in Flann O'Brien's *The Third Policeman*', *Éire-Ireland*, vol. 30, no.1, Spring 1995, 145–58

Sprinker, Michael (ed.), *Ghostly Demarcations: A Symposium on Jacques Derrida's Specters of Marx* (London: Verso, 2008)

Stanford Friedman, Susan, 'Definitional Excursions: The Meanings of Modern/Modernity/Modernism', *Modernism/modernity*, vol. 8, no. 3, September 2001, 493–513

Stephens, James, *The Charwoman's Daughter* (London: Macmillan & Co., 1912)

— *Here Are Ladies* (London: Macmillan, 1914)

— *The Crock of Gold* (London: Macmillan & Co., 1928)

— *James, Seumas and Jacques: Unpublished Writings of James Stephens*, Lloyd Frankenberg (ed.) (London: Macmillan & Co., 1964)

— *Letters of James Stephens: With an Appendix Listing Stephens's Published Writings*, Richard J. Finneran (ed.) (London: Macmillan, 1974)

— *Uncollected Prose of James Stephens*, 2 vols, Patricia McFate (ed.) (New York, NY: St Martin's, 1983)

— *The Poems of James Stephens*, Shirley Stevens Mulligan (ed.) (Buckinghamshire: Colin Smythe, 2006)

Stewart, Bruce, 'Lumberjacks and Surgeons' [rev. of *James Joyce: The Artist and the Labyrinth* by Augustine Martin; *James Joyce and the Politics of Desire* by Suzette A. Henke; *The Irish Beckett* by John P. Harrington; *Clongowes Wood: A History of Clongowes Wood College 1814–1989* by Peter Costello], *Books Ireland*, no. 154, November 1991, 215–17

Taaffe, Carol, *Ireland Through the Looking-Glass: Flann O'Brien, Myles na gCopaleen and Irish Cultural Debate* (Cork: Cork University Press, 2008)

Taubes, Jacob, *The Political Theology of Paul*, Dana Hollander (trans.) (Stanford, CA: Stanford University Press, 2004)

Thompson, Evan, *Mind in Life: Biology, Phenomenology, and the Sciences of Mind* (Cambridge, MA: Harvard University Press, 2007)

Tiernan, Sonja, *Eva Gore-Booth: An Image of Such Politics* (Manchester: Manchester University Press, 2012)

Tigges, Wim, *An Anatomy of Literary Nonsense* (Amsterdam: Rodopi, 1988)

Titley, Alan, *An tÚrscéal Gaeilge* (Baile Átha Cliath: An Clóchomhar, 1991)

Todorov, Tzvetan, *The Fantastic: A Structural Approach to a Literary Genre* (Ithaca, NY: Cornell University Press, 1975)

Tofts, Darren, 'A Retrospective Sort of Arrangement: *Ulysses* and the Poetics of Hypertextuality', *Hypermedia Joyce Studies*, vol. 3, no. 1, 2002, <http://hjs.ff.cuni.cz/archives/v3/tofts2.html>

Tóibín, Colm, 'Flann O'Brien's Lies', *The London Review of Books*, vol. 34, no. 1, 5 January 2012, 32–36

Valente, Joseph, *The Myth of Manliness in Irish National Culture, 1880–1922* (Urbana, IL: University of Illinois Press, 2011)

Valéry, Paul, *Variety: Second Series*, William A. Bradley (trans.) (New York, NY: Harcourt, Brace & Company, 1938)

Van Hulle, Dirk, *Modern Manuscripts: The Extended Mind and Creative Undoing from Darwin to Beckett and Beyond* (London: Bloomsbury, 2014)

Van Hulle, Dirk and Shane Weller, *The Making of Samuel Beckett's 'L'Innommable / The Unnamable'* (Brussels/London: University Press Antwerp/Bloomsbury, 2014)

Vaughan, W.E. (ed.), *A New History of Ireland: Vol. 6, Ireland under the Union, 1870–1921* (New York, NY: Oxford University Press, 1996)

Volpone, Annalisa, *Joyce, Give and Take* (Rome: Aracne, 2012)

Voltaire, *Candide ou l'Optimisme*, Thomas Baldischwieler (ed.) (Stuttgart: Reclam, 2007)

Von Koppenfels, Werner, *Der Andere Blick, oder Das Vermächtnis des Menippos in der Europäischen Literatur* (München: Beck, 2007)

Von Uexküll, Jakob, *Umwelt und Innenwelt der Tiere* (Berlin: Julius Springer, 1909)

— *Streifzüge durch die Umwelten von Tieren und Menschen: Ein Bilderbuch Unsichtbarer Welten* (Hamburg: Rowohlt, 1956)

Walsh, Townsend, *The Career of Dion Boucicault* (New York, NY: Benjamin Blom, 1967)

Wäppling, Eva, *Four Irish Legendary Figures in 'At Swim-Two-Birds': A Study of Flann O'Brien's use of Finn, Suibhne, the Pooka and the Good Fairy* (Stockholm: Almqvist och Wiksell, 1984)

Waugh, Evelyn, 'Felix Culpa?', *The Commonweal*, no. 48, 16 July 1948, 323

Wei, Li, *The Bilingualism Reader* (London: Routledge, 2000)

Weinbrot, Howard D., *Menippean Satire Reconsidered: From Antiquity to the Eighteenth Century* (Baltimore, MD: Johns Hopkins University Press, 2005)

Welch, Robert (ed.), *The Oxford Companion to Irish Literature* (Oxford: Oxford University Press, 1996)

West, Rebecca, 'The Strange Case of James Joyce', *Bookman*, no. 68, September 1928, 9–23

Wheatley, David, rev. of *Comhar: Brian Ó Nualláin: Eagrán Comórtha Speisialta*, *The Parish Review*, vol. 1, no. 1, Summer 2012, 28–33

Whitworth, Michael, *Einstein's Wake: Relativity, Metaphor and Modernist Literature* (Oxford: Oxford University Press, 2001)

Wills, Clair, *That Neutral Island: A Cultural History of Ireland During the Second World War* (London: Faber & Faber, 2007)

Windsor, Gerard, *The Mansions of Bedlam: Stories and Essays* (St Lucia: University of Queensland Press, 2000)

Wodehouse, P.G., *Over Seventy* (London: Herbert Jenkins, 1957)

Woolf, Virginia, *Orlando: A Biography* (Harmondsworth: Penguin, 1963)

— *Collected Essays, vol. 2* (London: Hogarth Press, 1972)

Yeats, W.B., *Fairy and Folk Tales of the Irish Peasantry* (New York: The Modern Library, n.d.)

— *Essays and Introductions* (New York, NY: Macmillan, 1961)

— *Explorations* (London: Macmillan, 1962)

Yildiz, Yasemin, *Beyond the Mother Tongue: The Postmonolingual Condition* (New York, NY: Fordham University Press, 2011)

Index